RYE

A History of a Sussex Cinque Port to 1660

The *Mermaid Inn*, Mermaid Street, Rye.

RYE

A History of a Sussex Cinque Port to 1660

GILLIAN DRAPER

with contributions by David Martin,
Barbara Martin and Alan Tyler

Phillimore

First published 2009 by Phillimore & Co. Ltd
This paperback edition 2016

The History Press
The Mill, Brimscombe Port
Stroud, Gloucestershire, GL5 2QG
www.thehistorypress.co.uk

British Library Cataloguing in Publication Data.
A catalogue record for this book is available from the British Library.

ISBN 978 0 7509 7026 6
Typesetting and origination by The History Press
Printed and bound in Great Britain by Marston Book Services Ltd, Oxfordshire

Contents

Dr Gillian Draper is an associate lecturer at the University of Kent and the Events and Development Officer of the British Association for Local History. She has a special interest in the history of towns in south-east England.

David and Barbara Martin are Historic Buildings Officers with Archaeology South-East, University College London, and the authors of *New Winchelsea Sussex: a Medieval Port Town* (2004).

Dr Alan Tyler is an archaeologist, retired museum curator and editor of the Romney Marsh Research Trust's newsletter.

List of Illustrations

Colour Plates

(between pages xvi and xvii)

List of Abbreviations

Cal. Docs France	Round, J. (ed.) 1899. *Calendar of Documents Preserved in France Illustrative of the History of Great Britain and Ireland, I, AD 918-1206.* [London].
Cal. Inq. Misc.	*Calendar of Inquisitions Miscellaneous (Chancery)* (7 vols). 1916-69. [London].
Cal. Lib. Rolls	*Calendar of the Liberate Rolls Preserved in the Public Record Office* (5 vols). 1917-64. [London].
CCLR	*Calendar of the Close Rolls Preserved in the Public Record Office* (59 vols). 1892-. [London].
CPR	*Calendar of the Patent Rolls Preserved in the Public Record Office* (33 vols). 1803-. [London]
HMC 5	Riley, H. 1876. *Manuscripts of the Corporation of New Romney, Second Notice.* Historic Manuscripts Commission, 5th Rep.
LPFD H8	*Calendar of Letters and Papers, Foreign and Domestic, of the Reign of Henry VIII, 1831-1932.* [London].
MED	Online Middle English Dictionary, University of Michigan.
Rough's Register	Murray, K. (ed.) 1945. *The Register of Daniel Rough.* Kent Archaeological Society Records Branch 16.
'Sussex wills'	Garraway Rice, R. and Godfrey, W. 1940-41. *Transcripts of Sussex Wills,* Sussex Record Society 4.
Sussex Chantry Records	Ray, J. (ed.) 1930. *Sussex Chantry Records*, Sussex Record Society 36.
VCH Sussex	*The Victoria History of the County of Sussex* (9 vols). 1905-37. [London].

VCH Kent	*The Victoria History of the County of Kent* (3 vols). 1908-32. [London].
PNS	Mawer, A. and Stenton, F. 1929, 1930. *The Place-Names of Sussex* (2 vols). [Cambridge].
PNK	Wallenberg, J. 1934. *The Place-Names of Kent.* [Uppsala].
Reg. Chich.	Jacob, E. (ed.) 1943-7. *The Register of Henry Chichele: Archbishop of Canterbury 1414-1443* (4 vols). [Oxford].
DB Sussex	Morris, J. (ed.) 1976. *Domesday Book: Sussex.* [Chichester].
DB Kent	Morgan, P. (ed.) 1983. *Domesday Book: Kent.* [Chichester].

Repositories

ESRO	East Sussex Record Office.
CCA	Canterbury Cathedral Archives.
TNA	The National Archives.
WSRO	West Sussex Record Office.

Note: documents of Rye town have a reference number commencing RYE and the repository, ESRO, is not given repeatedly in this study.

Foreword

This is one of two volumes arising from an integrated research project co-ordinated and managed by the Romney Marsh Research Trust. The idea of an interdisciplinary project centred on the town of Rye was first proposed by the then Chair of the Executive of the Trust, Helen Clarke, in 2004. Subsequently two strands developed, work on the domestic built heritage of Rye which, placed in the context of the town's history, has been published as *Rye Rebuilt: regeneration and decline within a Sussex Port Town, 1350-1660* by D. Martin, B. Martin with J. Clubb and G. Draper (Domtom Publishing) and work on the history of Rye from its origins until 1660. The present volume, which draws on the buildings research, is the culmination of the historical research funded by the Trust which was led by Gillian Draper and supported by local volunteers. The 'Rye and hinterlands project' was overseen by a Steering Committee comprising Martyn Waller (Chair), Terry Burke (Secretary), David Williams (Treasurer), Luke Barber, Caroline Barron, Gillian Draper, Barbara Martin, David Martin, Caroline Thackray and Alan Tyler. The Trust was able to sponsor this research and the publication of the two volumes as a result of very generous donations from the Colyer Fergusson Trust and the Hawkins Charitable Trust. Publication of *Rye: a History of a Sussex Cinque Port to 1660* was enabled through additional grants from The Aurelius Charitable Trust and the Sussex Archaeological Society (a Margary Research Grant).

The Romney Marsh Research Trust exists to promote, co-ordinate and disseminate research into the historical, social, economic and physical development of Romney and Walland Marshes and their immediate hinterlands. The Trust receives, raises and holds funds to meet grant applications to support and publish research into the Marsh and invites individuals to become Friends of the Romney Marsh Research Trust and to participate in lectures, conferences, field visits and research projects. Details of the Trust and membership are available on the website www.rmrt.org.uk.

Martyn Waller
Chair of the Executive of the Romney Marsh Research Trust

Preface

It is more than sixty years since an attempt was made to write the history of medieval Rye. Rather more attention has been paid to Early Modern Rye: Graham Mayhew wrote his excellent book on *Tudor Rye* in 1987 and Stephen Hipkin completed his doctoral dissertation on the economy and social structure of Rye between 1600 and 1660 in 1985 and has published a number of articles on Rye since then. Perhaps it was thought that between them, Leopold Vidler who brought out his *New History of Rye* in 1934, and L.F. Salzman who wrote a rich account of the town in the ninth volume of the *Victoria History of the County of Sussex* (1937), they had said all that could be said. But if this was the assumption, then Dr Gillian Draper and her team of volunteers have here proved them wrong. The work of archaeologists and the study of the built environment (see the companion volume to this book written by Barbara and David Martin) have produced a great deal of new evidence which was not available to Vidler and the *Victoria County History*. Moreover Dr Draper and her team have been able to trawl through more of the documentary material and to align this with the findings of the archaeologists and buildings' experts. Our understanding of Rye in this 500 year period has been enlarged by Dr Draper because she has been able to set the town within its economic hinterland which stretched to the north up the Rother into the Weald and as far as London, and south across the sea to Calais. In this account we are reminded that Rye was not the only Cinque Port, nor were the Cinque Ports the only harbours along the south coast of England. The economic fortunes of Rye are here examined against the larger picture of a society more often than not engaged in war of some kind with the men across the Channel and we are reminded that although warfare was often profitable for the inhabitants of Rye it could also, as in 1377, prove devastating.

There is nothing Whiggish in this account of Rye: its fortunes rose and fell in the later medieval period and rose again to new heights in the 16th century, only to fall once more as the harbour silted up and the focus of English trade moved westwards to the ports which funnelled men and goods across the Atlantic to the

New World. But the importance of Rye in the period covered by this book can be seen in its surviving administrative records, its fine church and the remarkable collection of surviving buildings (albeit sometimes hidden by later facades). These visual reminders of the 'glory days' of Rye's history are well illustrated in this book and, although we may not have portraits of the men who made medieval and Tudor Rye, we do have the witness of their buildings and their documents. This is not only an attractively presented book, it is also a careful and scholarly account of Rye which will prove to be the authoritative history of the town for the foreseeable future. The Romney Marsh Research Trust who funded this work have every reason to be proud of the outcome.

Caroline Barron, Royal Holloway College

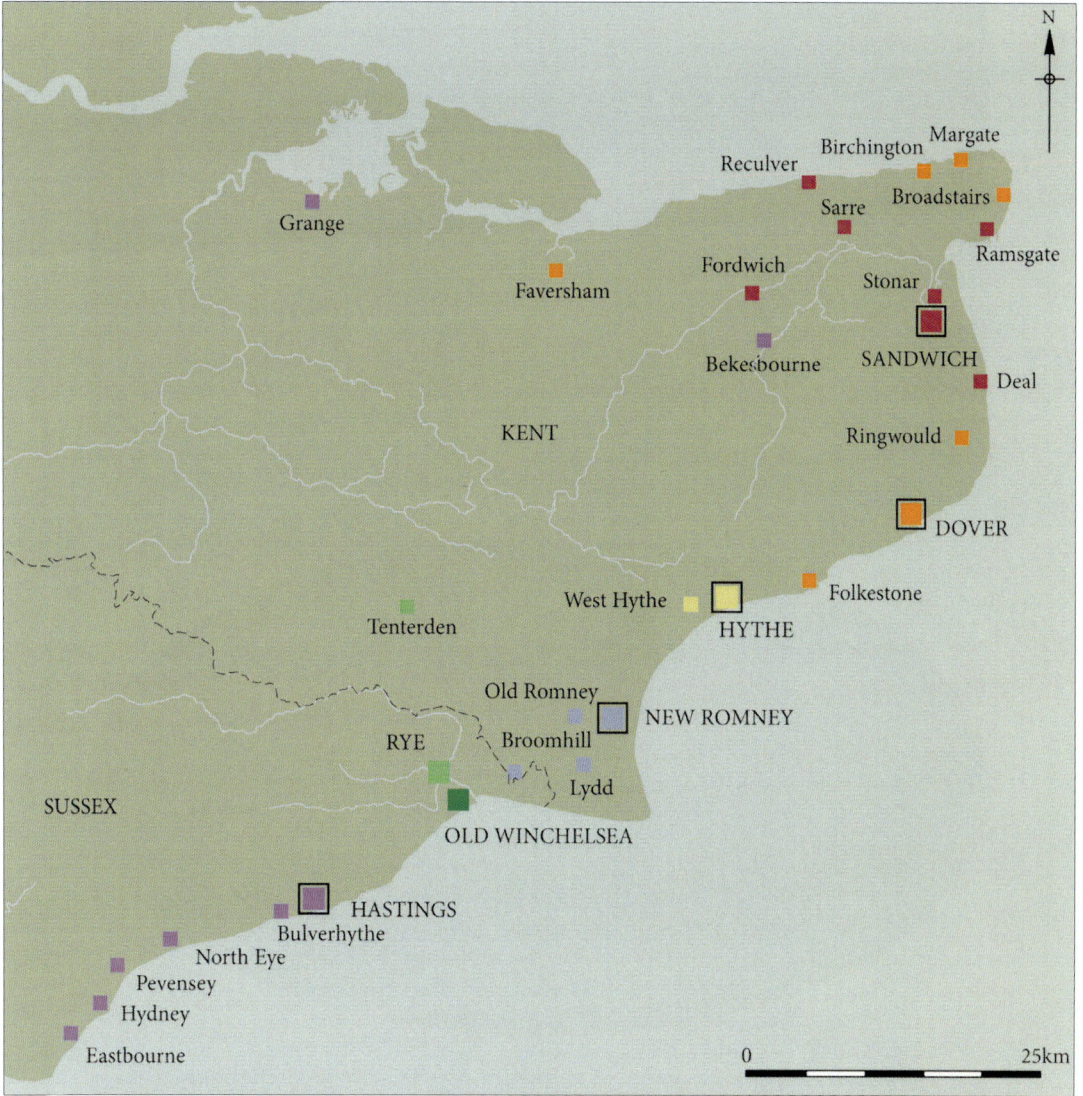

1 The Cinque Ports, Ancient Towns of Rye and New Winchelsea and the members of the confederation (Pre-Construct Archaeology).

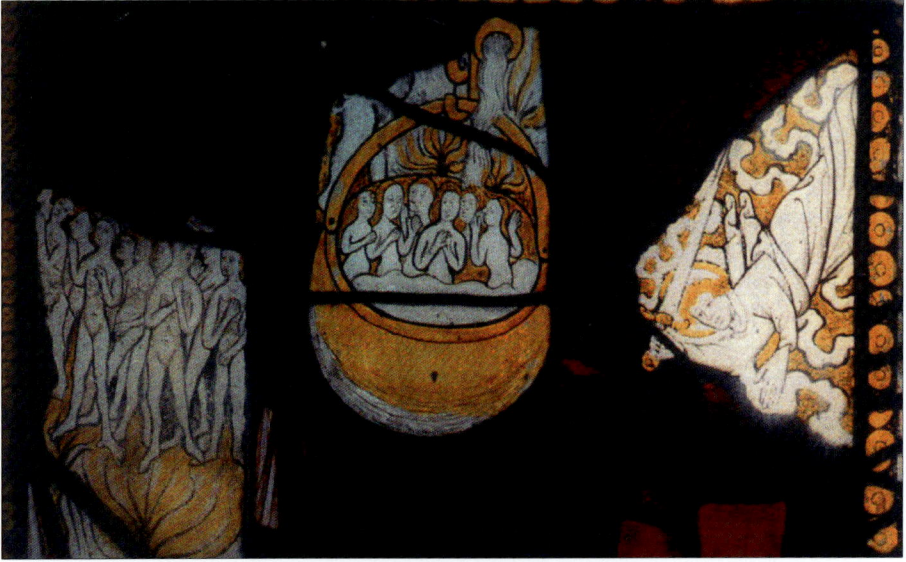

II Stained glass windows showing the fear of the Final Judgement and Hell. From Ticehurst church which lay on a pilgrimage route down the River Rother.

III The development of St Mary's Church, Rye (after J. Kirkham with permission of the Rye churchwardens).

① East Window
② Old school fireplace
③ Organ
④ Old carved panels
⑤ Benedicite Window
⑥ Lectern
⑦ Queen Anne's coat of arms
⑧ Pulpit
⑨ Font
⑩ West Window
⑪ Entrance to the Tower
⑫ Norman carved head
⑬ Original Quarter Boys
⑭ Tomb of Allen Grebell
⑮ Communion Table
⑯ St George memorial
⑰ North Door

Early 12th Century	■
Late 12th Century	■
c. 1220	■
c. 1250	■
14th Century	■
15th Century	■
16th Century	■
Victorian	■

IV Contours superimposed upon a map of the town and its immediate environs based on a town plan of 1771.

V Extract of map by John Prowez in *c.*1572, TNA MPF 212. North is at the lower edge. The castle is Winchelsea, later called Camber, Castle (see also Figure 2.5 showing a modern reconstruction of this area). Rye town is on the right-hand side of the map, and the open sea at the top. There is an extensive muddy area known as the Black Shore and a large area of sands where barrels of water, etc. were laden onto small boats to be taken out to larger vessels anchored in the channel next to the Black Shore. St Mary's Marsh is shown centre right in pale orange-brown, marked 'The Brache in to Mr Sheppardes marshes'.

Acknowledgements

Volunteer researchers brought a wealth of knowledge, hard work and enthusiasm to the Rye and hinterlands project. Material from printed and manuscript sources of the 13th to the 17th centuries was collected for entry into the Rye database which covers the town itself and 36 local settlements, as well as the more distant places with which historic Rye had connections. Photographs of buildings, maps and documents were obtained, books were loaned and copies of the final text were proof read. In short, the volunteers were involved from start to finish and I thank them all: Margaret Bird, Terry Burke, Rosalind Collier, Catherine Eady, Marion Gulliver, Ann Hignell, Ray Huson, Pauline Kingswood, Jo Kirkham, Sheila Maddock, Roger Nixon, Marion Pont, Jeremy Potter, Sally Potter, Tony Pratley, Pauline Pullen, Rene Regendanz, Susan Stratton and David Webb. A special acknowledgement is made of the contributions of Terry Burke who administered the project, while also carrying out research and acting as Secretary to the Trust, and of Stephen Draper who maintained the database and assisted in the preparation of the text and illustrations for publication. Without them this book would not have been produced.

Permission to reproduce illustrations has been given by Canterbury Cathedral Archives, East Sussex Record Office, the National Archives, Oxford University Press, Phillimore & Co. Ltd, the Churchwardens of Rye, the Victoria County History and individual authors, for which I am very grateful.

Rye Museum provided a place for meetings of the project team on numerous occasions. Many historians, archaeologists, archivists and curators have very generously offered information and help on various points which have greatly contributed to the project from the evaluation stage onwards: Dr Martin Allen, Dr Stuart Brookes, Professor John Blair, Professor Martha Carlin, Dr Helen Clarke, Dr Alan Dickinson, Allen Downend, Professor Barbara Harvey, Professor Mavis Mate, Dr Graham Mayhew, Dr Frank Meddens, Professor Carole Rawcliffe and Christopher Whittick. All the errors and opinions are of course mine. Particular thanks are due to those who offered welcome advice on the text and illustrations: Professor Caroline Barron and Dr Mark Gardiner.

Gillian Draper

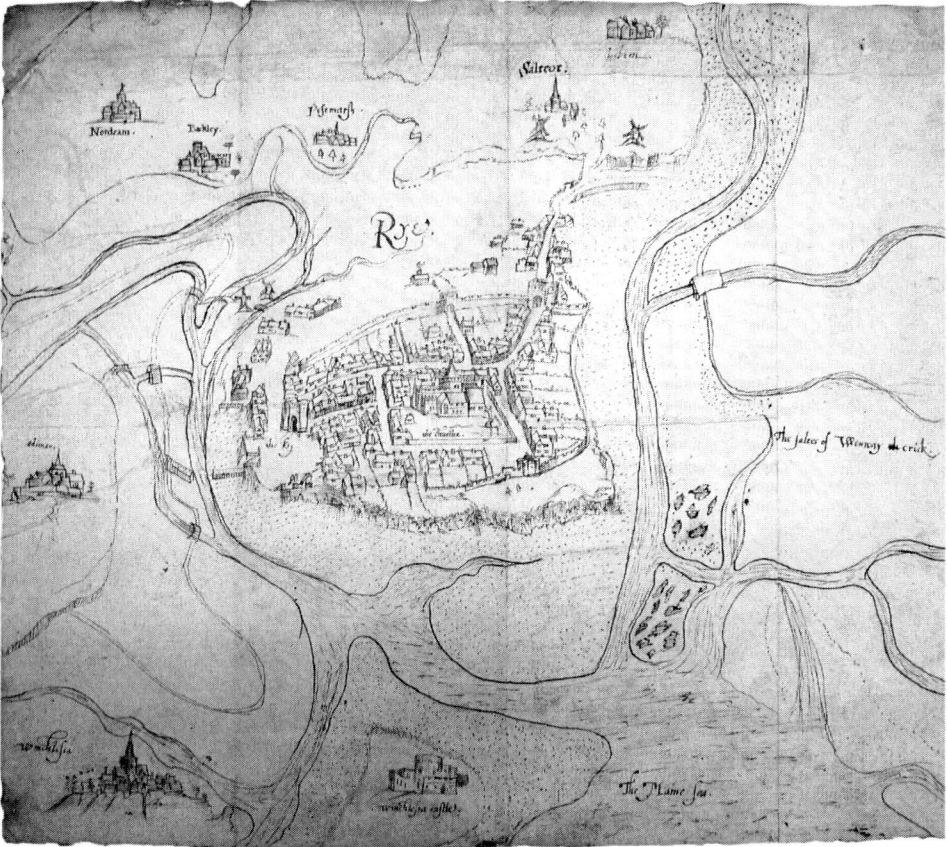

Fig. 1.1 'Plott of the Towne of Rye' of 1591, showing Rye, New Winchelsea town and castle (Camber), Udimore, Northiam, Beckley, Peasmarsh, Saltcote, Iden, and the Tillingham, Brede and Rother rivers, TNA MPF 1/3.

CHAPTER 1

The Origins of the
Town of Rye c.1000 to c.1250

Introduction

Rye was one of the towns which made up the confederation of the Cinque Ports in the 12th century (Plate I). The three major Head Ports of the confederation, New Romney, Dover and Sandwich, developed as towns after their establishment as beach trading places and fishing settlements in the eighth century. The two other Head Ports, Hastings and Hythe, were urban settlements in the mid-11th century. Neither Rye nor Old Winchelsea were among the original Head Ports but instead became full members of the confederation in the later 12th century, known as the Ancient Towns (Figure 1.4). The reasons for this are crucial for understanding the origins of Rye, particularly the important suggestion that Rye was a new town founded shortly after the Conquest and recorded under an estate called Rameslie in Sussex in Domesday Book (1086). Investigating whether this was Rye is the first step towards understanding the town's history, and draws on several other pieces of evidence: archaeological, architectural, numismatic and geomorphological. Reconstructing Rye's origins from this varied material can be likened to erecting a wigwam, a model taken by some urban historians of the 1980s when they examined the diverse evidence for prosperity and decline in medieval towns. The wide range of experiences of different towns led these historians to the simple wigwam. In this model 'there are several pieces of evidence each insufficient or untrustworthy in itself, [but] which collectively confirm a generalisation... Each pole would fall down by itself, but together the poles stand up, by leaning on each other'.[1] This chapter examines each of the evidential poles of the wigwam to see whether together they do in fact demonstrate that Rye was a new town founded after the Conquest, and how Rye's origins and growth compared with those of other coastal towns in Sussex and Kent.

The Settlements of Sussex and Kent before 1066

In Sussex some pre-Conquest coastal or estuarine settlements were places where people gathered for defence, communal organisation or trade; for example, they were estate centres, ports, *burhs* (defended hill-top sites), locations where coins were minted or meeting-places of the ancient civil units known as hundreds. Many of the settlements which had clusters of such features before the Conquest went on to develop into towns. Sussex was the kingdom of the South Saxons, whose influence spread from Chichester in the west of Sussex as far as Eastbourne or Pevensey in the east (Figure 1.2).[2] It did not extend further east to the territory or sphere of influence of an important group of people, the *Haestingas*. The *Haestingas* were still known under that name in 1011 in the Anglo-Saxon Chronicle. Their name connects them with Hastings, a settlement of which part is described in Domesday Book as having four townsmen (*burgensi*) belonging to the Norman Abbey of Fécamp (Figure 2.7).[3] At the far eastern end of Sussex, beyond the territory of the *Haestingas*, lay an important estate known by 1005 as Rammeslege, later Rameslie, where Old Winchelsea and, it is suggested, Rye became established (Figure 1.4).[4]

A defended site called *Eorpeburnan* is listed in the Burghal Hidage. The Hidage gives the names of *burhs* of the late ninth or early tenth century and the amount of land which was allocated for their defence in hides, nominally 120 acres. *Eorpeburnan* may have been located on the hill on which Rye later stood but more probably on Castle Toll, a hill to the north-east of Newenden in Kent, which had better strategic value (Figure 1.4).[5]

The future site of the town of Rye, on its distinctive hill or rock promontory, has also been proposed as the meeting place of a hundred in the period 650 to 1066. A hundred was a taxation, judicial and administration unit and an open-air court of freemen. The Saxon meeting places of the hundred were often at a prominent landmark which developed into informal markets as goods were traded where large numbers of people periodically assembled. The proposal that Rye was an early hundred meeting place derives from later documentary evidence and from the absence of a certain pre-Conquest meeting place in the hundreds adjacent to Rye. No early meeting place is known for Goldspur hundred which lay immediately to the north of the later town of Rye, nor for Guestling hundred which lay to the south west. However the boundaries of the hundreds underwent changes between the tenth and 13th centuries, including the incorporation of outlying settlements into them, particularly in eastern Sussex.[6] It is possible that Rye, on its landmark site with access by land and water, was an early trading site and hundredal centre but this cannot be demonstrated. Nevertheless the later evidence of Rye as a hundred is extremely significant (below).

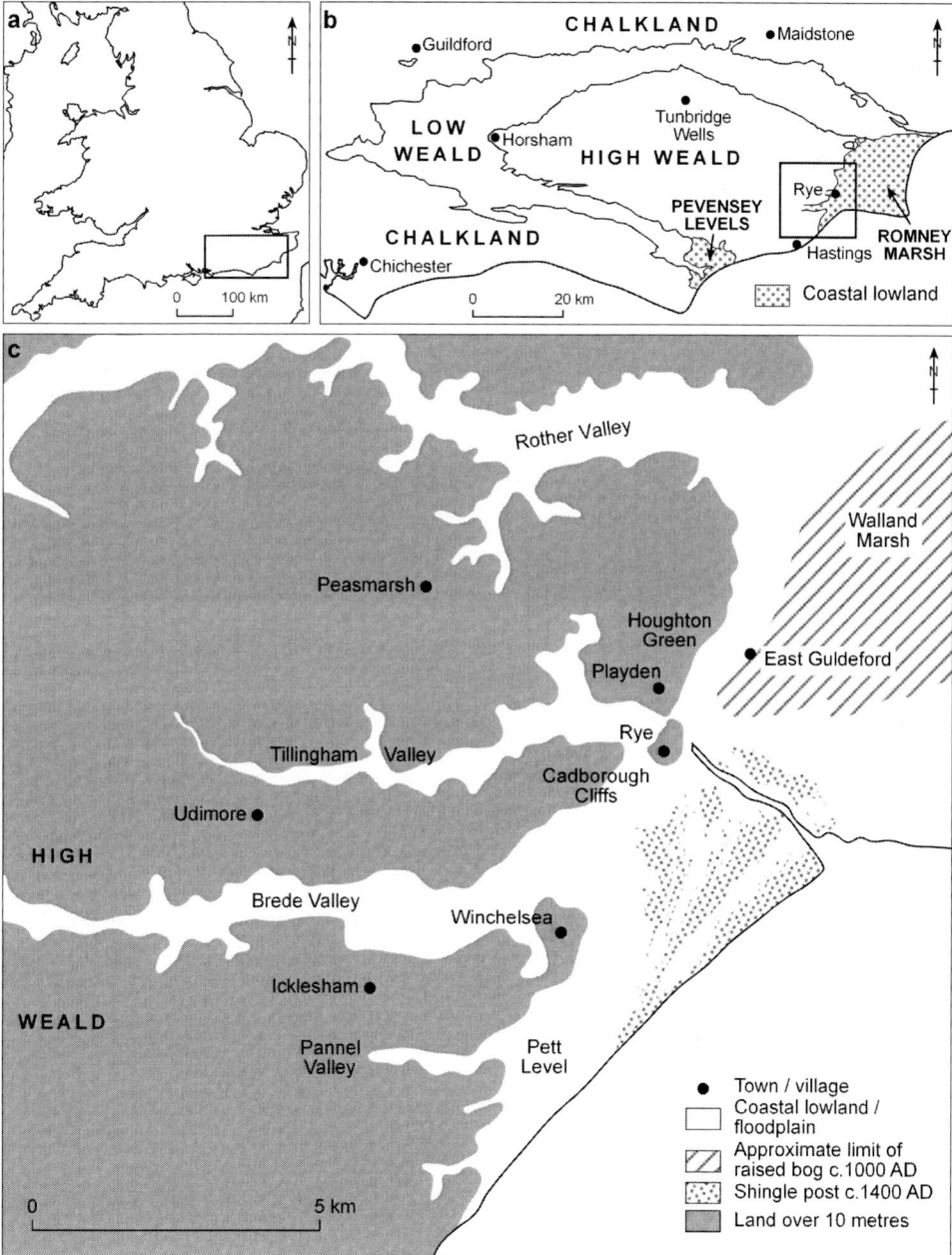

Fig. 1.2 Location map showing the *pays* of south-east England including the Weald, and Rye and its immediate hinterlands (after Long *et al*. 2007).

The early medieval trading places of Kent also need consideration. Several proto-urban coastal settlements lay to the north east of the location where the town of Rye was later established. These were trade and production sites known as *wics* or *emporia* in east Kent in the mid-Saxon period (*c.*650-850). Trade at Sandwich and Sarre on the Wantsum Channel, Fordwich, Dover, and *Sandtun*, near West Hythe, is indicated by the imported goods and boat parts found in burials in east Kent.[7] Little archaeological investigation has been made except at *Sandtun* and this trade may therefore have been more significant than has traditionally been suggested.[8] There is good evidence from coin finds for trade development in its primary phase to *c.*710 and particularly in its secondary phase. Trade was initially oriented towards eastern Francia and the Rhine mouth area. Coin finds make clear that each of the *wics*, those in east Kent connected to the Wantsum channel as well as those elsewhere, London, *Hamwic* and Ipswich, was the entrance from the North Sea or the Channel into its hinterlands.[9] Minting was concentrated in coastal areas and the need for currency in inland areas was met by coins from the coastal mints. There has been a small but significant number of early coin finds in east Kent at Folkestone which may or may not reflect a commercial context; Folkestone was part of the Cinque Ports confederation as a member of Dover from a very early period. One *sceatta* (small silver coin) dated between 500 and 600 has been found at West Hythe.[10] There are a large number of finds of coins from the second phase of trade. These coins were minted at places on the coast farther to the south west, Lympne, Hythe and Romney, and date from 924 onwards. Coin finds from Hastings date from the reign of Æthelred II (978-1016) and possibly from Old Winchelsea from the reign of Edgar (973-9).[11] The finds suggest that the trading significance of these two places in Sussex developed later than that of the east Kent *wics*, and reflects a re-orientation of English trade from the North Sea towards the ports of the lower Seine valley and Rouen. This re-orientation occurred firstly under the monastic houses based in the lower Seine valley such as Fontenelle and Jumièges in the eighth to ninth centuries, and then under the Viking displacement of Frankish merchants and traders and the repopulation of these ports by Scandinavians or Anglo-Scandinavians at the end of the ninth century.[12] In the next two centuries the importance of trade and travel between the continent and places on the south-east coast and the River Thames is reflected in the grant of Greenwich in 918 to St Peter's Abbey, Ghent, and of Rameslie and its port at or near Old Winchelsea to Fécamp Abbey between 1017 and 1032. Pre-Conquest grants of coastal and riverine lands such as these were designed in general to give the foreign monks easy access to their properties, and in the case of Fécamp to promote contacts and commerce.[13] Overall, coin finds suggest that the focus of trade moved from the early *wics* and *emporia* of east Kent to include coastal places a little further to the south west, New Romney from 741, and Old Winchelsea and then Rye in the 11th century.[14] These trade and production sites, from Sandwich in north-east Kent round to Hastings in Sussex, were the earliest origins of the settlements which developed into Cinque Ports and their members or 'limbs' during the 11th century.

Coastal change in the vicinity of Romney Marsh, the Dungeness foreland and the river valleys to the west is crucial to understanding the development of towns here. The extensive navigability of inland waters was fundamental to trade in the early medieval period and is particularly relevant to the development of the southerly members of the Cinque Ports confederation.[15] A model of the physical development of this locality between *c*.700 and 1250 held that a shingle barrier, permeated by salt water, existed across Rye Bay until breached in the late 11th century and finally broken down by storms of 1287 to 1288.[16] Recent palaeoenvironmental research has however provided new evidence of the physical development of this locality between *c*.700 and *c*.1250 (Figures 1.3, 1.4). By *c*.700-800 peat formation had ended and tidal waters had entered into the lower Brede valley to the north of Iham hill on which New Winchelsea stands, although active peat formation continued at the area later known as East Guldeford to the east of the future site of Rye (Figure 1.2).[17] There were tidal creeks to the south of the site of Rye in the Brede Levels and the Tillingham valley which probably connected to a breach in the shingle barrier to the south. At least as early as the 11th century a tidal inlet developed near the site of Old Winchelsea. There is also likely to have been a small channel to the east of the site of Rye, running towards Houghton Green to the north east of Playden. However, the predominant feature on the east side of the future site of Rye was a low dome formed by a large raised peat bog which was still extensive in *c*.1000. Some remnants of the peat may still have been in place in the 13th century making it unlikely, although not impossible, that the channel running past Playden connected with the main course of the Rother before storms of the 13th century diverted the river southwards to the Rye inlet. These storms are documented from 1236 but the storms of the middle and later part of the century seem to have been more severe.[18] There was also an inlet at Romney which is likely to have been connected by the Cheyne Channel to the Rother across northern Walland Marsh[19] and probably also to the breach near Old Winchelsea. Either the Romney or Old Winchelsea breaches would have provided easy access for a Danish raid and encampment near Appledore which occurred in 892.[20] The existence of a tidal inlet leading towards

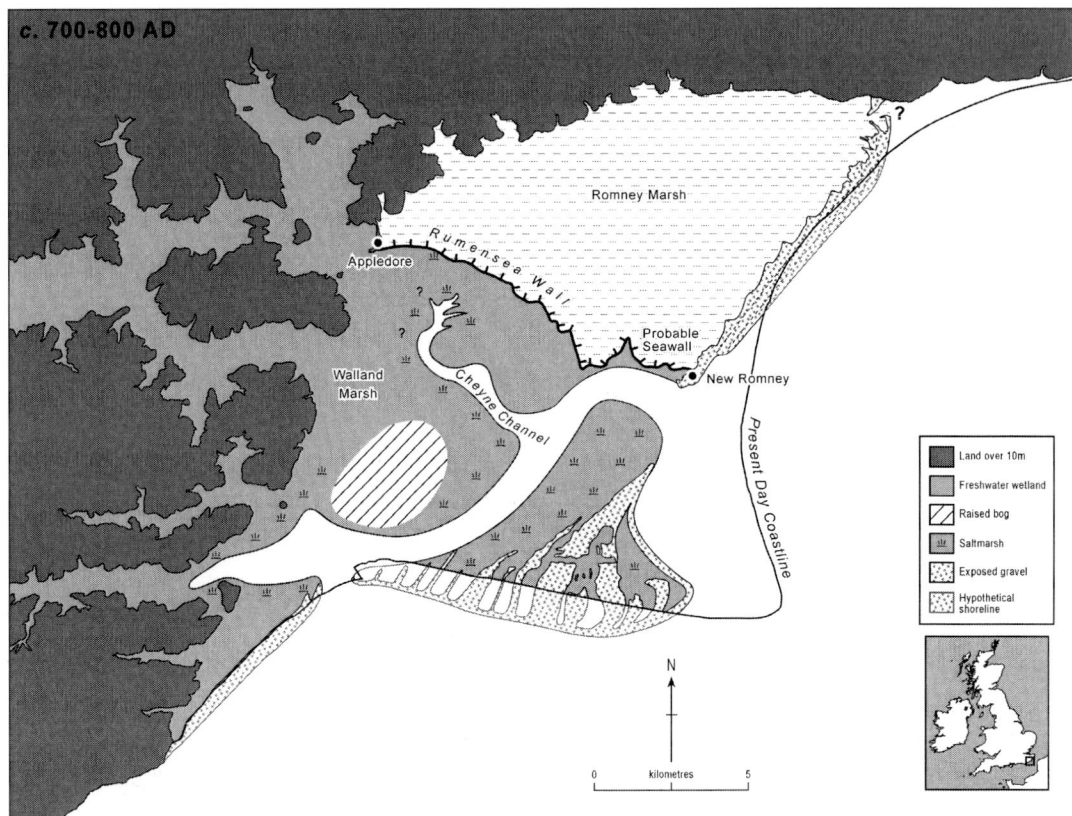

Fig. 1.3 Palaeogeographic reconstruction of Romney Marsh and Dungeness Foreland
c.A.D. 700-800 (after Long *et al*. 2007).

Rye by the 11th century, as opposed to the 13th, fits with the evidence of charters and Domesday Book which is examined next.

The Estate or Manor of Rameslie: The Evidence of Charters and Domesday Book

The development of Old Winchelsea and Rye is connected with the area on the coast at the eastern end of Sussex known as Rameslie (various spellings). The charter evidence from 1005 onwards is crucial for the identification of the new town of Domesday Book as Rye. Rameslie is first recorded in a charter of 1005 when it was granted to Eynsham Abbey in Oxfordshire. Eynsham Abbey was granted various lands, including Rammeslege, with its port or hythe, that is landing-place.[21] The charter is accounted genuine and was written partly in Latin and partly in English. Only Rammeslege itself was named, not Old Winchelsea nor Rye. No bounds were given for the estate of Rammeslege nor is there later evidence for them, although they are sometimes the subject of conjectural

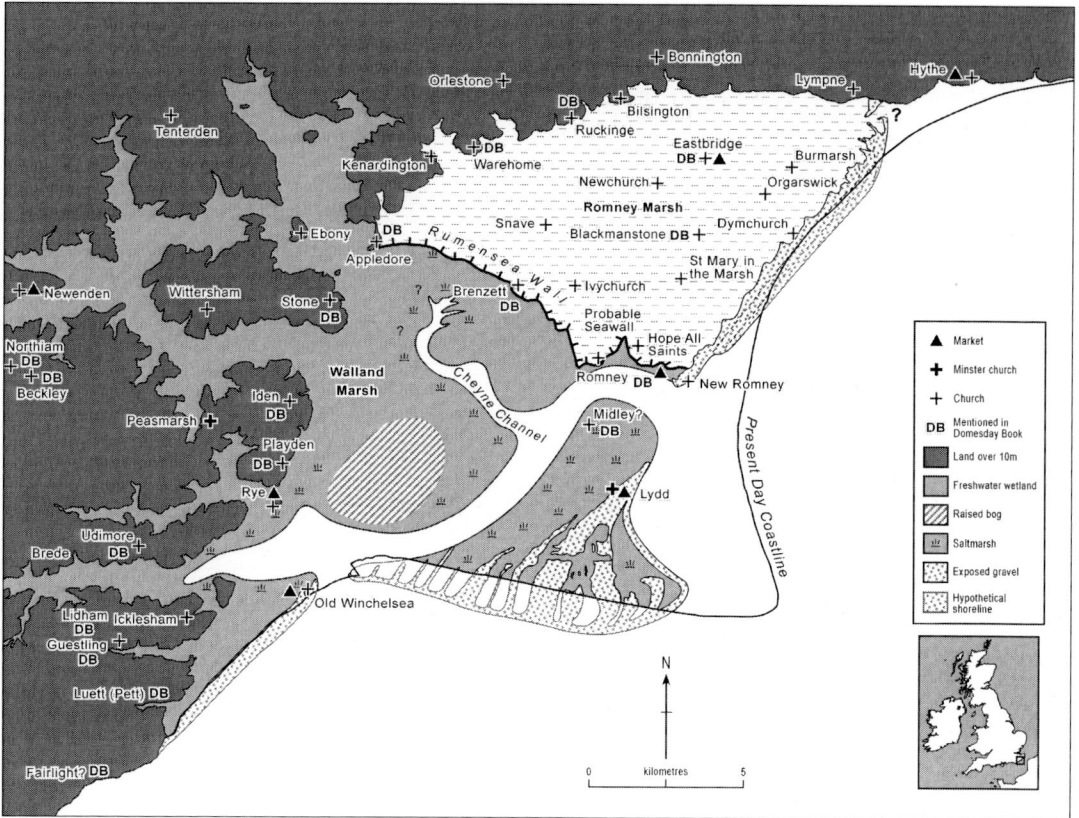

Fig. 1.4 The *c*. A.D. 700-800 palaeogeographic reconstruction with the addition of settlements of the 11th century evidenced by Domesday Book, church architecture and archaeology.

reconstructions including the proposition that land at Hastings formed part of Rammeslege. The mention of the port or hythe on this changing coastline was primarily a reference to the right to beach vessels and collect tolls rather than to the unalterable location of a landing place.[22] Between 1017 and 1032 Fécamp Abbey received 'the land called Rammesleah with its port' in a charter of Cnut, at the instigation of Cnut's wife Queen Emma. This grant was confirmed by his son Harthacnut who died in 1042 and there 'seems no occasion to doubt the original grant of Canute or the confirmation by his son'.[23] The charter survives only in a 13th-century copy, which brings together three distinct grants, that of Cnut and the confirmation by his son, and an amplification which recorded the grant to Fécamp of the farm (*tribuo*) and two-thirds of the tolls of *Wincenesel*, an early form of the place-name Winchelsea. Other land called Brede along the river valley from Winchelsea was included also.[24] It is now accepted that the existence of Old Winchelsea by 1042 is documented in this charter of Cnut and

Harthacnut.[25] Its tolls identify it with the port or landing place of the estate of Rammesleah, which Fécamp acquired by 1032, and indicate its main function as a place of trade, a function recorded again in 1130.[26]

There are two early, possibly contemporary, narratives of a journey by Abbot John of Fécamp to the Abbey's properties in Brede and Old Winchelsea in 1054. The narratives also record further grants of property in Sussex to Fécamp. Abbot John requested that Edward the Confessor grant the Abbey the church at Eastbourne which he did.[27] One of the two narratives recorded that the Abbey was granted saltpans, 12 houses and a plough-land at places in Sussex called Lamport (near Eastbourne) and Horse Eye (near Eastbourne or Pevensey), and a plough-land at *caestram*. This plough-land is possibly to be identified with the castle or fortified place at Hastings, *haestingaceaster*, or more likely with the former Roman fort at Pevensey.[28] Fécamp Abbey also claimed after the Conquest that it held the land of Steyning in West Sussex, but it is dubious whether it had held it in Edward the Confessor's time. In a charter of 1085 William the Conqueror confirmed the grant of Steyning despite his express doubts about the Abbey's claim to have held it before the Conquest. In the same charter William made an exchange with Fécamp of some rents in Hastings for the manor of Bury in Sussex, which may have been those of the plough-land at *caestram* (Hastings or Pevensey) which the Abbey held in the mid-11th century.[29] However, there is no suggestion in the narratives of this period nor the Eynsham charter of 1005 nor the Cnut/Harthacnut charter that any holding at Hastings formed part of the estate of Rameslie.

In Domesday Book Rameslie was included under the lands of the Abbey of Fécamp in Guestling hundred (Figure 1.5).[30] The Domesday entry stated firstly that the Abbot of Fécamp held Rameslie from the King and went on to summarise the taxable assets of Rameslie, which were assessed at 17½ hides. There was land for 35 ploughs, of which one plough was the lord's, and there were 100 villeins (servile tenants). There were five churches which paid 64s.; 100 salthouses (*saline*) which paid £8 15s.; seven acres of meadow, and woodland from which two pigs were owed as pasturage. The last entry under Rameslie is the record of a new town (*novus burgus*) with 64 townspeople (*burgensi*), who rendered £7 18s. Domesday Book moved on to record the holdings of Fécamp in the town and manor of Hastings.[31] For over a century scholars have recognised that the best interpretation of the record of the new town in the Rameslie entry is that it refers to Rye.[32] This is confirmed by new evidence for early minting at Rye. In 2002 a coin of Henry I type 11 (*c.*1115) of the Rye moneyer Ailward was found in a hoard from Pimprez near Beauvais (Oise). The hoard was deposited about 1140 and was discovered in the grounds of a house fifty kilometres north of Paris.[33] This find of a coin minted at Rye about the year 1115 fits well with its establishment as a new town by Fécamp Abbey in time to be recorded as such in Domesday Book in 1086.[34] Other early coins known to have been minted at Rye ('REIh') are two coins of a moneyer Eadweard of Henry I type 14 (c.1123-5). Other coins were minted at Rye ('RIEE') in the reign of Stephen (1135-54), the moneyer at this time being Randulf. These are similar spellings to the usual form of Rye in early documents, *Rie*. Two coins minted at Rye were discovered in Norfolk and one near Dover where they had presumably been carried, perhaps for trade.[35]

17 b TERRA ÆCCLÆ FISCANNENS. *IN GHESTELINGES HD.*

.V. A BBAS de Fifcanno ten de rege *RAMESLIE*.

7 de rege . E . tenuit . 7 tc fe defd . p xx . hid . modo
p . xvii . hid 7 dimid . Tra . e . xxxv . car.
In dnio e una car . 7 c . uilti un min hnt . xl.iii . car.
Ibi . v . æcclæ reddtes . lxiiii . folid . Ibi . c . faline de . viii.
lib 7 xv . folid . 7 vii . ac pti . 7 filua . ii . porc de pafnagio.
In ipfo m . e nouu burg . 7 ibi . lxiiii . burgfes reddentes
viii . lib . ii . folid min . In Haftinges . iiii . burgfes 7 xiiii.
bord reddt . lxiii . fot.
De ifto m ten Robt de haftinges . ii . hid 7 dimid de abbe.
7 Herolf dimid hid . Ipfi hnt . iiii . uillos . 7 iiii . cot . 7 ii . car.

5	LAND OF FECAMP CHURCH	17 b

In GUESTLING Hundred

1 The Abbot of Fecamp holds RYE from the King, and held it from King Edward. Then it answered for 20 hides; now for 17½ hides. Land for 35 ploughs. In lordship 1 plough. 100 villagers, less 1, have 43 ploughs. 5 churches which pay 64s; 100 salt-houses at £8 15s; meadow, 7 acres; woodland, 2 pigs from pasturage. In this manor is a new Borough; 64 Burgesses pay £8 less 2s; in Hastings 4 burgesses and 14 smallholders pay 63s. Robert of Hastings holds 2½ hides of this manor from the Abbot; Herewulf ½ hide. They have 4 villagers, 4 cottagers and 2 ploughs.

Fig. 1.5 Domesday Book entry for Rameslie and Rye from the 1976 edition, giving the Latin version and an English rendition. The Fécamp entry relating to Rameslie is clearly separate from the subsequent part of the entry dealing with Hastings.

Domesday Book describes landholdings as they were before the Conquest in the time of Edward the Confessor and then as they were in 1086. The implication of the words 'new town' is that Rye was established in the period after the Conquest and before 1086. From the early 12th century the names of some Rye townsfolk begin to be revealed: Ailward the moneyer in 1115, Robert de Rye in 1127 and, soon after, Agnes, widow of Hubert de Ria.[36] The townspeople enjoyed various privileges including paying a fixed annual cash rent to the lord, the Abbey of Fécamp, rather than carrying out the kinds of services provided by tenants on rural manors. They had the liberty to trade without paying tolls of the sort recorded at Old Winchelsea which were paid by outsiders. They were free to buy, sell, and bequeath land (below).[37] All these activities are documented once relevant records began to be made locally in the 13th century (*Chapters 4, 5*).

The Rye Inlet and the Surrounding Marshes

Rye's development depended on the existence of the tidal inlet (above) whose exact nature in the 11th and 12th centuries is unknown. It is nevertheless clear that by the late 12th century investment in marshland reclamation had already taken place in parts of the area to which the inlet led, Hope Marsh and probably White Fleet Marsh.[38] The word fleet refers to a channel through a marsh. Hope and White Fleet Marshes were parts of what came to be known as Cadborough Marsh; they lay below Cadborough cliffs and the hill on which New Winchelsea was later established (Figure 1.2). The area around Old Winchelsea must also have been reclaimed at this time since valuable tithes were due from the land there, to be paid by Laurence, the parson of Brede, and James son of Alard, a family based in Winchelsea.[39] In c.1220 a channel of water ran through the marshes of the Brede valley from Iham to the village of Brede where there was a bridge across the river, suggesting that land here too was reclaimed.[40] At this period the Rye inlet was described as 'the great fleet which goes towards Rye'.[41] It was widened to its maximum extent of four kilometres by the later 13th-century storms which necessitated further reclamation in the marshes through which its tidal water flowed.[42] As the Rye breach enlarged, deeper-water, higher-energy tidal channel conditions became established in the lower Brede valley.[43] Reclamation took place in this valley once again by 1332; this reduced the width of the tidal channels here, White Fleet, *Pipinesellefleet*, *Mareflet* and *Betelesflet*, and left productive and valuable marshland lying between these fleets.[44]

In the later 12th and early 13th centuries, men from Guestling, Old Winchelsea, Rye, Icklesham, Pett, Catsfield and Guestling exchanged and granted marshland around Rye, Old Winchelsea and Broomhill with a view to reclaiming it, partly prompted by the interests of Robertsbridge and Battle Abbeys in this locality. This activity seems to have been terminated by the mid-13th century when threats were perceived to newly enclosed marshes from marine flooding. Reclamation then took place again quite widely in the 14th century.[45] The names of some channels through the marshes such as *Finchesflet* and *Bradeflet* (Broad Fleet) are known but their locations cannot be precisely identified. *Finchesflet* was probably named from the wealthy Finch family of Winchelsea and Rye (*Chapters 2, 3*).[46]

Broomhill, Old Winchelsea and Romney

The tidal waters reaching northwards towards Rye penetrated via an inlet through the shingle between Old Winchelsea and Broomhill, as documents of the late 12th or early 13th century indicate.[47] Broomhill lay approximately one kilometre to the north east of Old Winchelsea and was in existence by 1129 (Figure 3.1). The earliest references to the place-name Broomhill are of the 12th century.[48] These references exist because of Battle Abbey's interest in the locality from this period; they do not mean there was no settlement there earlier. An excavation of a small part of the now destroyed church at Broomhill found four phases, none earlier than the mid-13th century, but there was evidence of earlier domestic activity which preceded the first construction phase, and it was proposed that future work may locate an earlier church building or indeed a village.[49] Broomhill church has been identified with the one known by 1129 as *Alscholt*.[50] Cooper in 1850 stated that *Alcotch* was the name of Broomhill in old deeds but failed to cite the deeds.[51] Gardiner noted that *Alcotch* is not otherwise known.[52] However it is probably identifiable with *Hocholte*, otherwise *Ockholte*, which is known as an early name associated with this locality in a deed of *c*.1220. The deed is a quitclaim to Gervase, son of Andrew of Old Winchelsea, from Hamo Bellede of Boxley, Kent, concerning all Hamo's lands with buildings which he held in Sussex and *Hocholte*. This was for a substantial consideration of 16½ marks of silver (£11). This quitclaim is undated but the parties and witnesses place it at *c*.1220. The witnesses included Henry Alard, from a family strongly associated with Old Winchelsea.[53] This documentary identification of the church of *Alschot* or *Alcotch* with *Hocholte* and Broomhill by 1129 contributes to the evidence of activity at Broomhill before the earliest phase of the destroyed church.

Old Winchelsea lay on a shingle ridge which was vulnerable to damage by storms and tides. In the early 13th century the economy of Old Winchelsea was based on wine-importing, milling, baking, fishing and shipbuilding.[54] In a charter of 1221 Hugh de Aleto, the prior of the Hospital of St John of Jerusalem, gave five specified tenements and a mill in Old Winchelsea (*Wincheles'*) to Fécamp Abbey. The charter points to the growth of Old Winchelsea since 1042. Fécamp was to exercise the same powers over the tenements and their tenants as it did by law and custom over its other tenements in Old Winchelsea. In return Fécamp Abbey agreed to pay various rents to the prior of the Hospital from these tenements, including 25d. for the tenement of Henry, son of Reynold, and the mill; 2d. for the tenement of Hugh de Dun', probably from a shipbuilding family known from 1305;[55] 6d. for the tenement of Henry Finch, presumably an early representative of the Finch family; 22d. for the tenement of William the baker, and 5s. 5d. for the tenement held by Martin Fetere (feter), Alwin, Jordan, and Albin King. In this locality a feter was a wholesale fishmonger.[56] The rents due from Fécamp Abbey to the prior of St John's Jerusalem were to be paid in London by its bailiff. The charter of 1221 noted that the rents of the tenements and the mill at Old Winchelsea were to cease to be paid if any of them were 'irrecoverably destroyed by the violence of the sea'.[57] This possible destruction became a reality by the mid-13th century. In

June 1244 Henry III granted the 'barons' of Old Winchelsea a toll on incoming wine ships in order to finance the construction of a quay for the defence and improvement of the town. This may represent an attempt to provide a suitable quay where cog ships could tie up in order to maintain Old Winchelsea's harbour facilities in the face of damage to its landing facilities.[58] Cogs became much more prevalent in the 13th century and needed a jetty or quay rather than merely being beached.[59] By the spring of 1251 the threat to Old Winchelsea from the sea was again noted, as well as to the danger of flooding in the surrounding marshes of Rye, Old Winchelsea, Iham, Icklesham, Fairlight, Udimore and Brede.[60] By 1271 a quay on the south side of St Thomas's church at Old Winchelsea had been carried away by floods and storms, and most of the church itself had fallen. By 1280 the site of Old Winchelsea was largely submerged and in that decade New Winchelsea was founded on the hill of Iham.[61]

The town and liberty of Romney comprised what became known as New Romney and Old Romney, which was a separate village. There may have been a *langport* or long port stretching down the tidal inlet between them which was the main outlet of the River Rother until the 13th-century storms. Charters and excavation make clear that Romney was by 741 a fishing settlement with an oratory dedicated to St Martin. By the later 11th century, Romney had clear urban characteristics demonstrated, for example, in its 11th-century mint and in its Domesday Book entry which describes an already established town and port with 156 townspeople (*burgensi*). The architecture of St Nicholas's church on the south-east margin of New Romney demonstrates that by the mid-12th century it was New Romney rather than Old Romney which was the settlement of growing significance. New Romney became a distinctively urban place, with two hospitals, a friary, three parish churches, a guildhall and a street layout which was renewed after 1234 to incorporate a new market space. There was a site of maritime activity on the beachfront to the north east of the town and a harbour close to the intensively used commercial quarter. Old Winchelsea and New Romney were in origin both beach trading places on inlets and both became early towns. There was a particular stimulus to the growth of New Romney in the reclamation of its very large marsh hinterlands from *c.*1050, in part for arable use. The analysis of pottery finds from a systematic programme of field-walking and pottery collection demonstrated that land use, population and the number of settlements grew greatly between 1050 and 1250.[62] However New Romney's location caused it to suffer much damage in the mid- to later 13th-century storms, particularly to trade and maritime activity on the beachfront. The loss of Old Winchelsea and the damage at New Romney set the scene for the further growth of Rye after its origins as a new town in the estate of Rameslie in the late 11th century.

The Foundation of Rye and Settlements in its Hinterlands

Why should Fécamp Abbey have wanted to establish a new town within its estate or manor of Rameslie after the Conquest? There are several reasons. Firstly it could establish a town which would emulate the development of other coastal or estuarine towns in the South East, or those just inland such as Battle.[63] A new town would make further economic use of the assets of Rameslie, particularly salt, which was heavily used in conjunction with herring fishing, and it would be able to exploit the potential of resources in the hinterlands.[64] Rye may have been a useful port for the trading and export of Wealden iron, and other products such as woad and other dyes, wood, pottery and stone. Before the 13th-century storms, the most direct route by water from the Weald to a port was to New Romney, and only subsequently to Rye, but the transport of iron by road to Rye was certainly possible from the time of the town's foundation (*Chapter 8*). Sussex was one of the centres of ironworking mentioned in Domesday Book and despite the limitations of the 11th- and 12th-century evidence, iron production in the Wealden hinterland of Rye and transport along the River Rother may have been significant. Iron and iron products were necessary for agriculture and weapons and the centres of ironworking 'would have sold raw iron and iron products to manors throughout England via the network of commercial institutions and, as the reputation of English ironworkers increased, to Europe as well'.[65] The iron industry depended on local resources, power supply and water transport, and supplied local agricultural and military needs, crucial to the defensive and shipping functions of the Cinque Ports. The iron industry flourished in this area in the second and third centuries and again in the Middle Ages, although the latter is not well researched. Where new archaeological and historical work on the Wealden iron industry exists, it emphasises its significance from at least the early 14th century when the commencement of the Hundred Years' War boosted the need for iron for boat fittings, weapons, armour and equipment for horses.[66] The industry was based on the local seams of ironstone in the Wadhurst Clay formation which are plentiful around the Wealden settlements of Mayfield and Rotherfield in Sussex and places to the east (Figure 3.1). Rotherfield is known as the site of late medieval iron production, and both Rotherfield and Mayfield had notably early churches; that of Mayfield dates to *c*.960 and that of Rotherfield to before 1100.[67] Mayfield is the location of the course of the upper Rother, with two watercourses joining from the Rotherfield direction, and the River Dudwell joining at Etchingham. The Rother flowed from its sources near Mayfield and Rotherfield, through Etchingham, Robertsbridge (Salehurst parish), Bodiam, Newenden, Smallhythe (Tenterden parish) and Appledore, and then reached the sea at first via the Romney inlet and later via the Rye inlet (Figure 1.4).[68] Iron production based on the availability of both ironstone and transport may have been one reason for the existence of these early settlements.[69] The surname of Gilbert de Maghfeld, the London ironmonger known in the 14th century, derives from Mayfield, suggesting that his family originated there and perhaps had earlier interests in iron production.[70]

The Domesday record of extensive salt production at Rameslie give no precise indication of the saltpans. To the north of Rye and south of Playden, under Point Hill, lies the settlement of Saltcote. Saltcote itself was on high ground and a lane, Saltcote Street, led down to another part of the settlement on lower ground next to the channel there (Figures 1.1, 7.1). The place name Saltcote refers to a specialised settlement concerned with salt production rather than with agriculture.[71] Saltcote may also have been a fishing settlement with beaching facilities for boats; two coins of Henry III's reign (1216-72) and medieval boat clinker nails have been found there.[72] The name Saltcote is first recorded in 1307 but the place may have existed earlier and it may have been the location of some of the 100 Rameslie salthouses.[73] In *c.*1100 the chronicle of Battle Abbey records that one Osbern, son of Isilia, gave Battle Abbey two saltpans and land for a third saltpan at Rye, for the benefit of his soul.[74] Before the 13th-century storms the tides probably flowed up past Rye to the area of Saltcote along a small channel, at the side of which the salt was made, as it was at New Romney where there was an area of saltmaking along the side of the tidal channel leading into the estuary and haven. Saltmaking at New Romney was recorded in the form of seven salthouses in the Archbishop of Canterbury's manor of *langport* in 1086.[75] The salthouses and saltpans of New Romney were however much less numerous than those of Rameslie, presumably including Saltcote, at the end of the 11th century.[76] After the 13th-century storms the Rother flowed south to the sea past Saltcote and Rye, and the creation of this estuary is likely to have changed the character of Saltcote significantly (*Chapter 8*).

By the mid- to late 11th century Rye had many settlements in its hinterland for which Fécamp could expect its new town to be the local, if not the regional, market. These settlements have been mapped from those recorded in Domesday Book, and from the archaeological and architectural evidence of churches in this locality (Figure 1.4).[77] The eastern geographical hinterlands of Rye were the Romney and Walland Marshes to which direct access was by boat. Immediately to the east of Rye lay the tidal inlet from the area between Old Winchelsea and Broomhill. To the east of Rye there were eighth-century settlements at Lydd on Dungeness and at Romney, and in the ninth century an estate at Misleham on Walland Marsh, which lay approximately one and a half kilometres to the south west of the later Brenzett church.[78] Colonisation of the Misleham area with precautions against flooding were recorded in the mid-12th century.[79] However, this flooding, the river course running towards New Romney and the raised peat bog account for the relatively sparse settlement immediately to the east of Rye and the absence of churches on Walland Marsh recorded in Domesday Book. The town of New Romney in any case provided the main market for settlements on Romney Marshes.

The western hinterland of Rye was, in terms of landscape, quite different. It was an area of ridges of high land deeply cut by rivers backing the western coastal strip around Hastings and Pevensey, where William the Conqueror landed. The settlements in the western hinterland include many known as manors from Domesday Book, and several marked by churches, including a suggested minster at Peasmarsh. Routes probably joined these settlements, running along the ridges and towards Newenden, an early bridging-point. Access from Rye to most of these places would also have involved ferries over or along watercourses.[80] However, Rye's most important asset as a new town was a narrow isthmus or land bridge leading north towards Playden approximately along the line of the current road from the (later) Landgate. This route was the shortest one across the boggy area to the north of Rye which was known before 1247 as North Marsh and later as St Mary's Marsh (*Chapter 9*); coring has revealed that this route may have originally lain on the bedrock.[81] Channels flowed around the west, east and south of Rye but the town was connected to the inland by the land bridge which was generally a dry route. Beyond North Marsh and Playden this route gave access to the Weald, particularly the area around Tenterden. A great growth of population and land use began in the mid-12th century in the Weald, including its south-east corner around Tenterden, and particularly from there south towards the Rother.[82] Thus by the later 11th century the immediate hinterlands of Rye were full of settlements, churches, markets and salt workings. The potential for a new town with good inland as well as coastal connections is clear, and Rye had these connections in a way which Old Winchelsea did not.

As the only overlord of its new town of Rye, Fécamp had sole control of the income from the rents of townsfolk, the income of the church, the tolls from trade and the profits of fishing. This undivided lordship at Rye was in contrast to some of the other towns, Hastings, New Romney, Hythe, Fordwich and Sandwich, where lordship and urban profits were divided between more than one lord.[83] In the late 11th century Rye offered the potential to develop the trading rights which Fécamp already had through its charter of Rameslie and the Old Winchelsea tolls. Little is known of Old Winchelsea in the late 11th century, apart from its origins as a trading place on a shingle bank. When 11th-century fleets sailed it was preferable for them to be anchored in an estuary rather than beached or tied up.[84] Since a tidal inlet had developed to the south of Rye at least as early as the 11th century, it is likely that Fécamp intended to exploit the potential of such an inlet or estuary between Old Winchelsea and Rye to offer a safe anchorage for merchants and fishermen, both coastal and cross-Channel. Records of the early 13th century onwards show this usage for vessels of the Cinque Ports and royal fleets, although it is difficult to reconstruct the nature of that inlet and anchorage closely between *c.*700 and *c.*1330 from either the physical or historical evidence (*Chapter 2*).

Rye: A Non-Feudal Island in a Feudal Sea

Rye is a good example of Postan's claim that medieval towns were 'non-feudal islands in the feudal seas'.[85] Fécamp Abbey held Rye from the monarch but in return for an annual cash payment released the town from direct control and allowed the leading townsmen, the *prudhommes*, to develop urban institutions which were largely run by them. A document in the Fécamp Abbey cartulary of the mid- to later 12th century recorded the grant from the Abbey to the men of Rye of some rights which characterised feudal or manorial tenure, *ledschet* and *childwite feld*. In return the townsmen were to pay 2½ marks (33s. 4d.) annually to the Abbey. This payment was secured on some rents of town property and if the rents were in default the townsmen in common were to make the payment of 2½ marks. At the same period the townsmen made an agreement with the Abbey of Fécamp about sharing the profits from fishing, the major economic activity at Rye at this time (*Chapter 2*).[86]

The townsfolk went on to establish a leper hospital (St Bartholomew's) and an associated fair. They negotiated the arrangements for choosing the priest of the hospital with Fécamp and also the profits of a fair, if they could persuade the king to allow the hospital to have one. The town's leper hospital was established a short distance outside the town but close to the route from Playden into Rye via the land bridge (*Chapter 8*).[87] The hospital was in existence by the time of

Abbot Ralf of Fécamp (1189-1219) when an agreement was drawn up between the Abbey and the leading townsmen of Rye.[88] In this Simon the priest and the brothers and sisters of the hospital acknowledged that they had received the chapel and houses of the hospital from the Abbey and half a virgate of land, nominally thirty acres.[89] In return Simon and the occupants of the hospital were to pay 2s. yearly to Fécamp at Christmas in place of the rents, services and dues from its lands. The Abbey retained the right to appoint the priest from among their own number with the advice of the *prudhommes* of the town. This suggests that Simon the priest was himself from Fécamp or certainly appointed by the Abbey; subsequently the choice was effectively that of the townsmen (*Chapter 7*). The charter also stated that if Simon and his brethren could obtain the right to hold a fair at Rye from the king, the Abbey would receive all the tolls of the town and port while the fair lasted, and Simon and the hospital inmates would share the profits of the fair on their ground with the Abbey. A charter of the same period concerned the very valuable custom of *aletal*, probably a toll on ale exacted at the fair; this was leased from the Abbey by the men of Rye for 120 marks (£80).[90] The charter was confirmed by the communal seal of Simon the priest and his brethren and the seal of the barons of Rye (an honorific term for Cinque Port townsmen, *Chapter 5*).[91] The fair appears to have been held at Fairfield to the north side of Rye, on a fairly flat site near the hospital lands.[92] Other suburban hospitals, such as St Bartholomew's, Dover, were given permission to hold fairs in the 13th century. A spacious site on a well-used route near a port or town which was a centre of population and production offered both commercial and charitable opportunities for fund-raising for a hospital.[93] There were many productive trades and crafts in Rye for which the fair would be an outlet, not least pottery, which was made near the site of the hospital and fair (*Chapter 5*), and it is clear from the lease of the custom of *aletal* that not only the hospital but also the townsmen expected to benefit from the fair. (For the location of the hospital and its later history, see *Chapter 7*).

These marks of liberty from Fécamp's direct overlordship were paralleled by the freedoms granted by the monarch which gave it the basis on which to develop its corporate status as an Ancient Town of the Cinque Ports confederation. In 1191 the town of Rye received a royal charter, one of many granted to members of the Cinque Ports confederation, which confirmed its freedom from the control of the shire (county) and hundredal system.[94] From that time on Rye was regarded as a hundred in itself, and had a seal matrix or die made which expressed a new corporate status, the seal of the hundred of the whole vill or town of Rye (*sigille hundredi*

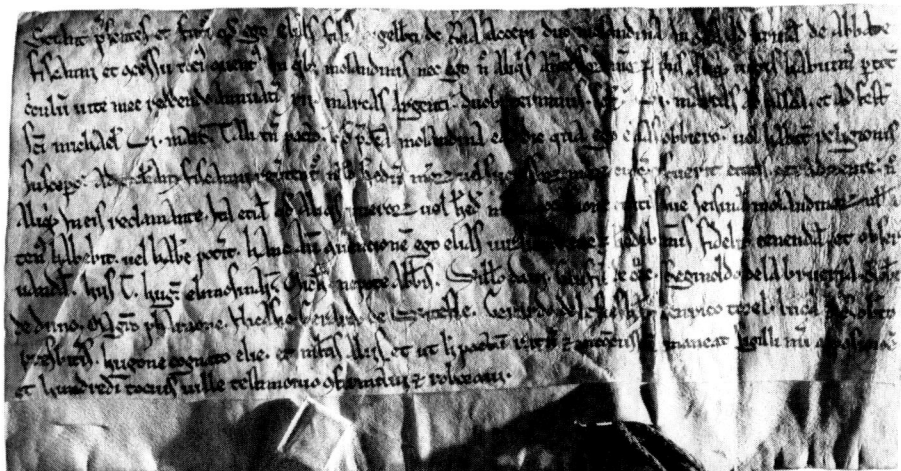

Fig. 1.6 The deed of Fécamp Abbey and Ellis of Rye with the early corporate seal of Rye, *c.*1190, ESRO AMS 4947.

totius ville) (Figures 1.6, 1.7) The seal was used on a charter between Fécamp Abbey and one Ellis de Rye which was witnessed by some leading townsmen of Rye.[95] The compilers of the later Rye custumal looked back to the hundred of Rye as the basis of its system of self-government. Rye had a mayor by *c.*1289 and, by the time of the compilation of the custumal at least, he was elected at the full and open hundred at the churchyard cross (*Chapter 5*).[96]

Ship Service and the Cinque Ports Confederation

The charter which Rye received in 1191 from Richard I confirmed rights which had been granted by his father Henry II (1154-89). The charter was granted jointly to Old Winchelsea and links the two towns to important developments in the Cinque Port confederation in the mid-1150s. These developments built on the provision of

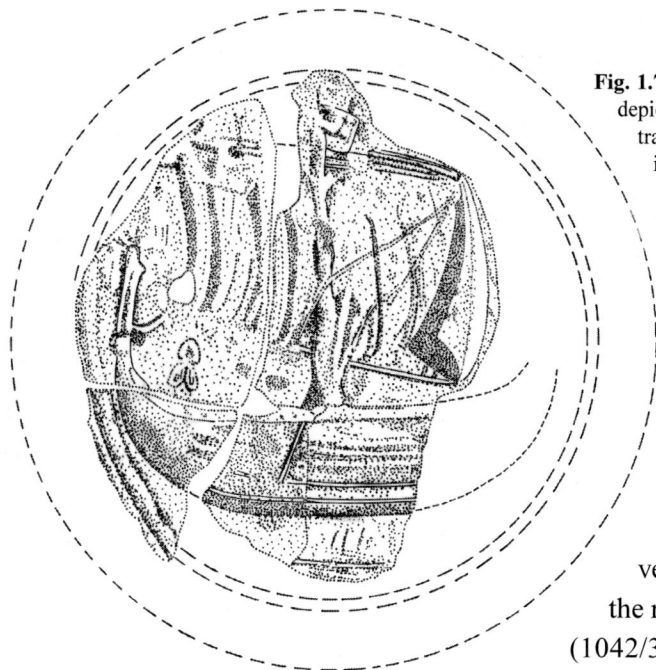

Fig. 1.7 Drawing of the *c.*1190 seal depicting a clinker-built ship in full sail travelling from left to right. There is a prominent stern-post with a steering-oar also visible and two ropes flapping from the spar carrying the sail. A member of the crew is shown in the stern and possibly one at the top of the mast.

mariners and ships for service at sea by the Head Ports of Dover, Sandwich and Romney from the reign of Edward the Confessor (1042/3-66).[97] Ship service became more significant once William's Conquest finally established England as part of an Anglo-Norman kingdom. Subsequent cross-Channel traffic and invasions required the south-eastern ports, having the shortest crossings, to provide transport for the king and his forces, as well as protection against raids. The Ports' service can be summarised as a total of 57 ships for a fortnight a year. The ships had twenty mariners and a steersman. These were too small to be warships, and may have been used for scouting in the Channel or to transport perhaps sixty soldiers.[98] Ship service was also provided by the two other Head Ports, Hastings and Hythe. All the Head Ports were aided by 'limbs' or members, small coastal settlements generally nearby, which provided some of the vessels and sailors. Lydd and Dengemarsh, for example, were members of Romney, and Rye and Old Winchelsea were at first members of the Head Port of Hastings.

The Head Ports received individual charters shortly after the coronation of Henry II which confirmed liberties they already possessed in return for ship service.[99] It was usual for newly crowned monarchs to confirm rights in this way but in addition Henry II was proposing a visit to Normandy and planning the conquest of Ireland, and needed transport ships for both. During Henry II's reign Rye and Old Winchelsea developed and then eclipsed Hastings in economic and maritime importance and, like the Head Ports, they began to receive the liberties which are known from the charter of 1191. The most important liberty for the development of urban government was freedom from the control of the shire system of taxation and justice, but Rye and Old Winchelsea were also freed from tolls such as *lestage*, *passage* and *rivage* on trading or landing at other coastal towns or passing through them. Together with Hastings and the other Head Ports they had joint rights to appoint a bailiff to oversee the Yarmouth herring fishery and yearly fair. Mariners from Hastings, Rye and Old Winchelsea held land on the shore at Yarmouth where they landed and sold fish. These rights of 'den and strond' were granted to the Portsmen as early as 1218 in return for supporting Henry III against the king of France and if necessary against his own rebellious barons; the rights were an ongoing cause of friction and violence between the men of these ports.[100] By 1247 Rye and Old Winchelsea were called 'noble members of the Cinque Ports' and later Ancient Towns.[101] As part of their change of status, the number of ships they supplied for royal service increased. Rye originally supplied two out of Hastings' 21 vessels, although it supplied four in 1337, at which time Old Winchelsea supplied ten.[102] The numbers supplied depended on the occasion for which ship service was required, with marked changes occurring in the numbers supplied between the early 13th and the early 14th centuries by the various ports of the confederation, and also by ports elsewhere (*Chapter 2*).

The development of the Cinque Port as a confederation and its period of greatest political influence derived from the loss of Normandy in 1204, the civil war and invasion of Louis the Dauphin in 1215 to 1217, and ultimately the loss of Poitou in 1224. The events of 1215 to 1217 exemplify the crucial roles of Rye and Old Winchelsea as entry and exit points to the kingdom. When King John died in October 1216, his nine-year-old son was crowned Henry III with the support of the Pope and English bishops. Half of Henry's kingdom, London and the eastern area, was nevertheless controlled by Louis to whom rebel earls and barons had offered the crown in spring 1216. The townsmen made important choices over whether to support the Dauphin Louis or the young Henry III and his justiciar Hubert de Burgh who was also Constable of Dover Castle, who had a crucial role in controlling the Cinque Ports; like the other supporters and opponents of the boy king the townsmen chose and changed sides according to a mixture of loyalty and self-interest. The King's supporters were William Marshal, Earl of Pembroke, and regent between 1216 and 1219, some great magnates including Hubert de Burgh, aliens such as Peter des Roches, Bishop of Winchester, and English sheriffs and castellans such as Philip de Albini (d'Aubigny). The King's opponents were many of the great earls and barons, including Gilbert de Clare, lord of Tonbridge castle and subsequently also Earl of Hertford and Gloucester.

The invasion of Louis the Dauphin in 1216 was based, as was usual in 13th-century warfare, on the capture of towns, especially those with castles, as strategic strongholds in which food supplies and English soldiers were concentrated. Control of the towns of the Cinque Ports confederation was also vital in order to keep open options for entering or leaving England, and these towns themselves controlled a large number of the vessels which were used for crossing the Channel. When Louis arrived in the spring of 1216 following the rebels' invitation, he landed at Thanet. This was perhaps to avoid Portsmouth, John's preferred port, and also Hubert de Burgh's stronghold at Dover. Dover was the military headquarters of the Cinque Port confederation, and Hubert de Burgh, who had personal interests in remaining loyal to the crown, was undoubtedly influential in ensuring that the other Cinque Ports in Kent supported the royal party too.[103] On Louis' arrival King John resumed Rye into his own hands from its overlord Fécamp Abbey and placed two of his own men, Aubrey de Den and Geoffrey de Craucomb, as keepers.[104] In the summer of 1216 John found it necessary, too, to offer additional privileges to the confederation ports of Hastings, Pevensey, Rye and Old Winchelsea to secure their loyalty, and also to Shoreham.[105] Despite John resuming Rye from Fécamp and attempting to secure the loyalty of the Cinque Ports, Louis landed at Rye with a large following from La Rochelle. He captured the town without too much resistance and placed it under the command of Baduin de Corbeil.[106] Rye was thus captured, or at least under the influence of Louis' forces, in the summer of 1216. At this time goods and chattels belonging to the men of Old Winchelsea, including wine, which had been taken to Rye, were detained by men of La Rochelle.[107] After the death of John and coronation of his young son in the autumn of 1216, the new King's captain Philip de Albini established himself at Rye, assisted by the Cinque Ports and by men of the Wealden forest under the organisation of William of Cassingham, a place near Rolvenden; William was also known as Willikin of the Weald and appears as a kind of Robin Hood figure there.[108] Albini managed to confine Louis and his vessels at Old Winchelsea. Rye was a useful strategic base because it allowed Philip de Albini access to the shared anchorage between Rye and Old Winchelsea and, via the route leading north out of Rye, to the Wealden hinterland where men who supported him were in control.

The regent William Marshal and his forces travelled in the course of the autumn and winter of 1216 to 1217 towards Old Winchelsea and Rye. However, when they reached Surrey (Chertsey or Dorking) on 28 February 1217 Marshal was told by Albini that Rye had been retaken, that a French fleet had broken the blockade of Old Winchelsea, and that Louis had sailed away to France. This success by Louis was temporary, and the final stage of the civil war was the battles at Lincoln and off Sandwich. Louis returned to England in the early spring of 1217. Since Hubert de Burgh had prevented Dover castle being captured in the previous year Louis started to besiege it again on 12 May 1217, an action which occupied many of his men. Thus when Henry's forces began to threaten the town of Lincoln, only part of Louis' supporters were available to defend it, and Lincoln fell to the Henricians. They then debated whether to march on London or to Dover to relieve the castle which was still being held by Hubert de Burgh. In fact they did neither, but by June 1217 Louis faced the likelihood of final defeat and started peace negotiations in London. The next two months were occupied by minor military actions, and the submission of some of Henry's former opponents to Henry's regent. A planned great council at Oxford on 25 August was forestalled by a sea battle off Sandwich after reinforcements of the French fleet, organised by Louis' wife, were spotted arriving from Calais on 24 August, St Bartholomew's day. Hubert de Burgh led out a fleet of ships from Dover and other Cinque Ports and, with the aid of a 'great cloud' of irritant lime dust hurled in pots from a cog onto the French flagship, finally defeated the French fleet headed by one Eustace. Eustace was known as 'the monk' and was formerly the bailiff and seneschal of the count of Boulogne, a pirate and traitor, at least in the sense of transferring his allegiance from King John to Louis. Louis himself was not present at the battle off Sandwich and sued for peace on 26 August on hearing of the disastrous end to his campaign.[109] The people of Sandwich are said to have attributed the victory to a sudden storm and to the intervention of St Bartholomew to whom they dedicated a hospital in the town.[110]

Rye, Winchelsea and the Loss of Poitou

Between 1217 and 1223 Henry III, his regent and his advisers concentrated on suppressing internal conflicts and rebellions in England. In 1223 Louis the Dauphin succeeded Philip Augustus to the French throne as Louis VIII and a truce with Henry III was ended. In 1224 Louis overran Henry's territory of Poitou and La Rochelle, threatening that he would do the same in Gascony.[111] In that year, in preparation for renewed fighting in Poitou, Henry ordered the bailiffs and 'honest and worthy men' of the Head Ports and Ancient Towns and elsewhere to keep all their ships in port, and to prepare them for service. They were not to permit any ships with merchandise or anything else to leave port without the king's special permission, and they were to halt all men and ships coming to their port from across the sea.[112] In the same year the bailiffs of the ports around the coast from Lynn (Bishops, later Kings, Lynn) as far as the Thames were ordered to allow barons of

Old Winchelsea and the other Cinque Ports to buy grain for their sustenance. The bailiffs were to take bonds that the barons of the Cinque Ports would take the grain only for their own use.[113] In 1225 Louis threatened to invade England, and although the threat was not carried out, Henry visited the Cinque Ports to seek their advice on co-ordinating defence measures.[114] Mariners from many Cinque Ports and eastern ports were ordered to bring their ships to Portsmouth to travel to Gascony with the fleet of the King's brother Richard, with the names of individual mariners who led the vessels being recorded (*Chapter 2*).

The Final Resumption of Rye and Old Winchelsea into Royal Hands

The regent Hubert de Burgh suggested in the 1220s that Henry III reclaim Rye and Old Winchelsea from Fécamp Abbey, and the King started to negotiate to resume the two towns in 1226, specifically because he intended to have a castle built at Rye (*Chapter 8*).[115] However the resumption of these towns did not happen immediately and in 1238 Henry III confirmed the position of the abbot of Fécamp as overlord. In the 1230s and early 1240s Rye, Old Winchelsea and Head Ports were called to provide ships for service, including for the feudal and dynastic struggle known as the Saintonge War of 1241 to 1242. Henry III supported his half-brother Hugh de Lusignan XI against Louis IX of France in a conflict centred on the coastal territory to the west of Saintes, the area immediately to the north of Bordeaux and Gascony, and south of La Rochelle and Poitou. On 14 July 1243, at the end of this conflict, a mandate was sent to the barons of the ports of Sandwich, Old Winchelsea, Hythe, Hastings, Dover and Romney 'to come to the king with ships well manned and equipped with good men, to take the king happily back to England'.[116] But Louis had in fact been the victor in the Saintonge war, marking Henry's acceptance of the final loss of the lands in Poitou. After this Henry resumed Rye and Old Winchelsea into his own hands between 1245 and 1247 in exchange for four inland manors and hundreds in Gloucestershire and Lincolnshire since it was crucial for him to be in control of these ports.[117] Even so he left Fécamp Abbey with land outside Rye on the northern side, known as Rye Foreign, as well as the manor of Brede.[118] From 1247 Rye town was therefore subject to the monarch rather than Fécamp as overlord. The townsmen however remained in control of Rye's internal affairs, and the king's bailiff and keeper or warden directed its role in defence and providing ship service, particularly in times of conflict (*Chapter 5*). The early 13th century saw the development of offices such as Keeper of the Coast to oversee and control both the king's own small fleet and the ship service of the Cinque Ports and other ports in the south and east. A Keeper of the King's Galleys and Ports is also known from 1224 when Geoffrey (Godfrey) de Lucy was appointed. He was to keep the peace at sea and punish crime, including piracy, and his functions were shared with those of the Warden of the Cinque Ports whose remit covered the coast from Pevensey eastwards. The role of Keeper of Galleys and Ports ceased to exist in the mid-13th century and was replaced by the more general one of Keeper of the Sea, an office held by 'obscure persons, probably practical mariners, such as Jeremiah of Rye'.[119] This change went alongside the growing importance of the role of the Warden of the Cinque Ports.

The Boundaries of Rye at the Time of the Resumption of the Liberty from Fécamp Abbey in 1247

The boundaries of the liberty of Rye at the time of its resumption by the crown were confirmed in a charter of 15 May 1247.[120] They can be partly reconstructed as running on the north side of Rye along a lane from the land of the leper hospital to the lane which ran west from the area outside Landgate to Blikewell or Blykewell; Blykewell was also known as Dodeswell, the form in which the bounds give it (*Chapters 8, 9*). The bounds then ran westwards past two places now lost, the cross of *Horbergw'a* and *Fingerline*. At *Fingerline* there was a gutter (sluice) through the middle of the dyke, here meaning wall rather than ditch, which can probably be identified with the western end of North Marsh. The bounds then ran to the middle of Colemersh 'as an old dyke runs'. Colemersh may be the 'saltmarsh called Colpit near the Wish in St. Mary's Marsh', which lay to the north-west of Rye.[121] On the west side the bounds continued up to the fee of William de Etchingham and then along that fee down to the sea, probably to be identified as the area to the west of Rye known as West Strond in the 14th century.[122] The charter noted that all the water on either side of the town belonged to Rye. The bounds also included the sea going up from the entrance to the mill race to the fee of James de Northeye, and along the king's highway to the steps on the fee of Brice Palmer (*Chapter 6*). The only king's highway was the route towards Playden and the steps may refer to this route, or to steps up the cliff on the eastern side of Rye. There are sufficient known points in these boundaries to be clear that on each side they enclosed a small area below and north of the hill on which Rye stands, as well as the town itself.[123] Lands further to the north of Rye were *forensecis terris* (Rye Foreign) and not within the bounds of the liberty, but they remained part of Fécamp's holdings, and included the site of the leper hospital and fair. In 1248, the year after the formal resumption of Rye, Henry III confirmed that Fécamp's bailiff, rather than his own, should be in control of Rye Foreign.[124] This left Rye and its Foreign as classic bipartite structure of the kind sometimes formed from the foundation of a new borough within a manor or estate. The Foreign lay outside the town proper but retained quasi-urban characteristics such as tax exemption for its residents.[125] The town proper, called the liberty, comprised the area of urban streets, market place, church site and the part of the marshy area to the north (North Marsh) which lay between it and the Foreign (*Chapter 9*). An arc of marshland from the north west to the north east of Rye is marked as Liberties of the Town of Rye on an early 20th-century Ordnance Survey map, reflecting a general knowledge of the location of the liberty but a lack of precision due to marshland reclamation and the large changes in the estuary since the Middle Ages.

Fig. 2.1 Ships shown on the seals of the barons of Rye in the 14th century (after Ross 1865 and Boys 1792).

CHAPTER 2

Mariners, Pilgrims and Pirates

Rye's Contribution to the Cinque Ports Service in the 13th and 14th Centuries

Rye's economy was based primarily on the sea, as the town seals suggest, and fishing was important enough to be the subject of a major agreement between the townsmen and Fécamp Abbey in the 12th century (Figure 2.1).[1] Fishing and trade of many kinds involved the seamen of medieval Rye in maritime activity over long distances in small or large vessels. The availability of mariners and ships underpinned Rye's growing importance as a member of the Cinque Ports confederation, a growth demonstrated in the contrast between the numbers of vessels supplied for ship service in 1225 and in 1337.

In 1225 Henry III was on the point of losing the province of Gascony and its two major towns, Bordeaux and Bayonne, to Louis VIII of France. A decision of great importance was made to fight to retain Gascony, which then remained in English hands for the next 225 years. It was made possible by sending a very large number of troops under the command of Richard, Henry III's teenage brother and Earl of Cornwall, and the Earl of Salisbury. The cost of this successful campaign was very high and was financed by a new tax which raised £40,000. The retention of Gascony however meant that its wine trade dominated the English market from 1225 onwards and produced large profits for the merchants of the south-east ports, most notably Winchelsea. From the summer of 1225 fleets of ships were sent yearly by the barons of the Cinque Ports to bring home the Gascon wine. It was a trade which subsequently brought in thousands of pounds to the monarch in annual customs levied on the export of wine at Bordeaux. This was a major force behind royal support for establishment of New Winchelsea once Old Winchelsea

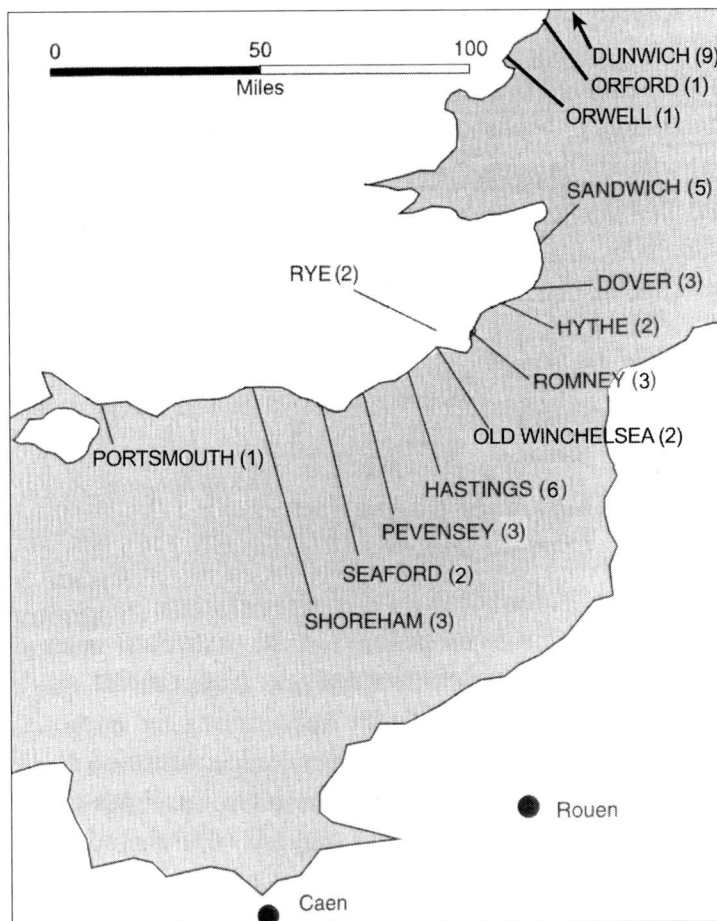

Fig. 2.2 Ports of origin of ships sailing on the king's service in 1225 (after Martin *et al*. 2004).

had been lost to the sea, and the former became the main centre for the import of Gascon wine.[2]

The assembly of the fleet in 1225 provides important information about the number of mariners and ships from various ports which travelled to Gascony with Richard, Earl of Cornwall.[3] These can be compared with the ports of origin of ships assembled at Sandwich in 1337 at the start of the Hundred Years War (Figures 2.2, 2.3).[4] The most striking point is the absence, in 1225, of vessels from the south and west of England and the presence of 11 vessels from the east coast, nine of them from Dunwich, a major port later severely damaged by storms and tides, particularly between 1287 and 1293.[5] Of members of the Cinque Ports confederation, Rye contributed four ships in 1337 as against two in 1225, but Hastings, of which Rye had been a member, contributed significantly fewer, six ships in 1337 compared with 10 in 1225. Old Winchelsea contributed two ships in 1225 but its replacement town New Winchelsea contributed 25 ships in 1337.

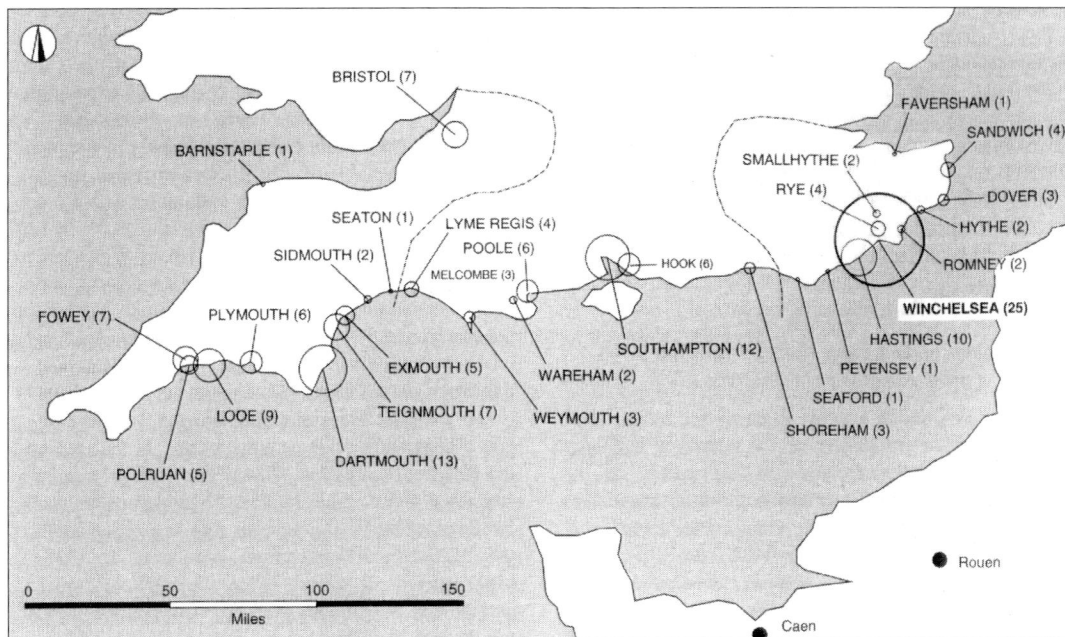

Fig. 2.3 Ports of origin of ships assembled at Sandwich in 1337 at the start of the Hundred Years War (after Martin *et al.* 2004).

Sandwich, New Romney and Seaford contributed one fewer vessel each at the later date, and Pevensey two fewer. Two ports which had not contributed vessels in 1225 did so in 1337, Smallhythe (two vessels) and Faversham (one vessel). Faversham was a member of Dover, and Smallhythe would in time became a member of Rye, as part of Tenterden. The purposes for which the ships were summoned in 1225 and 1337 were not identical, but the differences in the ports of origin reflect what is known about the fate of the harbour and beaching areas of the various Cinque Ports over this period, as follows. There were three hythes (landing places) belonging to Hastings. Two were 11th-century hythes of which one was part of the original settlement of Hastings and the other at Bulverhythe, some three miles distant. The third hythe is a conjectural quay at the beach area of the 'new town' of Hastings of *c.*1200.[6] This quay, together with the beach area and southern part of the new town, was subsequently lost to the sea. By the early 14th century Hastings did not have a safe anchorage nor did it attract foreign merchants to trade. Seaford was a landing place with rights of jurisdiction which were defined in 1262 but which perhaps originated in the 11th century. It became an early member of Hastings and sent two men to Parliament from 1298. It provided a small number of men and vessels for fleets in the 13th and first half of the 14th centuries but was much less important after the 1360s as it was damaged by coastal change. The same applied to the port of Pevensey from the early 14th century. The harbour of New Romney had been severely damaged in the mid- to late 13th-century storms, particularly that of December 1287. Of the easterly Cinque Ports, Hythe developed rapidly from the late tenth century and replaced a trading settlement at Lympne due to coastal change. In 1086 Hythe was recorded as having 230 burgesses (townsmen) and thus appears a flourishing new town. However Hythe's harbour was silting up by 1230 and after the storms of 1287 and 1288 sandbanks appeared in front of the anchorage there. Digging works in the harbour were ordered in 1412. The loss of the harbour was a slow process but had occurred by the mid-15th century, as it did at New Romney. Dover was forced to rebuild its harbour after the late 13th-century storms.[7] At Sandwich there was an early settlement to the east of the present town which grew up on a new, but nearby, site sometime after *c.*1000. New sandbanks built up across the entrance to Sandwich's excellent harbour after the storms but the harbour nevertheless continued to function, with the town reaching the peak of its trade between 1377 and 1400.[8] The decreased contribution of vessels in 1337 by Hastings, Seaford, Pevensey, Hythe, New Romney and even Sandwich is thus largely explained by the fate of their landing places and harbours, on which their trading and fishing economies depended. The increased contribution by Rye of four ships and by Winchelsea of 25 ships depended not only on the establishment of the new town at New Winchelsea but also on the shared anchorage between them and their individual port and landing areas.

The Shared Anchorage and Harbour Facilities at Rye and New Winchelsea

Between the 13th and the early 15th centuries royal instructions often commanded fleets composed of ships from the Cinque Ports and other ports to assemble at 'the port of Winchelsea'.[9] The port of Winchelsea comprised the sheltered anchorage between Rye and New Winchelsea (Figure 2.4), the successor to the harbour area between Old Winchelsea and Rye which was blockaded by sea in 1216 (*Chapter 1*). The sheltered anchorage was known by 1330 as the Camber.[10] Contemporaries described it sometimes as the port of Winchelsea and sometimes as the port of Rye, reflecting its location between the two towns.[11] The significance of the anchorage in the late 14th century was such that Rye was named as an alternative to Southampton for some imports from Ireland in 1364.[12] In 1374 John atte Wode, captain of the New Romney town barge, was arrested for refusing to give up goods taken from Italian merchants and resisting capture at the Camber by Rye.[13] A complaint of 1399 about merchants dumping ballast in 'the port of Winchelsea' described it as including the channel or course of the Rother from Camber to Bodiam. Traders arriving daily in ships and smaller vessels at the port of Winchelsea to collect goods were condemned for depositing stones, sand and other ballast in this channel. This was said to harm both the town of New Winchelsea and its adjacent haven (*Chapter 3*, Figure 3.4).[14] The anchorage was actively in use in wartime in 1423 when vessels of between 20 and 200 tons from Southampton, Dorset, Devon and Cornwall were ordered to be assembled there.[15] In the early 15th century Venetian traders assembled small numbers of galleys in the Camber, or outside it perhaps, when the tides were out. On a chart of 1436 by Andrea Bianco showing harbours the Camber (*camera*) was depicted simply as a large sheltered semi-circular bay with inlets running up towards Winchelsea, Rye and Romney.[16] This anchorage lay in the liberty of Winchelsea which included the area to the north east of New Winchelsea and the River Brede, between New Winchelsea and Rye, in the area where the castle (Camber Castle) now stands. In the 14th and 15th centuries the anchorage

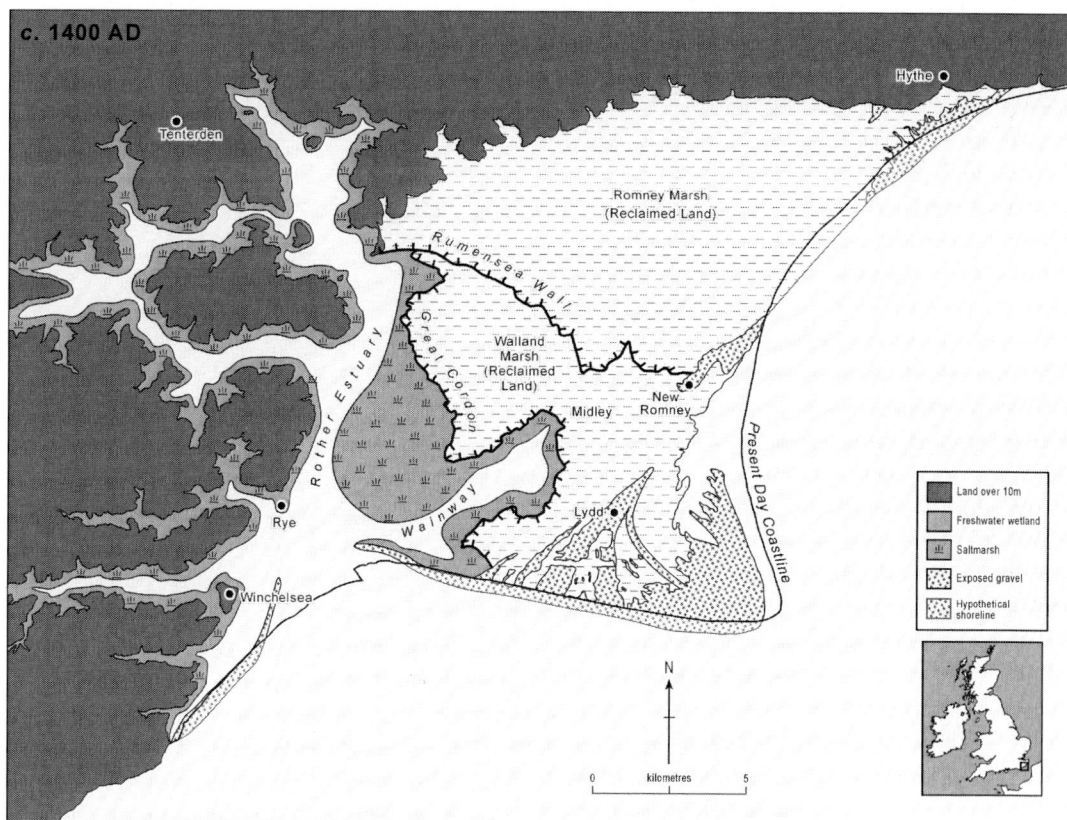

Fig. 2.4 The locations of Rye and New Winchelsea in the late Middle Ages; the shared anchorage lay between them (after Long *et al.* 2007).

was protected by a spit of shingle which was being newly formed or reworked to the east of the Dynsdale Sewer which lay to the east of New Winchelsea (Figure 2.5; see also Plate V). In around 1500 the Guldeford family made the defensive tower which later became part of Camber Castle on the headland at the end of this spit, in order to protect the estuary and harbour better. The area between New Winchelsea and the site of Camber Castle, i.e. the end of the headland, was salt and fresh marsh which were increasingly silted. In 1528 a long bridge was built across the Dynsdale sewer to reach the headland.[17] To the east of the spit and headland, access to Rye by water was maintained throughout the 16th century, and was the basis of its flourishing harbour until the early 17th century. As depicted by John Prowez in *c.*1572, large ships anchored on the main sea to the south-east of Camber Castle and in the 'Channell up toward bromehill [Broomhill] called the Camber'.[18] Smaller vessels anchored in Rye Creek on the west of town (Plate V, Figure 9.1) .

Landing Facilities within Rye and New Winchelsea

In addition to the Camber, medieval Rye had strands (beaches) where vessels could be drawn up: the east strand was damaged by inundations in the mid-14th century and the west strand, the area later known as Rye Creek, continued in use (*Chapter 8*). New Winchelsea had private harbour plots for merchants which were laid out under the cliffs of the town on its northern side. The estuary of the River Brede flowed past these harbour plots (Figure 2.5). However the estuary probably consisted of tidal mud flats and salt marsh which were overflowed at high tide in the late 13th and 14th centuries. The main navigable channel was probably narrow, and in this it was comparable with the inlet and harbour at New Romney.[19] The channel gave access to the harbour plots of New Winchelsea only at high tide and by 1344 nearly half of the plots had been abandoned, presumably because the channel had moved and no longer gave access to them. From the establishment of the town of New Winchelsea, both resident and foreign ships also used the separate common quay at the strand area to the north-east of the town, an area described in August 1324 as one in which several vessels could land at the same time on account of its size.[20] However by 1440 the diminished size of channel here too meant that fewer vessels could moor at once, and in order not to block access up the River Brede they were only allowed to do so while loading or discharging. By the 16th century this quay at New Winchelsea was simply a tidal mooring inlet.[21]

Until the 13th century many of the vessels using these facilities were galleys, and thereafter cogs, the usual transport ships of the 13th century, which could be converted into warships if necessary. Sometimes a simple distinction was made

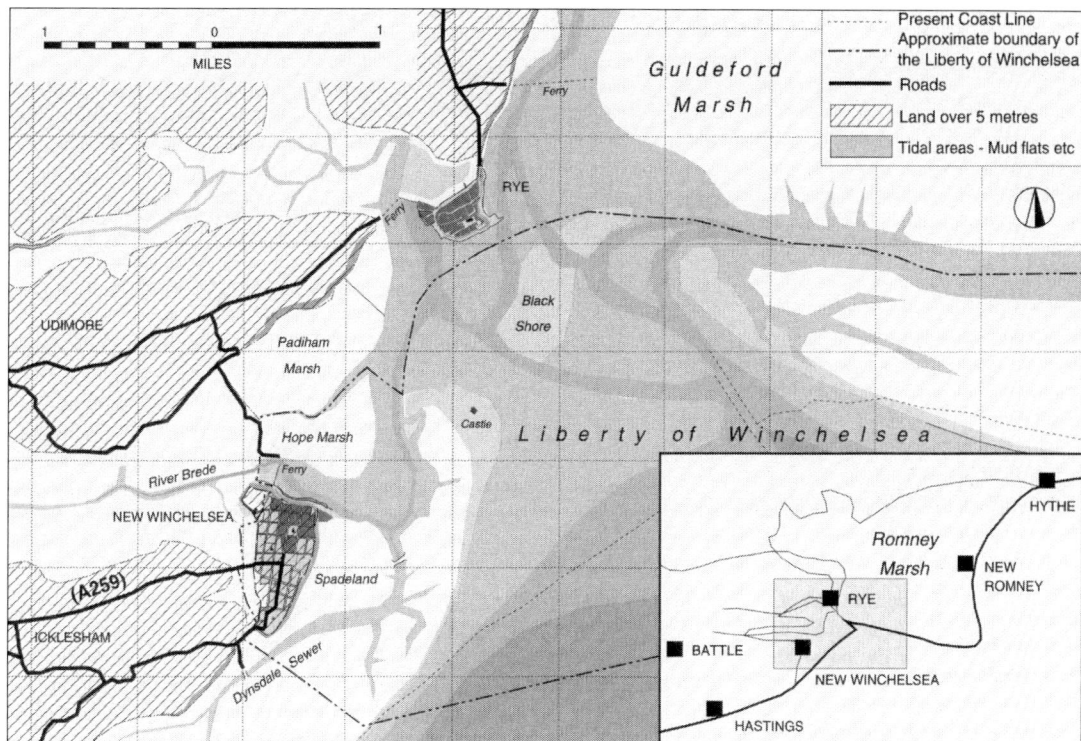

Fig. 2.5 Modern reconstruction of the locations of Rye, New Winchelsea, and the Castle (Camber) which was built after 1500 in the area of the sheltered anchorage (after Martin *et al.* 2004). The Black Shore is also shown on the Prowez map of *c*.1572 (Plate V).

between ships and boats, *naves* and *batellae*. Other vessels used in the southerly Cinque Ports in the medieval period included balingers, barges, crayers and shallops. The size of vessels using Sussex ports increased in the second half of the 14th century, but the larger types of later medieval vessels, hulks and great cogs, did not use the southerly Cinque Ports.[22] Other large cargo and merchant vessels, carracks, carvels, dromonds and tarrits, were used in the 15th century by Genoese merchants at Sandwich where the harbour and economy were flourishing. On occasion tarrits and carracks were captured by pirates off Rye and their goods were brought into the port on smaller vessels. In the summer of 1374, for example, wool, cloth and other goods taken from three tarrits belonging to merchants of Catalonia, Genoa, Milan, Florence and Naples were unloaded into boats and barges and taken into Rye. The masters and mariners of the barges of Lydd, Broomhill, New Romney and Folkestone were involved and were ordered to help in the recovery of the goods.[23] In 1406 a carrack recently taken at sea by Henry IV's son, Thomas, was in the keeping of the mayor and bailiffs of Winchelsea, but carracks did not use this port regularly.[24] Shipping activity at New Winchelsea, particularly the wine trade, was greater than that recorded at Rye from the late 13th to the late 15th century.[25] However, Rye's shipping was not insignificant as may be seen in the range of vessels for which Rye was the home port between 1212 and 1404 (Figure 2.6).[26] The names of Rye vessels are unknown throughout most of the rest of the 15th century but seven Rye vessels were listed in 1492, ranging from a fishing boat to a carvel.[27]

Fig. 2.6 Ships of Medieval Rye.

Ship name	Year	Some details
Unnamed	1212	Masters/owners: Robert Mainnard and Michael Arnald of Rye
Unnamed	1212	Masters/owners: Martin Freard and Godfrey Dun of Rye
Unnamed	1225	'Led' by John Crundel
Unnamed	1225	'Led' by James Mainard
Robert de Salern's	1225	Carrier of wine
Of Herebert de Rya	1225	Bringing wine to sell along coast of England and Flanders
La Salvee	1235	Led by Henry Pichepap (and a ship of Ralph Barlet, maybe of Rye), licensed to carry wine
Henry Pichepap's	1242	? = *La Salvee*
Pinnock	1242	Master Andrew de Poddepyrie (Potepirie)
A shout (*scouta*)	1295	Hired from Rye to carry timber to Dover
Nostre Dame (a shallop)	1299	Master John le Man; on the king's service preventing a crossing from Flanders to Scotland
St Thomas (a cog)	1299	Master Stephen le Lung (Longe); on king's service preventing a crossing from Flanders to Scotland
'A snake' [warship]	1300	Part of the Cinque Ports fleet, Master John Kittey
The Godyere	1300	Part of the Cinque Ports fleet, Master Robert Michel
The Rose	1300	Part of the Cinque Ports fleet, Master Reginald Baudethon
Vessel of Elias Muriel	1307	Used to export grain and import wine
John Torel's	1307	Seal with (merchant) ship on
Robert Bredeware's	1311	Seal with (merchant) ship on
Two barges	1323	Belonging to Thomas Muriel and others of Rye
240-ton *la Michel*	1336	Part of the Cinque Port fleet

170-ton *la Edmund*	1336	Part of the Cinque Port fleet
60-ton *La Palmere*	1336	Part of the Cinque Port fleet
La Katerine	1346	On king's service; master Walter Salerne of Rye
120-ton *La Nicolas*	1336, 1352, 1361	Owners Richard Baddyng and Paul de Portesmuth, master Walter Salerne, all of Rye
Various fishing boats	1362-3	Flewers, tramelers, tachons, herbows
Le Cristofore, balinger	1404	Master Richard Wyndesore, piracy
La Trinite, balinger	1404	Master William Beneyt, piracy
La Marie, balinger	1404	Master Thomas Langle, piracy

The names of many Rye vessels and their masters are known because they were part of the Cinque Ports fleet, or transported grain, wine or other merchandise across the Channel, or attacked merchants and plundered goods of great value.[28] For example, Master Stephen Le Lung, a relative of Thomas Longe, together with John Sampson, attacked merchants on the coast of Brittany in 1266 and plundered 121 tuns of wine valued at 600 marks (£400).[29] Others are known for the more peaceful and smaller-scale activity of fishing.

The names of the earliest vessels are unknown since the vessels were typically described by the man who 'led' them. In 1212 a vessel was captained or owned by Robert Mainnard and in 1225 a vessel was led by James Mainard, otherwise called James son of Mainard of Rye. The shared name, Mainard, suggests that these three men were related and points to the inheritance of vessels as valuable assets which is well known later in the Middle Ages. Another Maynard, Robert, was a baron of Winchelsea in 1268.[30] The wine transported in the vessel of Herebert de Rya (of Rye) in 1225, which was sold either in the Low Countries or England, presumably came from Gascony. The same vessels were used both for transporting wine and on ship service, for example *La Salvee* which Henry Pichepap of Rye led. In 1235 four citizens of Bordeaux were licensed to send merchandise to England in *La Salvee*, and to trade there. Seven years later Henry Pichepap of Rye was granted a safe-conduct for action at sea for the period of war with the king of France, together with the men whom he brought with him on the king's service. The action was described in the usual terms, 'to grieve the king's enemies by sea and land', and, although the ship's name was not specified, it was presumably *La Salvee*. Mariners like the Pichepap family were among the few families to lend their names in the long term to tenements or streets in medieval Rye, perhaps because their maritime activity was so well known and important locally.[31]

Many of the Rye vessels named in the table are the larger ones which are known through their contribution to ship service, originally two vessels. Two residents of Rye in the early 14th century, John Torel and Robert Bredeware, had personal seals with which to confirm their property transactions. Both seals showed a single-masted ship, in one case with a furled sail. The seals are exceptional among those on Rye deeds; Torel and Bredeware can be taken to have been owners of vessels and probably small-scale merchants and carriers.[32] Their vessels may have been those known by name at this period. Of the ships whose names are given in the records, two ships are known in the 1240s, two in 1299, two in 1300, three in 1336, two in the 1340s and 1350s, and three more in 1401. There may have been many more unrecorded vessels. The number of different names suggests that vessels were replaced quite frequently at Rye, perhaps because of storms or piracy. There is nothing to suggest that Rye vessels had a working life of around 75 years, like those plying the Thames.[33]

The tonnage of *La Michel*, *La Edward* and *La Palmere* bears comparison with that of New Winchelsea vessels which imported wine and ranged from thirty tuns to two hundred tuns in the first decade of the 14th century.[34] *La Nicolas* was a notable ship of mid-14th century Rye, one of whose owners had interests in milling in the town. *La Nicolas* was used to transport grain to Gascony, probably carrying 400 quarters on one voyage.[35] Since a quarter may have weighed 384 pounds and, with a little over five quarters making one tun, *La Nicolas* carried around eighty tuns of grain on its journey in 1352, plus whatever other goods were laden; it was recorded as of 120 tuns in 1336. Boats (*batellae*) plying coastal and inland waters often carried fifty quarters and are estimated to have been about twenty yards long and three yards wide, with a draught of two yards.[36] *La Nicolas*, which was a sea-going vessel, would have been proportionately larger, in order to transport 400 quarters of grain plus other goods. Fishing vessels of Rye were of between 14 and 20 tuns.[37]

Pilgrimage from Rye

On 30 March 1361 the owners of *La Nicolas* were licensed to take pilgrims to Santiago de Compostela from the port of Rye. Richard Baddyng and Paul de Portesmuth, the owners, were part of the town elite of Rye in the period after the Black Death. Both men were mayors in the 1350s and Baddyng was the one of the town's first named MPs (*Chapters 4, 5*). Since it was wartime the licence specified that pilgrims must not take with them materials of use to the enemy: sterling, silver, armour or horses.[38] Ships such as *La Nicolas* transporting pilgrims had to be licensed because

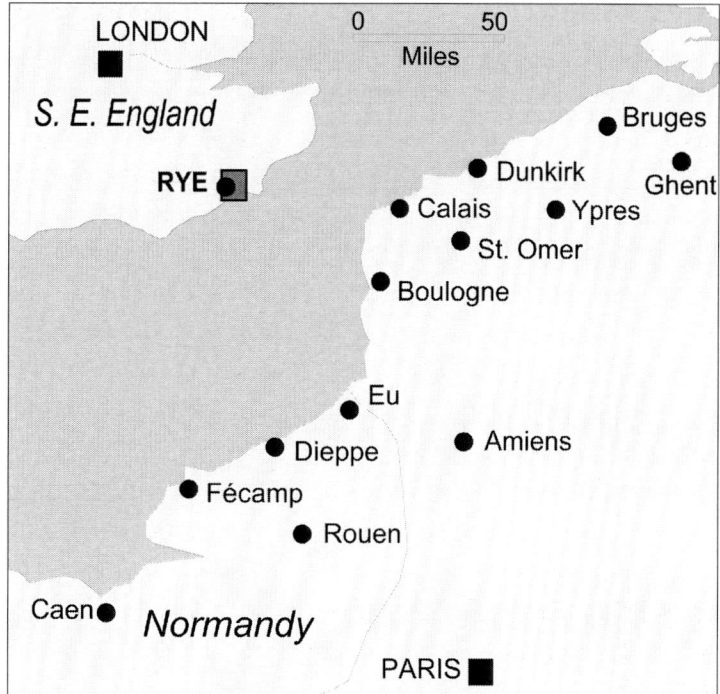

Fig. 2.7 Cross-Channel location map.

there had previously been mandates or proclamations limiting the departure ports. In 1335 Edward III ordered that pilgrims should set sail only from Dover under the penalty of one year's imprisonment, but this order was ineffective and New Romney, New Winchelsea, Rye and other ports continued to be departure points for pilgrims.[39] In 1381 Dover petitioned Richard II for the re-establishment of its monopoly, and he confirmed Edward's order in a charter to Dover of that year.[40] Many pilgrimage sites across the Channel such as Boulogne, Amiens and St Omer were within easy reach of the southerly Cinque Ports (Figure 2.7), but pilgrims also ventured much farther. New Romney had two taverns named after the major pilgrimage sites of Jerusalem and Rome, which probably served as meeting points, boarding houses or hostels for those gathering to make journeys.[41] Pilgrims left from New Winchelsea for Santiago de Compostela, probably via Dieppe, until about 1455.[42] However, in the 15th century western ports such as Bristol became the major points of departure for Santiago; not only was the sea voyage shorter, but the western ports accommodated larger vessels.[43]

Pilgrimage could be local or long-distance and was frequently carried out in a series of short journeys by road or water, along rivers and around the coast. Pilgrims travelling to the major English or European shrines stopped off at more minor sites to pray, give alms or find accommodation. Pilgrims coming to Rye on foot passed

St Bartholomew's Hospital where they could express their religious devotion and give thanks for a safe journey through the Weald by offering prayers and money; the inmates of the hospital possessed documents showing the indulgences which they could offer in return (*Chapter 7*). Pilgrims arriving at or leaving from the port of New Romney found that the road between the harbour and the town centre led directly past the gate of St John's Hospital, whose inmates were thus well placed to seek alms from them. The pilgrims may also have visited the town's other hospital which had been dedicated to St Thomas Becket soon after his martyrdom.[44]

The evidence for pilgrimage often lies not in documents but in artefacts such as a pilgrim badge, possibly originating in Lucca, which was found in the silts of the moat just outside the main gatehouse of Bodiam Castle on the River Rother (Figure 2.8).[45] Pilgrimage was widespread from the beginning of the 14th century and was prompted in part by the fear of purgatory as the doctrine was developed.[46] Excessive deaths in the outbreaks of plague which occurred in the mid-14th century also concentrated people's minds on practical ways to shorten their time in purgatory, in particular by obtaining papal indulgences by visiting pilgrimage sites such as Rome. The fear of purgatory is illustrated in the stained glass from the church of Ticehurst, a country parish which bordered the River Rother (Plate II, Figure 3.1). As pilgrims used the river as a route to travel to Rye or New Winchelsea, they are likely to have stopped to visit and pray at such churches. At Rye no stained glass survived the Reformation and the puritanical enthusiasm of the town government for destroying the remnants of Catholic beliefs and practices such as purgatory and pilgrimage (*Chapter 6*). However, an important local notable, Sir Richard Guldeford, left a remarkable record of his pilgrimage to the Holy Land from Rye in a narrative written by his chaplain.[47] Sir Richard belonged to the Guldeford family which is first known in the Wealden parishes of Benenden and Rolvenden in 1388. His father, Sir John, was instrumental in the rise of the Guldefords to the status of a leading gentry family by the 1450s. Both father and son supported Henry Tudor, and Sir Richard was a royal official, becoming comptroller of the household and sheriff of Kent and MP in 1494 to 1495. Sir Richard was an administrator and engineer and oversaw military campaigns, the building of royal ships and coastal fortifications. He built up landholdings in the Weald and in the area between Rye and Hastings, and received the manor of Iham, part of New Winchelsea. He was also responsible for the reclamation of Guldeford Marsh or Level and, most importantly, for the creation in 1505 of the new parish and church there, East Guldeford. The church building reflected the austere devotion of the Guldeford family which was inspired by humanist thought and connections. In 1506 Sir Richard decided to make a pilgrimage to

Jerusalem, perhaps seeking an answer to the serious financial and political difficulties into which he had fallen as well as an opportunity to express his piety. Henry VII pardoned Richard's debts, some arising from the offices which Richard had held, a pardon which may have been precipitated by his decision to go on pilgrimage.

The journey to the Holy Land was well known to be dangerous and during a short stay at Rye Sir Richard took the precaution of making his will. George Mercer, the former town clerk of Rye and servant to both Henry and Richard Guldeford, was one of the witnesses. Richard then sailed from Rye just before Easter, accompanied by his own chaplain, and the Prior of Guisborugh in Yorkshire and other pilgrims. They travelled to Venice where they spent seven weeks being impressed by the sights, especially the Corpus Christi celebrations with its crowds of children carrying lights. Sailing on to Palestine, they landed

Fig. 2.8 A pilgrim badge found in the silts of the moat just outside the main gatehouse of Bodiam Castle on the River Rother, showing a clothed Christ on the Cross, an image associated with the cult of the Volto Santo in Lucca.

at Jaffa on 27 August and then reached Jerusalem a few days later where both Sir Richard and the Prior fell ill and died in the Hospital of St John. However the narrative of the pilgrimage was completed by the chaplain, covering his return journey through winter weather and dangerous seas to the port of Dover.

In writing this memoir the chaplain drew heavily on one of the many standard accounts of pilgrimage to the Holy Land which were printed in the late 15th and early 16th centuries, that of Breydenbach of Mainz, parts of which he translated into English from Latin. However, the chaplain moulded the account to reflect the religious sensibilities of the time, the humanistic piety of the Guldeford family and the nature of the Weald and the Romney Marsh area, where criticism of two aspects of medieval pilgrimage was strong: indulgences for visiting holy sites and the fascination with saints' relics. Sir Richard Guldeford was an influential man in the Rye area, not least at East Guldeford. The memoir of his pilgrimage, like his own piety, had many traditional aspects but also anticipated the religious changes which reached a fractious climax in the early movement of the Rye town government towards Protestantism in the 1530s (*Chapter 6*).

Piracy, Wrecking and Smuggling

The men of Rye and other members of the Cinque Ports confederation often turned to piracy after periods when their ships had been required in conflicts or to deliver provisions to Gascony, Calais or Scotland (*Chapter 3*). At times the monarch allowed the Cinque Portsmen a relatively free hand to attack shipping in the Channel; at other times political events and the demands of merchants required a crackdown. Part of the Cinque Ports' ship service was keeping the seas and could be directed towards protecting favoured merchants who were being held to ransom by pirates. In wartime this aspect of ship service was described as grieving the king's enemies by sea or land or resisting the malice of the king's enemies, a cross between naval service and attacks on shipping themselves verging on piracy.[48] Such attacks were effectively licensed: for example, on 10 May 1267 five mariners of the port of Winchelsea and Rye were deputed to patrol the coast around the south-eastern ports: John Andrew, John de Horne, Reynold Alard, Thomas de la Nesse, Robert Sampson and John le Marchaunt. With the agreement of the merchants of both sides of the Channel, these mariners were permitted to pursue and attack one Henry Pechun and his accomplices, 'the king's enemies', between Thanet and Old Winchelsea. The mariners were also permitted to take one mark from every laden ship, and half a mark from every empty ship, for guarding the coast and for their own maintenance and that of their associates.[49]

In the second half of the 14th century piracy was known as *skumerie* in the Cinque Ports. *Skumerie* developed a particular meaning as semi-licensed piracy, or privateering, in which the royal right of prize was allowed to the pirates while Lord Warden of the Cinque Ports turned a blind eye.[50] The term *skumour* derived from the French both for piracy and a kind of light ship or barge. John Trevisa, writing in the 14th century, called such pirates 'strong skumours and see theues' (sea thieves).[51] The term *skomerfare*, used in the Ports, perhaps suggests that the Portsmen considered that there was a 'fare', the local word for season, for piracy just as there were different seasons for fishing. The royal commissions which were on occasion set up to deal with piracy were concentrated in the summer months, the very time when the mariners were not occupied in fishing and when merchants were at sea and vulnerable to attack. English vessels, including those of the Cinque Ports, were victims of such piracy as well as protagonists. Thirty-nine ships were captured or destroyed by Spanish vessels in August 1375 while loading salt at La Baie de Bourgneuf.[52]

There were three periods in which piracy was especially prevalent and which demonstrate the development of piracy in the Cinque Ports and its wider context: the 1230s, the early to mid-1320s, and the 1350s to 1370s. The involvement of the mariners of Rye and other ports of the confederation in piracy becomes clear in the records from the 1230s. Some of the earliest pirates known in this locality were the brothers William and Robert *de Mariscis*, i.e. of Romney Marsh. In 1212 Robert received a galley captured in Normandy as prize or bounty. However, in 1237 Robert and his brother, together with some accomplices from Scotland, attacked merchants and others crossing between England and Ireland; they killed and wounded some of them and demanded heavy ransoms for others.[53] These events make two points which are echoed later: that although such mariners sometimes acted with royal approval, at other times they turned to independent and threatening behaviour, and that these mariners often acted in groups whose members were drawn from a wide area, making control of their actions by the king difficult.

The 1320s, a time of war in Gascony, produced many accusations by alien merchants that they were terrorised by mariners of Rye and New Winchelsea when they came to England with their goods.[54] These mariners travelled as far as Dartmouth and Harwich to attack merchant ships, mostly those transporting valuable cargoes from some distance but on occasion attacking English merchants who were taking part in the coastal trade.[55] In 1322 Gervase Alard, junior, of New Winchelsea, together with Henry Alard, and other mariners from Sandwich and Greenwich, boarded a ship belonging to a merchant of Almain (modern Germany) which was anchored at Harwich. They assaulted the merchant and his men, and took away the ship and its goods.[56] Gervase Alard was previously mayor of New Winchelsea and admiral of the Cinque Ports fleets.[57] Such attacks continued and in 1323 Edward II ordered three commissions to be set up to investigate the complaints of merchants from St Omer that Portsmen were terrorising them and other alien merchants. Pirates had attacked the Spanish ships that the merchants were using which they had ordered to be laden at La Rochelle with wine and other goods such as tallow and bacons for transport to Calais. The first ship was attacked near Guernsey by a group of men led by John Hardyng of New Winchelsea and the goods were taken and divided up among the pirates at that town. The second ship was being crewed by mariners from Dover. Thomas Muriel of Rye and some pirates of Somerset and Dorset attacked it using two barges and took the goods to Weymouth to divide them up. The third ship, *The Ship of St Juliana of St Sebastian*, was attacked by the same group of pirates when it was anchored in Dartmouth. Of the 184 tuns of wine on board, the pirates took 44 tuns for themselves, but did not bother with the 22 bales of tallow which were also being carried.[58] Thomas Muriel's immediate forebear, probably his father, was Elias Muriel, a baron and mayor of Rye, who owned a vessel which he used to transport grain to Gascony and to bring back wine.[59] Thomas Muriel held a tenement on the east strand of Rye where presumably he beached or moored the barge which he used to attack merchants (*Chapter 8*).[60]

Again in 1323 a joint attack was made by two men from Redyng near Appledore and two men from Smallhythe in conjunction with others from Sandwich, Gravesend, Borstall, Grain, Hoo, Milton, Faversham and Seasalter on the Thames estuary. They attacked a ship belonging to merchants of the Society of Peruzzi (Peruchi) of Florence which was carrying wool from London to Sandwich.[61] The next year there was a complaint by a Spanish merchant, Nicholas Dominici, that several mariners had captured two ships and their goods which he had had locked in the ships in Spain with the intention of bringing them to England. The mariners were named as John Hardyng of New Winchelsea, John de Shotele, Walter Robyn, Simon Faron of Rye, Adam Charles and others from Southampton. These mariners had captured the ships and goods at New Winchelsea, taken them to Portsmouth and divided them between themselves.[62] Of these pirates, Simon Faron or Pharon came from a well-known and extensive family of Rye which was active there between 1258 and 1325 as members of the town government, one of whom held a tavern there (*Chapter 4*).[63] John Hardyng of New Winchelsea was later chosen in 1336 as an MP for Chichester, in a parallel with the choice of William Longe, privateer, as MP for Rye in the early 15th century.[64]

In the summer of 1326 seven men of New Winchelsea, Sandwich and London carried out a huge act of piracy on a vessel belonging to four merchants of Dinaunt (in modern Belgium). They included Benedict Cely who was at that time described as of New Winchelsea but later of Rye (*Chapter 6*). The merchants loaded a ship with a large amount of goods at Waterford in Ireland and it set sail for Bruges. The seven pirates met the merchant ship near the Isle of Wight in a large ship, boarded it and took an immense and varied amount of valuable goods said to be worth £600. The pirates took the ships and goods to the Downs by Sandwich and distributed them as they pleased. They also forced the merchants to sign a letter saying that they required nothing in return for these goods. At the first attempt at royal justice in 1326, John Badding of Rye and Benedict Cely showed the letter to Edward II, attempting to suggest that this had been a simple case of salvage. However, a more strenuous attempt at justice was made in 1327 under Edward III, who was keen to placate and gain the support of the Duke of Brabant, his kinsman, and that of the towns of Bruges, Liege and Dinaunt. He appointed the Lord Warden of the Cinque Ports to investigate, and finally an order was made to imprison Cely and take his ship into custody too.[65]

Among the Cinque Ports mariners, those from New Winchelsea, together with those of Dover and Sandwich, were the most frequently recorded carrying out acts of piracy between 1322 to 1326, no doubt because these Ports had had the largest numbers of vessels and mariners. In contrast the men of the ports of Hythe, New Romney and Lydd specialised in luring merchant vessels onto the shingle spit of Dungeness, wrecking and then plundering them. These mariners capitalised on their local knowledge of this part of south-east coast, the nature of the tides and the difficult entrances to harbours to profit from both wrecking and smuggling.[66] In an example from 1361 some merchants, masters and mariners of La Rochelle loaded a cog with wine to sell in Flanders. However, the cog was driven off course by storms and wrecked near New Romney, presumably on Dungeness. Although the mariners escaped alive, the men of New Romney and of the places around cut the ship into little pieces and then carried away the wines, tackle and timber of the ship on horses and in carts and boats.[67]

The third notable phase in piracy in the Cinque Ports was in the 1350s to 1370s. In October 1351 Edward III announced that he had taken some merchants of Genoa who were living in Bruges under his special protection. This followed an attack by some mariners of New Winchelsea and elsewhere on a ship freighted with 917 ox-hides as it sailed past Dieppe. The mariners took the ship to New Winchelsea or somewhere nearby where they helped themselves to the goods.[68] The King's special protection involved giving his serjeant-at-arms permission to travel around the Cinque Ports to find out the names of mariners involved, locate the goods and report back speedily.[69] In the late 1360s and 1370s there was a crucial change in political alliances which caused the role of the Cinque Ports mariners to change. In 1369 Louis de Mâle, Count of Flanders (1346-84) decided to abandon his alliance with the English and throw his lot in with the French. Louis' heir Margaret married Philip, Duke of Burgundy and brother of Charles V, the French king, and with this change of alliance Flanders ceased to be part of England's sphere of influence. The Count's new alliance outraged the Flemish weaving towns of Bruges, Ypres and particularly Ghent, which depended on supplies of English wool and also on exporting cloth to England. The mariners of English coastal towns, in whose hinterlands wool production was vital, also vented their anger on the Count by attacking Flemish shipping.[70] This was a self-defeating move as far as the transport of wool and cloth was concerned but perhaps a useful excuse for piracy.[71] Most of the Cinque Ports were involved, capturing wine and other goods at sea and bringing it into port under the pretext of demanding payment of the king's custom or subsidy. As Edward III complained, the mariners who were attacking merchant shipping should have been on his service, and in addition many were being paid by him; he called them 'evildoers of the realm'. In 1374 they captured four tarrits belonging to some merchants and subjects of the King of Aragon, Edward III's ally. The tarrits were laden with merchandise and were sailing to and from Flanders and Aragon, having received safe conducts from Edward III. The pirates put into the port of Rye, carried away the goods and burned one of the tarrits. The four owners of the tarrits pleaded with the King for speedy justice, the restoration of their merchandise and recompense for their damage and losses. Edward III ordered a commission to find out the names of the pirates and those who had received the goods from the sheriffs, mayors, wardens, bailiffs and constables of the Cinque Ports. These officers were also ordered to prevent the goods being further distributed and return to the merchants any goods which they could prove to be theirs. The penalties for the pirates and the people who had acquired the merchandise were to be severe: 'heavy compulsions and distraint, incarceration and [the] sale of goods'.[72]

Edward III's response to piracy in 1374 was a high-level one and it points up the complications of piracy. Sometimes the evildoers were people who had been practicing *skumerie* in earlier years when political alliances were different. Trade was carried out between merchants of several countries, some of them acting at least partly as carriers of goods between ports which were not their places of origin. The Portsmen were prepared to attack carriers or merchants whether or not they were now the king's allies or enemies. The king could issue safe conducts but they did not always protect the vessels or merchants in question. Most of the mariners practising *skumerie* were embedded within the urban society of the Cinque Ports, hence the royal request to question the town officers after the attack at Rye in 1374. In the 13th century the ship service of the Cinque Ports had been called on to protect merchant ships whom the king wished to favour when they were threatened by pirates. It was very easy in the 14th century for the masters of barges and other vessels of the Cinque Ports, including those used for ship service, to turn to piracy when it suited them.

From 1410 Henry IV was keen to control what was effectively an unofficial war raging in the Channel between English and continental privateers. The activities of the privateers Sir John Prendergast, who was linked to New Romney and Lydd, and of William Longe of Rye, interrupted maritime commerce and damaged relations with Flanders. Henry, Prince of Wales, was appointed Lord Warden of the Cinque Ports and captain of Calais and a crackdown on attacks on Flemish shipping by men of the Cinque Ports ensued: one William Worthe, a New Winchelsea shipowner who was involved in illegal privateering, was imprisoned at New Romney. This provoked local resentment there and also at New Winchelsea, Sandwich and Rye, where the privateer William Longe was chosen as the town's MP and took up smuggling (*Chapter 5*).[73] In further manifestations of resistance to the changes being imposed, New Romney and Lydd made an agreement over the ransoms of Frenchmen, and New Romney sought Sir John Prendergast's 'friendship' with a gift of wine in this period.[74] In 1411 the Lord Warden as Admiral punished the vicar and a fisherman of Lydd for sheltering and supplying a group of pirates under Prendergast's command.[75] From 1415 the energies of the Cinque Port pirates and privateers were redirected to protecting the coast and supplying Calais, Harfleur and Guisnes. Richard Clitherow of Sandwich, forebear, presumably father, of Richard Clitherow of New Romney, was prominent in organising supplies to Harfleur.[76] However, in 1441 the Court of Chancery and Admiralty held in Dover was still dealing with felonies committed by the pirate Prendergast.[77]

Fishing at Rye

In the 12th-century charter the men of Rye made an agreement with the Abbot of Fécamp concerning two matters: rights and property in the town (*Chapter 1*) and the profits from fishing. The importance of this agreement is emphasised by the fact that some of the townsmen travelled to Fécamp to meet with the Abbot and, when there, took an oath on behalf of their heirs as well as themselves to keep to its provisions.[78] They also promised that when they got home they would make the rest of the townsmen swear to keep to the agreement. The agreement was intended to reinforce a traditional arrangement whereby the fishing profits were divided by shares, an arrangement known in ports in Sussex, Kent, eastern England and Normandy.[79] The share system allowed the master and the crew to divide the profits from the catch according to their contribution as master and owner of the vessel or as oarsmen and fishermen.[80] The agreement also allowed the Abbot of Fécamp to get a cut as the lord of Rye town and rector and patron of the parish church, a share later known as 'Christ's share' or St Mary's share.[81] Instead of the catch being divided simply among the master and mariners, say twenty-one men, it was divided into a larger number to allow for the lord's share.

The charter recorded the abbot's cut as part of the shares due from ships of various sizes, measured at this period by the number of oars, that is of oarsmen who rowed them. The largest vessels had 26 oars(men), the next largest 22 or 20 oars, and the next 18 or 16 oars, with each one also presumably having a steersman. There were also some smaller fishing vessels whose profits were shared. The two largest categories comprised vessels big enough to provide Rye's ship service in the 12th century, i.e. 20 men and a steersman. Vessels of this size were then the standard requirement from all the members of the Cinque Port confederation.[82]

Shares were due not only from fresh fish landed and sold at Rye throughout the year for local consumption and marketing, but also from the profitable catch at the Yarmouth herring fishery and fair which lasted from late September to mid-November. The Cinque Portsmen had rights to hold land, sell fish and dry their nets on the strand at Yarmouth, and controlled the herring fair by their own bailiff, rights which were strongly resented in Yarmouth. This herring fishery was at the height of its importance in the 13th and early 14th centuries, at least as measured by the fights and disputes between the sailors of Yarmouth and the Cinque Ports.[83] The evidence about Yarmouth fishing shares at Rye and Old Winchelsea comes from the late 13th century, by which time the lord's shares went to the king rather than to Fécamp.[84] It shows that in the 1260s and 1270s Old Winchelsea's fishing industry was twice the size of that of Rye, as measured by the number of vessels participating in the Yarmouth fair.[85] The income to the lord from shares at Old Winchelsea averaged about £25 a year in these two decades. From Rye in the one year in the 13th century for which a record survives (1272 to 1273), the royal shares amounted only to £5 8s. 2d.

After the establishment of New Winchelsea in c.1290, the royal share income from fishing fell at both Rye and New Winchelsea, averaging £2 a year at Rye and £17 at New Winchelsea in the years up to 1304 to 1305. This fall can be attributed to damage by the late 13th-century storms. By the early 1340s the situation, as measured by the shares, was changing. In 1342 the value of Rye's shares to the crown was at the level of the 1260s and 1270s at roughly £5 a year while those of New Winchelsea were only £2 a year.[86] This fall in royal income from shares at Winchelsea compared to Rye is substantiated by the number of fishermen paying shares in the years 1343 to 1358: between five and 14 fishermen at New Winchelsea and between 20 and 56 fishermen at Rye.[87] At both places however fishing was on a downward trend as measured by the amount which fishermen paid in shares between 1343 and 1357, despite a 50 per cent rise in herring prices over the same period. The average payment by a Rye fisherman in these years fell from between 7s. and 9s. a year to between 2s. and 5s.[88] This serious situation can be attributed to the decline of the Yarmouth fishery, to numerous plague deaths and more generally to the conditions of war. Yarmouth's own harbour and town, whose prosperity was based on fishing, were severely damaged from the early 14th century by the combination of factors also well known in the Cinque Ports: storms, shifting shingle, silting and the growth in the size of vessels.[89] The extent to which fishing actually experienced a downturn at New Winchelsea in the early 14th century is difficult to assess but had certainly occurred by mid-century.[90] At Rye, Yarmouth shares were still being paid under that name in 1343 but not in 1362, perhaps suggesting that the damage to the fishing industry caused by the Yarmouth decline had by the 1360s reached Rye as well as New Winchelsea.[91] The late 14th century saw, in the place of the Yarmouth herring fishery, the large-scale development of the fishing industry of Devon and Cornwall. It occurred for several reasons: rising domestic incomes which allowed greater purchases of fish; an expanding Mediterranean market which the south west was well positioned to exploit; the adoption of new Flemish and Dutch fish-preservation systems which allowed the catch to be kept for longer and transported farther; and perhaps less regulation in the ports of the south west than in those of the south east. By the mid-15th century mariners of the south west were selling fish in significant amounts at Lydd and Dengemarsh (Dungeness), and also in Sussex and Norfolk. This growth took place at the expense of mariners of eastern England from Scarborough to Dunwich, and of the south east, notably those of Rye, all of whom had depended heavily on the Yarmouth fishery.[92]

In the 13th century, and indeed up to the time of the Black Death, Rye fishermen participated in four fishing seasons: the autumn herring season based around the Yarmouth fair, the much less valuable pre-Christmas season; the post-Christmas season culminating in the provision of fish for Lent; and the spring and summer fishing season. The Rye mariners departed for Yarmouth at the start of September: in 1305 the date of the Rye fair was moved from 8 September to 15 August at the petition of the townsmen because by 8 September the fishing season had begun.[93] The spring and summer season may have been mackerel fishing in the Channel or the annual voyage to Scarborough for herring and cod after the mackerel fishery.[94] It was a valuable season since herring formed the largest part of the yearly catch (over half) followed by plaice, mackerel and sprats.[95] After the Black Death, there are records of share payments for fishing only at three terms; the valuable spring or summer season has disappeared.[96] In the Black Death and subsequent plague epidemics there was a mortality of forty per cent or more among the inhabitants of

Rye (*Chapter 5*). It seems that in the changed conditions of the 1360s, with fewer people and a greatly reduced demand, Rye mariners abandoned fishing in the spring and summer and found more profit in attacking merchants, the *skomerfare*.

Fishing Vessels at Rye

Four different types of vessels took part in fishing at Rye in the 14th century (Figure 2.9). The sea-going flewers and trammelers, named after their nets, fished for herring. The 'tachons', defined by the Middle English Dictionary as 'some kind of fishing boat', caught fish in the run-up to Christmas. The fishing vessels called herbows or harbews were named after the kind of hooks employed, i.e. 'harbour hooks'.[97] John Lytewerk fished with such hooks and his name may suggest that his fellows did not consider harbour fishing very demanding. Boats of three of the four types known at Rye in 1362 caught fish for eating in Lent, the period of high demand during fasting from meat.

Fig. 2.9 Rye fishermen in 1362: their vessels and amounts paid as 'Christ's share', from the bailiff's account of William Taillour, TNA SC6 1028/15.

Season	Forename	Surname	Kind of Boat	s.	d.
Autumn	Robert	Bernhand	For share in one flewer	8	4
Autumn	Richard	Beselyn	For share in one flewer	6	8
Autumn	Matthew	Sam[s]on	for share of tramelers	4	0
Autumn	John	Mentour	for share of tramelers	7	6
Autumn	Jacob	Brok	for share of tramelers	3	6
Pre-Xmas	William	Ryder	for tachons		15
Pre-Xmas	Robert	Fynch	for tachons		12
Pre-Xmas	Stephen	Portour	for tachons		6
Pre-Xmas	John	Merker	for tachons		6
Lent	Robert	Bernhand	for share of tramelers	13	0
Lent	John	Mentour	for share of herbows and tachons	18	6
Lent	John	Lytewerk	for herbows	8	10

The table shows the amounts which the fishermen paid as 'Christ's share' in 1362. These amounts appear to be realistic assessments of the value of the catch at a rate of a tenth; the parson stated at this time that Christ's share was a tithe of fish.[98] The total of Christ's share was £3 17s. 4d., giving a total value of £38 13s. 4d. for the fish sold in town. However, this is a bare minimum of what the fishermen caught, and the fishermen are likely, by comparison with those of New Winchelsea, Dover,

New Romney, to have sold some of their catch, fresh, salted or smoked, not just in Rye but at more distant markets and fairs.

Over twenty kinds of specific names for fishing boats are known from medieval Kent and this may suggest that at Rye in the 1360s there was a limited number of types of fishing vessel being used.[99] Many types of fish were caught in the southerly Cinque Ports and off the coast of Romney Marsh. A large variety was caught at New Romney in the second half of the 14th century, where a fishmonger supplied his local customers and more distant markets with sprats, porpoise, salmon, haddock, lampreys, mackerel, codling, conger eel, shrimps, herring (red and white), whiting, whelks, tench, eels, oysters, crabs, trout, 'pickerelle' (young or small pike), stockfish (dried and cured cod or other fish) and gurnards. The distant places supplied included London, Hertford, Dover, Bury, St Albans, Cambridge, Newmarket, Walsingham, Wallingford, Kirkby and Uxbridge.[100] New Romney also had a thriving kiddle (shoreline) fishery at this period, of which there is no mention at Rye.[101] Cartloads of fish from New Romney were taken to inland markets in this period, much cod was sold, and porpoises were sold both at retail in the town market and wholesale out of town.[102] It is likely that the fishing industry of Rye and New Winchelsea, which was based on a limited number of species, did not compete well with that of New Romney in the later 14th century, which flourished in a period of higher disposable incomes and increased demand for a greater variety of foodstuffs after the Black Death. The picture of a declining fishing industry at Rye in the 1350s and 1360s seems to be borne out by the comparisons with the very different state of the industry at New Romney. But fishing at Rye revived later and it enjoyed what seems to have been its most flourishing period between the mid-15th century and the 17th century (*Chapters 5, 9*).[103]

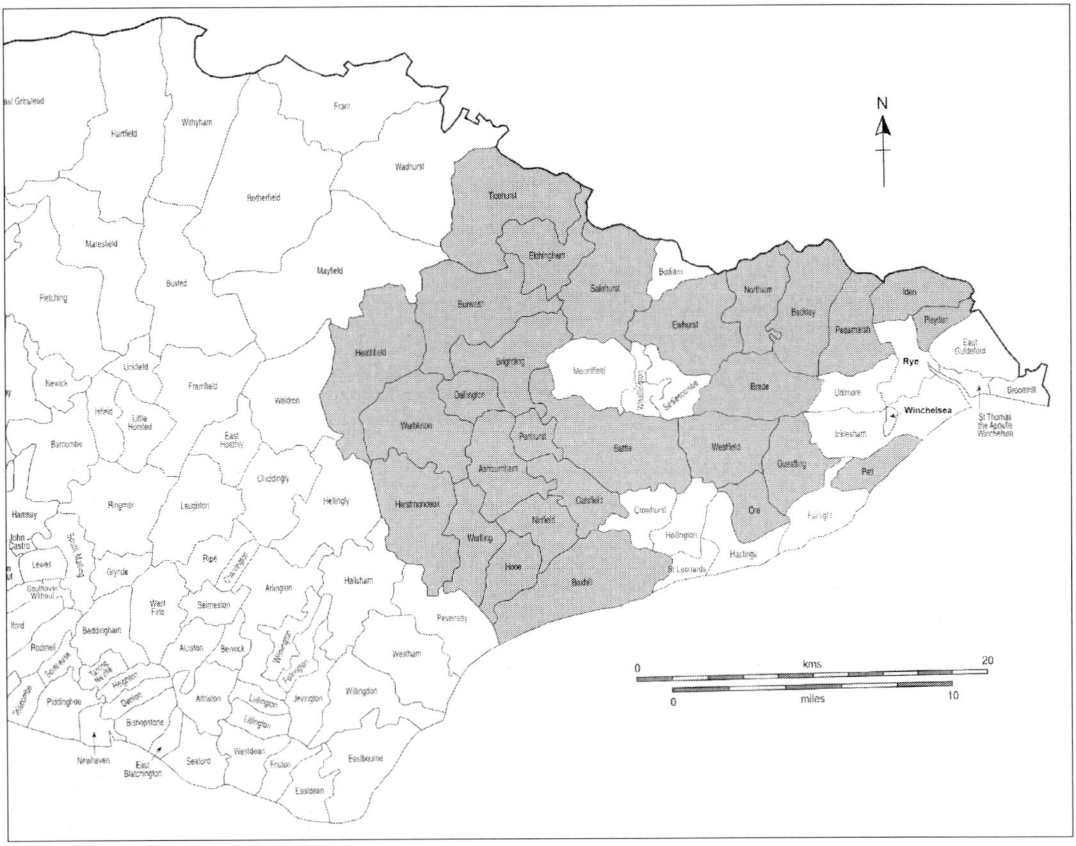

Fig. 3.1 Eastern Sussex between the coast and the River Rother to the north showing the parishes where Queen Philippa had woodland in 1351 (after frontispiece in *An Historical Atlas of Sussex*, 1999).

CHAPTER 3

Rye and its Hinterlands
in the Middle Ages: War and Trade

Introduction

The control which the royal family exercised over Rye and New Winchelsea from the mid-13th century onwards was crucial in three ways: politically, militarily and economically. This is very clear in the late 1320s when control of these two Ancient Towns and the Cinque Ports was essential to allow Edward III free access to and from his own kingdom, not least to exploit the possibilities and advantages of his alliance with Hainault in the Low Countries through his marriage to Philippa of Hainault.[1] The resumption of war with France in 1337 demanded that Rye and New Winchelsea were able to provide their ships and send them to join the fleet wherever it gathered, often off Sandwich. The sheltered anchorage shared by New Winchelsea and Rye frequently provided the initial gathering point for ships of the southerly members of the Cinque Port confederation in the 14th century, providing better harbour facilities than Hastings, New Romney, Hythe and Seaford. However, it was not only the sheltered anchorage at Winchelsea-Rye which was important but also the production of the crucial wartime products of timber and fuel in the hinterlands of these two towns. This production was also largely under royal control.

The Availability and Use of Timber in Rye and its Hinterlands

Rye and its hinterlands to the north and west were a focal point for the supply and use of timber and wood in the 13th and 14th centuries.[2] The many uses of woodland in this locality reveal that its importance was not a simple matter of availability but that royal and knightly lordship and the existence of Rye as an outport were also critical. The towns of both Rye and Winchelsea (Old and then New) were in the king's hands after 1247 and were under the direction of his bailiff. On occasion the revenues of Rye and New Winchelsea were granted to the queen consort with the towns remaining under royal control.[3] Much of the woodland in the Rye hinterlands was held in the 14th century by the queen consort, first Philippa of Hainault and then Anne of Bohemia, the wife of Richard II.[4] Other woodland there was held by the royal supporters Sir William de Etchingham and Sir Edmund Pashley.[5] Another important factor was the existence of accessible and convenient water transport by river to the sea. The Ewhurst and Northiam area which was particularly notable for its woodland had water transport via the river Rother; this was where the woodland of Rye hospital lay (*Chapter 7*). In 1389, when William Batlesforde leased to Roger Aschbournham 35 acres of woodland in Ewhurst parish, it was recorded as being adjacent to a watercourse running from Bodiam to Newenden, i.e. the Rother.[6] Similarly Brede parish was important for its woodland and the River Brede for water transport (below). The River Tillingham and its major tributary bordered Peasmarsh and Beckley parishes, both notable for their woods.

In the mid-14th century Queen Philippa, consort of Edward III, held woodland in the parishes of eastern Sussex as part of the revenues which supported her household (Figure 3.1).[7] These parishes, comprising the far eastern end of the High Weald, had a large proportion of woodland, a feature usually attributed to its poor soils. Arable and sheep farming, and to a lesser extent cattle farming, were concentrated further west in medieval Sussex.[8] It is clearly the case that the eastern Weald lay on poor soils, but the existence, maintenance and exploitation of woodland in the hinterlands of Rye was also prompted by the wide variety of valuable uses for timber and wood, and by the importance of the families who held it and their opportunities to use and sell it, particularly in wartime. Woodland provided timber both for shipbuilding and other construction and wood for fuel; it represented power in both senses of the word.

Timber was used in building the timber-framed houses of the late 14th to the early 16th centuries, those in Rye and also those in rural parishes such as Northiam where there is a cluster of early survivals of such houses.[9] Timber was also used to build mills in Sussex and Kent. In 1295 timber was carried by boat from Rye to Dover Castle to build a tower windmill there.[10] In 1350 the agent of Fécamp Abbey was licensed to fell oaks and other timber in Sussex up to the value of 100 marks (£66 13s. 4d.), for sale or to build or repair mills and houses.[11] The timber was most probably used at Fécamp's properties in the county: Rye, New Winchelsea, Iham, Steyning in West Sussex and nearby Warminghurst.[12] Wooden hurdles formed the side of the bridge crossing the lower River Brede to the west of

New Winchelsea.[13] As well as being used directly in buildings and other structures, timber was also used in the construction process of stone fortifications, cellars or undercrofts and bridges, notably in the 14th century. Stone structures needed timber as frames, scaffolding and support as they were built, in particular the large number of cellars and vaults under the medieval houses of New Winchelsea (at least 51) and the smaller number (ten) at Rye (Figure 3.2).[14] Wine was imported into Rye, for example by Elias Muriel, and Rye's cellars are likely to have been used for its storage.[15] Sixty oaks were required for Pevensey Castle in 1358 as well as 619 oaks for Dover Castle.[16] Timber from Brede and Crowhurst, and probably the 79 great oaks from the woodlands of the Rye hospital which were felled in 1380, were used in rebuilding the fortifications of Rye after the disastrous French raid of 1377 (*Chapter 7*).[17] These woodlands lay approximately 11½ km to the north west of the Rye hospital at Broklonde, otherwise known as Speteslond (1406) and now Spittal Wood.[18] They lay on the eastern side of Ewhurst parish and a small stream led northwards down to the Rother, which is about 1½ km away.

Timber was supplied from the far eastern end of Sussex to places as far apart as Dartmouth in Devon and Boston in Lincolnshire.[19] In autumn 1358 John, Earl

Fig. 3.2　Some stone cellars at New Winchelsea whose construction required timber supports.

Fig. 3.3   The Landgate, part of Rye's fortifications (unattributed postcard).

of Richmond, the fourth son of Edward III and Queen Philippa, was proposing to build a bridge at Boston, where he held the main part of the town. This fenland river port and important medieval town had two major bridges, Stone Bridge and Town Bridge. The timber which went to Boston in 1358 for the building, or more probably rebuilding, of one of its two bridges came from Sussex.[20] The shipping of the timber was organised by the bailiff of Hastings who was ordered to hire additional vessels from New Winchelsea, Sandwich, Dover and other unnamed places along the coast to transport it.[21] The vessels used to transport the timber were described as crayers, i.e. flat-bottomed barges, which were sometimes sea-going but often used for fishing in estuaries and creeks, and were suitable for carrying trees.[22] In 1387 when more timber was sent to Boston from eastern Sussex it was specified as being shipped from Rye.[23] The connection between eastern Sussex, Rye and Boston lay in the fact that they were all in royal hands in the 14th and early 15th centuries, a time largely of war.[24] The importance of this was demonstrated by the royal response to the serious French raid on New Winchelsea and the area around in March 1360.[25] The bailiff of Boston was ordered to organise a fleet of the great ships and barges of the town. The merchants of Boston were to make a loan so that the vessels could be furnished with armed men, archers and seamen, and victualled for one month. When they were ready they were to be brought to Sandwich where the King had ordered a fleet to be gathered in order to attack his French enemies.[26] Activity by this fleet was however forestalled by the signing of the Treaty of Brétigny in May 1360 which was followed by nine years of peace.

Royal shipbuilding for the king is known at Rye from 1223 when the export of timber was forbidden as the king was planning to build ships and galleys.[27] In 1254, when the king required the vessels of the Cinque Ports confederation, he specified those which could carry 16 horses or more, since horses were used in the great battles of the medieval period.[28] In 1297 a huge English fleet sailed from New Winchelsea which was said to comprise 1,500 cavalry and 50,000 foot soldiers.[29] Transporting the horses for the cavalry alone would have required nearly 100 vessels of the minimum size specified in 1254, and many more were needed for provisions. Making vessels fit for boarding and transporting horses was yet another use of wood. In 1341, following the battle off Sluys, Edward III planned 'his next progress on the sea', and supplies of bridges, hurdles, boards, rafts and other items necessary for shipping horses were to be sent from as far as Somerset, Southampton and Surrey as well as Kent and Sussex to Winchelsea, where the western fleet was to gather.[30] Timber was needed not only for the equipment to embark the horses, but also, together with leather, to build internal structures in vessels such as compartments for the horses.[31]

Timber was needed not only for the hulls of vessels but also for the tackle. The value of this is emphasised in the frequent royal demands that the tackle of vessels wrecked on this coast must be rescued, accounted for and re-used; for example, the fate of *La George* at New Winchelsea was a particular royal concern in 1346. *La George* was a sea-going vessel which sometimes crossed to Gascony on the king's service laden with victuals.[32] In July 1346 the King ordered *La George* to be sent from Caen to New Winchelsea in the care of its master Robert Salmon and Thomas de Snotesham, who were to deliver it to Stephen de Padyham and Henry Finch of New Winchelsea, a former mayor.[33] On 13 August 1346 Padyham and Finch were ordered to collect the tackle and timber of *La George* and put them in a safe place, and to make orders for the safety of the hull, since the ship had been severely damaged in the port of New Winchelsea. The next day, when the ship was still aground in the port, the deputy of the Lord Warden of the Cinque Ports was also ordered to secure the tackle and rescue the remains of the hull, and to find out from the townsmen how the ship came to be damaged. Nearly a fortnight later the King expressed his anger that this had still not been done. In the spring of the next year the mayor and bailiffs of New Winchelsea were required to deliver up all the tackle and apparatus of *La George* to a new man appointed to deal with it.[34]

Once the Anglo-French war resumed in 1369, lords from east Sussex such as William de Etchingham (II), knight, and others who held woodland wished to sell their timber and planks to anyone willing to buy, either native or alien buyers.[35] These buyers wished to ship their purchases of timber overseas but Etchingham and the others were prevented from shipping the timber by the mayor, bailiffs and burgesses of New Winchelsea right up to the late 1370s. In this they relied on a writ of 1367, made shortly before war was resumed, in which the Lord Warden of the Cinque Ports had forbidden them to allow timber exports.[36] The fortifications of Rye were being strengthened after the 1377 raid (*Chapter 8*) and raids were occurring or threatened on other coastal towns from Portsmouth to Gravesend. The town government of New Winchelsea may have preferred to see timber sold for the construction of local defences rather than to alien buyers.[37]

Supplying Calais with Timber

Wood from east Sussex was also used in the provisioning of Calais: men of the town government of Rye such as the Longe family were appointed to act on the king's behalf. Members of this family in the late 14th century included John Longe, bailiff of Rye, William Longe, privateer, mayor and MP for Rye, and Thomas Longe junior, also MP and one of the soldiers of the town of Calais (*Chapter 5*).[38] In March 1381 John Longe, holding the office of the king's carpenter, was appointed to take carpenters and workmen to cut down a wood in Bodiam Park and have the timber carried to the sea. This wood had been bought for the town of Calais for £120 by the royal treasurer and the chamberlain of the Exchequer on behalf of Edward III in 1376.[39] Calais was the English staple port for wool from 1363 to 1558 and as such its fortifications had to be continually maintained and upgraded because its site was naturally vulnerable. From 1347 the occupants were mostly English and needed to be supplied from England with essentials, particularly firewood. Timber and firewood were supplied from east Sussex where they were more plentiful than in the immediate area of Dover or east Kent which had a shorter sea route to Calais.[40] In 1347 Adam of Brede and his heirs were, like many others, granted an inn in Calais on condition that they were loyal to the king and carried out their duties for the safekeeping and arming of Calais.[41] It can be envisaged that not only was Adam of Brede part of the very important English repopulation of Calais but that his origins in a manor and village of east Sussex noted for its timber and firewood supplies were relevant. In 1367 timber was transported down the Rother on shouts (barges for rivers or short coastal journeys) from Bodiam bridge to a place called *Waterwassh*, near Rye (Figure 3.4). The precise location of *Waterwassh* is unknown but its name gives the sense of a place washed by the tides. Here the timber was loaded onto sea-going vessels to be taken to Calais for work on the harbour.[42]

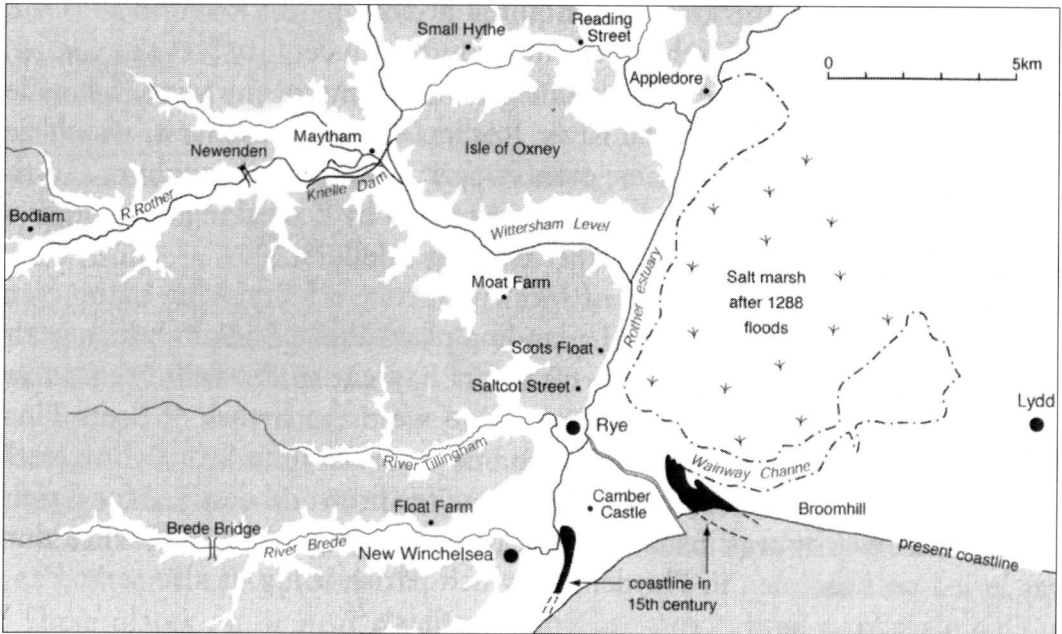

Fig. 3.4 Hythes (quays) on the Rivers Rother and Brede between the 13th and 15th centuries (after Gardiner 2007).

Wood for Domestic Fuel and the Iron Industry

Another other use of woodland was for domestic fuel. Wood from east Sussex was undoubtedly used locally but it was also exported from Rye for use at a greater distance. Firewood from Brede wood was taken to Queen Philippa's residence in London in the early winter of 1351, and probably transported by water down the River Brede, around the coast and up the Thames.[43] The distance and cost of transport to London, however, meant that in the 14th century Rye and New Winchelsea more frequently exported billets of firewood across the Channel rather than to London.[44] The large-scale export of billets from Rye in the early modern period is well known but it also occurred much earlier. The royal customs accounts record the export of billets from New Winchelsea, Pevensey and Seaford from 1307.[45] New Winchelsea was clearly much the most important wood-exporting port recorded in 1323 but Rye's exports may have been subsumed under New Winchelsea in the record. Later in the 14th century Rye may have largely replaced New Winchelsea as the main outport for the eastern Weald.[46] Detailed ('particular') accounts survive from Rye and New Romney for 1371 but not for New Winchelsea. In this year New Romney exported billets of wood worth over £150 while Rye exported billets worth only £41 8s. 6d, which amounted to 232,000 in number: they were sent to ports such as Schiedam near Rotterdam, Dordrecht, Nieuport and Flushing.[47]

In 1362 traders from Damme and Dunkirk in Flanders came to buy firewood at Rye. The bailiffs of Rye, who accounted to the king for payments for marketing goods in the town or on the quay, recorded local landing dues and purchase or export taxes on firewood, which was known in these accounts as talwood, and measured in thousands.[48] Talwood was good-quality logs for burning, although the term was sometimes used to mean the small, cheaper firewood known as billets.[49] In 1362 Arland Perssone of Dunkirk paid 14d. in dues 'for three barrels of herring sold and 14,000 of talwood bought'. William Machon of Damme paid 2d. for the due called anchorage and 3d. for the custom on 12,000 of talwood which he had purchased. John Morys, who may have been English, bought 12,000 of talwood and paid 6d. in local dues and 4d. for landing and loading. The total on which dues were paid in this account of 1362 is 38,000 of talwood. This falls far short of the 232,000 billets of wood recorded in the customs accounts of 1371, and the local dues paid on the talwood of 1362 may therefore represent only the wood exported by aliens. Alternatively talwood, the term and unit used in the bailiffs' accounts, may not directly equate with billets, used in the customs accounts; or in 1361 the exports of firewood may have been badly hit by plague epidemics at Rye in 1348 and in 1361 itself.

The customs accounts record the places from which traders came to Rye, New Winchelsea and New Romney to buy billets as well as timber and other woodland products such as oak bark. Throughout the 14th century the same places appear: Wissant, Calais, Dunkirk and Dieppe and 13 other cross-Channel ports. From 1371, when English as well as alien traders exporting wood were also recorded, the overwhelming majority of wood exporters were still aliens, and the English largely hired ships belonging to aliens. At the end of the 14th century wood for fuel was by far the most valuable kind of wood exports, followed at a great distance by timber. But wood products described as processed in some way, such as sawed board, began to appear more frequently, perhaps suggesting an increase in manufacture rather than just felling. Most importantly the numerous exports of wood indicate that the 14th century saw the large-scale cutting of trees in the Wealden forest, probably on the hills nearest to water courses, which would have contributed to the silting of the Sussex rivers.

The alien traders and carriers who came to buy wood at Rye and New Winchelsea in the 1360s and 1370s are not recorded as bringing in cargoes of goods from the Low Countries and northern France. They may therefore have often carried ballast such as stones and sand and deposited them in the Camber and in the Rother as far up as Bodiam, contributing to the damage of the port, as was suggested in 1399 (*Chapter 2*).[50] Although Smallhythe on the Rother had some functions as a place of sale and export, it did not become a town and simply remained a settlement within Tenterden parish, providing its local port facility. In 1398 Canterbury Cathedral Priory's wood at *Drofden* near Tenterden produced 100,000 billets which were sold at Smallhythe and three vessels from Smallhythe exported wool between 1379 and 1399.[51]

Soap, Steel and Straw Hats: Other Imports and Exports at Rye

Although forest products, notably fuel, were by far the most extensive and valuable export from Sussex, there was some trade in other goods: salt, wool, wool-fells, hides, manufactured leather goods, cloth, wax, iron, grain and the major import, Gascon wine. The main series of customs accounts does not distinguish between imports and exports before 1393, although the one detailed customs account which survives for Rye from 1371 does so. This records that woad, madder, alum, Seville oil, grain, black soap, steel, wainscot, paper and straw hats were brought in, listed in order of value. The import of 186 tuns of woad, for dyeing cloth, was by far the most valuable, at £599 of the total assessed value (£1,122 17s.). The vessels which brought these goods came from Schiedam (five vessels), Nieuport (two vessels), London, Dordrecht, Flushing, Newhythe, Coxyde (Koksijde, Belgium) and Sluys (one vessel from each). From 1393 the import of wine and beer flavoured with hops is noted in the customs accounts. The most substantial export was 16 shiploads of billets of firewood; in addition there were shipments of salt, eels, garlic, cloth and nuts. Although only one export shipment of salt was made, at £80 it was worth nearly twice that of the 16 shipments of billets.[52] However there was a gradual increase in imports of salt over the 14th century, possibly for preserving fish. High-quality imported salt seems to have supplemented the use of that from salt pans like those of Rameslie, perhaps as changed conditions in the channel at Saltcote made salt production unfeasible or unprofitable. The men of eastern Sussex, and particularly of New Winchelsea, became importers of salt, especially from La Baie de Bourgneuf. Simon Salerne imported salt from La Baie in *La Katerine* of New Winchelsea in 1387, and Gamelin atte Watere in *La Nicholas* of New Romney did so in 1350.[53]

Occasionally it is possible to learn more of the goods traded through Rye. The export of wool and the import of cloth and wax was concentrated in the west Sussex ports and New Winchelsea between 1300 and 1350.[54] Wool exports from Sussex fell heavily in the latter part of the 14th century, partly as war with France resumed and conditions of piracy prevailed in the Channel, but primarily because of the development of the English cloth industry.[55] The number of merchants involved in exporting wool declined and the wool trade became concentrated in the hands of a small group of merchants, including the Cely family. A specialised export from the area of Rye and its hinterlands was that of shoes. The processing of leather and the making of leather goods is known at Rye from the 13th century (Figure 3.5) (*Chapter 4*). In the 1390s one William Elmet exported a variety of goods from eastern Sussex, but most notably large quantities of shoes. The goods were shipped in vessels from New Romney (*Seyntmariebot of Romney*, master Thomas Elys of New Romney) and in *La Katerine*, which may have been Simon Salerne's ship from New Winchelsea or a vessel of the same name from Rye. Elmet used six different vessels in total to export goods, of which two or three may have been Low Countries vessels with men of Flanders as masters, and one a vessel of Calais, *Cristofore*.[56] A trader from Dunkirk brought a small amount of herring to sell at Rye in 1362 when he purchased a large amount of billets. Other cross-Channel traders from Dieppe and Le Tréport sold fish at Rye without buying firewood on the same trip, paying 10d. or 12d. as the custom on the fish sales and 2d. to anchor at Rye.[57] One merchant or trader from Piacenza on the Lombardy shore of the Po river in modern Italy, Pers de Piacenza, also landed and traded in salted fish and maybe cloth at Rye in the same year.[58]

In times of war, and perhaps more generally, Rye men exported grain, which was sometimes linked to the import of wine. In 1307 a licence was issued to Elias Muriel of Rye to export corn and other victuals to Gascony because he intended to bring back wine (*Chapter 2*). Similar licences were issued to barons of the other Cinque Ports such as Dover, Sandwich and New Winchelsea.[59] In the last years of his reign Edward I required large amounts of corn to provision the army which was attacking Scotland, and the export of corn was forbidden.[60] These licences therefore suggest a special favour to the barons of the Ports at a time when Edward

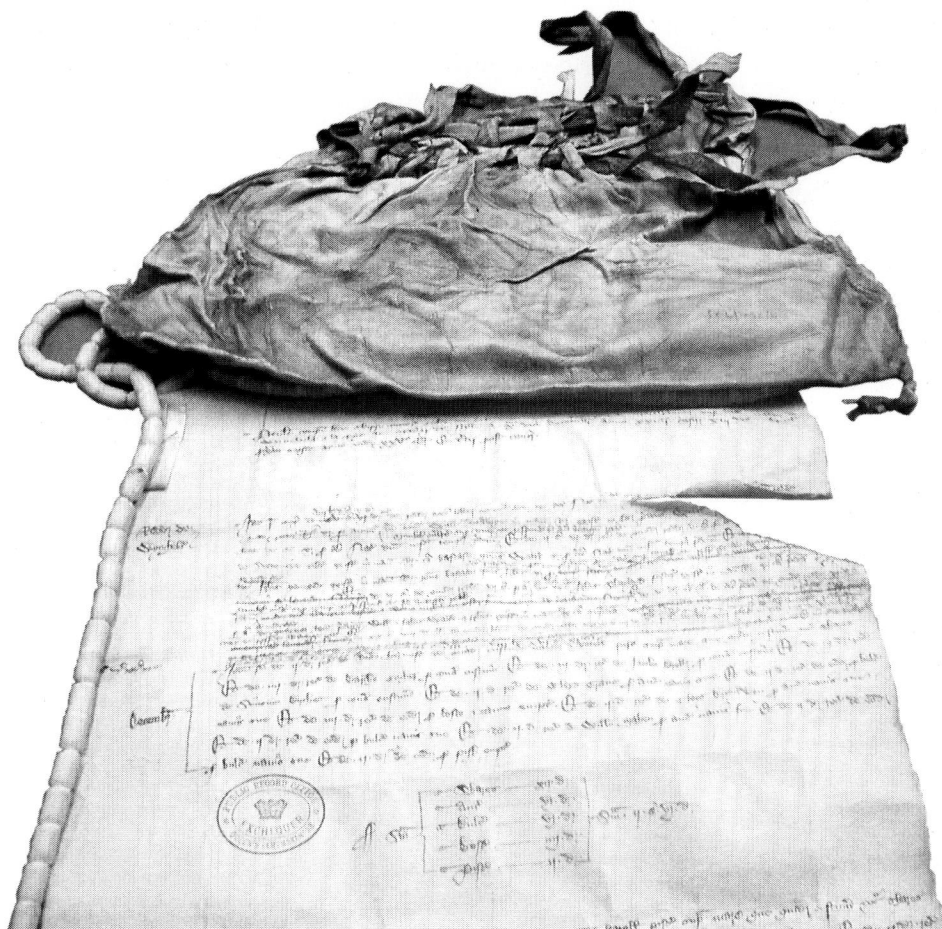

Fig. 3.5 Bailiff's account recording trade and rents in the town in 1350-1, together with its original leather bag, TNA SC6/1032/6. Similar bags also survive for the customs accounts in TNA E122.

was dependent on their service, and their vessels, to form part of the royal fleets on expedition to Scotland.[61] Grain was again required in Gascony in the 1340s and 1350s to supply the city of Bordeaux and the surrounding countryside.[62] In 1346 William Clapitus, an important Londoner, acquired a licence to buy 100 quarters of wheat and 200 quarters of oats in England and take them to Gascony in a ship called *la Katerine* of Rye of which Walter Salerne of Rye was the master.[63] The oats may have been bought locally since they were grown on Romney Marsh, and on the upland of Udimore parish and of the Isle of Ebony to the north of Rye.[64] However, although the grain was to be transported in a Rye vessel with a Rye master, it may not necessarily have departed from that town: William Clapitus was required to find security before the bailiffs of the town from where the corn was shipped that it would be delivered to Gascony.[65] On 7 November 1352 Walter Salerne received a royal licence to load 200 quarters of corn in a ship called *La Nicolas* of Rye and have it exported from the port of Rye in order to sell it in Gascony. The next month another merchant, Walter de Bynedenne, received a similar licence. Two men, including Richard Baddyng of Rye, gave guarantees that both Salerne and Bynedenne would unload and sell the corn only in Gascony. Both licences lasted until Whitsun and it is likely that they were for the same voyage. In 1374 another important, indeed notorious, Londoner, Richard Lyons, was licensed to load 200 quarters of oats into ships and have them carried from Rye to Bordeaux.[66] The licences point to the use of Rye as a port from which to ship grain, perhaps grown locally, with the trade sometimes in the hands of local merchants and sometimes London ones.

The production and use of iron in the Weald was a growing industry in the 14th century, one that itself required fuel in the form of charcoal. Iron was the second most important material in shipbuilding after wood. In the Sussex Weald, the iron industry was based in the parishes of Mayfield and Rotherfield which had access to wood for charcoal, water power and water transport in the head waters of the Rother. After the great 13th-century storms, the estuary of the Rother lay to the east of Rye and New Winchelsea rather than at New Romney. The rise and prosperity of Smallhythe as a royal shipbuilding centre depended on this route down the Rother to the sea. The import and export of iron in the Rye hinterlands is not well documented but it is mentioned in relation to shipbuilding at Smallhythe in a memorandum of 1390. This records a fine paid by one William Newenden, master of a ship called *la Alice* of Smallhythe and holder of a tenement at Rye, for taking 'two thousand of iron' in *la Alice* from London to Calais instead of straight to Smallhythe. It was suspected that William had disposed of some of the iron in Calais instead of providing it all for the building of royal ships at Smallhythe.[67]

The trade of eastern Sussex and Rye depended on the resources of the Rye hinterlands, such as wood, iron and salt, and on the access which the ports of Rye and New Winchelsea had to rivers which reached deep into the Weald. The royal family kept the crucial wartime resource of wood largely in its own hands and those of its supporters. With the ports of Rye and Winchelsea in the king's hands, timber was conveniently available for shipbuilding, and other lesser quality wood for fuel both in England and in Calais. Once at the ports, wood was easily transported around the coast, up the Thames and notably across the Channel. The import of Gascon wine was very significant at New Winchelsea, but the trade of Rye was mostly with the Low Countries and northern France: it consisted mainly of the export of billets of firewood carried in vessels belonging to non-Englishmen. In this it was similar to London where a large proportion of trade was with the Low Countries and northern France in the 14th century, and in small vessels belonging to Dutch masters or carriers, and not with more distant places.[68] War disrupted imports and exports but invasion scares or times of acute warfare, such as the 1330s, 1370s and early 1380s, increased the demand for timber. Indeed, except when Rye was raided by the French in 1339 and 1377, the aggressive policies of Edward III were probably beneficial to the economy of the town.

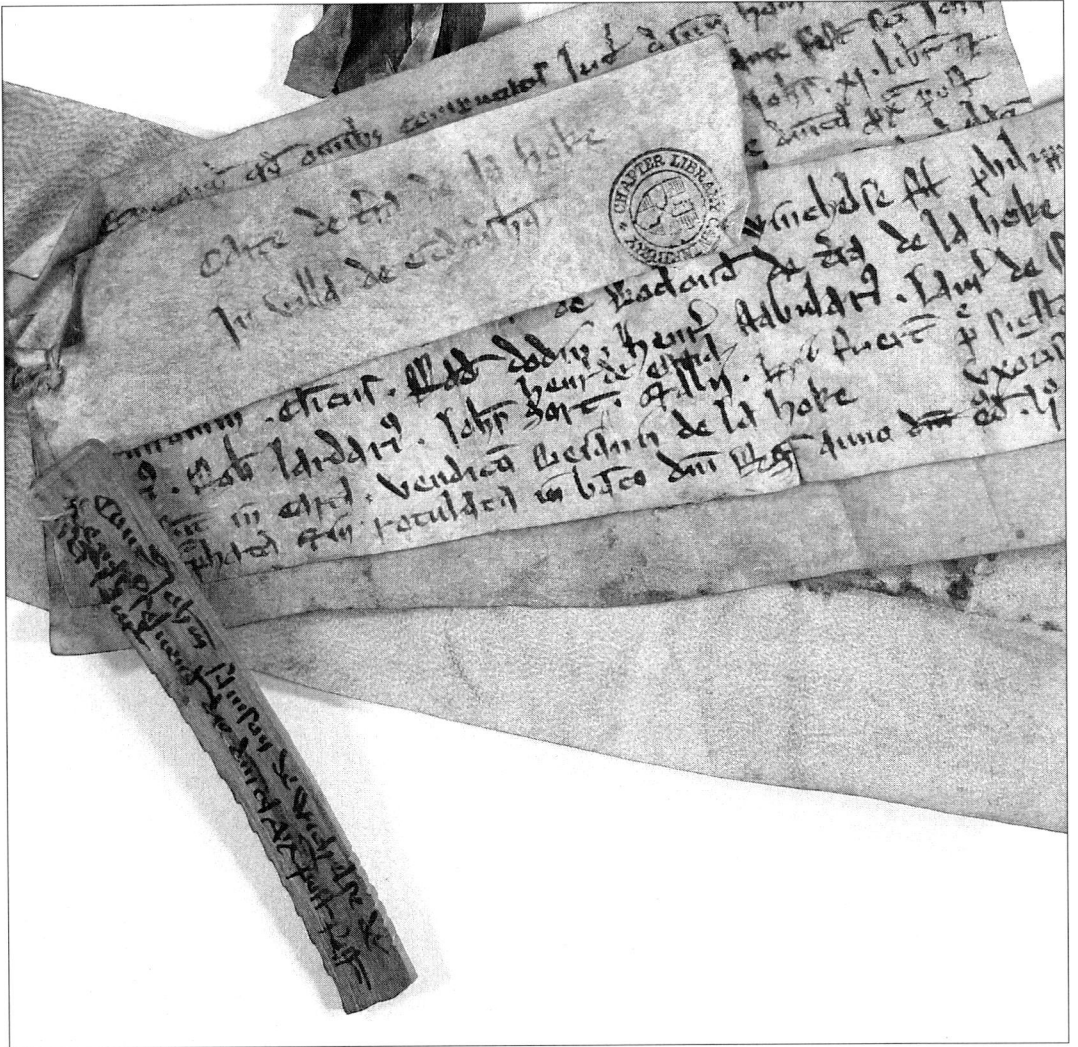

Fig. 4.1 The wooden tally stick recording money to be paid by John Sampson on 12 August 1268, CCA DCc CA G138A, 1-5, reproduced with permission.

CHAPTER 4

The People of Rye: Economic and Occupational Activity c.1260 to c.1660

Introduction

This chapter and the next examine the lives of the people of Rye between the 13th and the later 17th centuries, and the changing prosperity of the town. Every urban centre has its own story of rise and decline but that of Rye has not previously been explored in detail for the medieval period. Some themes are always prominent in town histories: the ways in which people earned a living, the differences between the lives of men and women, and between poor and rich, the houses in which the townsfolk dwelt, and the public buildings and open spaces by which they were surrounded. All towns vary, however, and these two chapters draw some comparisons and contrasts with three other towns which had different chronologies of prosperity following the Black Death.

The origins of a town and the nature of its lordship in the medieval period influenced the records which it kept. There are relatively few useful national records of taxation or customs for the Cinque Ports and Ancient Towns, since they largely managed to maintain their exemptions from such payments throughout and beyond the Middle Ages. However the early development of these towns and especially the rights which they gained to self-government have left a 'mighty mass of municipal records'.[1] These can be exploited together with royal records to open up the history of economic and social activity in Rye through the use of a database, a standard tool for historical urban analysis.[2] Individuals and families come to life again because it is possible to reconstruct many aspects of their lives, not only of the small number of wealthier townsfolk but to some extent of the numerous other people on whose labour everyone relied.

The chapter opens by examining the nature of the houses and other buildings and features of the town at the end of the 13th century, including the market. It investigates those who worked and traded there, and the debt and credit arrangements on which both poor and rich depended. Some medieval towns have extensive material about the occupations of the townsfolk. This includes Rye, and those chosen for comparison: New Romney, the nearest Cinque Port to Rye; Exeter, the estuarine port of Devon whose rise and prosperity in the late Middle Ages was partly dependent on the decline of the fishing industry of the Cinque Ports; and a rather different, inland, town, Coventry. The history of Rye in comparison with that of the other towns of the Cinque Ports confederation has been examined elsewhere.[3]

Occupations uncover the nature and scale of economic activity and give pointers to the location of certain commercial and industrial activities. The records sometimes reveal how the control of commerce and trade developed and the means which were used to sustain it, such as marriage alliances, inheritance, and investment in assets and marshland reclamation. By the late 13th century the men who headed the important and profitable crafts and trades formed the Rye town government. The strong rights which Rye possessed to organise and govern itself led to the emergence of an identifiable urban elite whose constitution and characteristics were then transformed by the plague mortality of the mid- to later 14th century (*Chapter 5*).

The Nature of Rye at the End of the 13th Century

A rental of Edward I's reign (1272 to 1307) provides a vivid picture of the town at the end of the 13th century. It records rents due to the king from a variety of houses, 'lands' and other property.[4] These rents were generally small ones of the type known as quit rents which were fixed at a date close to the foundation of the town, the mid- to late 11th century. There were rents worth 33s. 7d. payable at Michaelmas and a payment of 2½ marks (33s. 4d.) due from the mayor and commonalty at the term of St Andrew (30 November). Together these represent the rents of the earliest holdings in the town (*Chapter 1*) and in addition other rents worth over £7 were due each year by the time of Edward's reign. Some of these rents were noted later as being those of the free tenements and represent the growth of Rye over the course of two centuries.[5] All these rents seem to have remained at the similar levels over time and had changed little by 1670. They bore no resemblance to the much higher considerations which Rye inhabitants paid to each other or to outsiders on what were effectively the sales of some of these properties, up to 10 marks (£6 13s. 4d.).[6] There can however be no certainty that the rents in the Edward I rental covered all the holdings in or around Rye. Approximately 211 individuals are named in the rental but the nature of its evidence and a lack of information about family or household size preclude an estimate of Rye's population.[7]

The rental describes Rye in terms of dwellings, commercial and industrial buildings, and different kinds of lands. The lands had various descriptions including *terra stathe*, suggesting a hythe or quay, and *terra pleisance*, suggesting a garden. This may be equated with the pleasant open hilltop in the town overlooking the estuary which became known as the Gun Garden from the 15th century.[8] However, some of the lands, notably a valuable meadow (*pratum*), were clearly agricultural and must have lain outside the built-up area of Rye which was surrounded by cliffs and the town fosse (*Chapter 8*). Of the dwellings there were two or more burgages (the holdings of *burgensi* or townspeople), 19 principal tenements (*tenementa*), 120 other tenements and a house (*domus*). There were a tavern and a tenement *stabiler'*, i.e. a tenement possibly with stables, called *Rostejambe*, which suggests a place providing food and accommodation. Rents were also paid on five plots or open spaces (*placea*) including the Courton, a tannery, 26 other 'lands', two pieces of salt land, a dike, perhaps the fosse, and a corner (*cornerio*). There were also five entries relating to mills or mill land, two salthouses, a stone wall and a gate. In addition 31 rents were paid for holdings whose nature is not specified. There are 221 entries in total, with two or three covering more than one holding such as 'all the tenements of the heirs of John Bone'. The number of burgages is low; although one entry is in the plural ('from Lovetot and sister for their burgages') the level of the rent suggests it was only for two or three burgages.[9] The other entry for a burgage notes that it was held by Walter de Ratkeleye, a member of the family which provided Rye's first known mayor.[10] These entries for burgages, probably three or four in total, are a reminder that the number of *burgensi* recorded in Domesday Book for Rye (64) was, as at other towns, part of a financial assessment, not a count of burgages, nor of so-called burgess plots, nor a good basis for population estimates.[11]

The term tenement was probably applied to a house with a yard or garden area. The principal tenements were the main dwelling of their holders who in most cases had at least one other property which was sublet: Brice Morekyn, John Wyte, Robert Michel, Robert Marchant, John More, Paganus Andreu, William Geylard, Pharon Ion and John Torel. Torel, a merchant, had four tenements in addition to his principal one, and two pieces of land. Of the four tenements, which he sublet, one was said to be small (*petit*), and one was held by a chantry priest of Rye, Roger (*Chapter 6*). The principal tenements commanded the highest rents of the dwellings, up to 20d., and one of them was noted to be in the market place. Many of them were held by wealthy men who formed part of the town government such as John Ambroys, John Kyttey, John Torel, Robert Marchant, James Marchant, Pharon Ion and Henry Sliphe. One woman paid the rent on half of the principal tenement which had been her father's. The holder of the *Rostejambe* held the other half of her principal tenement and must have sublet it since he dwelt at the *Rostejambe* (*in quo manet*). The tenement which John Kyttey held but let out was also subdivided into two, with one part called a 'Cote', that is a peasant's cottage, hovel, hut, or a shelter for domestic livestock.[12] As might be expected, subletting in some cases resulted in small and subdivided tenements.

The rents of the 120 ordinary tenements, as opposed to principal ones, generally ranged between 4d. and 12d. although a few tenements held by wealthy members of the town government had higher rents. For example, Geoffrey Solas, who also held one of the mills (*Chapter 8*), paid a rent of 2s. and Robert Paulyn, who was the bailiff, paid 40d. John, son of Robert Paulyn, was living in a tenement which had formerly been the house of the Friars of the Sack (*Chapter 6*). In total the king's bailiff was due £9 2s. 9½d. from the various rents, an amount similar to that recorded in the bailiffs' accounts of the mid-14th century.

One principal tenement and two other tenements were located in the market (*in foro*): Hamo Robert paid 20d. rent for his principal tenement there; Richard de Portesmuthe junior, sometime mayor, paid 10d. rent for his tenement there; and John Torel, the merchant, paid only 3d. rent for his, which had formerly been Robert Pharon's. One more tenement was held by Matilda atte market, presumably at the market, and later by Richard le Webbe, who paid 10d. She may perhaps be identified with Matilda, the wife of Reginald de Rakele, of the mayoral family. These four tenements in the market may be linked to the four shambles (*shamell'*) in the market place which are recorded in the bailiff's account of 1272 with a payment of 10d. for each shamble. It is likely that the shambles were temporary stalls put up outside the tenements on market days. This number of stalls and the payment appears to have been fixed, like the other rents; the 'farm of the stalls' at a total of 40d. yearly was still being recorded between 1355 and 1359.[13]

The Rye market catered not only for the inhabitants of the town but also for those of the villages nearby which did not apparently have markets: Saltcote, Iden, Playden, Peasmarsh, Brede, Udimore, Beckley, Ewhurst and Northiam.[14] The market provided a weekly outlet for the products of artisans of the town. Residents did not have to pay tolls to trade there but those paid by outsiders reveal that Rye was an important market for fuel brought in from local places. John de Legh of Peasmarsh, for example, paid 8d. to the town court in 1343 'for the customary right of carrying a box (or basket) to the town for selling for the period of summer'.[15] He was assessed as selling fifty faggots of firewood. Hugh Wodegate, Thomas Bellesherst, and Benedict Knelle, all from places in Beckley parish, were assessed too at fifty faggots. Others such as Thomas Berghham (in Etchingham) were assessed as selling twenty-five faggots and paid 4d. Although the assessments are clearly round numbers, perhaps Bergham brought a smaller amount of faggots to sell as he had a greater distance to transport them. Five other men paid a similar amount for bringing in firewood between June and September 1343. The next summer 11 men also brought faggots into Rye to sell. Many were the same individuals as the previous year but also included Thomas Crepwod, from a place in Penhurst parish, to the west of Battle and Mountfield parish. Penhurst was about twelve miles from Rye and there were nearer markets at Robertsbridge, Salehurst, Bodiam, Bulverhithe, Battle, Hastings and New Winchelsea and other places.[16] This suggests that Crepwod, and possibly the others, were professional traders in fuel who visited various markets on different days. Two men brought in bundles of broom to sell in addition. Two others, including Robert de Oxenbruge, brought in talwood, another kind of firewood, perhaps logs. They were assessed on 200 pieces, which were tiny amounts compared to the amounts which traders from the Low Countries came by ship to buy (*Chapter 3*). The fact that all these sellers of fuel paid a trading toll to the Rye court in the summer may suggest that the fuel was for local industrial, rather than domestic, purposes. The market also had a small number of people bringing bundles of unspecified goods to sell there, paying a market toll (*de tolneto mercati pro uno fardell*). Richard Parker of Lewes paid 2d. for such a bundle in the summers of 1343 to 1345, and Walter Webbe in 1343 only.[17] None of these traders appear in the account which survives from after the Black Death for the year 1362. Perhaps the traders did not wish to enter a town which had experienced a very high level of plague mortality or perhaps there was simply little demand for their goods (*Chapter 5*).

The Debt and Credit Network, Small and Large

Small and large-scale trading and craft activity at Rye depended on loans in the later 13th century and first half of the 14th century, for which there is very clear evidence. In the 1270s two men were involved in the small-scale debt and credit network whose existence is clear from the bailiffs' accounts, Paganus gavelere and Luce plegger.[18] A gavelere was a moneylender or usurer and possibly also a tax collector. Plegger was a byname, perhaps a nickname, related to the word pledge, a guarantor or surety to appear in court, which was a common proceeding.[19] The Rye town court heard pleas for the non-payment of debts which were incurred in the course of trading. For example, on 23 July 1343 it heard the case of Adam Strongebogh versus Laurence le Taverner on a plea of debt and Strongebogh was fined 6d. On 20 August 1343 Robert Marchaunt was fined the same amount for making a false claim against William Boly on a plea of debt.[20] When fines were levied they were recorded as part of the town income in the bailiffs' accounts. The pleas point to a much wider credit network where such debts were part of ordinary commerce, were paid promptly and did not come to the attention of the town court. Sixteen pleas of debt were dealt with between 1344 and 1345. Five pleas involved people with bynames derived from trades: butcher, goldsmith, taverner, candeler and makemete (a preparer of food or meals). Several of the pleas concerned women, who almost never have occupational bynames in the Rye records, but may have been supplying or making goods, like Parnel Lamb, said to be in debt to John makemete.[21] The fines of 6d. which were usually levied represented about two or three days' wages for a male labourer at this time and place. Some of those fined may therefore have had to turn to a small-scale moneylender or a surety like Luce plegger. Towns of the Cinque Ports confederation had substantial populations of poor people, particularly widows, who depended on small loans from other townsfolk to tide them over until their next cash income came in from by-employments such as spinning.[22]

There were also other moneylenders, often Jewish, like Aaron de la Rye, who operated on a vastly greater scale, enabling the large-scale and profitable trades such as milling and leather processing, merchant activity and even the payment of customs and taxation to take place.[23] Moneylending is well known in large towns between *c*.1070 and *c*.1240 when Jewish inhabitants were involved, alongside Christians, in exchanging foreign coin, moneylending, goldsmithing, and dealing in plate and bullion, not least because Jews were largely barred from most artisanal occupations.[24] In the 13th century Jews had a separate legal status from Christians as a result of growing royal dependence on Jewish loans. Throughout the century Jews were increasingly suspected and hated by the monarchs, queen consorts, magnates and knights who used their credit services. Forced taxation (tallages) were imposed on Jews in England and in Gascony by Edward I, and on occasion were so heavy that contributions were made to tallages on Jews by members of the Christian population. Royal and popular suspicion and hatred of Jews eventually resulted in their formal expulsion from England in 1290. There were Jewish populations in many towns including London, Oxford, Stamford, Hereford and Canterbury.[25] The presence of Jews in smaller towns, including the Cinque Ports, is little studied, although the money-changing and moneylending in which they were concerned would have been vital to trade, and it was well understood that Jews had assets in these ports.[26] There were one or two Jewish inhabitants of New Romney in the late 13th century, possibly connected with the commercial quarter.[27] The existence of Jewish inhabitants is indicated at Rye and Winchelsea from the late 12th century[28] and money-changing is in evidence at Old Winchelsea in the late 13th century. Thomas Legat and Clement Langsters of Old Winchelsea exchanged money with Moses the Jew, as did a 'certain stranger', i.e. a man who was not a baron of the Ports, William Chaplin of Ebony, a village to the west of Appledore.[29] In January 1273 the king ordered the barons and bailiffs of Old Winchelsea to expel the Jews who were said to have moved into the town recently, on the grounds that 'according to custom of the king's Jewry', Jews should live only in cities, boroughs or towns where they had traditionally done so. On this occasion he ordered that no damage was to be caused to the Jews or their goods by their expulsion.[30]

Aaron de la Rye is prominent in the records of Jewish moneylending in the later 13th century. His byname indicates that he, and his brother Abraham, originated or at some time lived at or near Rye, as did his debtors, who included William de Ore and Walter de Tillingham (1277).[31] In 1268 Aaron compounded a debt of 120 marks owed to him by William de Ore, a parish approximately ten miles to the south west of Rye. Aaron's loans and property ownership extended well beyond Rye and in the 1270s his home was in London. In 1273 he granted all his houses, rents and tenements in the city of London to Gamaliel of Oxford, except the house in which he lived. He may have been among the many Jews executed in 1278.[32]

Men with the name Samson or Sampson are known at both Rye and Old Winchelsea in the late 13th century: Samson de Levelishamme (Leasam) known in 1304, John Sampson of Old Winchelsea, known in c.1260 to c.1268, Robert Sampson and Sampson Sliphe. Samson was a name often used in Jewish families as a forename or byname.[33] It may suggest the Jewish origins of the Sampsons in this locality, although some had forenames more typically used by Christians, John and Robert; intermarriage was not uncommon between Jewish and Christian families. John Sampson held a tenement in Rye which is likely to have been sublet.[34] By 1260 Sampson also held land at Rye which was adjacent to the tavern of Henry Sliphe at the strand, where vessels are likely to have been beached.[35] He took part in a large-scale piratical attack on merchants in 1266 and probably owned or part-owned the vessel involved (*Chapter 2*). In 1268 he lent money in association with a transaction of some property near Canterbury which belonged to Alice of Winchelsea, perhaps security for the loan.[36] The loan and transaction were recorded on four small pieces of parchment and an associated wooden tally stick, an unusual survival (Figure 4.1).

They were agreed at Canterbury and this may suggest that Sampson was acquainted with the large Jewish community there and its moneylending activities.

In the 13th century the king was provided with loans not only by Jews but also by (Christian) Italian merchants. Such merchants are known to have traded at Rye in the 14th century (*Chapter 3*) and it may be that they offered credit there in the 13th century. In 1278 merchants were accused of taking silver plate, clipped money or other broken silver out of England without special permission. An order was made for the barons and bailiffs of Old Winchelsea to search such merchants wishing to pass through the port. The order noted that these merchants might be native or foreign, and either Christians or Jews.[37] In the 1270s William de Rye, not apparently a Jew, made several large loans of between twenty and forty marks to men with lands spread across England. He also witnessed a deed of Adam de Basinges concerning property in London. William's byname clearly suggests that he came from Rye and he may have been the cleric who was in dispute with the parson of Rye church, Henry de Holm, in 1282 and who subsequently himself became vicar of Rye. In 1286 the Bishop of Chichester was ordered to pardon William, vicar of the church of Rye, of the arrears of the taxes called twentieths and fifteenths which had been extracted from him. The king had now pardoned William this sum, which may suggest that William not only lent to lay landholders but also to the king.[38] Such loans were vital to activities based in medieval Rye: the prosecution of war, merchant and large-scale artisanal activity, and property conveyances. The deeds recording these transactions never note that the substantial considerations involved were financed by loans, but it is likely that many were.

Occupational and Economic Activity

The records of Rye provide very good evidence of the occupations of the male inhabitants between the 12th and the 17th centuries.[39] Fishing was the primary occupation of the townsmen in the 12th century but in the 13th and 14th centuries many other occupations are also known from the rental of Edward I's reign, the Rye bailiffs' accounts, tax assessments, and the deeds of property transactions which were witnessed by members of the town government (*Chapter 5*). Occupations are revealed in bynames since these were not yet fixed and inherited surnames. The occupations were either given in Latin forms, for example Laurence *tinctore* (dyer), or in English forms which had become a byname, for example Laurence le Deghere.[40] Stephen Skinner, as he appeared in the rental, was described as Stephen called Skynnere in a deed of 1315.[41] Bynames like this were generally descriptions of real occupations until the mid-14th century when, for example, the lists of names of those who paid the lay subsidy (tax) specified if a person with an occupational byname such as smith had in fact a different occupation.[42] After this period bynames became inherited surnames but because trades were often passed down in families they might still represent actual occupations well into the 15th century.[43] Some bynames were nicknames rather than occupational descriptions but still derived from an economic activity such as those of Elias Makerell, Robert Makerall, William called cod, Henry le Cod, and Peter Harang (herring).[44]

The names of fishermen, mariners, ship owners and masters, merchants and carriers of wine and other goods are known at Rye from 1212 onwards (*Chapter 3*).[45] The many craftsmen and artisans who are known from the later 13th century were often substantial men who headed commercial and trading activity in the town and took part in its the government. They can be compared with Daniel Rough, the town clerk of New Romney, who was called a fishmonger. He was no mere holder of a stall on the quayside but had a substantial business selling many kinds of fish at a wide variety of places in southern and eastern England.[46]

Between 1258 and 1332 Rye men were involved in butchery, in trades which prepared and utilised leather, in milling and/or baking, in cloth-making (weaving) and in the spice trade. These important industries and trades are discussed below. There were also three or four tailors: Stephen le Thaylur, Philip the tailor, William his son, and William called Godman, tailor, who married Juliana, Philip's granddaughter. The tenement of Philip the tailor was next to the market place and was subsequently held by his son William, and then by Juliana and William Godman, tailor. At least three generations thus held this tailor's tenement in the market.[47] Several potters are known, for example Robert Croker (potter) in 1344. Some, perhaps all, of these potters worked at the kilns on the hill to the north of Rye on the route to Playden where land called *Crockeresfeld* lay.[48] These kilns were operational between the mid-13th and the mid-14th centuries (*Chapter 7*).[49] William Potter and Thomas Potter inherited a tenement from their father before 1358 but Adam Voghel of Playden then acquired it and sold it to William and Agnes Taillour of Rye in 1361. After this date, there are no occupational names which suggest that Rye inhabitants continued to make pottery. Rye or Rye-type pottery wares are found on coastal sites in Kent and Sussex, for example at New Winchelsea and New Romney, in the latter at the leper hospital, North Street, Prospect House and the Southlands School site (the former beachfront). These finds largely date from the late 13th or first half of the 14th centuries and this seems to confirm that the mid-14th century saw the end of the pottery industry at Rye.[50]

Between 1258 and 1332 there were also a barber and two bloodletters,[51] four carpenters,[52] a clencher who inserted nails into vessels,[53] a salter,[54] a ditcher, a cook and two chapmen (merchants or their agents, or peddlers and hawkers),[55] and a makemete, a spicer, two smiths,[56] a carter and four taverners. The bailiffs' accounts of 1343 to 1345 reveal some further occupations at a slightly later period: a shipman, another clencher, a maker of glass, possibly stained glass, a candeler, another smith, a goldsmith, and a soukere, perhaps a leech, i.e. physician.[57] Of all these various occupations, the carpenters may have worked on buildings or vessels. The salter is likely to have been one of many salters who provided the raw material for preserving fish, perhaps working at one of the two salthouses mentioned in the rental. A cooper, John Knyght, known in 1408, provided barrels which could be used for fish or wine. Knyght was one of three feoffees (trustees), who conveyed an acre of land to Stephen de Wye of Rye which abutted on 'the cave of Rye', suggesting a place where wine was stored.[58]

Service Trades

There are in total five taverners known in Rye between the mid-13th and mid-14th centuries: one named William, John le taverner, junior and senior, Laurence le Taverner, and Henry Sliphe who held a tavern at the strand, a location which suggests that it may have provided accommodation, at least, for visiting mariners, as well as drink and food.[59] In addition Pharon Ion held the tavern which had once belonged to Brice of Rye, the founder of the chantry in Rye church (*Chapter 6*). Both Pharon Ion and Henry Sliphe had principal tenements, their main dwellings, in the town, and their taverns may perhaps have been leased to another man such as John le taverner. The taverns seem to have generated income for Ion and Sliphe rather than being their work places or homes.[60]

In 14th-century Rye there were several medical men: two bloodletters, a leech, and possibly an apothecary (below). There was also a barber, Thomas Barbour, who may have practised some surgery, i.e. as a barber-surgeon. In 1340 he held a tenement in Rye which may have lain in the market area.[61] In 1415 men surnamed John Barbour and Roger Barbour were taxed in Market Ward: they may still have operated their trade there although by this date their surname cannot be taken as a definite indication of their occupation.[62] All these men must have responded to a need for medical attention by mariners in port as well as by inhabitants, not least in times of plague. This was an ongoing need and in 1572 the town government was extremely exercised about the imminent arrival in town of men whom they regarded as 'two abusers of the Divyne gefte of God in Medicene' who had been practising in Ashford, Kent. Later the need was met by three chyrugeons (surgeons) and the vicar, John Allin, who practised medicine (*Chapter 6*).[63]

The Supply of Food: Milling and Baking

The mills of medieval and early modern Rye were important and valuable assets supplying both the local and export market, especially in wartime (*Chapter 3*). Ellis de Rye had a lease of mills, probably tide-mills, near Rye. Ellis's lease was of two mills at an annual farm of £8, a large amount.[64] The importance of the deed of acceptance of this lease is underlined by its witnesses.[65] They included the almoner of Fécamp and the Abbot's nephew, and 12 others, several of whom were wealthy men from Rye: Master Pharon, Nicasius, Henry Torel, Gerard de Witeflet (White Fleet), Gerard de Leflesham (Leasam), Hugh, a relative of Ellis, and William Davi, possibly from the shipbuilding family Davy known in this locality from 1326.[66] As well as the mills Ellis had widespread interests in marshland reclamation around Rye as did several others in the early 13th century (*Chapter 1*).

One street in Rye was named after a miller, *Milnerstrete*, and before the Black Death there were at least four windmills in the town, owned by wealthy people, members of the Hallere, Portesmouth, Rakele and Nesse families (*Chapter 8*). The actual operation of the mills, the production of milled grain and its processing for food were carried out by others on behalf of these families, for example by Nigel the miller of Rye known in 1234 and Thomas called Pyron, miller, known in 1315.[67] Sometimes these men were recorded in Latin as *pistor* (miller or baker) or in English as baker, emphasising the close integration between the operation of the mills and the production of food. Two *pistors* appear in the rental of Edward I's reign and Walter Belde, *pistor*, and John Bakere appear in deeds of the 1320s and 1330s.[68] Walter Belde had a relative who conveyed a valuable tenement in Rye to a baker of New Winchelsea.[69] In 1339 John Bakere held land on the north side of Rye next to the highway leading out of town where there is known to have been a mill later (*Chapter 8*).[70] Mills were valuable assets and two men who guarded or kept the product of a grain mill are recorded in Rye, Nicholas meleward in the Edward I rental and John Muleward in an account of 1343 to 1344.[71]

The French attack in 1339 which included the burning of a mill, followed by the Black Death, led to the loss of some Rye mills and the disappearance of the wealthy families who owned them. These families were replaced by a new, and much smaller, town elite which included William Taillour, the mayor (*Chapter 5*).[72] In 1358 Taillour acquired rights in a half (moiety) of the windmill on the cliff at *La Nesse* from Thomas Bakere, probably John Bakere's descendant.[73] The process of acquisition is clear. Following the severe mortality of the Black Death, the Hallere family disposed of their share in this windmill to Richard Gayllard, probably because of the death of Thomas Hallere. Gayllard sold this share to Thomas Bakere and his wife Joan, who then sold it to William Taillour.[74] A member of the new town elite thus acquired one of the assets of the town traditionally held by the rich families. But the loss of population and demand for grain after the onset of plague may have caused this windmill at *La Nesse* and the others to fall out of use in the second half of the 14th century when they cease to be mentioned in the records. A rent for one mill from Robert Dyne is recorded in the chamberlains' account of 1405 which survives in very poor condition.[75] The only mill at Rye mentioned in the later medieval period (1480) is *Hothemill* which lay to the north of the town, and this may have milled all the grain which was needed. Demand picked up by the early 16th century when some new mills are known (*Chapter 8*).

Cloth-making

The presence of two families of weavers are recorded in occupational names at Rye from the mid-13th century until the 1360s, and possibly into the early 15th century. The property transactions of these weavers indicate the location of their industry. In 1258 Parnel, daughter of Richard le Webbe or weaver (*textoris*), received a payment to give up her inherited rights in land which appears to have lain on the outskirts of the town.[76] Richard le Webbe is recorded in the Edward I rental as holding a tenement which Matilda atte market had held previously, and Richard presumably sold his textiles in the market. Richard was dead by 1304 when his two other daughters, Emetota or Emma and Margery, received payments for their inherited property as their sister Parnel had done. The description of this property as 'in Rye next to the tenement of La Lee' locates it on the northern outskirts of Rye.[77] Emetota and Margery had sufficient property and wealth to possess their own seals with which to confirm this transaction: the legend on one seal ran *S' EME LE WEBBE, which is an exceptional instance of a woman identified by a craft in Rye. The legend on the other seal was *S' MARGERI: RECOTE, since Margery had married one John Recote. The custom in Rye was partible inheritance or gavelkind, as it was in the adjacent county of Kent, and meant that Richard's daughters would have inherited in the absence of brothers. In 1304 Emetota and Margery sold their rights in the inherited land to Thomas Ricard of Rye, whose name suggests he may have been a son or other relative of Margery's husband, John Ricote or Recote. By 1304 Emetota, Margery and John must all have been elderly, since Parnel, Richard's other daughter, had disposed of her rights in 1258. It is thus possible that Emetota had run the family business of weaving as a single woman in the late 13th century, accounting for the name on her seal, Le Webbe.[78] There is no evidence that Thomas Ricard was involved in the cloth-making industry. He was a member of the Rye town government in the 1310s. A property transaction of c.1325 in which he acquired the inherited rights of two other sisters in land at La Lee suggest that his wealth and status were based not on commerce but on the tenure of manorial land on the fringes of Rye.[79]

The premises of Benedict le Webbe and his heirs were at the area called *Le Teynton*, or tenter-ground, a place where milled cloth was stretched with tenterhooks on a wooden frame to prevent shrinkage. This was an industrial activity which required some space and so was not likely to be carried out in the town centre. *Le Teynton* lay on the north side of St Mary's Marsh, Rye (*Chapter 9*), and to the south of the route called Blikelane which led to Blikewell (Figure 7.1).[80] To the south of *Le Teynton* was a meadow called Kingswish which lay behind the Landgate suburb on the western side of the road between Rye and Playden. In this suburb were four messuages (houses with an associated enclosed area) belonging to wealthy people: two belonged to Matilda de Pigevirle, widow of William de Pigevirle, one to Robert Alard, and one to the heirs of Benedict le Webbe, suggesting that his messuage was close to his tenter-ground.[81] In 1363 *Le Teynton* was granted to William Storm of Cadborough, a man with no known connections to cloth-making, and weaving may already have ceased at this location.[82]

Limited evidence from the first decades of the 15th century suggests the final disappearance of cloth-making at Rye by this time. There are no occurrences of people called weavers nor of the name Webbe apart from Robert Webbe, who was taxed in Nesse Ward in Rye in 1415 and involved in piracy with William Longe (*Chapter 2*). His lands and tenements at Pypeneselle in the marsh of Cadborough to the west of Rye were granted away to a man of Brede and then to Robert Onewyn (I) (alias Taylour), the mayor of Rye, by 1431, and possibly some time earlier. Robert Webbe's other lands, said to be upland and marshland in Rye, Udimore and Brede, were also bought by Robert Onewyn.[83]

The Trade in Spices

Jordan le Spycer of Rye is recorded in 1315, his byname indicating that he either dealt or traded in spices or was an apothecary.[84] Jordan is the only spicer known in Rye before the Black Death, but there was also a valuable spice trade at New Winchelsea in which a London citizen and spicer invested.[85] Jordan and his wife Gymmota seem to have been a wealthy couple, since after she was widowed

Gymmota was able to purchase a tenement in Rye to provide a rental income for herself and inheritances for her two daughters. The daughters married non-Rye men and sold their shares in the inherited tenement to Ralph, son of John Blodletere, and to Ralph's wife Christine, receiving considerations of 20s. and one mark of silver (13s. 4d.) respectively.[86] Robert le Spicer held a tenement in Rye in the 1360s and 1370s, which lay in a crowded area where shipmen and a 'crabber' also had tenements, and which was therefore perhaps down by the quayside. This tenement may have been the base for the import of spices into Rye. This was an area which underwent change after the Black Death, with members of the town elite, first William Taillour and then Stephen Andreu, buying up a tenement there in 1363, the one adjacent to that of Robert le Spicer.[87] It is not possible to say whether in the 1360s and 1370s Robert's byname represents his occupation or an inherited surname; the same applies to Richard Espiccer, who was mayor in 1437.[88] On very special occasions such as the entertainment of the Lord Warden of the Cinque Ports in 1455 by the town government, the chamberlains' accounts record the purchase of spices as well as other luxury foodstuffs such as crab and cream but there is no indication of where the spices were obtained.[89]

In the late 14th century one Robert le Mustarder held a plot in the market place, and he may have been a maker or seller of mustard. Mustard was regarded as an especially suitable accompaniment to mackerel, one of the types of fish caught by Rye fishermen: it was said that 'Mustard is metest with…Salt ele, salt makerelle'.[90] However by 1395 Robert le Mustarder had ceased to pay his rent and the plot was vacant, an indication of the downturn in trade at Rye in this period.[91] (*Chapters 3, 8*)

The Leather Trades: Skinning, Tanning and Dyeing

Between 1272 and 1332 there were several men involved in trades which prepared leather: two skinners, four or five tanners, and two dyers.[92] Others utilised their products, Helyas le Corvayser, a worker in leather or a shoemaker, Moses, a cordwainer and perhaps a Jew, and John de Toulveherste, also a cordwainer.[93] Cordwainers were specialised workers in Cordovan leather making shoes, in particular, from the hides of horses, goats, sheep or pigs which had been tanned with alum, sulphur or sumac to produce a light-coloured leather. The best brilliant red Cordovan leather was dyed with kermac. Cordwainers used only new leather, in contrast with cobblers, who were mainly repairers who used old leather.[94] Two more cordwainers and a glover were recorded in Rye in 1334 and 1335.[95] They presumably sold their goods in the market place which was near the Butchery, the source of the leather hides which they used (*Chapter 8*).

Stephen Skynnere held a property from the town on which he paid a rent of 3d. and also leased another messuage in Rye from Agnes called Sonke, which he subsequently conveyed to Thomas called Pyron, miller.[96] Some of the mills of medieval Rye were on the low-lying eastern side of town and tanning may also have taken place here: it was a smelly activity needing a water supply and so was often found on the outskirts of towns. Large amounts of ashes for tanning were imported into the port of Winchelsea until 1351.[97] Stephen Ambrois paid rent for a tannery (*tanerie*) in Rye but was not himself called a tanner.[98] He came from the Ambroys family, part of the town government and elite, and it appears that, as with milling, there were wealthy families owning industrial plant who employed others to carry out the work. The processes of preparing leather by tanning and making leather goods made human connections between those in related trades, both within and beyond Rye; for example the glover known in 1335 conveyed a plot with buildings to one of the cordwainers.[99] The daughter of Stephen Skynnere, Alice, was married to Thomas Pokel of Canterbury, a member of a remarkable family of professional carriers of letters between London and Canterbury in bags or sacks, presumably made of leather.[100] After Stephen Skynnere's death, which occurred by 1343, the family tenement in Rye was held in equal shares by his widow Margery and daughter Alice, who was his heir in the absence of a son. Both Margery and Alice conveyed their shares in the tenement to William Baker of Appledore, and thus by family circumstances Skynnere's tenement, perhaps the base for his trade, passed to a tradesman of Appledore (Figure 1.4).[101] Appledore was a small market town and since William does not reappear in the Rye records, it is likely that he continued to pursue the trade of baker in Appledore and sublet the Rye tenement. After 1363 the leather producing and processing trades of skinning, tanning and dyeing disappeared from Rye as known occupations or occupational names, and it may be that demand for leather goods shrank until the late 15th or 16th centuries (below).[102]

The example of marshland at *Levedimerss* in Iden indicates the relationship between leather processing in Rye and the holding of marshland around the town. A family called Kechenore was named from a settlement in Iden or Beckley, the area with which they remained associated.[103] They are recorded in deeds from 1303 as grantees and witnesses, mainly in connection with a very substantial marsh called *Levedimerss* in Iden. In 1303 William, son of John de Kechenore, owned land in *Levedimerss*, and acquired some more marsh which lay next to it from Adam de Bosenye.[104] In 1330 William de Kechenore transferred this holding in *Levedimerss* to Thomas Dyges. Dyges then transferred a half of *Levedimerss* to Stephen at Leghe of Rye, a tanner, who paid a consideration of 20s. Five years later, John Roger, a cordwainer of Rye, acquired this half of *Levedimerss* from Stephen atte Leghe, the tanner. John Roger then transferred it to John de Kent, cordwainer of Rye, for a much increased consideration of four marks of silver (53s. 4d.), who transferred it to Elias atte Halle of Rye in 1341.[105] In the 1330s, then, *Levedimerss* was held by a tanner and two cordwainers of Rye, and it is likely that it provided grazing for the animals on which their trades depended. The Kechenores went on to rise to the status of minor rural gentry after the Black Death, but part of the foundation of their wealth seems to have been prudent investment in marshland at *Levedimerss* in Iden before 1303, its value partly realised by granting some of it to artisans in the leather industry of Rye.[106] *Levedimerss* may later have suffered the fate of some land and heath at *Le Hole*, on the north side of Rye, which seems to have been used for grazing the animals of Rye butchers before the Black Death, but which passed into the hands of the minor gentry Tychebourne family at the end of 14th century (below).

Butchery

The market place in Market Street and the Butchery was strongly associated with the sale of both meat and leather (*Chapter 8*). Individuals and families involved in the butchery trade at Rye are known from the late 13th century when Thomas Bochard, presumably butcher, appears in the Edward I rental, holding a principal tenement.[107] In 1305 a tenement next to the market was held by Henry the butcher and then by Adam de Tuysdenne, butcher, and Parnel his wife. The tenement was let to them by Peter de Heghtone, the town clerk, and his wife for a substantial yearly rent of 8s. and an initial consideration of 40s.[108] Richard Beneyt, another butcher, was a witness to two property transactions in Rye in 1316. One of the transactions concerned property at *Pigges-Lane*, rather suggestive of an area of butchery.[109] Beneyt himself was involved in a conveyance of property to a couple who were part of the town elite, the Kytteys (*Chapter 5*). He possessed a personal seal with an image of a hawk on its prey, an image which was becoming common in the period after 1300.[110]

Peter Bocher is known at Rye in the mid-1340s from a variety of small debt and trespass cases heard in the town court. Bocher was fined 6d. for a false claim against William Langport for trespass and Robert Bernehond was fined the same amount for a false claim against Bocher for debt.[111] For several decades the butchery trade of Rye was in the hands of the Bochers, apparently members of a single family: Robert senior and Robert junior, Reginald and another Peter. In the late 14th century they were all were witnesses to property transactions and thus identifiable as members of the town government.[112] In 1374 Reginald Bocher held a shop (*selda*) near the market place or the Butchery. This shop temporarily passed to Stephen de Wye, butcher of Rye, via William Taillour senior, who was the founder of the new civic elite family of this name. Ten years later, when this shop was held by Robert Bocher junior, it was described simply as a plot of land, as were two others around the market place, probably an indication of the loss of active trade.[113] A feoffment of 1384 recorded that Thomas Taillour received the plot 'by award according to the ancient law of the town', and passed it on to Robert Holstok and his wife, who were neither Rye residents nor butchers.[114]

In 1398 Robert Bocher junior held a tenement called *Le Hole* with three pieces of land and heath or scrub attached to it amounting to 18 acres. *Le Hole*, although located in Rye, lay on the north side of the town towards Leasam and near *Wellefield* (*Chapters 8, 9*). Robert thus appears to have been a grazier as well as a butcher, a typical conjunction of activities. The land and heath at *Le Hole* which Robert Bocher held passed in 1398 to Richard Tychebourne of Rye and Joan his wife after a brief tenure by William Kechenore of Iden and Juliana his wife.[115] Neither the Kechenores nor the Tychebournes are known as butchers in Rye, but rather were part of the new rising gentry of Rye and the surrounding rural parishes who were participating notably in the 14th-century property market there. Richard Tychebourne was, in addition, deputy to the mayor (*locum tenens*), John Baddyng, in 1397.[116]

In the early 15th century nobody was described as a butcher in Rye although men surnamed Bocher, Walter and William, still lived there. Walter Bocher held a tenement in Market Ward in 1415 on which he paid 20d., a fairly large amount in this ward.[117] However William Bocher's tenement was in Watermelle Ward, not Market Ward, suggesting that he was not active in the butchery trade. It may be that in a period of economic decline at Rye Walter Bocher and one or two others continued to supply meat to the inhabitants but butchery, like leather processing, does not seem to have been thriving again until the very end of the 15th century (*Chapter 5*).[118]

William Eston was known as a butcher in 1492 in the period when economic activity in Rye was growing; what is known of his family suggests that butchery was once again becoming a profitable trade.[119] John Eston senior, William's forebear, was collector of the maletotes, a local tax on trade, in 1475 and was MP in 1477 to 1478. The family was first recorded in Rye in 1431 when Thomas Eston, presumably John's ancestor, was a witness to a conveyance of Robert Webbe's land to Robert Onewyn II alias Taylour.[120] In the 16th century the Estons were one of the notable and prosperous jurat families, for example owning the kiln which supplied 10,000 bricks for the building of the town's almshouse in the 1550s.[121] By this time butchery was re-established as an important trade, supplying a much increased population, a revitalised port and the large number of inns and victualling houses in the town. Butchers continued to be among the wealthy members of the town elite and government until at least the 1660s (below).

Alien Craftsmen in the 15th Century

The record of other occupational activity is not extensive in 15th-century Rye but that of the alien craftsmen working in and around the town is notable.[122] Alien craftsmen were sometimes welcomed and sometimes suspected in the Cinque Ports depending on political and military conditions. In 1436 there were a number from places in modern Germany and Holland, including Cologne, Utrecht, Amsterdam and Rotterdam. Those with named occupations were an armourer living in Rye, a skinner and a weaver who were living in Appledore, a haberdasher and a cordwainer both living in New Winchelsea, occupations which were typical of the Cinque Ports. Four other aliens were recorded living in Smallhythe, presumably working in shipbuilding or marshland drainage there. Two more were recorded, without occupations, as living in Appledore, three more in Rye, and 14 more in New Winchelsea, and four others in places on Romney Marsh.[123] The presence of these aliens suggests that the long-term connections formed by trade with the Low Countries prompted the arrival of some craftsmen who knew of and took up specialist opportunities in this locality.

From 1441 various poll taxes were levied on aliens living in the Cinque Ports although at this time only Sandwich had significant numbers of aliens recorded, mostly wealthy Genoan merchants or factors.[124] Rye and Lydd however dutifully noted the costs of a man carrying the 'alienes mony' from their towns to Dover in 1457.[125] By 1483, when only 'Dutch' aliens were counted, Rye had nearly as many as Sandwich, with five alien householders and 14 lodgers (non-householders) compared with Sandwich's eight householders and 18 lodgers.[126] In 1525 Parliament granted a subsidy on the lands, goods and wages of aliens and an assessment for Rye survives (the native inhabitants were exempt). Fifty-three aliens were assessed and of those whose nationalities were given, 12 were Frenchmen, two were Normans, one was an Italian and one a Spaniard. The names of some others suggest they came from the Low Countries but the nationalities of most of the 53 were not given, nor the occupations of any. Eleven were assessed to pay on goods or ready money, and four on yearly wages of between 15s. and £3 a year. Most, however, paid only 8d. 'hede money', the amount due from those not receiving yearly wages, and two were assessed as too poor to pay anything.[127] In 1538 there were said to be over a hundred resident aliens in Rye who were in dispute with the native fishermen over such tasks as mending nets.[128] These various records of aliens were not made on the same basis and cannot be used for direct comparisons but it seems clear that the numbers of aliens rose in line with those of the population of Rye in the late 15th and early 16th centuries.

Trades and Crafts in the 16th and 17th Centuries

The types of occupational craft and trade activity in early modern Rye were strikingly similar to those of the medieval town. Once again the occupations which can be identified are mainly those of the wealthier sort, the freemen, in 16th-century terms. Over forty per cent made their living primarily from the catching, sale and distribution of fish. Merchants, textile workers and those preparing and selling food and drink were other major categories by percentage. Workers in shipbuilding and house building, leather and metal trades formed one or two per cent of the total in each category.[129] The occupations in the different categories were rather more specialised than in medieval Rye. There were also some new trades, partly reflecting the more numerous and various sources but mainly the active economy and demographic circumstances in Rye and the higher disposable incomes of individuals. (*Chapter 5*). The new trades included brickmakers who worked on local examples of avant-garde brick buildings: East Guldeford church, built in 1505, Smallhythe chapel, rebuilt shortly after 1514, and the new Rye almshouse of the mid-century (*Chapter 6*).[130] There were also plumbers who were probably involved in the extensive works on Rye's new water supplies or conduits. The first two decades of the 16th century saw an increase in the import and manufacture of fashionable French-inspired headgear by hatters and cappers, another new trade. Although weapon-makers such as the alien armourer were known earlier, they were more numerous in the 16th century, and in the 1560s included bowyers, fletchers and arrow-head makers, reflecting Rye's anxieties about the defence of the town at this time (*Chapter 8*).

In the 1560s to 1580s there was strong local demand for the building of ships and houses with, for instance, arrangements for the building or leasing of ships between Rye and London men particularly noticeable in the late 1570s and 1580s.[131] In the spring of 1585 John Hamond of Rye, carpenter, obtained 100 tons of oak timber from *Lymewood* in Northiam from Richard Brigden of Ewhurst, a yeoman.[132] In this period a large population of Rye residents and visiting mariners needed to be supplied with foodstuffs, mainly bread and beer, and fulfilling this need occupied many Rye men.[133] The demand was catered for at its peak in 1575 by 37 people licensed as beer tipplers or vintners and four unlicensed ones. In 1574 94 beds were available to accommodate visitors in Rye's licensed premises.[134] In January 1589 the brewing trade was still strong: Richard Portriff of Rye, beerbrewer, bought logs for his fire from as far away as the woods of Richard Baker in Rolvenden in the Weald.[135] John Hamond was a carpenter in the 1570s and 1580s, during which period he had several apprentices. However, by 1592 he held the Blue Anchor, one of the lesser victualling houses of Rye, apparently changing his occupation or taking on an additional one, as many Rye men did in the late 16th century. Hammond's tenure of the Blue Anchor may have been taken up in retirement from his carpentry business or as an attempt to supplement his income as a time when Rye was passing its peak of economic activity.[136]

There is little evidence of a thriving leather industry in Rye in the 15th century with simply one record of a townsman, John Bayle, being paid in 1449 'for making a little sack of sheep's leather' to hold pellet powder (*pulveris librillarum*) for the town's old guns, which were laid in a pit by the Landgate.[137] However, it is in the 16th century that there is evidence of an active trade in leather goods, particularly shoes, with cordwainers second only to tailors among the artisanal occupations.[138] They provide a case study of the nature and location of craft activity in Rye at this time. In 1575 Thomas Radford junior, cordwainer, who lived in Landgate Ward had a shop which was under the town wall outside the Strandgate and near the New, i.e. Strand, conduit.[139] This was one of the shops which had been built here by the town government in the mid-1480s, sometimes on vacant land (*Chapter 8*).[140] By 1587 Radford also held a long narrow strip (24 feet by two feet) in front of his shop on which a stall had been erected. He also acquired a plot of land about fourteen feet square behind his shop and stall, perhaps to use as a work area. Radford paid the town an annual rent of 12s. for his shop together with Mr Francis Harris, who contributed the same amount. Mr Harris was a mercer and jurat and may have sublet his shop at the Strand, perhaps to Radford, since the jurats were usually older men who had ceased to be active in commerce.[141] Noye Radford was the town drummer, perhaps because his family supplied and fitted the skins for the drums; he used the drum to call the townspeople to and from the great works on the harbour sluice in 1596 to 1597.[142] Other men who held shops at the Strand were the jurats Mr John Bredes and Mr William Tolken of Landgate Ward, a wholesale fishmonger.[143] By 1575 Mr Bredes was dead and the shop was let to widow Chapman for 10d. a year. Anthony Cocke, a French merchant, held a large plot of vacant land next to the work area on the Strand belonging to Thomas Radford.[144]

In the late 1650s there were still at least four cordwainers active in Rye: Abraham Hanson, Moses Peadle junior and senior, and Bartholomew Breads.[145] Abraham Hanson and his wife Margaret owned a house and garden on the north side of Longer Street (also known as Lower Street, and now as High Street and the Mint, *Chapter 8*). The Hansons occupied this property themselves, in contrast to many properties in Rye at this period which were sublet, and it may have been used for Abraham's trade. His surname indicates that he was descended from Hance Hanson, a Huguenot immigrant of the late 16th century and one of a number of merchants and craftsmen who, like Antony Cocke, the French merchant, became denizens and settled permanently in Rye. Abraham, the cordwainer, and his wife conveyed their property to Francis Younge, a grocer, for a substantial consideration of £50 10s.[146] A previous Francis Younge, perhaps the grandfather of the grocer, was a yeoman of Iden. His son John Younge was apprenticed in 1624 to William Starkie, jurat and a tallow chandler of Rye.[147]

Moses Peadle junior, the cordwainer, and Aaron Peadle, a tailor, were the sons and heirs of Moses Peadle, the elder, also a cordwainer of Rye. In 1658 they conveyed their father's house and shop in Market Ward for a consideration of £30 to another cordwainer, Bartholomew Breads, who was already in occupation. The northern boundary of the property was the 'common street called Butchery'.[148] In 1661 Moses Peadle junior, then described as a glazier and a gentleman, acquired another property in the market place and it seems that he chose not to continue working and trading as a cordwainer.[149] Other trades using leather such as glovers and saddlers were still known in Rye in the mid-17th century, for example Edward Bourne, saddler, John Martin, glover, and Benjamin Martin, fellmonger.[150] One Rye freeman only is known as a tanner in the Tudor period but tanning remained an important activity at Iden until at least the mid-17th century.[151]

A detailed analysis of those who had their property transactions recorded in the town court book as grantors or recipients between 1651 and 1661 inclusive provides a wider picture of the range of occupations in Rye:[152] a baker, a blacksmith, two butchers, a cloth-worker, a glover, a currier (leather dresser), three surgeons, a goldsmith, a glazier, a husbandman, a joiner, a seaman and 13 mariners, a salter who had earlier been a wholesale fishmonger, a shipwright, three ship carpenters, three tailors, a tallow chandler, a victualler, two yeomen, two labourers, a beerbrewer, a cooper and one soldier ('Captain').[153] This range of occupations is very similar to that found in Rye deeds between *c*.1551 and 1640.[154] The 'statistical darkness' which then prevails in the 1640s and 1650s and the nature of the town court record book as a source precludes any real quantitative assessment, but the number of those apparently involved in Rye's maritime economy between 1651 and 1661, 13 mariners and a seaman, is remarkable given the suggestion that this period saw the town's final decline.[155] The presence of three ship carpenters and one shipwright in this period also demonstrate the ongoing importance of shipbuilding at Rye. The assessments for local and national taxation of 1660 to 1663 show that, of 47 households deemed wealthy, seven were headed by seafarers and allied occupations.[156]

The Poll and Hearth taxes of 1660 and 1664 indicate the size of the houses of some people recorded in the town court book between 1651 and 1661, both the very rich and the less wealthy.[157] Those with large houses were often described by their status rather than their occupations: four jurats, the mayor, and three gentlemen out of the eight who appear in the court book.[158] The surgeons of Rye were also rich and had money to spend on their homes. John Allen, a goldsmith of Rye, sold two messuages and gardens in the Butchery to John Kevell of Rye, surgeon. The property was inherited by his son Francis Kevell, another surgeon, who by 1653 had the two messuages made into one, together with their gardens. Francis Kevell was an unusual instance of the property owner being also the occupier, rather than subletting. Together with his wife, Francis, he sold the house to a third surgeon of Rye, James Welsh. This was a valuable property for which Welsh paid Francis Kevell a consideration of £56.

At the other end of the scale of wealth, as measured by the considerations paid, was a blacksmith, Richard Younge senior. He owned a messuage or tenement in the Fishmarket, i.e. between the town crane and the rows of shops which lay to the north west of the quay and the Strand (*Chapter 8*). It is likely that the blacksmith made specialist iron products for vessels such as anchors and chains. He left half of this messuage to his son Thomas who was involved in another maritime occupation, as a ship carpenter of Rye. The other half of the property was inherited by the blacksmith's other son, Richard junior, a mariner of Rye. Subsequently Bridget, the daughter and heir of Thomas the ship carpenter, married a yeoman of the nearby parish of Peasmarsh. Together with her husband she sold her half of the messuage to her uncle Richard, the mariner, in 1657. This is a typical transaction involving a women's inheritance of which there are many more examples. Bridget was examined 'diligently and solely' in the town court before the mayor and jurats, a long-established practice intended to demonstrate that she was alienating her inheritance voluntarily.[159] A consideration of £8 was paid by Richard the mariner to acquire his niece's half of the property. This is the second lowest sum mentioned in these deeds.

Women had strong property rights in Rye through the partible inheritance system, rights which are evident by the 13th century. The procedures in the town court were strikingly similar in the 17th century to those of the 13th, at which time women's property was sometimes conveyed for large considerations; for example, 10 marks was paid for a tenement which Robert Bredware, merchant of Rye, had acquired from Joan Dore and shortly afterwards passed to another man and his wife.[160] The names of the parents from whom women inherited were given in deeds; conveyances named wives as well as husbands; and some women, such as Joan, wife of Robert *faber* (smith) of Rye, sealed the deeds with their own seals.[161] Subletting of property was a common feature even in the 13th century, making it feasible for mothers such as the widow Gymmota to ensure their daughters received an income or a dowry from subletting. Where a family had no sons, inheritance by a daughter might on occasion contribute to the apparent disappearance of a trade or craft from Rye, as in the case of Alice Pokel. In a different example, William Godman seems to have inherited his trade by marriage, becoming a tailor like his father-in-law. Careful choice of marriage partners with proper records of the transfer and conveyance of women's inheritances seems to have reinforced the retention of property, money and town office within a small group of families. When the Rye merchant John Torel conveyed a field at the pottery kilns just outside the town to Richard de Portesmouthe, mayor of Rye, he gave power of attorney to the man whom his daughter had married to deliver formal possession of the property.[162] The women of medieval Rye were seldom marked out as participating in trades and crafts by being given an occupational byname, with Emetota Le Webbe being the only exception. Nevertheless their marriages and their rights as heirs helped in the formation of an early town oligarchy and its maintenance over time; these are examined in Chapter 5.[163]

Occupational Activity in Rye compared with other Medieval Towns

Rye was in many ways well placed to fulfil the ambitions of its lord and become both a local market and a specialist urban centre in the 12th and 13th centuries. The local villages to the north and north west did not apparently have markets and thus looked to Rye for goods which were required weekly, and for other items which needed to be purchased less often such as cloth, clothes or shoes. Rye's market hinterland effectively stretched from Robertsbridge on its west to New Romney on its east. Almost everything sold in the Rye market was made in or around the town, with the fuel brought in from neighbouring villages being the significant exception. Rye, however, was a small place compared with an inland town such as Coventry which dominated trade in its much larger regional hinterland in the 13th and first half of the

14th centuries, a dominance reflected in the greater diversity of occupations there. For Coventry 628 different occupational categories have been discovered between 1200 and 1299, partly because there is a greater variety of source material but mainly because it was a much bigger place. The occupational categories were similar to those of Rye but included a much greater degree of specialisation within each category, for example 12 kinds of workers in metal rather than simply 'smiths'. At Coventry distributive traders, including merchants and especially wool merchants, grew in numbers and significance in the 14th century as inland trade and specialisation in wool exports from London and Boston occurred, partly replacing exports from the Cinque Ports where piracy was rife. Coventry also managed to preserve its cloth manufacturing which became increasingly profitable from the mid-14th century. Although the inhabitants of Coventry died 'in droves' in the Black Death, there was significant demographic and economic growth over the next three decades. The merchant class thrived, relying on a complex system of credit and debt and the recently formed merchant guilds. The masters and officers of the guilds took over the reins of town government from the Benedictine Priory. Before Coventry suffered an economic setback in the 1440s it enjoyed sixty years of prosperity and population growth, becoming the fourth largest city in England after London, Bristol and York.[164] Its history was thus very different from that of Rye, and a more direct comparison for Rye might therefore be Exeter, the estuarine port town and marketing centre of the South West, whose population was about 3,100 in 1377.[165]

Exeter was relatively prosperous in the late Middle Ages, partly because of the development of the fishing industry of Devon and Cornwall at the expense of the south-eastern ports (*Chapter 2*).[166] Late medieval Rye was perhaps only about one-third the size of Exeter.[167] Exeter, like Coventry, has an exceptional amount of material relating to occupations, although mainly from the 14th century and particularly its second half. It shows the occupational diversity of most medieval towns, especially when the activity of all members of the household, and of the poor as well as the rich, are considered. This highlights the extent to which many medieval households depended on a variety of incomes, not merely the main one of the male 'householder'. The provision of food and drink and mercantile activity were particular features because of its role as a port, regional capital and cathedral town.[168] It is clear from the examples of Coventry and Exeter that local factors and the geographical situation of medieval towns were crucial in how they fared in the 14th century. Rye was important as a market but had no administrative functions nor great abbey or cathedral to attract visitors. Its fishing industry was in decline by the mid-14th century and suffered from the competition from the south-western ports.

The piracy in which its mariners indulged may have brought some of them large, if intermittent, gains but overall it damaged cross-Channel trade in valuable goods. As a port Rye was particularly vulnerable to plague, and the occurrence of French raids and fear of future ones helped prevent the population levels recovering.[169]

In the middle decades of the 14th century all the productive and service activities of the town seem to have been badly hit by the inundation, famine, plague epidemics and French raids: pottery, milling and baking, cloth-making, tailoring, leather producing and leather processing (skinning, tanning, dyeing, making shoes, bags and other goods), butchery, medicine and inn-keeping. Rye was worse placed to recover from the Black Death than the nearby Cinque Port of New Romney, which had already been badly affected by the 13th-century storms but then recovered to some degree. The butchery trade of New Romney, for example, was far more extensive than that of Rye, probably because of the town's immediate and very extensive marsh hinterlands where animals were raised. In 1340 thirteen shambles were assessed for a local trading tax at New Romney, and even after a loss of population and a decline of trade in the second half of the 14th century, 10 butchers still paid this tax in 1414; furthermore butchers became among the chief families of the town in the 15th century.[170] In contrast at Rye only one or two butchers continued to operate in the town after the plague and French raids and there is certainly no evidence of a rise in their status. In addition the stagnation of the important leather processing and butchery trades at Rye in the late 14th century resulted in grazing land passing into the hands of gentry families. Animals may still have been raised there but the direct connection between grazing stock and the use of their products by the artisans of Rye seems to have been lost. In all, Rye was significant as one of the urban centres in the South East which pre-dated the widespread growth of English towns in the later 12th and 13th centuries.[171] Its market was important at the eastern end of Sussex but its trade could not withstand the damage of external events in the middle decades of the 14th century, leading to prolonged stagnation in the late Middle Ages. There is little sign of production or service trades being re-established in the 15th century, when the town income, from mid-century when evidence survives, was largely dependent on maletotes from the export of billets, from the ripiers who traded fish overland to places beyond Rye, a payment called poundage from the fishermen of Saltcote, and enforced payments from foreign fishermen or other traders.[172] An ordinance made in 1456 that ale brewers and beer brewers should also pay a maletote may indicate the development of what became part of the important victualling trade of early modern Rye, and a forerunner of the recovery of other trades which occurred from the late 15th century.

Fig. 5.1 The seals of the office of mayor of 1378 and 1574 (after Boys 1792, plate following 782.)

CHAPTER 5

Mayors, Barons and Bailiffs: the Government and Prosperity of Rye

As early chartered towns, the Cinque Ports developed their own forms of government, independent of their overlords, and also sent representatives to Parliament from the 14th century. Self-government assisted in the formation of an urban elite which ran the town as well as holding the major economic assets, such as mills, and heading the main commercial and productive industries. The composition and the fortunes of the elite were linked to the town's prosperity which is therefore also examined in this chapter. Each member of the Cinque Port confederation had a different form of government depending on the number and nature of their overlords and on the competition for power between the bailiffs of the lords and the Port's own officials. Contemporary evidence about the activities and choice of town officials is often lacking for the Middle Ages, and on occasion commentators assume that they were the same as in the early modern period; however, this was not necessarily the case and a close examination of the roles of the town officials demonstrates change over time.[1]

From the mid-12th century the worthy men (*prudhommes*) of Rye made a yearly payment of 2½ marks (33s. 4d.) to Fécamp Abbey, the lord of the town, which freed them from manorial-types dues and allowed them over the next century to develop a degree of independence in running Rye's internal affairs.[2] The *prudhommes* developed a formal system of government headed by a mayor, with the name of the earliest mayor known before the end of the 13th century, in a deed of *c.*1289. This was the first Rye deed in which the official roles of the witnesses were given. The witness list was headed by Robert Paulin, who was called bailiff; Henry de Rakele was the fourth witness and was called mayor.[3] Subsequently, from 1304, it was the mayor and not the bailiff who was the first witness, and the mayor thus came to be seen to head the town government (Figure 5.1).[4] This is in contrast to New Romney where the innovative appointment of a mayor in *c*.1270 led to a dispute with the bailiff of the Archbishop of Canterbury, one of the town's overlords. The New Romney townsmen were attempting to emulate other members of the Cinque Ports confederation such as Sandwich, Dover and Fordwich which acquired the right to have a mayor during the 13th century.[5] The dispute reached the king and the office of mayor at New Romney was suppressed, and the town remained subject to the Archbishop's bailiff throughout the Middle Ages. However the king was much more dependent on the goodwill and ship service of Rye than of New Romney by 1289, since New Romney's maritime facilities had already been heavily damaged by storms. Edward I probably took the view that to allow the townsmen of Rye to have a mayor, a desirable mark of urban independence, was much more important than having his own bailiff acting as the apparent head of the town; it may also have been a favour to Rye at the time when New Winchelsea was founded. In any case control of the town in aspects which really mattered to the monarch, external relations and warfare, was in the hands of the Warden of the Cinque Ports and, when necessary, a local warden appointed for Rye and for New Winchelsea.

The men of Rye were known as the commonalty, for example in the rental of Edward I's reign where, together with the mayor, they were responsible for making the payment of 2½ marks. However, the lists of witnesses to the many conveyances of property within Rye which are recorded in deeds from the early 13th century suggest that there was also a select body of men which confirmed property transactions and effectively formed the town government.[6] From the end of the 14th century they were occasionally called the jurats, or 'sworn men'.[7] Books of customs are a major source of information about the form of government in medieval towns. However, the earliest Rye custumal dates from *c*.1550 and while it incorporates earlier material it was moulded by post-medieval developments and thought, as a heading makes clear: 'These byn [are] the usages of the Comynalty of the Towne of Rye used there of tymme out of mynde whiche mens myndes cannot think to the contrary'.[8] The production of the Rye custumal reflects the politics of 16th-century Rye when the Lord Warden of the Cinque Ports tried to quell factionalism and disputed elections by restricting those who chose the mayor, jurats, parliamentary representatives and town officers to a common council rather than all the commonalty or assembly (mayor, jurats and commons).[9] Unlike, say, Exeter, which has a surviving custumal of *c*.1240, there is no evidence from Rye about how the mayor was chosen until 1474 when it was stated in the town accounts that the mayor was chosen by the assent and consent of the whole commonalty 'in the place from of old accustomed'.[10]

The Rye custumal refers to the mayor choosing 12 'prudents' as jurats on the day of his election, surely a reflection of the early term *prudhommes*.[11] However, the custumal codified practice over centuries and cannot be taken to indicate that this was how the mayor was elected or the jurats were chosen at an earlier period. There is slightly more extensive material for New Romney than for Rye on the membership and election of the town government. By 1242 there was a group of 12 men who were the leaders of the town in the sense of taking responsibility for defence. The king commanded the townsmen ('barons') of Romney to send 12 men of the town with the bailiffs to make arrangements about defence with the other Ports at Shepway in east Kent, where one of the confederation's courts was held. The king's primary interest was in the ship service which the 12 would organise and they are therefore likely to have been men who had ships, merchants, carriers or fishermen.[12] The townsmen of New Romney stated in 1309 that they elected the mayor and 12 jurats, claiming this was an old right, a claim which was rejected.[13] At Rye at this time the witnesses to deeds, often 12 men and later called jurats, may have been elected as at New Romney, or chosen by the mayor as the 16th-century custumal stated. It is impossible to be certain and preferable to think of the mayor and witnesses of Rye from *c*.1220 not as a governing body with a clear constitution but as a town elite.[14] The deeds make clear that they were all Rye townsmen, and that many were by birth or marriage; a number were involved in craft or commercial activity. Ten men with occupational bynames, and also three fishermen, were among the witnesses before the Black Death, as was John Torel, merchant. In addition members of four of the five families involved in milling provided mayors (Portesmouthe, Rakele, Marchaunt and Nesse), as did the merchant family the Muriels. At least six members of the Marchaunt or Marchaund family are known between 1258 and 1351, of whom three were mayors for extended periods. Their byname indicates their merchant origins and source of wealth.[15] Pharon Ion, holder of one of the Rye taverns, an important asset, was mayor in 1305. The tavern was previously held by Brice of Rye, who was first witness to a deed in *c*.1264, an equivalent position before the office of mayor is known.[16]

The mayor and *prudhommes* of Rye were assisted by a clerk or chaplain, who was sometimes named thirteenth in the witness list, a common practice.[17] Named local scribes are known as early as *c*.1220 from the Rye deeds, which were concerned with property transfers in and around the town; for example in *c*.1220 one Nicholas wrote a charter in a local court concerned with Fécamp Abbey's property in the manor of Brede near Rye.[18] The existence of the town clerk's office is clear by the very early 14th century when Peter de Heghtone was clerk between 1300 and

1330. Peter was not a simple chaplain; he was married and possibly had a son who followed him as town clerk. He was familiar with writing grants, quitclaims, bonds, feoffments and letters of attorney, all requiring different formats. The documents make clear that Peter was a Rye man although his byname indicates that he or his family originated in Heghtone in the nearby parish of Beckley.[19] The office became known as that of common clerk or town clerk, and its holder acquired even greater significance and powers as urban government came to depend ever more heavily on written records. At the height of Rye's prosperity the town clerks had an influential and lucrative office in the first half of the 16th century at the head of about a dozen other town officials. They were elected yearly, and except in times of acute political crisis, usually held their posts for some years, notably so as Rye's economy declined. By the time Samuel Jeake the elder was town clerk between 1651 and 1661 they were a force for stability, or at least conservatism, in the running of the town (below).[20]

The Chamberlains and other Officers

By 1474 chamberlains accounted to the mayor and jurats for the town income, taking over from the collectors of the dues or maletotes, or treasurers, who are known by 1429.[21] Bread and wine were provided on the occasions when the chamberlains laid their book of accounts before the town government for auditing.[22] In 1478 it was agreed that one chamberlain should be a jurat and one a member of the commonalty, but this caused great rancour and the following year the whole assembly of the town agreed that the two chamberlains should both be members of the commonalty. Those chosen as chamberlains were obliged to accept the office on pain of 10 marks but received one mark (13s. 4d.) in wages for their year in office. In 1479 the governors and officers of the town were the mayor, 11 jurats, the two chamberlains, the two collectors, the serjeant-at-mace and the town clerk. In the early 16th century the two chamberlains were denoted 'land' chamberlain and 'sea' chamberlain reflecting the different sources of town income which grew in a period of prosperity, leading to more complex accounting. This separation of roles continued until at least 1606, and the office of chamberlains is known until 1659.[23]

Barons and Bailiffs

From the reign of Henry II the charters of the Ports gave the men of Rye many freedoms in relation to trade, taxation and local justice but the male inhabitants were not called freemen in the Middle Ages; the usual term was commonalty or commons. The monarch used the expression 'baron' as an honourable and convenient term of address for the men of the Ports but, like commonalty, it was a general term and was not restricted to any particular group, nor was it a synonym for jurats or freemen. Although royal communications addressed the men of Rye as barons, the word was very seldom used in documents written within medieval Rye. There are two deeds which are exceptions to this. Richard Portesmouth was called 'baron of Rye' in a deed which recorded his receipt of an acre and more of agricultural land at *Westwissche* in the parish of Rye in 1312.[24] In 1330 four men, John Paulyn, Robert Marchaund, James Marchaund and John Ambroys, were described as barons of Rye when they witnessed a conveyance of an important area of marshland at *Levedimerss* in Iden parish. The other seven witnesses were the chaplain of the leper hospital and men of locally notable status from the area outside Rye such as John de Kechenore and John Oxenbridge.[25] It seems that the term baron was applied in this case to make clear why the four Rye men were witnesses, and to reinforce their own status compared to that of the other seven. The four men, like Richard Portesmouth described as baron in 1312, did all come from families which provided bailiffs or mayors, or were extremely rich Rye men, but such people did not usually need to reinforce their status by having the clerk refer to them as baron. It was sufficient for them and others to know that they ran the town, while in communications about ship service or the assembly of the fleet the king usually covered all sensibilities by addressing the inhabitants as mayor, barons and bailiffs.

The bailiffs were often appointed to cover not only Rye but also Winchelsea (Old or New) and the manor of Iham, which lay at New Winchelsea. The earliest known bailiffs of Rye, Old Winchelsea and Iham were Mathew de Hastings and one Haltone(?), who were in office between 1267 and 1273.[26] Henry Paulyn was bailiff in 1276 to 1277.[27] A man of the same name was mayor of Old Winchelsea in 1306.[28] In addition to the detailed accounts of Rye, Winchelsea and Iham, there are some other accounts of 1282 to 1290 of men described as king's bailiff or serjeant of Rye. These officers accounted primarily for the farms of places in the honor (estate) of Aquila in Kent and in Sussex and were not local men, Luce de la Gare and Walter of Horsham (Sussex). Rye is not mentioned in every year in their accounts and the accounts contain little detail when it is.[29]

John de Glende of New Winchelsea was bailiff of Rye town in 1343 to 1344; he is not otherwise known among the Rye records. He was followed the next year by Stephen de Padyham, from a family well known at New Winchelsea (*Chapter 3*). Paul Marchaunt was bailiff in 1350 but died in office and Adam Skipsy, rector of Playden and executor of his will, accounted in his place.[30] Marchant's will itself does not survive. John Longe, a member of the family which was frequently involved in piratical attacks on merchant shipping, was bailiff of Rye, New Winchelsea and Iham in 1351 to 1352 (*Chapter 2*).[31] Thomas de Wynchelse apparently followed John Longe as bailiff of Rye town for up to four years in the late 1350s, when the town's income and expenditure were greatly disrupted after the onset of plague.[32] The final surviving bailiffs' accounts are those of 1361 to 1363 when William Taillour and Benedict Cely, the mayor, accounted for the gear of a ship broken up at New Winchelsea.[33] Taillour and Cely were among the men of Rye who were commissioned to scrutinise for the illicit export of money and bullion in 1364.[34]

The bailiffs' first duty was to receive and account for the profits (farm) of Rye. After the resumption of Rye into royal hands in 1247 the profits of the town were farmed out (leased) to various individuals and on occasion to the barons of the town, for large amounts, up to and beyond seventy marks. The farm was usually granted with that of Old Winchelsea which was regarded as much more valuable, at 130 marks. In 1266 the farm of Rye was briefly recorded at £40 at the end of a long and detailed account of Old Winchelsea.[35] There is no evidence that the farmer of Rye paid the £40 or indeed that the town produced an income which would have enabled the farmer to do so. On occasion part, or all, of the profits of Old Winchelsea and Rye were assigned to others by the monarch, and the sum assigned suggests a more realistic view of what the towns could produce by way of income. In 1254, for example, £5 from the income of the two towns was granted to a Hastings man for his services by sea and land.[36]

From the late 13th century the profits of Rye were assigned to the dowager Queen Eleanor and in the 14th century to the queen consort (*Chapter 3*). From this period the bailiff accounted only for the income from specific sources, not the farm: the rents on free tenements, fishing shares, market tolls on goods such as bacon, wool and salt, and other customary taxes on trade, particularly for loading and unloading goods. The bailiff also accounted for profits of the court dealing with residents, strangers and fishermen, and the assize of bread. The court was held on Sundays and Wednesdays, the latter being one of the market days (*Chapter 8*). The account of 1343 shows that pleas of debt, trespass, covenant and dowry were dealt with at the court which was held two or three times a month.[37] In 1327 a grant was made for life to Queen Isabella of the king's town of Rye which was valued at £15 a year, a realistic amount similar to the actual receipts recorded in the bailiffs' accounts, rather than the earlier farms.[38]

The bailiffs were also expected to receive and act on the king's orders, particularly in relation to attacks on merchants, preventing the export of goods or the departure of certain categories of people; the orders were usually addressed to the mayor also.

The bailiff was to co-operate with the Warden of the Cinque Ports and to account for the tackle and timber of ships damaged and broken in the Rye-Winchelsea anchorage. In addition the bailiffs were called on to co-operate with wardens appointed for the towns of New Winchelsea and Rye when French attacks were expected: in 1324 William de Echyngham was appointed for the former and Edmund de Passeleye (Pashley) for the latter.[39]

The Bailiffs between the 1370s and 1520s

In the 1370s the profits were assigned to the mayor, bailiffs and commonalty of Rye to help strengthen the town defences (*Chapter 8*). In the late 14th century and first two decades of the 15th century non-local men sometimes described as king's servant or esquire or serjeant-at-arms were appointed as bailiff, with the incentive of collecting the income of the town of about £18 for themselves. However, the office was not especially attractive and on 9 May 1381 Edmund de Tettesworth, the new bailiff, was required to reside in the town and to take steps to defend it, as well as to supervise the purchase of fish for the royal household.[40] The next year the revenues of the town were again assigned to the mayor, barons and commons to repair the defences. On occasion local men were appointed bailiff and they sometimes performed other roles in Rye too. They included Richard Baddyng, mayor in 1367 and bailiff in 1375 and 1378, and John Baddyng, who was bailiff in 1389 and mayor in 1391. Richard Baddyng was, with William Taillour, the first named MP of Rye.[41] In the period of Rye's post-Black Death decline, these men had greater involvement with the town government and defences than the non-local men who were bailiffs at the beginning of the 15th century such as William Catton (1411), Thomas Burcestre and Thomas Phelip (both 1413). By the mid-15th century one Babilon Grauntford was bailiff. Although he appears to have been from a non-local family, he lived in Rye for many years and was active in its government. In 1451, for example, he provided horses for the town government when messages had to be sent to London, perhaps taking the messages himself.[42] In 1457 Babilon was named first in a list of jurats and two years later he rode to William FitzAlan, the Earl of Arundel and the Lord Warden of the Cinque Ports, to 'excuse' the town, presumably for their support of the Earl of Warwick, Richard Neville, the 'kingmaker'.[43] Babilon became mayor in 1463 and again in 1465, 1466 and 1474, and bailiff in 1459 and 1466, together with his relative John Grauntford, who was also bailiff in 1474 and mayor in 1479.[44] Babilon Grauntford, as mayor, seems to have had a role in helping Rye at the beginning of its period of economic recovery when demand for grain, leather and meat began to grow again, for example by renting out a plot at the Strand in 1466 on which a shop was later built (*Chapter 8*). In 1474 he himself had a workshop (*opella*) in the market and a workshop at the Strand, and organised some reclamation ('inning') at the 'gutt', a sluice whose location was unspecified.[45] John Grauntford participated enthusiastically in the hospitality which the town government provided for travelling groups of minstrels attached to royal or noble households, for local groups of players, for the Lord Warden or his deputy, and for members of the governments of the other Cinque Ports when they met on various official occasions. These costly entertainments were funded from the maletotes and customary payments largely on the trade in fish, salt, firewood and ale which were collected in the town 'boxes'. The costs, and the fees paid to the mayor and officials, suggest that these trading activities were producing a good income in the mid-1470s.[46] At the quarterly opening of the boxes, the mayor's wife, the 'mairesse', made a dinner for the town governors and was given 6s. 8d. to cover her expenses.[47] In 1480 the town income was in absolute terms about three times higher than it had been before the Black Death and four times higher than in 1361, although purchasing power in general declined as wages rose over this period.[48] John Grauntford's son-in-law, the courtier Sir John Shirley or Shurley, was bailiff from 1501 to 1524 and held a very large stock of property in and around Rye, which were the profits of office and evidence of Rye's burgeoning economy: 24 houses, seven shops, six gardens, three acres of land and a large mansion.[49] Subsequently the office of bailiff came into the hands of local magnates who took an oath in front of the mayor and commonalty that they would uphold the franchises of the town. The office was then granted to the town corporation which apparently suppressed it in *c.*1704.[50]

The Meeting Places of the Town Government

In the 13th century the town government of Rye consisted of the bailiff, mayor, town clerk, and the men, often 12 in number, who witnessed deeds in the town court. As well as overseeing the market, the court was the forum for the writing and witnessing of deeds, which was mostly carried out on Sundays or Wednesdays.[51] Holding a court at which records are made is usually an indoor activity and probably therefore took place in a communal building, perhaps the church or a common hall. By 1348 the court met at the Courton, originally an open space between the market and St Mary's church; by 1374 a communal building appears to have been built on part of this area (Figure 5.2) (*Chapter 8*).[52] By 1478, however, the town held meetings on some occasions in the church, a parallel with New Romney.[53] The meeting or court of the mayor, jurats and commonalty in 1478 which confirmed the appointment of chamberlains was held in the Lady

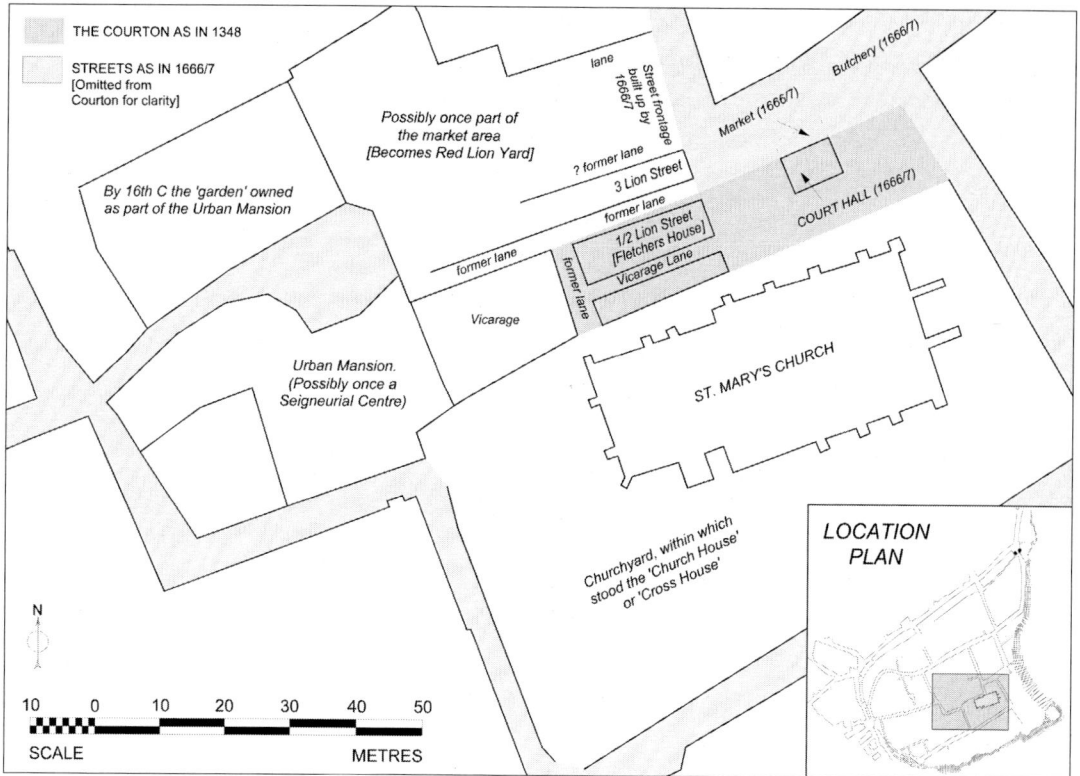

THE COURTON AS IN 1348

STREETS AS IN 1666/7
[Omitted from
Courton for clarity]

Possibly once part of
the market area
[Becomes Red Lion Yard]

By 16th C the 'garden' owned
as part of the Urban Mansion

lane

Street frontage
built up by
1666/7

Butchery (1666/7)

Market (1666/7)

? former lane

3 Lion Street

former lane

former lane

1/2 Lion Street
[Fletchers House]

Vicarage Lane

COURT HALL (1666/7)

former lane

Vicarage

Urban Mansion.
(Possibly once a
Seigneurial Centre)

ST. MARY'S CHURCH

Churchyard, within which
stood the 'Church House'
or 'Cross House'

LOCATION
PLAN

N

10   0   10   20   30   40   50

SCALE   METRES

Fig. 5.2   The area called Courton immediately to the north of the church where courts, the medieval market and the choosing of the mayor were held. This area was partially enclosed and built over from the late 14th century.

Chancel of St Mary's church, and this may have been a usual arrangement. Rye had a building known as the court hall which was reconstructed in 1514 or 1515, and called the town hall in 1526. This or another building at the Courton was rebuilt in 1742 to 1743, and is the building now surviving as the Town Hall.[54] Although there was some trade and craft activity at Rye before the Black Death the town was too small for fraternities of merchants or merchant guilds with their own buildings to develop as they did in large towns like York or King's Lynn.[55] Instead, the freedom of self-government which Rye possessed allowed the town's institutions and buildings to fulfil the ceremonial and corporate roles which their wealthy male residents enjoyed, while the parish church and the new Austin Friary provided them with a religious focus (*Chapters 6, 7*).

Medieval and Early Modern Oligarchy

Many medium and large medieval towns had a freedom or liberty organisation whose membership was limited. At Exeter, for example, there was a category of townsmen who held the freedom, a category known from the early 13th century. Entry to the freedom was by birth, patronage, payment, gift, service or apprenticeship. The main privilege was to trade at retail and the freedom was highly restricted: about twenty per cent of all householders and under four per cent of the total population held the status of freeman in 1377, a status which gave access to civic power and membership of a clearly identifiable oligarchy.[56] Medieval Rye in contrast had no concept or organisation of a restricted freedom, and all the adult male commonalty was entitled to the liberties of the town which were laid down in the charters. Membership of the commonalty was not defined in contemporary sources beyond 'the men of Rye', which clearly excluded women, young people, foreigners and aliens.[57] However, just as at Exeter, in Rye commercial power such as that of the millers, taverners, merchants, weavers, leather processers and spicers, provided the foundation for political hegemony in the 13th and first half of the 14th centuries (*Chapter 4*).[58] Oligarchy in Rye at this period did not need to be bolstered by a limited freedom but was based on commerce, wealth passed on by inheritance and marriage, and membership of the town government. In the second half of the 14th century many medium-sized and large towns tried to maintain or increase membership of the freedom in order to sustain trade and the town's income. This option was not open to Rye where no restricted freedom existed and which in any case suffered much greater economic stagnation than towns such as Exeter between the Black Death and the end of the 15th century.[59] During this period a form of oligarchy was maintained at Rye by the new town elite, particularly families such as the Taillours who took opportunities to buy up assets such as mills. This new town elite could, however, be regarded not so much as an oligarchy but as a small group of wealthy well-wishers who, in taking on roles in town government, did their best for Rye under difficult circumstances, especially the maintenance of its defences (*Chapter 8*).

The evidence for an oligarchy in many towns appears greater in the 16th century than in the Middle Ages because of the larger number and greater variety of records created at the later period, some of which were explicitly concerned with reinforcing the rule of a small privileged group. The development of oligarchies which were 'closed' specifically in relation to town government is apparent in the late 16th century, notably at Rye.[60] The number of paid town officers also increased greatly at Rye, partly as a result of new statutes. A period of vigorous growth in trade and population in 16th-century Rye also gave the town government, chosen by an increasingly restricted franchise, new ideas and opportunities for exerting control, for example over the lives of the poor, servants, immigrants and women.

At Rye religious weight was added to the armoury of control wielded by the town government through the town's adoption of a puritanical form of Protestantism, which contrasted with other towns around such as New Romney, Dover and Ashford, whose town governments resisted the Protestant preaching imposed on them, and whose inhabitants maintained their traditional religious practices and 'superstitious' entertainments for much longer than at Rye (*Chapter 6*).[61]

Medieval maritime towns, whether in the South East or the South West, were especially likely to have commerce and government dominated by a small network of rich individuals and families since overseas and coastal trade required plenty of capital, risk-taking and human connections. The risks arose from factors such as storms, piracy and the disruptions of war, and the geographical position of towns in the Cinque Ports confederation meant that risks, and opportunities, were concentrated in the English Channel.[62] Until the 1360s wealthy Rye men such as Elias Muriel, merchant and mayor, and Walter Salerne, master of *La Katerine* and *La Nicolas*, seized the opportunities of wartime to supply grain and timber. William Longe seized those of piracy and his relative John Longe organised the supply of timber to Calais.[63] But apart from the activity of the Longes, Rye's economy entered a prolonged period of decline when the major industries disappeared completely or shrank dramatically (*Chapter 4*). Decline is suggested by the use of urban space for the new Austin Friary of 1378 on the edge of the built-up area of town within the walls, which was still surrounded by vacant plots until the 1480s and early 1490s (*Chapter 6*).[64] The initial impetus for the decline in many towns was the Black Death. However, Exeter's economy withstood the deaths of numerous inhabitants in the Black Death, and the economy of New Romney was less severely hit than Rye's for two reasons: it did not suffer additionally from the effects of French raids, and the townsfolk were able to turn to agriculture in the immediate vicinity of the town as an alternative occupation.[65] The reasons for the severe downturn at Rye and its consequences for the town elite are explored next.

Mortality at the Black Death and its Consequences

Rye was severely hit by the plague epidemic known as the Black Death of 1348 to 1349, as were other towns and ports. There was a mortality of approximately forty per cent among the men who composed Rye's town government, the mayor and jurats and town clerk.[66] This is evident from an analysis of the numbers of witnesses to transactions of Rye property who, before the Black Death, usually numbered twelve or thirteen, and occasionally sixteen or more, with the inclusion of the bailiff or other notables (Figure 5.3). There were forty per cent fewer witnesses to deeds in the period 1348 to 1476 than there had been in the period *c.*1200 to 1347, despite the fact that the official composition of the witness group did not change.[67] The mayor, jurats and clerk of Rye were among the wealthiest of the residents and therefore those who were best fed and best housed. Among the poorer people living in less spacious accommodation the mortality of the Black Death may have been greater. Rye may also have been affected by the wet weather and famine which occurred in England between 1315 and 1318, and certainly was the victim of a French raid in 1339 and an inundation in *c.*1342 (*Chapter 8*).[68] These may account for the fall in witness numbers which began in the 1330s.

In the second half of the 14th century the income which the town received from its fishermen and market traders fell substantially, confirming both this loss of population and the loss of demand which was one of the consequences of the plague (Chapter 4). From as early as 1360 the names of the great majority of families who had formed the town elite before the Black Death, providing mayors, witnesses and sometimes bailiffs, about forty families altogether, disappear altogether from the Rye records.[69] They were replaced by a much smaller number of new families, about a dozen, including Baddyng, Eston, Goldheve, Lounceford, Macop, Onewyn, Otringham,

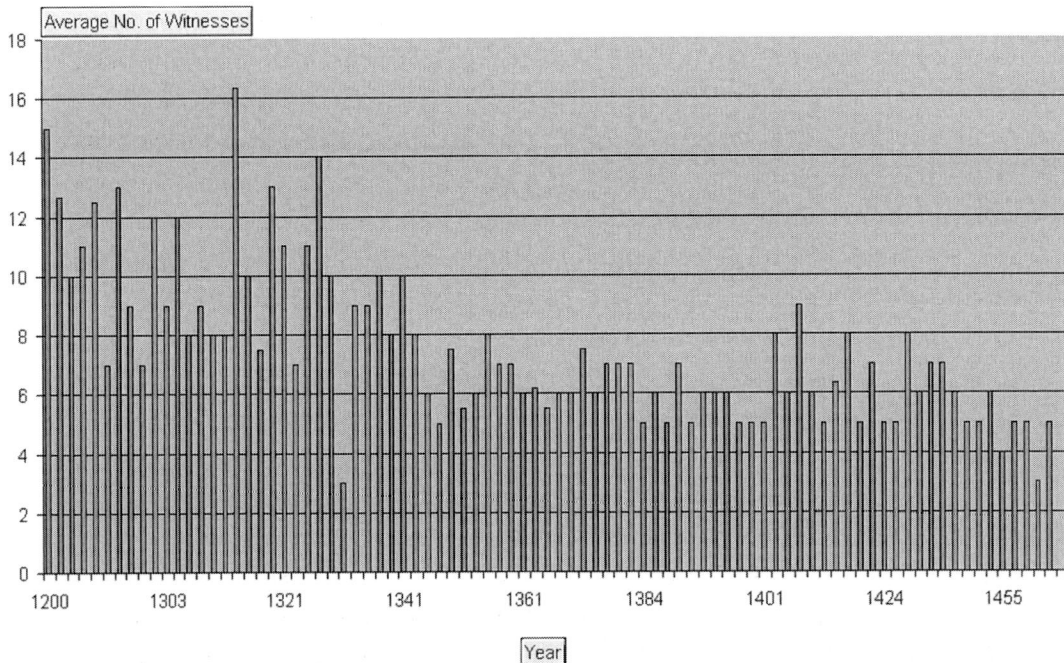

Fig. 5.3   The number of witnesses to transactions of Rye property between *c.*1200 and 1476.

Oxenbridge, Pope, Salerne and Wymond. Most of these families did not appear in the Rye records before the Black Death and those few which did had not been part of major governing families.[70] The only exception was the Longe family which had a significant presence among the town governors from the early 13th century right through to the mid-15th. Notable among the new town elite, by 1361, were William Taillour, the bailiff, and his friend Benedict Cely, the mayor. The first use of the mayoral seal of Rye was on a private deed of the Taillour family in 1378 when John Baddyng was mayor.[71] William Taillour was mayor in 1373 and Thomas Taillour in 1375. William Taillour and Benedict Cely were the movers in the foundation of the new Austin Friary inside the town walls, an institution intended to protect the souls, if not the lives, of the population by its presence and its prayers (*Chapter 6*). Of the dozen or so families who formed the new town elite in the later 14th and early 15th centuries, only a few survived as such in Rye into the 16th century. Many disappeared over the course of the 15th century, undoubtedly as a result of continued epidemic disease and a devastating French raid in 1377. Epidemics are recorded in England in 1361, 1369, 1375, 1390, 1405, 1413, 1433, 1444, 1448-50, 1452, 1454, 1464 and 1471. They continued in 1479, 1485, 1499 to 1500, 1505 and 1521. There were also food shortages after bad harvests in 1438-9.[72] The precise nature of the epidemics is unknown and they may have been more localised than the Black Death. However some of these epidemics may have affected Rye and caused the population to remain low throughout the 15th century and into the early 16th century. The number of those paying as 'advocants' to enjoy the privileges of Rye inhabitants with regard to trade appears to have declined sharply between 1448 and 1483.[73] Even in the first two decades of the 16th century there were often as few as six or seven jurats instead of the official number of twelve.[74] This may suggest not only that the population was still low but that urban office was unpopular. In the early 1520s Rye's population was something over 2,000 people, about the same as the town ranked fortieth in England, Hull. Rye's population then quickly rose to perhaps double that number by the 1550s, i.e. a little over 4,000, despite ongoing outbreaks of plague. The arrival of Huguenots and their crafts and trades in 1570s further boosted the population, although only temporarily, and numbers overall were sharply reduced at the start of the 17th century.[75] Even so, in 1660 Rye remained much larger than Battle, the nearest comparable Sussex town, and nearly as large as the county town of Lewes.[76]

Among the elite families who survived into the 16th century were the Estons, Oxenbridges (*Chapter 7*) and the Wymonds. The Wymonds became 'of considerable note' from the 1530s. They resided at the Grene Hall (58 and 60 Church Square), a house of status previously owned by Sir John Shirley and later by Thomas Greenfeild, a jurat and royal official. From the early 17th century the Wymond family appears to have moved to New Winchelsea where between 1603 and 1633 three family members served as mayor.[77]

Rye's Resurgence

Rye had a temporary resurgence not only in population but also in economic activity and wealth between 1490 and 1580 after more than a century of stagnation. This temporary boom is attributed to both local and wider factors. New Winchelsea declined with the final loss of its wine trade to western ports and the almost complete choking of its harbour in the second quarter of the 16th century. It may be that its merchants and fishermen moved to Rye, where there is evidence of extensive building of domestic dwellings in this period.[78] The wider factors include the use of the port for cloth exports to Rouen in the 1520s and 1530s during the European religious wars; this was linked to the role of the fish carriers known as ripiers. Fish was taken to London and cloth was brought back to Rye.[79] The provisioning of Calais and Boulogne, especially with billets of wood for fuel, temporarily reinvigorated Rye's role as an outport for products of the Wealden hinterland as Figure 5.4 demonstrates.

Fig. 5.4 Billets of wood exported per year from Rye in the early modern period.[80]

Year/decade	No. of billets	To where	Notes
Early 1490s	<1,000,000		
1490s-1540s	c.1,000,000		Usual peacetime level
1543/3	908,000	Mostly Calais	Only 20,000 billets went elsewhere than Calais
1545/6	782,000	Calais	
1545/6	92,000	Boulogne	Recently captured by Henry VIII
1548/9	2,390,000	Calais	Renewed hostilities with France
1548/9	169,000	Boulogne	Renewed hostilities with France
1549/50	4,083,000	Calais	
1549/50	451,000	Boulogne	Loss of Boulogne in 1550
1558/9	<1,000,000		Loss of Calais
1560s	c.1,000,000		
1570s	c.1,000,000		
1580s	c.1,000,000		
1590s	c.20,000		

After the silting of the haven at Sandwich in the 16th century and before the artificial harbour and virtual free port at Dover were developed in the early 17th century, Rye was the only remaining harbour and cross-Channel port of any significance in Kent and Sussex; for example, the customs revenues of Rye and New Winchelsea together formed 77 per cent of the total revenues between 1490 and 1550, with those of Winchelsea falling very significantly by 1530.[81] As the major south-eastern harbour, Rye enjoyed royal support, particularly in wartime. Rye's significance as a port was revived with the military and naval activity of the Tudor monarchs, both general warfare and action against pirates, including Scottish ones and those operating in the Channel. Rye provided several ships on five occasions between 1481 and 1557, mainly for transporting troops. Provisioning armies and naval ships supported the town's merchants, the cast-iron cannon industry in the Weald was developed, and a large number of Rye inhabitants (122) contributed to a benevolence of 1545. Royal encouragement of privateering by Rye shipowners in 1544, as in the case of ships from West Country ports, meant that it was difficult to suppress in later decades.[82] As measured by the total tonnage of its merchant shipping, Rye ranked eleventh among English ports in 1570.[83] The capture of ships at sea, sometimes with the involvement of Rye fishermen, was closely linked to the sale of the ships' goods in or around Rye. In 1573 William Fyrral of Strandgate ward was obliged to transport the Lord Ambassador of England's gelding from Rye to Dieppe in his barque. On board was Thomas Grene, merchant of New Winchelsea, who bought or otherwise acquired five barrels of white herrings in mid-Channel, and persuaded Fyrral to load them on the barque. In Dieppe the owner claimed the herrings, saying that he had been 'pyratically robbed' of them, Thomas Grene slipped away and Fyrall was imprisoned in irons for many weeks. He appealed to the Lord Warden and the mayor for justice.[84] The freebooters of the 1570s and 1580s, including French Huguenots and Dutch Sea Beggars, were in general popular with Rye's inhabitants and they were to some extent protected by the town government in defiance of the privy council. Francis Bolton, who between 1572 to 1600 was town clerk of New Winchelsea and then of Rye, was linked to both Huguenot pirates and to the Sea Beggars.[85] Violence sometimes arose, however, between Dutch pirates visiting the homes of Rye inhabitants such as Francis Russell, shoemaker, and Rye mariners who pleaded innocence when caught assisting the freebooters.[86]

Rye's resurgence was however temporary: four factors contributed to its final decline. The loss of Boulogne (1550) and Calais (1558) reduced the export of billets for two decades. The trade recovered temporarily in the 1560s to 1580s but then finally decreased sharply in the 1590s. The decrease was relatively unimportant for the town revenues as the dues on billets were low but it was more damaging for the individual merchants involved.[87] Secondly, the control of the cloth and other trades such as fish was in the hands of London, not local, men; a similar situation had existed in 15th-century Sandwich.[88] Thirdly, Huguenots departed from Rye, either returning to France or moving on to other south-east towns and taking with them the vitality and profits of their crafts (*Chapter 6*). Fourthly, changes in Rye harbour marked the end of its effective use for any sort of large vessel by the late 16th century, leaving only a fishing port.[89] Until at least 1628 the town, with royal support, tried to raise thousands of pounds to maintain its position as 'the most convenient passage between England and France' and 'the chiefest sea town providing fish for the royal household' but to no avail.[90] A brief period of prosperity for Rye's maritime trade, transit and fishing industries occurred in the 1630s, principally as a result of continental warfare, but the English Civil War and further harbour deterioration then put paid to it.[91] Silting in the anchorage called the Camber or Puddle made access difficult even for the smaller vessels which undertook both fishing and trade and without both of these activities neither was sufficiently profitable.[92]

In response to these difficulties the focus of Rye's town elite became narrow and local. As at Sandwich, the Rye merchants who formed its town government seem to have liked being big fish in a little pool. Connections with London, despite the ripier trade, are hard to detect and it seems London men held the important economic strings. Rye men did not apparently move to London nor seek to exploit connections there, although the City might have been the destination of the poorer people who do not appear much in the records. Instead wealthy Rye families invested money and marriages in surrounding rural parishes and in the Cinque Ports in the 1650s: in Kent these parishes included Benenden, Marden, Rolvenden, Hythe, Lydd and Deal. In Sussex they included Battle, East Guldeford, Guestling, Heathfield, Hellingly, Ewhurst, Peasmarsh, Westfield and New Winchelsea. In addition some families, once the 'urban gentry' of Rye, and certainly the richer ones who are easiest to detect such as the Tokeys, the Fagges, the Palmers and the Oxenbridges (*Chapter 6*), refocused on their rural property in Sussex or Kent and physically relocated there.[93] In 1543 John Tokey requested a burial in Rye church marking his high status and that of his family: he was to be buried in the chancel on the south side of the church, 'at the ende of my seate', with a stone to be laid over him.[94] Yet by the later 16th century members of the Tokey family seem to have been feeling the effects of Rye's decline, diversifying and moving away as others did.[95] Robert Tokey held tenements in Watchbell ward in Rye but was known as a yeoman of New Winchelsea in the town sesse of 1576, a local assessment or rate. In 1587 Robert held three messuages in the Wishe at Rye which he granted to a husbandman of New Winchelsea, suggesting they were both living partly on rents. Thomas Tokey, a tailor, held a tenement in Strandgate ward opposite the Red Lion in 1576 for which he paid 10s. in the sesse, at the higher range of payments in this ward. However, two members moved or lived elsewhere, John Tokey of Guestling, who made his will in 1560, and John Tokey, yeoman of New Romney, who made his will in November 1599. Agnes Tokey, a widow of 60 years, held the *Three Mariners* in Rye in 1592, an inn frequented by foreign seamen, including some accused of theft.[96]

In the 1570s John Fagge (I) was a resident of Rye, a butcher and ship owner, a jurat and mayor. He also had a lease of valuable property at Playden, a messuage called Grove, a barn, outhouse, orchard, garden and five pieces of land totalling 17 acres.[97] He was leader of a puritanical faction in the town government, concerned with drunkenness and women's morals in particular. John Fagge (II) married a daughter and heir of Clement Cobb of Canterbury, and died in 1639. John Fagge (III), esquire, was a wealthy Puritan mayor of Rye between 1642 and 1643, dying in 1646. His son Sir John Fagge (IV) was elected MP for Rye aged 18, supported by the prominent Independent Herbert Morley, and he later purchased Wiston House, West Sussex. He continued to have sufficient influence at Rye, however, to ensure that he was selected as one of the barons to attend the King's coronation in April 1661 and to carry the royal canopy there. There is a 17th-century family tomb at Brenzett church, Romney Marsh, which records their move from the Rye town elite to rural gentry.[98]

The last of these three families, the Palmers, is of great interest since their home, 31 Mermaid Street (earlier Middle Street), is one of the few standing houses in Rye about which a significant amount of historical material survives: it later became known as Hartshorne House (Figure 5.5). The Palmers are discussed as the final case study of this chapter.

The House of Palmer

The Palmer family is known in Rye in the 16th and 17th centuries. Members of this family may also have been part of the town elite and government in the 13th and 14th centuries.[99] The story of this family in the early modern period exemplifies aspects of the town government and finances, the role of the churchwardens, apprenticeship, investment in property and inheritance. There were several members of the Palmer family whose exceptional wealth in the early 17th century seems to have derived from wartime provisioning (Figure 5.6).

Fig. 5.5 The House of the Palmer family at 31 Mermaid Street, otherwise Hartshorne House or The Old Hospital from its use as such in the Napoleonic War, ESRO AMS 6022/2, reproduced by permission.

John Palmer I, cordwainer, d.1576

John Palmer II, jurat, d.1628 = Elizabeth

Thomas I = Joan   John III   Richard   Mark   Joseph   Benjamin   And five daughters

haberdasher, jurat, mayor, gent. d.*c.*1673

Thos II   John IV   Anne   Mary

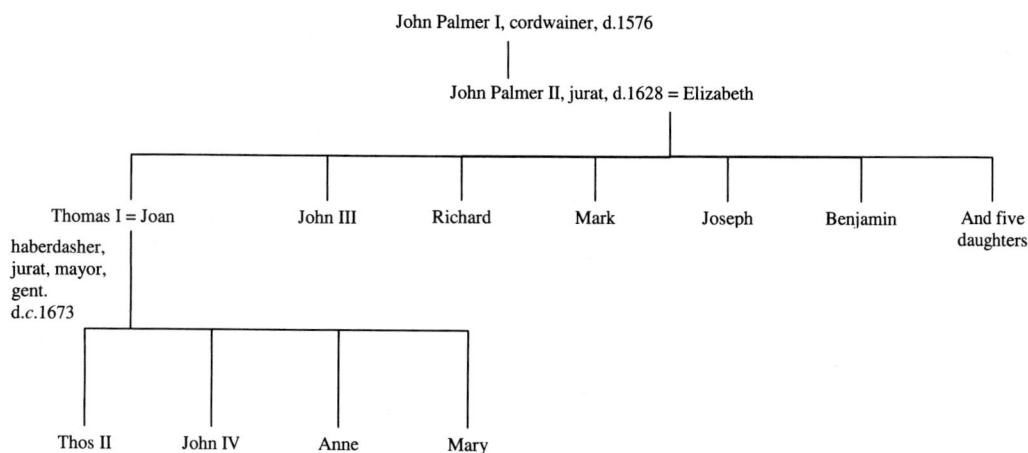

Fig. 5.6   Some members of the Palmer family.

John Palmer (I) was a cordwainer of Rye whose goods were valued in 1576 at 55s., a low sum in the range of surviving Tudor inventories.[100] He was also taxed at only 3s. 4d. in Market Ward in the town assessment of 1576.[101] His inventory is unlikely to relate to the later Palmer family home at 31 Mermaid Street, since this was in Middlestreet Ward, not Market Ward. There was also a William Palmer, fisherman of Rye, who in 1609 made an agreement together with two other Rye fishermen, Richard Oke and John Swayne, for John Riall, a shipwright, to build them a ship.[102] William Palmer was a churchwarden and in this capacity witnessed a bond of £20 from George Pyper, a husbandmen, to Rye town. In this bond Pyper agreed to maintain an illegitimate child of one Catherine Deane without charge to the town since he was the reputed father.[103] Three years later William Palmer himself was obliged to give the town a bond of £40 for maintaining the child of his own illicit union, who had been born to Christian, the wife of Martin Chesher, in her husband's absence.[104]

John Palmer (II) was a very wealthy resident of Rye in late 16th and early 17th centuries. He is often recorded as a jurat but no other occupation has been found, and it may be that he was so wealthy, as his will suggests, that he did not have one. His home can be identified as 31 Mermaid Street, built in 1576, around the time at which John Palmer (I) died. It is not an especially large dwelling but is one of the best preserved and most opulent merchant houses in Rye, particularly its façade.[105] John's surname suggests that he was related to Sir Henry Palmer, the naval commander of the 1580s and 1590s and commissioner for the maintenance of

Dover harbour, and this may explain John's wealth.[106] In spring 1597 Sir Henry Palmer sent a shipload of grain to Rye to relieve an acute shortage.[107] John Palmer (II) was a frequent witness to apprenticeship indentures of the 1610s, sometimes in his role as churchwarden. The indentures which he witnessed concerned the apprenticing of five young women as maidservants to Rye fishing families, and of three young men, two to fishermen and one to a feter, or wholesale fishmonger.[108] John (II) was also a jurat of Rye, was elected mayor in 1620 to 1621 and re-elected in the next year.[109] He made a loan of £80 to the Rye corporation on 11 January 1628 as a mortgage secured on 32 acres at St Mary's Marsh which the corporation had acquired in 1617 (*Chapter 9*). This loan was made six weeks before he made his will and was presumably intended to provide his wife with an annuity, which amounted to £6 8s. a year.[110] He specifically bequeathed his annuities to her. John made his will on 20 February 1628 and it was proved in June that year.[111] He may have died at quite a young age since none of his 11 children had achieved their majority. At death he had six sons under the age of 21 and five daughters under 18 years. He made cash bequests to his children. Each was to receive £60, the boys at the age of 21 and the girls at the age of 18 or when they married, whichever was first. John bequeathed the family home in Middle Street to Elizabeth his wife for life, and then to his three eldest sons, who were also joint residuary legatees if any one of them died underage without legitimate heirs. John's eldest son was named Thomas (I), his second son John (III), and his third son Richard. John (II) had purchased another house in the Butchery and a parcel of land near the old churchyard from Mr Thomas Ensinge, jurat, and sometime mayor. These he bequeathed to his three younger sons, Mark, Joseph and Benjamin.[112]

Thomas Palmer (I), haberdasher, jurat and mayor, was described as a gentleman of Rye. He took an interest in the maintenance of the town's water supply and the grammar school in the 1630s and 1640s and again in 1661. Thomas, his wife Joan, and Ann and Mary, his daughters, appear under Middlestreet Ward in the Poll Tax of 1660 and Hearth Tax of 1664. Their house was assessed at seven flues, the second highest assessment in this ward and third highest in the whole of Rye.[113] Thomas (I) died in 1673 or 1674, and his sons and co-heirs, Thomas (II) and John Palmer (IV), sold the family home in Middle Street immediately after his death, possibly because Thomas (II) planned to leave Rye.[114] This house in Middle Street may be identified with the one described in John Palmer's (II) will of 1628 as 'my howse or Tenement wherein I now dwell with all other the buildinges thereunto belonginge backsides, Gardens and other Appurtenances scituate in the Midle Strete of the saide towne'. The boundaries of the property as given in 1674 enable it to be located more precisely and identified.[115]

This Palmer family home was sold in 1674 to Richard Hartshorne of Rye, gentleman, and his wife Barbara, after which it became known as Hartshorne House.[116] Richard Hartshorne was the Master at the Free School, Rye in 1673, and husband of Barbara.[117] Samuel Jeake the younger, who married Elizabeth Hartshorne, received this important house as his marriage portion from Barbara Hartshorne, Elizabeth's mother, who was by that time a widow. Samuel Jeake moved to Hartshorne House with Elizabeth and his father Samuel Jeake senior. (Jeake junior later built a new storehouse further along Mermaid Street which is now known as Jeakes House.)[118] The elder Jeake's large and exceptional collection of radical religious and political books and pamphlets was relocated from the previous Jeake home into Hartshorne House.[119]

Fig. 6.1 St Mary's Church from the south east.

CHAPTER 6

Religious Rye:
the Parish Church and the Friaries

Introduction

Rye had one parish church, two friaries and a hospital, which was founded originally to care for lepers (*Chapter 7*). This was a small number of ecclesiastical institutions in comparison with other members of the Cinque Ports confederation and other medieval towns and ports in Kent and Sussex. Many of these had more than one overlord which encouraged the development of a number of churches. Rye's one parish church was built under the auspices of its lord, Fécamp Abbey. The town covered a small area (36 acres, or 14.6 hectares) and had a relatively low medieval population.[1] Its parish church, St Mary's, was nevertheless large and impressive: it was, for example, nearly twice the length of the church of the neighbouring rural parish of Playden.[2] The design of St Mary's made it a truly urban church with a central tower, a crossing and transepts, as well as aisles to the chancel and the nave (Figures 6.1, 6.2). All these were constructed by *c*.1250, by which time the church was under the lordship of the crown which did not act to improve the church further.[3] The subsequent changes and additions to its architecture reflected the fortunes and concerns of the townspeople, particularly the need for commemoration and prayer for the dead. The central, elevated, position of the church and its tower made it both a useful vantage point and an obvious target for raids. In the French raid of 1377 the bells and lead of the church were taken but recaptured by the men of Rye in a revenge raid the following year. The chronicler Thomas Walsingham stated that Rye was reduced to ashes in 1377, both houses and church ('of extraordinary beauty'), although the survival of large parts of the 12th- and 13th-century church structure suggests that this was an exaggeration.[4]

The Growth of the Parish Church

The growth of the building is shown in Plate III and Figure 6.2. Following the building of the stone church in the early or mid-12th century, the nave was extended in the late 12th century. The entrance was via a north doorway next to which are the remains of a piscina (a niche near an altar for washing ceremonial vessels). An aisle to the north of the chancel was added about 1220. This is now called the Clare Chapel, but may previously have been dedicated to St Nicholas.[5] Another aisle was added to the south of the chancel about 1250. These major structural developments took place during part of the period of Rye's greatest medieval prosperity and there was subsequently limited building development until the 19th century.

In the 14th century some buttresses, and what is now called the Vestry (previously the Lamb Vault), were added. The Vestry was the original south porch and is of two storeys. The lower storey consisted of two vaulted bays, of which one, with an exterior door and a door into the church, formed the porch proper. The stonework of the quadripartite vault and doorways was of high quality and finely moulded. The adjacent vaulted bay, which was accessed only from the

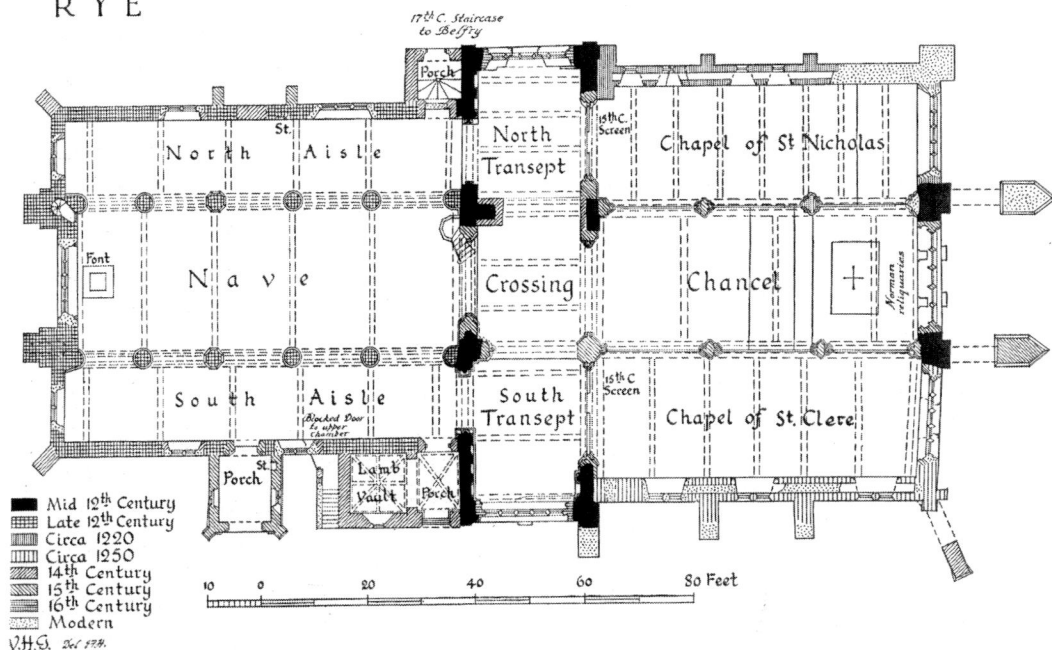

Fig. 6.2 Plan of St Mary's church (after *VCH Sussex* 9).

Fig. 6.3 Two seals of medieval Rye showing the church, the depictions apparently partly conventional and partly realistic (after Boys 1792; Ross 1865).

first bay, the porch, was a plainer chamber with a large quatrefoil window (it should be noted that there was a glassmaker in 14th-century Rye, *Chapter 4*). The upper storey consisted of one chamber, whose entrance was via a door and stairway from inside the church. This complex structure may have been built not only as porch but also as a chantry, providing accommodation for a chantry chaplain and a space for teaching.[6] The existence and importance of education is clearly indicated in medieval Rye. Like other members of the Cinque Ports confederation, Rye had an early literate culture which is demonstrated in many ways. Examples include the existence of the office of town clerk, which was held by a local man, Peter de Heghtone, from *c*.1300, the early deeds and the personal seals of the townsfolk, and the use of wills and testaments from the 13th century. Furthermore the special relationship of the Ports with the monarch in wartime was articulated through the use of written instructions to the town government, and it is thus no surprise to find urban record-making, underpinned by education by chaplains, in Rye. Before Peter de Heghtone began his thirty-year stint as clerk, town deeds were witnessed by chaplains including Walter, who was called in *c*.1260 'notary of this writing', and by Robert, probably the chantry chaplain known in *c*.1290 (below).[7]

A north porch was also constructed in the 14th century and the earlier north doorway was blocked. This new porch was of two storeys like the south porch, and may also have accommodated a chaplain. It contained a stairway and door which may have led to a passage through the wall on the south side of the transepts and crossing.[8] In the 15th century the chancel pillars were rebuilt and a second south porch was added. The fact that a second south porch was constructed suggests that the 14th-century south porch and its ancillary accommodation may still have been in active use at this time for a chaplain and teaching. One or other of the south porches was also a chosen spot for burial. This pattern of development fits with wider aspects of Rye's history. The church as constructed by the mid-13th century provided a very adequate space for the worship of the townsfolk throughout the Middle Ages, and even for the performance of religious plays between the 1470s and 1530s.[9] However, the only significant new constructions after the mid-13th century were porches, of which at least one was probably also a chantry. The tower may have been reconstructed at the end of the 14th century. Although there were no major structural changes to either the late medieval or early modern church, yet it should be noted that many windows were inserted into the church between the early 15th and early 16th centuries: a large window of high quality in the east wall of the chancel, clerestory windows in the nave, and a large five-light transomed window with tracery in the north wall of the north aisle. The insertion of a large window in the south transept about 1500 destroyed an earlier double processional doorway. A similar window was inserted in the north transept. There are surviving wooden 15th-century screens with doors between the transepts and the chancels, and a wooden bench-end of the same century. The new high-quality windows and screens of the 15th century made a strong visual impact in the church. They demonstrate that there were some individuals among the new town elite with sufficient funds to make impressive gifts to the building, probably during their lifetimes rather than as bequests at their deaths (below).

The religious controversies which affected the town and its government from as early as the 1520s made the church building a controversial space. Annual civic and religious rituals, such as the celebration of the feasts of St Anne, the Transfiguration and the Holy Name of Jesus, were held in the church and churchyard in the 1530s under the influence of the traditionalist curate, William Inold, until he was removed and imprisoned in 1538 on the instructions of Thomas Cromwell. The celebrations were opposed by a vigorous faction among the town government led by Thomas Birchett (II), who was the town's first Protestant MP in 1539. Birchett's position was consolidated by his appointment as mayor in 1545, under the influence of

Cromwell, and its confirmation under Edward VI in 1548. Between 1546 and 1548 the churchwardens and the new staunchly Protestant vicar, Edmund Scrambler, enthusiastically removed the rood loft and three tables next to the high altar on which certain 'idolles' stood.[10] The early triumph of the Protestant members of the town government meant that there was little investment in the church building, and in the 16th century the only addition to the church structure appears to have been two pillars at the sides of the door into the north transept.[11]

After the Reformation the two chapels (the south and north chancels) were separated from the rest of the church and put partly to secular purposes. The north chancel was used for storage, including smuggled goods perhaps, although burials continued to be made there in the 18th century. The south chancel was used for guns and stores from 1585 and in 1637 a complaint was made that it was used as prison and for the execution of punishments. It was later divided into two floors, and the upper one was used as a school for poor pupils. From *c.*1638 Rye also had a free school in Longer Street 'for the better Educateing and Breeding of Youth [boys] there in good Literature'. It was founded by Thomas Pecocke in his will with the support of the town government, but represents the continuation of schooling in the town which had been carried on earlier by the chantry chaplains and, in the 16th century, by two masters employed by the town.[12]

The Chantry Founded by Brice and Elena of Rye and other Rye Chantries

A chantry in St Mary's church was funded by the will and testament of Brice le Palmer of Rye, son of Nicholas, dated *c.*1275, with the consent of his wife Elena.[13] It was then established in 1281 by Brice's executors who included his grandson and heir, John Bone of Icklesham, son of Henry Bone of Rye, and James Marchaunt, mayor of Rye.[14] In his lifetime Brice held a tavern in Rye which was held later by another member of the town elite, Pharon Ion. Brice was also responsible for the repair and keeping of the royal galleys at Rye, which were committed to him in 1242 and 1252 together with Paganus le Palmer, Thomas Pharon, Henry Buchard and William Beufiz.[15]

Brice's testament provided for a sum of money to be used to purchase a rental income to maintain two priests to celebrate mass and other offices in the parish church daily for the souls of himself and Elena. The lands purchased were at Peasmarsh, Brede and Udimore and a tenement in Rye (below).[16] Brice wished half the rent to be assigned to Robert le Paumere or Palmer of Pevensey, a clerk, who may have been related to Brice and who in time became one of the two priests. Brice requested that Robert be admitted to the higher clerical orders of sub-deacon,

deacon and priest, and this was agreed by the Bishop of Chichester.[17] In 1281 John Bone petitioned for the right to choose the chantry priest and, as Robert le Paumere had by then been ordained, he was admitted as such.[18] In c.1290 Robert the chaplain, presumably Robert le Paumere, witnessed a deed in which John Bone, as Brice's heir, conveyed a large amount of valuable marshland around Rye, mostly in Cadborough Marsh, to Richard Portesmouth.[19] John Bone himself was a wealthy landholder at New Winchelsea and gave some of his land for the establishment of the Friars Minor there.[20]

Brice's instruction was that two priests were to celebrate mass in honour of God, the glorious Virgin his Mother and all saints, and for the souls of himself and Elena.[21] There is no physical structure in the church to locate the chantry. Its dedication was expanded before 1419 to include St Nicholas, and this may have occurred by the end of Edward I's reign (1307) when a rent of 4d. was paid to the king's bailiff from 'the tenement of St Nicholas', which may represent some property given to endow the chantry.[22] Unlike the early 14th-century Alard chantry at New Winchelsea, which contained family tombs and was clearly a mausoleum within the church, the chantry of Brice and Elena at Rye was primarily the funding of prayers and lights, perhaps carried out in what became known as St Nicholas' chancel.[23]

The rental of Edward I's reign refers to the holdings of two priests in Rye, Roger le Prest and Stephen Prest, who may have been the two chantry chaplains following Robert le Paumer.[24] By 1354 John, the son and heir of Robert Alard of New Winchelsea, had acquired half (a moiety) of the advowson of the chantry from John Ambroys of Rye, whose family died out in the Black Death.[25] John Alard probably took turns with the holder of the other moiety of the advowson to nominate the chaplain or chaplains.[26] In time John Alard sold his rights in the advowson to John Petevyn, who was mayor of New Winchelsea and also held messuages at the west strand of Rye and in *Potepirie Street*, Rye (*Chapter 8*).[27] This share in the advowson and lands of the Rye chantry passed to Agnes, John Petevyn's daughter, and then to Alice, Agnes's daughter. Alice married Nicholas Monyn from Dover and in 1415 they conveyed the advowson and lands to their son John.[28] The right to choose the chantry priest thus continued to be passed on by inheritance, although after the Black Death it seems to have been shared with the town governors, William Longe and Thomas Longe, described as 'the true patrons'. In 1419 one John Casselake was chantry priest and on his death the Longes presented in his place *dominus* John Bevere through his proctor (agent) and relative, Stephen Bever, who was a Rye resident and mayor in 1429.[29] In the next year, on John Bevere's death, the Longes presented John Moreyeve.[30] When

John Moreyeve was dead, Thomas Pope, bailiff, mayor of Rye and MP, presented John Walewyn as chaplain in 1429.[31] Walewyn was inducted in the person of his proctor Richard Clerk, which suggests that he was not resident at Rye and may not have been active as a chantry chaplain.[32]

The absentee chaplain and the lack of further references to Brice's or St Nicholas' chantry suggest that by the 1430s it was less active as a site of commemoration. Prayers were refocused on the new chantries in the south porch and maybe the north porch in the 14th and 15th centuries and also on the new Austin Friary (below). The heavy mortality of the mid- and later 14th century prompted updated ways of remembering the dead, carried out in new sacred spaces. Their construction and financial support came from contemporaries in the new town elite and not from the endowments of the long dead like Brice and Elena. Despite the wish often expressed by the founders of chantries that prayers should be said for them forever, remembrance was often in reality limited to one or two generations who had known the founders personally, and chantries within a church were re-founded by others over time. The chantry of John Lynot at Ivychurch on Romney Marsh, for example, although given sufficient endowment in the 1360s, died out by the 1420s and another one was set up in the same church by Robert Stonestrete in 1449. It is difficult to follow the whole history of early chantry foundations from their origins to their suppression since, with rebuilding and alterations to the church fabric, the sites of the altars were changed and the original beneficiaries were replaced by others.[33] This happened at Rye when in his will of 1497 Robert Crowche, a jurat and mayor in 1479, 1489 and 1493, set up another chantry in St Mary's, whereby he contributed a part payment of 6s. 8d. towards a priest's wages for him to be 'yerely synging for my soule, my fader and moder soules and for alle christin soules in the church of Rye'.[34] Crowche also funded a yearly payment for the Paschal candle, the central item in the Easter rituals. In addition he provided for a suitable new house for the priest to be built, perhaps because the old accommodation for chaplains in the south or north porch was no longer considered fitting; Crowche, however, did ask to be buried in the south porch. The priest whose wages were to be funded was to be chosen initially by the vicar and mayor and subsequently 'by the more part of his [the priest's] brethern', indicating that there were a number of clerics at the church in the late 15th century. In the previous year (1496) Adam Oxenbridge, also a jurat, and mayor in 1487 and 1496, had willed that an honest priest be found to say mass and prayers in the Lady Chapel for his soul, and those of all Christians, for seven years, stating that the priest should have 10 marks for his wages (£6 13s. 4d.). The Lady

Chapel was probably on the south side of the church, where the altar of Our Lady stood in 1521. Oxenbridge also asked to be buried in the Lady Chapel, near the place where he normally sat, specifying 'afore my setle'.[35] One meaning of settle was a special chair reserved for the holder of a position of authority or special dignity, perhaps here the office of mayor. Crowche and Oxenbridge were the two wealthiest and most important men in town; in 1483, as barons of Rye, they had carried the canopy over Richard III at his coronation, and brought home four silver spears and bells from the ceremony. At the end of their lives they co-operated to re-establish chantry provision in Rye church with their two endowments.[36] They ensured that the chantry priest would receive £7 a year which, although at the lower end of what such priests usually received, up to £12 a year, was boosted by the provision of a new house in addition. Over the following half-century several rich Rye residents bequeathed sums for the saying of prayers for their own and others' souls (below), and these no doubt went to the chaplain.

This chantry, 'the foundation of Robert Crowche', was set up only fifty years before the formal suppression of all chantries in 1547.[37] At the suppression property which produced an income to support chantries, religious fraternities, lights, lamps, obits, anniversaries or similar 'superstitious' causes was seized for the crown by means of the Court of Augmentations with the stated intention that the property be used for 'good and godly causes' such as education. The commissioners of the Court first investigated which chantries and property existed, identifying in Rye a tenement out of which Crowche's part-payment of 6s. 8d was paid, and another tenement, four stables and three cellars which produced a rental income of £6 16s. 8d., the rest of the priest's stipend at that time. In the course of assessing the pension which the former chantry priest, John Fullers, would receive, it was noted that these tenements, etc, did 'lye alle in old ruinate houses and the repaireng of them yerlie will be verie chargeable'.

The Court found that obits and lights also produced a yearly income of £2 7s. 8d. from the rents of various other tenements in Rye. There was also a religious fraternity in the church which had an income of £4 yearly but there was no other record of it, and the commissioners for Sussex simply made a memorandum saying 'loke in the old boke for the remembraunce hereof'. The total yearly income for these various causes was £13 11s. This compares with a total of £21 8s. 4d at New Winchelsea and nearly £31 at Hastings, where these large sums include the property of early chantries such as that of the Alards. The total for Rye does not seem to include anything derived from its early chantry, that of Brice and Elena.

The Act under which the suppression of chantries took place protected the property of boroughs and towns from confiscation, and some town governments, such as that of Hastings, interpreted this to mean that they could take possession of chantry lands and proceeded to do so. As a result, the crown later investigated 'concealed' property which was judged to have supported chantries and so on, but which had slipped into private hands or those of urban corporations, including Rye and New Winchelsea as well as Hastings. Concealed property was to be confiscated and would have to be repurchased from the crown. The Rye town government seems to have had difficulty in distinguishing between property which it held for the support of the church or parish causes from that which supported chantries, or perhaps it did not wish to distinguish them. Some tenements and marshes in Rye were judged to have been 'concealed' and the town possessed the deeds to many of them, but these deeds do not make clear which were parish or charitable endowments and which were chantry endowments. The commissioners recorded that the churchwardens of Rye owed the crown 22s. 4d. a year for income from chantry property but made a note to investigate how this charge came into being, since it had apparently not been paid from the time of the suppression. Similarly the commissioners recorded that the rent of a tenement in Watchbell Street which ought to produce 26s. 8d. yearly was not being paid. In all, the crown's search for concealed chantry property in the 1580s was complicated at Rye by the early foundation of one chantry, the subsequent foundation of others in the 14th century evidenced only by church architecture, and the later foundation of a chantry set up by Oxenbridge and Crowche in their wills and then supported by other general bequests for commemoration. It was further complicated by the widespread practice of endowing chantries and pious causes with property which in Rye then frequently changed hands or was sub-let. During the investigations into concealed property the town clerk made an attempt to sort out the deeds to this property, some dating back one hundred and fifty years, by annotating several of them with names of previous holders, such as 'Cokefield's tenement late mother Ashes and now the Churches'.[38] However it is not clear that the town government ever really established who held what property for which purposes, certainly not to the extent that the crown could successfully claim that the properties should be forfeited because they had been used for superstitious purposes.

Devotional and Pious Practice

Wills and testaments reflect civic and economic status and reveal devotional and pious practice in the 15th and 16th centuries, particularly changes over the period of the Reformation.[39] Wills were made in Rye as early as the late 13th century, as the example of Brice Palmer shows. However, other testamentary evidence does not survive until late in the 15th century, apart from one will of 1417, that of John Standen. His will suggests he was a single man or a cleric and other evidence indicates that he was wealthy. In 1415 Standen was assessed for a half scot (local tax) in Market Ward at 6s. 8d., a far higher sum than other residents in that ward and in other wards of Rye.[40] He desired to be buried in the churchyard of St Mary's of Rye and left 10 marks for a chaplain to celebrate his soul in the church for a year. He left bequests of 6s. 8d. to its high altar and the small sum of 6d. to the window of St Richard of Chichester, probably in the cathedral there or possibly in Rye church.[41] Standen bequeathed substantial sums, 20s. each, to the high window and the fabric of St Mary's. To the service of the altar at Rye he left 6s. 8d., and 20s. to that of Playden. A similar sum was devoted to the repair of a lane leading to the rectory of Playden, suggesting that he may have been the rector there. Notably Standen made no bequests to any saints' cults in Rye church apart possibly from St Richard's window, nor to any in Playden church.

There are a few surviving wills of Rye residents between 1473 and the end of the century but from 1500 the number of wills increases dramatically.[42] The fact that Standen's will is the only one identified before 1473 is suggestive of the economic stagnation of Rye which prevailed throughout the middle decades of the 15th century. The 148 Rye wills which are known to have been made between the late 15th century and 1560 compares with 55 surviving wills made by the inhabitants of New Winchelsea, and is another pointer to the growing size and importance of Rye at the expense of the latter in this period.[43] Rye wills proved in the Prerogative Court of Canterbury between 1500 and 1599 form a very significant proportion of all the wills made in Sussex and Kent towns.[44] The numbers confirm the dominant, and recent, role of Rye as 'easily the largest and most prosperous town' in these two counties in the 16th century, a dominance which is clear in other evidence, notably customs revenues, taxation and benevolences.[45]

Saints' Cults and Burials in the Church

From the late 1530s reformist thinking was expressed in Rye wills and became increasingly specifically Protestant.[46] However, the bequests for spiritual purposes in them demonstrate that the traditional practices of masses and prayers for the soul such as obits, month's minds masses and *diriges* remained popular choices with some residents over the period of religious reformation. Obits were yearly prayers for the souls of the testators on the anniversary of their deaths, and month's minds were a remembrance one month after the date of death. *Dirige* is an antiphon that opened the Matins service in the Office of the Dead from Psalm Five. Of the fifty wills surviving from the crucial years of religious change between 1540 and 1550 18 testators bequeathed sums for these traditional forms of remembrance.[47] Nevertheless this represents fewer than one third of the wills for this decade, and is in line with other indications of widespread support for reformed beliefs and practice in Rye, where there was strong criticism of belief in purgatory, prayers for the dead and to the Virgin and saints, pilgrimage and fasting. Joan Blacke in her will of 1550 asked for a solemn sermon at her funeral and while she also wished *Te Deum* to be sung, this was to be done in English to the praise of almighty God. The priests and clerks who sang *Te Deum* were to have 3s. 4d. shared between them for their pains. In the reign of Mary and Philip two testators felt able to request the old services. Walter Steward, who also wanted to be buried inside the church, relied in 1558 on 'the use and custom of this realme' to ask for *dirige* and mass to be sung at his funeral, even though the re-introduction of the mass in 1554 had produced a riot in the church.[48] In the same year Edward Cheston too asked for mass and *dirige*, and also for a group of women to pray for his soul and for all Christian souls, bequeathing them 6s. 8d. each. He left the same amount to Sir (*dominus*) Thomas Lame, presumably also for prayers.[49] But Steward and Cheston were exceptional and from the mid-1540s most Rye testators had left money not for masses and obits but for the poor, especially after 1547 when Edward VI's injunctions on religion recommended this.[50] The wording of these bequests strongly suggests the influence of the scribe, probably the town clerk Alexander Wellys, in the repeated use of the phrase 'I wille to the chest for the poor people' between 1548 and 1552. Some testators bequeathed goods rather than money to the poor, perhaps feeling that goods could not be misspent, or at least were fulfilling a known need, for example a bequest of billets of wood worth 20s. to be given at Christmas, and shirts and smocks worth 20s. to be given at Easter.[51] The poor were, as elsewhere, perceived as numerous and particularly problematical in 16th-century Rye, a perception increased by the steep rise in the population.

In the 15th century only the possible cult of St Richard (above) is known in Rye church although there may have been other saints' lights and altars. In the early 16th century there were altars dedicated to St Mary, St Peter and St John the Baptist. Testators left bequests for the Holy Rood light, the sacrament light, a light called 'Wensham' and the Jesus altar (the Holy Name). However, bequests to these saints' lights and altar were few in number and ceased to occur early, all but one by 1506; the other was a bequest to a light before Our Lady of Pity in 1521. The cult of the Holy Name of Jesus, which was centred on Christ as opposed to a saint, was very popular in England between 1450 and 1550 and particularly in this locality, for example at Tenterden and New Romney. Devotion to this cult, expressed in bequests for obits or prayers at the Jesus altar, continued at Rye until 1546.[52]

Requests to be buried before the altar of St John the Baptist disappeared by 1504. From then on, bequests for burial in a particular spot in the church referred to the structure of the church rather than to saints: in the south porch, the north chancel, the 'myddel pase' (probably the main aisle or central part of the chancel), the south side of the church, or 'as near the west dore as may be'.[53] Those who requested burial in the church, as opposed to the churchyard, were the town elite in terms of wealth and civic status, such as jurats and mayors.[54] Requests for a burial in church, as opposed to one in the churchyard, began in Rye in 1473 with John Grene, who also left half a mark to the vicar. Grene had previously received a grant of a very large piece of town land at the strand; this was an early example of the grants of vacant parcels there which were made in increasing numbers by the corporation from the 1480s as the town's economy recovered (Chapter 8).[55] In the late 15th century requests for a church burial were also made by Adam Oxenbridge and Robert Crowche.[56] In 1518 Thomas Birchett (I), baker, and father of Thomas Birchett (II), the Protestant MP and mayor, made a simple request for burial in the church without specifying an exact place, and eschewed any requests for traditional services or gifts to altars, including the customary payment to the high altar in lieu of forgotten tithes. Others who wanted a church burial in the 16th century included members of the Wymond family, Robert, John and William (Chapter 5), and John Fletcher (1546), who was a jurat, mayor, MP, merchant, sea captain, collector of intelligence on behalf of the government, and royal purveyor of fish.[57] Richard Fletcher, merchant and jurat, also requested a church burial, in 1559. His descendant, presumably his son, Richard Fletcher (II), was from 1575 to 1581 the preacher or lecturer appointed by the corporation. From 1571 to 1594 the corporation appointed various lecturers to remedy the deficiencies in preaching which they perceived in the men appointed as vicar by the Sackville family after the Reformation. Fletcher himself was then apparently appointed vicar but left Rye in 1581, going on to become a chaplain to the Queen and future bishop of London. His treatise on the Ten Commandments typified the well-established attitude in late Tudor Rye that the practice of reformed religion and the control of sins, such as drunkenness, idleness and lewdness, by the town magistracy should go hand in hand.[58]

Alexander Wellys, town clerk and jurat, also wanted to be buried in the church. As town clerk he conveyed property to the town for the establishing of an almshouse in 1551. This had been envisaged as a project of the mayor, jurats and commonalty in the will of Joan Ashe in 1546. She gave £10 towards the almshouse, but if the town would not agree to the almshouse then the money was to be spent on principal vestments for the church. Joan Ashe was very wealthy or generous in her bequest. William Wymonde gave half this amount (£5) at the time the almshouse was actually set up in 1551. Alice Dier, a generous and presumably wealthy testator, who also wanted burial in the church, left a mattress, a bolster, a pair of sheets, a blanket, an old coverlet and 10s. in money. Subsequent bequests were typically smaller ones of bedding or fuel for the maintenance of the inmates of the almshouse. In 1559 Alexander Wellys' widow, Joan, who wanted burial in the church too, left a very large bequest of £50 to be invested in land for the benefit of the poor of Rye, although she did not specify that it was for those in the almshouse.[59]

Rye church has few monuments in the form of brasses or stones remaining from the 15th or 16th centuries, in contrast, say, to Lydd, a large urban church on Romney Marsh which is in many ways comparable. Only two brasses survive at Rye.[60] One possibility is that many monuments were destroyed after the Reformation or in the 17th century. But in general the absence of monuments mirrors that in wills: it was exceptional for Rye testators to make arrangements for a monument; John Tokye who asked in 1543 for a stone near his seat is a rare example. Some people did ask to be laid next to members of their family. George Mercer, jurat and town clerk, specified in his will of 1541 that he wished to buried next to the tomb (*sepulturam*) of his wife. The mother of Robert Wymond had a tomb in the church near which Robert wished to be buried (1510). William Wymonde wanted to buried beside his father, John Wymonde (1541). Their requests suggest there was an area in the church set aside for the burials of this rich family. The same applies to members of other families, at least husbands and wives: Joan Blacke and her husband, and Alexander and Joan Wellys. Out in the churchyard, too, where the great majority of townsfolk requested to be laid, there are indications that the burials of members of particular families such as the Swans and Woods were gathered together.[61]

William Wykwyke or Wikwik, MA, was a vicar of Rye who made his will in 1495.[62] He left 10 marks for the commemoration of himself and his friends in the church and 20s. for the repair of the roads around Rye. He also bequeathed his book *Catholicon* to the church. This was an English-Latin dictionary, with treatises on orthography, etymology, grammar and rhetoric, effectively an encyclopaedia, which was first arranged by Johannes Balbus of Genoa in the late 13th century. *Catholicon* was one of the first books to be printed, running to three editions in the 1460s and 1470s. It was used extensively in the late Middle Ages to interpret the Bible and for general knowledge. It does not reappear in wills of later vicars of Rye and it therefore probably remained in use for the clergy of Rye and perhaps the parishioners for some decades.[63] Other churches of the Cinque Ports confederation and even the rural parishes of Romney Marsh possessed religious, liturgical and legal texts from *c*.1200. These are known from the survival of fragments reused as covers and fly-leaves on Cinque Ports records after the Reformation.[64] No books owned by medieval St Mary's church appear to have survived the drastic and destructive changes of the 16th century in Rye but it must be taken that Rye's educated clergy and parishioners, too, possessed texts for liturgical and wider use. Several sheets of medieval music apparently from a 15th-century antiphonary were reused as covers for Rye town records, probably in the 1560s.[65]

Bequests of vestments or vessels to Rye church were, like offerings to the saints, very few and mostly ceased before the end of the 15th century. John Eston and Robert Crowche bequeathed chalices in 1484 and 1497 respectively. In the 16th century (1526) only Sir John Shurley, the wealthy king's bailiff, did so, and he was in any case an outsider at this time, living at his manor of Isfield (Place), near Lewes.[66] He made the traditional bequest of a rich man of a chalice or other ornaments to Rye church, with the intention that the parishioners should pray for his soul and that of his wife. Like the early disappearance of bequests to the saints, the lack of value placed on church ornaments and vestments prefigured the early move of Rye church towards Protestantism.[67] Those who could not accept this move, like some members of the Oxenbridge family, moved away from Rye (below).

Rye's coastal location and its largely Protestant nature made it a place which welcomed large number of Huguenots from 1562 onwards, many from Dieppe and Rouen. Many Huguenots returned home as religious conditions allowed but returned again under conditions of persecution. There were 641 Huguenot refugees in the town after the St Bartholomew's Day massacre of 1572. The Huguenots established a French Church in the town which had its own ministers and system of poor relief and registers, and held services in St Mary's church. Although most of the Huguenots left after the Edict of Nantes (1598), some Dutch and French families, mainly from Dieppe, were temporarily present in Rye in 1622 on account of renewed persecution, and at least one Dutchman (Walloon) moved to Rye from the Stranger community at Sandwich.[68]

Religion in Rye in the late 16th century can be described as a kind of 'advanced Protestantism' as expressed, for example, in 1575 in the will of Robert Shepherd (II) (*Chapter 9*). Shepherd committed his 'soule unto god and to his unspeakable mercye belevinge without any doubte that by his grace and merites of Jesus Christ and by virtue of his passion and resurrection I have and shall have free remission of all my sinnes and offences and therebye Do belyeve to have resurrection of my bodye and soule according as it is written Job i 9', which he then quoted.[69] However, extreme puritanical views received little support in the late 16th century and when, in 1591, a group of Rye residents tried to reject one of the town preachers they were condemned as a 'a small sect of Puritans now of late sprung up among us'.[70] By the early 17th century, however, Rye corporation was largely Puritan, attempting in 1631 to keep Sundays as a day 'which ought to be wholly kept to be spent in the service and worship of God' and therefore moving the election of the mayor and town officials from a Sunday to a Monday.[71] Throughout the Civil Wars, the Commonwealth and Cromwell's Protectorate both the town government and vicar remained Puritan and supported Parliament. The 'Engagement to the Commonwealth' of 1650 required those who held office to undertake to be 'true and faithful to the Commonwealth of England, as it is now established, without a King or House of Lords'. It was signed or marked by a large number of Rye men, 168; notably this included a staunch Royalist, Anthony Norton.[72]

Samuel Jeake the elder, a highly educated and influential common clerk and preacher, strongly supported Presbyterian worship in the town from the 1650s. The pamphlets which Jeake possessed mark him out as a religious and political radical but personally he seems conservative, and 'an amphibious creature between an attorney and a scrivener'.[73] The strength of the Presbyterian meeting seems to have discouraged the presence of more radical groups such as Baptists and Quakers until late in the 17th century.[74] Jeake's records as town clerk show great concern for proper procedure, a reliable legal record and acknowledgement of the status of the town and its governors. John Allin, the vicar of Rye from 1653, was obliged to leave Rye after the Restoration, and went to London where he practised medicine; however he kept in touch with Jeake and his friends in Rye by extensive correspondence. There was an intellectual milieu in mid-17th century Rye underpinned by letter-writing, book-collecting and education at the grammar school. There are, for example, 268 surviving letters to Philip Frith (d. 1670), lawyer and serjeant-at-mace of Rye; many concern religion and were sent to him mainly by Londoners. Jeake's son, also Samuel, married the daughter of Richard Hartshorne, schoolmaster. Jeake the elder was persecuted for his failure to support the established church after the Restoration. He was deprived of office as town clerk in 1662, his religious meetings were suppressed in 1681 and he left the town until the declaration of indulgence of 1687.[75]

The Friary of the Sack, Rye

Friaries were notable institutions and buildings in the towns of Sussex and Kent from the mid-13th century onwards and were concentrated in coastal and estuarine towns.[76] There were two friaries in Rye of which the Friary of the Sack was the earlier. This was an order which lived by begging, hearing confessions, preaching and performing the burials of non-parishioners.[77] Little survives by way of documentary or buildings evidence about the Sack Friars in Rye. They were granted a chantry function in 1263 by which time they were already established in the town. This was a 'grant for the salvation of souls and the increase of divine service, to the Friars of the Sack, that they may dwell in peace in the place which they have in the town of Rye'. They were permitted 'so far as concerns the patron' (the king) to have a chantry there, provided that they obtained the consent of other interested parties.[78] In 1274 the Council of Lyons ordered the discontinuation of some of the smaller orders of friars, including the Sack Friars. However, it was some decades before all the houses of Sack Friars disappeared, with those in York, London, Stamford, Lincoln and Norwich surviving until the end of the 13th century or just beyond.[79] At Rye the existence of one tenement (house) which had formerly belonged to the Friars of the Sack is recorded in a rental of Edward I's reign (1272-1307). Since the rental is not precisely dated, this gives no exact date for the disbandment of the Sack Friars at Rye but it had certainly occurred by 1307 at the very latest. When the rental was drawn up, John, son of Robert Paulin the bailiff, was occupying the former Sack Friars' house and paying a quit rent of 4d. to the king's bailiff on it.[80] Old Stone House (40 Church Square) which has traditionally been identified as the home of the Sack Friars, then that of John Paulin, still survives as a private dwelling although much altered. The identification of the Old Stone House with the Sack Friars house depended on the fact that an early quit rent of 4d. was still paid on this property in a rental of 1670. However the early rental recorded 19 quit rents at this rate and the 1670 rental recorded only three such rents. Of these three rents, only one applied to a property in Church Square, described as 'vicarage house and gardens'. This vicarage, as shown on the 1874 OS map, is the house now numbered 66 Church Square, not 40 Church Square. Very little of the original stone building of the latter survives. Externally the surviving stone window has a 19th-century replacement of a decorated style head which might be of 13th- or early 14th- century date; internally the original stonework of this window is more reminiscent of 14th-century than 13th-century work.[81] Old Stone House therefore cannot be identified as the Sack Friars house.[82]

The 'Hermit' Friars and Austin Friary, Rye

In contrast with the Sack Friars, the Austin Friars and their surviving building on Conduit Hill are well known. In the spring of 1364 papal licences were issued which allowed new foundations of the Austin order of 'hermit' friars (*Ordo Eremitarum Sancti Augustini*) in cities and considerable towns where 'many faithful' desired them.[83] The licences specified the nature of the buildings, the numbers of the friars and the preservation of the rights of the parish church, and are all relevant to Rye.[84] The foundation there was the first successful one in England and Wales after the Black Death, being established promptly after the papal licences were issued. There were other successful foundations at Atherstone (1375), Newport (1377) and Thetford (1389). There were also unsuccessful attempts at founding Austin friaries at Coventry (1363), Tawstock (1385) and Barnard Castle (1381). Apart from Rye, these foundations all had aristocratic patrons.[85] Rye in contrast was established and patronised by the town elite, with the support of Edward III who was not only the lord but relied on the town's facilities in wartime. Heavy plague mortality seems to have been a stimulus to the foundation of the Rye Friary, which was originally established on a vulnerable site outside the town. The devastating French raid of 1377 then induced the townsfolk to relocate the Friary within the safety of the defences which received attention to strengthen them after the raid (*Chapter 8*).[86]

The Austin Friary was first established in *c*.1364 on two acres of land held in chief from the king for a payment of 2s. 10d. yearly.[87] There had formerly been five messuages there, but they had become submerged by water and were worthless. The messuages may have been among the 18 tenements, some or all on the east side of Rye, which were noted by the king's bailiff in his accounts as submerged from 1341.[88] The nature of the buildings erected on the first Friary site is unknown, although the documents of 1364 refer to a proposed oratory and a manse (*mansio*). A community of friars was certainly established since it possessed both a communal and a prior's seal in 1368 (Figure 6.4).[89] The nearest geographical parallel for the subsequent relocation is New Winchelsea.[90]

The Friary was established and then supported by families who were members of the town elite, the Taillours and the Zelys or Celys, also spelt Celi and Sely. The individuals involved were named on 10 January 1364 as Benedict Zely, Henry Zely and William Taillour. The aim was that the friars should increase the worship of God, celebrate divine service for the well-being ('good estate') of the king and the founders, and also pray for their souls, and those of their parents and heirs, after their deaths.[91] An interesting question is the extent to which these men were acting as private individuals or on behalf of the town. Royal documents

Fig. 6.4 Seals of the Austin Friary, Rye, 1368, RYE 134/1. Left: the seal of the community showing St Augustine(?) on a throne and three figures below. The legend reads [SI.]COMUNE: CONVET: DE RIE ORD[INIS] FRM: HEMITAR:SC[I]: [AU]GUSTINI]. Right: the seal of the prior showing a mitred figure holding staff, with left and right hands raised in benediction, standing on a shield bearing the arms of the Cinque Ports, the legend reading SIG: PORIS: DE RIE ORDIS: FRM: HEMITAR: SCI AUGUSTI.

and Rye deeds dovetail to give some detail about their roles in the town, both at the initial foundation of the Friary and then at the time of its relocation. In 1362 William Taillour, as bailiff, and Benedict Zely, as mayor, listed the rope and gear of the cog ship *Katherine* at Rye which had once belonged to John Lytle and Alan Frere, both of the city of London. John Lytle was perhaps the fishmonger known as sheriff of London in 1353 to 1354, since Rye supplied London with fish.[92] The cog, formerly in the service of a man of New Winchelsea, was broken up and the gear bought for the king's use.[93] William Taillour was at various times in the 1360s and 1370s mayor, bailiff and MP of Rye, and (with Vincent Finch of New Winchelsea) Cinque Ports bailiff to Yarmouth. Several members of the Taillour family are known among the town elite from 1354 but not earlier.[94] From 1366 members of this family, as well as being active in Rye, leased the important manor of Mote in Iden from the knightly Pashley family. In 1367 William Taillour and his son Thomas bought a wood in the manor of Mote from Sir Piers de Brewes, knight, Henry Aucher, William Stantton, clerk, William Olmestede and Robert Covert, chaplain, for 40 marks of sterling.[95] This purchase was recorded in an acquittance which was written in French, apparently to mark the status of the parties; Henry Aucher, for example, came from a minor knightly family based at Lossenham near Newenden on the River Rother.[96] The manor of Mote contained a Pashley family chantry which had been set up in 1304 and whose chapel was located in c.1320 in the gatehouse of manor. Arrangements were made for feoffees, who included Robert Covert, to ensure the continuance of the Pashley chantry after the Taillours leased the manor.[97] In setting up a chantry in the Rye Friary, the Taillours, as new urban gentry, were emulating more traditional rural gentry landholding and activity of the pre-Black Death period, which is epitomised in the Pashley chantry at their rural manor in Iden. The Taillours cease to appear in the Rye records after 1394 and it can be conjectured that they moved out to Mote manor in Iden which they had held since at least 1378.[98]

The Zelys were, like the Taillours, new to Rye's town government after the mid-14th century, and are likely forebears of the wool merchant family of that name which was crucial to the control of the Calais staple in the late 15th century. Histories of the Cely family do not fully trace its members back before Richard Cely senior, known from 1449 when, with other London staplers, he made a loan to Henry VI for wages of the garrison at Calais in return for the remission of subsidy dues on some shipments of wool and fells. Richard Cely's forebears are suggested to have been either London merchants who 'sank in the social scale' or from a villein (non-free) family from 'some provincial town' who rose economically after the Black Death.[99] The latter suggestion fits with a notable early 14th-century deed of manumission which freed 'Benedict of Rye with all his family' from villein status. He may be identified with Benedict Cely since the forename is very rare in Rye records of the 14th century.[100] One Stephen Cely was imprisoned with other wealthy Rye men as a hostage in Fécamp following mutual raids in 1377 and 1378.[101] In 1397 another Benedict Cely, then called knight, was granted the manor of Iham for £40 a year.[102] Sir Benedict is taken to have been a descendant of Benedict Cely of Rye and Henry Cely of New Winchelsea, MP for that town, who were founders of the Friary with William Taillour.

The chantry function of the Friary was of great importance. It was confirmed in 1368 by a grant between the prior of the new Friary and William Taillour, baron of Rye and Agnes his wife. They bestowed a sum of money and other current and future benefits in return for an obit, the friars' prayers and other divine exercises, and specifically a friar who was also a priest to celebrate daily at the altar of St Nicholas in the parish church. This priest was to pray for the healthful estate of the Taillours and their children, and their souls when dead, and in addition for the soul of William's brother John who had already died. In naming the family members, the grant emphasises the fear of illness and death under which the people of Rye were living.[103] At the time of this grant the Friary still lay on its first, low-lying, site outside the town, the site which had been granted by the king in 1364. This may account for the provision of a friar to celebrate daily in the parish church rather than in the Friary on its undesirable extra-mural site. The unspecified benefits to be bestowed by William and Agnes Taillour may have included helping ensure the provision of land for the relocation of the Friary within the town. The grant was witnessed by the local dean, the vicar of Rye, the mayor and 12 other men of the town government. Clearly the operation of the Friary was supported by the parish church and the town governors.

Other grants of the 1360s and 1370s indicate that the town governors and the churchwardens were transacting land in the aftermath of the plague visitations and the French raids with the intention of relocating the Friary inside the town at a place called La Halton.[104] Thomas Taillour, who was one of the churchwardens, specified in 1366 that the land was being transacted with the agreement of the whole community, perhaps because it was church property.[105] William Taillour held land next to it and other members of the Taillour family and Richard Badding, mayor, may have done so.[106] The site at La Halton was in a quarter of the town which in 1334 had consisted of, or included, a plot of land with buildings belonging to people in the leather-working trades, a glover and a cordwainer.[107] Reconstruction of La Halton site indicates that it was a large area on the north-east side of Rye town.[108]

The raid of 1377 prompted urgent action to relocate the Friary within the relative safety of the area enclosed by Rye's fosse, walls and towers. On 8 July 1378 the mayor and barons of Rye made the grant which confirmed the new large town-centre location for the Friary. The friars were to receive the place called La Halton, leaving a sufficient space by the town fosse (probably a bank and a ditch) for building, or rebuilding, the town wall and a way to it. A clause stated that if the friars left the place, or were unwilling to inhabit it, then the donors could resume it.[109] The witnesses to the grant included men known as local lords or minor gentry from the surrounding countryside, since the mayor and barons could not witness it themselves: William Batisforde, William Horne, Robert Ore, Robert Etchingham, William Guldeford and John Edwarde. The reservation of space for the town wall and way next to the new Friary precinct suggests that part of the corporate motive in supporting this relocation was linked to Rye's defences. There had been a serious French attack on Rye in 1339 as well as the one of 1377 which was part of a wider attack. In June, shortly after Edward III's death, a combined fleet from France, Portugal, Monaco and Spain attacked and destroyed or seriously damaged Rye, Folkestone, Rottingdean, Lewes, Portsmouth, Dartmouth and Plymouth. The attack on Rye was devastating, with slaughter in the streets, wealthy men like Stephen Cely taken ransom, the buildings burnt, the church entered and its bells stolen; the bells had been used, not least, to summon men in and around Rye in times of attack.[110] The nearby town of New Winchelsea had been burnt by the French in 1360.[111] The townspeople of Rye thus had reason to be frightened in the 1360s and 1370s. Not only had they suffered losses of population in the Black Death and subsequent epidemics, but also they were always in danger of French attacks. The founding and relocation of the Friary, as well as providing a chantry for the Taillours and Zelys, looks very like a spiritual response to these events by the town community.

The surviving building of the Friary on Conduit Hill is taken to be the chapel. At the lower end of the hill was the postern gate of the town. The route via Conduit Hill and the postern gate led to the extra-mural springs which supplied the town's inhabitants with water in the medieval period. In the 16th century the collection of water by hand was replaced by conduits, cisterns, taps and pipes, hence the name Conduit Hill (*Chapter 8*).[112] At the top of the hill is a street, once called Lower or Longer street, which became known as the High Street. Neither the surviving building nor the precinct of the Friary have been subjected to a modern survey or professional excavation, but a plan of the chapel, which is about 65 feet long, was given in the *Victoria County History* (Figures 6.5, 6.6, 6.7).[113] The other buildings seem to have consisted of north and east ranges only, without a west range on Conduit Hill.[114]

The relocated Friary had a particular relationship with the defences of the town. The western window of the Friary chapel on its new site fronted onto Conduit Hill leading down to the postern gate.[115] The fosse and the way to it were on the north-west side of the new Friary site. This way was reserved to give access to the town fosse in order for the town wall to be built there.[116] The reserved way survives as a lane (Turkeycock Lane) running alongside the section of wall which was built alongside the fosse, apparently after the Friary's relocation.[117] By the late 14th century, and in response to the raids, the town's defences consisted of the fosse and the length

Fig. 6.5 Drawing of the Austin Friary by S. Grimm *c*.1785.

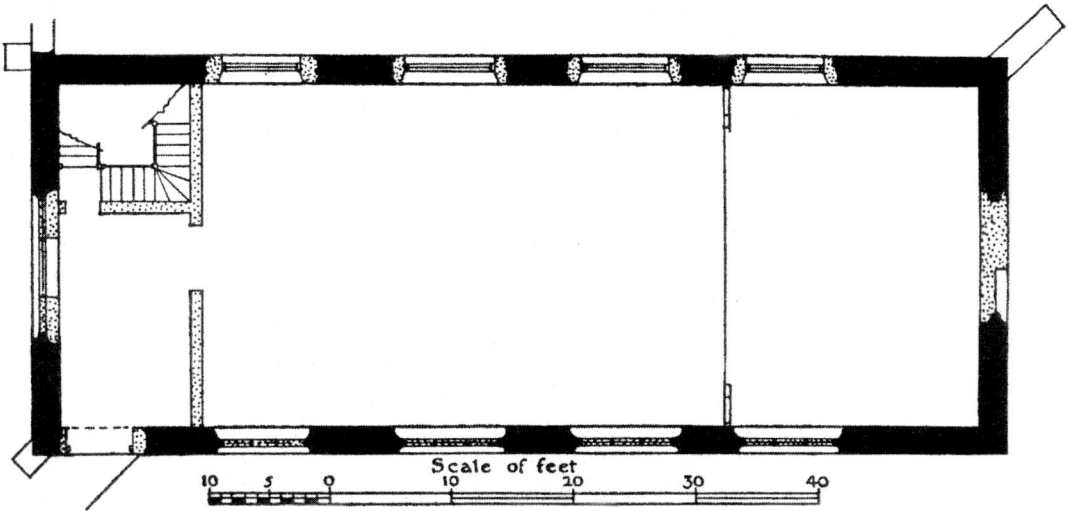

Fig. 6.6 Plan of the surviving building (chapel) of the Austin Friary (after *VCH Sussex*, 9).

of wall which supplements the natural protection of the cliff which runs around the east and southern sides Rye, as well as the Landgate, the Strandgate and Badding's or Ypres tower. The Landgate was Rye's main gate and is overlooked by the Friary chapel (*Chapter 8*).

The Friary precinct lay on the north side of the surviving building. In 1380 at least two pieces of land on the eastern side of the Friary at La Halton remained in the hands of an individual owner. The eastern boundary of the Friary precinct is not precisely identifiable because the cliff there has slipped or been eroded, apparently taking with it some other properties and a way. At this period the Friary, while re-sited within the town, was still on the edge of the built-up area. A century later, the situation had changed. Immediately to the south-east of the Friary chapel and garden

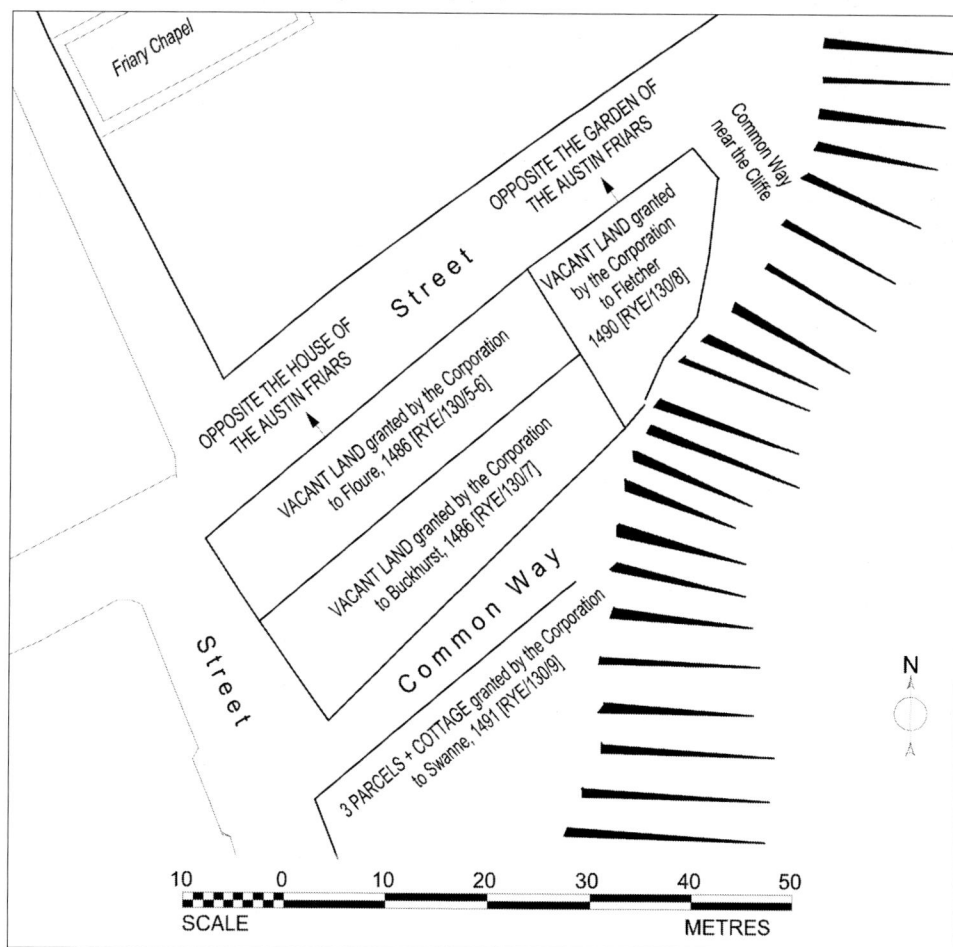

Fig. 6.7 The Halton area of Rye showing the vacant plots opposite the house and garden of the Austin Friary which were granted out by Rye corporation in the late 15th century.

was a street, the eastern end of what is now the High Street (Figure 6.7). In the 1480s and 1490 lay three plots here which the mayor and corporation granted out. They were described as vacant land opposite the house and garden of the Friars and were adjacent to at least one cottage. More land for housing or economic activity was being taken up in this part of Rye as it entered a period of growth.[118]

Bequests to the Austin Friary

Between 1368 and 1535 there were several bequests to the Austin Friars of Rye. Some were made by townsmen such as Robert Bawdwen, Robert Crowche and the mayor, William Byspyn. Others were made by wealthy men from nearby parishes, with a dozen bequests from Iden, Brede, Playden, Ewhurst, Northiam, Ore, and three from more distant places such as Ardingly, Burwash and Battle. Some of the wealthy testators such as Adam Oxenbridge and John Shurley had interests in both Rye and rural property in the hinterland. In 1496 Adam Oxenbridge left a bequest of to the Austin Friars of Rye (6s. 8d.) as well as others to the Friars of Lossenham (Carmelites), and the Friars Minor of Winchelsea. Robert Oxenbridge of Brede, whose will was drawn up in 1483, bequeathed 6s. 8d. to the Austin Friars of Rye, and 6s. 8d. each to the Friars Minor and the Dominicans of Winchelsea, as well as 20d. to the shrine of St Richard at Chichester, and money, clothes and vestments to the parish church. Leaving money to a range of local houses and to St Richard's shrine, as well as to the Rye friars, was typical of wealthy testators. Four bequests came from clerics: Robert Rede, Bishop of Chichester, and the rectors of Iden and Playden, and of Snargate on Romney Marsh. Fifteen bequests were unconditional, with the sums bequeathed ranging between 3s. 3d. and 10s. A further eight bequests were made in return for commemoration, such as individual friars to pray or sing, often one trental, for their souls, obits or anniversaries. These eight included the bequest of 13s. 4d. from John Shurley for the Austin Friars to pray for his soul, that of his wife, and those of their ancestors and all Christian souls; similar sums were left to the two orders of friars of New Winchelsea.[119] In 1427 Thomas Colpeper, knight, bequeathed 40s. to the Austin Friars of Rye to hold his obit and anniversary. He lived at the manor of Bayhall near Bayham Abbey in the Weald on the Kent-Sussex border in Frant, where he was to be buried. Like other knightly families of the Weald at this time, Colpeper mostly bequeathed money to parishes and religious houses in the nearby area, and in fact mainly in Kent, i.e. to the Abbot and Convent of Bayham £35 6s. 8d.; to the church of the nuns of Malling 40s.; to the Priory church of Tonbridge 20s., and to the friars of Aylesford 20s. Besides Bayham Abbey, the Rye Friary was the only house at which obsequies were requested in return for the bequest, suggesting its importance as a site of commemoration, at least in the range of places supported by such knightly families.[120]

In 1435 two brothers of the Rye Austin friars were ordained in Canterbury Cathedral, John Ricard as acolyte and sub-deacon, and John Lucas as priest.[121] However, there appears always to have been only a small number of friars at Rye, with a low point in the mid-15th century when the Friary was described as almost without brethren, perhaps reflecting the state of the town's economy.[122] Nevertheless, quite a large number of burials, i.e. finds of skeletons, have been reported within the chapel, precinct and Friary garden, and this may reflect the regard which Rye townsfolk placed in the Friary for remembrance.[123] These burials may of course have taken place over nearly two centuries between the Friary's foundation and the Dissolution. The evidence of the foundation and of bequests to both the parish church and Friary by the same individuals, for example William Byspyn and Robert Crowche, suggest there was little competition between the Friary and the parish church.[124] The graveyard of Rye parish church was encroached on by market and civic functions on its north side and in the period of growth from the late 15th century the Friary may have provided a useful additional burial area.[125] However, although there were many bequests to the Friary, no testators specified burial there.

In 1493 the town governors (jurats) of New Romney called on a friar of Rye to come to New Romney to hear the confession of a prisoner, presumably before execution, and paid the friar 1s.[126] New Romney no longer had a friary of its own, and thus there was no friar in the town to perform this typical role of confessing an outsider.[127] In the 16th century support for the Austin Friary and its buildings became part of the well-documented struggle between religious traditionalists and reformers at Rye. In the first three decades of the century the friars and their chapel continued to attract financial support, for example in 1514, when John Kyrkeby of Rye, draper, bequeathed 20s. to the building of the church of the Austin Friars in Rye.[128] This cannot be taken to indicate the first building of the chapel but does suggest a significant renovation. In the 1520s the Friary buildings seem to have been leased out since a note in the Rye town account book records that on 4 September 1524 the roof (*tegumentum fabrice*) of the Friars Heremites was erected (presumably a substantial repair following neglect) at the expense of William Marsh, its farmer, i.e., lessee.[129] John Marche, jurat between 1537 and 1541, was identified as among the religious traditionalists of Rye known from the 1530s.[130] This suggests the possibility that William Marsh, of the same family, had taken over the Friary and repaired it in 1524 as an expression of devotion. The same support for and interest in the Friary was shown both before and after the Dissolution by members of the traditionalist or recusant family of Oxenbridge (below). In the fourth decade of the 16th century the Friary played a part in the struggle between traditionalists and reformers in Rye. On 23 October 1533 the mayor and jurats of Rye advised Cromwell that they had received his order to 'put in safe keeping one freer and one prest: for that they shuld have spoken as well certeyn cedycyus and heynous wordes ayenst the Kynge's Highnes as ayenst the Quene's Grace'.[131] Subsequently, tenure of the Friary buildings by the Oxenbridge family briefly became an expression of support for traditional beliefs as may have been the case with William Marsh in the 1520s.

At the Dissolution in 1538, the Austin Friary and precinct were described as a garden, orchard and small close containing one acre and were valued at 8s. 4d.[132] On 26 September 1544 Thomas Godwyne leased the site of the late Austin Friars with a close there in the tenure of William Oxenbridge.[133] Subsequently the premises known as 'the Friars' were for some decades held by this wealthy Oxenbridge family of Rye and Brede, a parish to the west of Rye. Brede (or Forde) Place was the family seat where Sir Godard Oxenbridge, sheriff of Sussex, lived. His younger brother, Adam Oxenbridge was an active member of the Rye town government between 1485 and 1495, collector of customs in the 1490s and MP in 1496. At his death Adam had extensive landholdings in Rye, Winchelsea, Hastings and eight other neighbouring Sussex parishes, and the White Horse at Southwark; as noted, he helped establish a chantry with Robert Crowche and bequeathed a cash sum to the Rye Austin Friars. Adam's son John, his nephew William, and another relative, Thomas, followed him as jurats of Rye.[134] However, the Oxenbridge family retained traditionalist religious views into the 1540s and 1550s and so chose to bring its close involvement with Rye to an end.[135] The family retired to its seat at Brede Place and its interests in law, and mirrored in east Sussex the small but influential number of Catholic gentry families known in west Sussex.[136] It was a servant of Sir Robert Oxenbridge who brought a copy of the proclamation of Mary as Queen to Rye on 21 July 1553, and in the second half of the 16th century the family was part of the local Catholic gentry.[137] Despite retiring to Brede, members of the Oxenbridge family still held the former Friary in the 1560s and 1570s. In 1564 a tenement in Rye abutted 'north on the lands of Sir Robert Oxenbridge, knight, called the Friers', and a Mr Oxenbridge was assessed, as a non-resident, in 1576 'for the Friors' in Landgate ward.[138] It is interesting to speculate that the Oxenbridge tenure of the Friars in Elizabeth's reign derived from their attachment to the buildings and sentiments of the old religion and perhaps reflected their hopes for its restoration.

In 1580, an entry in the burial register which records 'a Frenchman out of the Friars and a child who died there' suggests that the Friary chapel may have been a place of residence for Huguenots.[139] Subsequently the Austin Friary and precinct came into the hands of the Norton family. Despite being described as owners they were presumably, like Thomas Godwyne earlier, actually lessees of the property in the complicated pattern of tenure and occupation found in medieval and early modern towns and amply demonstrated in Rye between 1405 and 1670 in the rentals, deeds and early chamberlains' account.[140] The area around the Friary and its precinct seems not to have been heavily built up in the mid-1580s. In 1584 the mayor and jurats leased a void plot 'besides the Fryars tight against the house of Robert Farley, merchant' to Robert Gillam, feter, which he was to fence and enclose.[141] Anthony Norton, the Royalist, held the former Friary by the mid-17th century.[142] A stable and orchard, part of a messuage called The Friars, was purchased by Ralph Norton in 1720.[143] In the following centuries the surviving Friary building was used as a theatre for itinerant players, a wool and dairy store, a barracks, a church house, a Sunday school, a hospital in the First World War, a centre for evacuees and entertainments in the Second World War, a cinema and, most recently, a pottery.[144]

So at Rye after the Dissolution the Austin Friary remained in use for the townspeople in a variety of ways, a usage reflecting its origins. The friars were apparently few in number but well supported by the townsfolk, and their buildings were a notable part of the town's topography with a significant relationship to the town fosse, wall, main gate, postern gate, and the supply route for water. The Friary offered a new focus for devotion, chantry functions, and an alternative to the parish church and its graveyard as a burial place. In its foundation and its pre-Dissolution functions there are perhaps parallels in miniature with the London mendicant houses. In the 13th century the friars in London, notably the Dominicans and Franciscans acquired land, extended their precinct and moved site. This was to bring about distinctive adjustments in London's topography, including the relationship of the convents to the town defences and the obstruction of routes. The extension of the precinct included buildings purely or largely for the friars' use (chapter house, dormitory and refectory) and other constructions which had a wider use in the community (enlarged Friary churches, and even the water supply). The friars also brought a new form of spiritual life although the response of Londoners to it is unknown. Support from the monarch, urban office holders, wealthy citizens and, presumably, poorer ones was important.[145] On a smaller scale, but similarly, the Austin Friary of Rye, was erected with the support of the townspeople, and then was relocated and adapted over time to respond to the needs of the urban community.

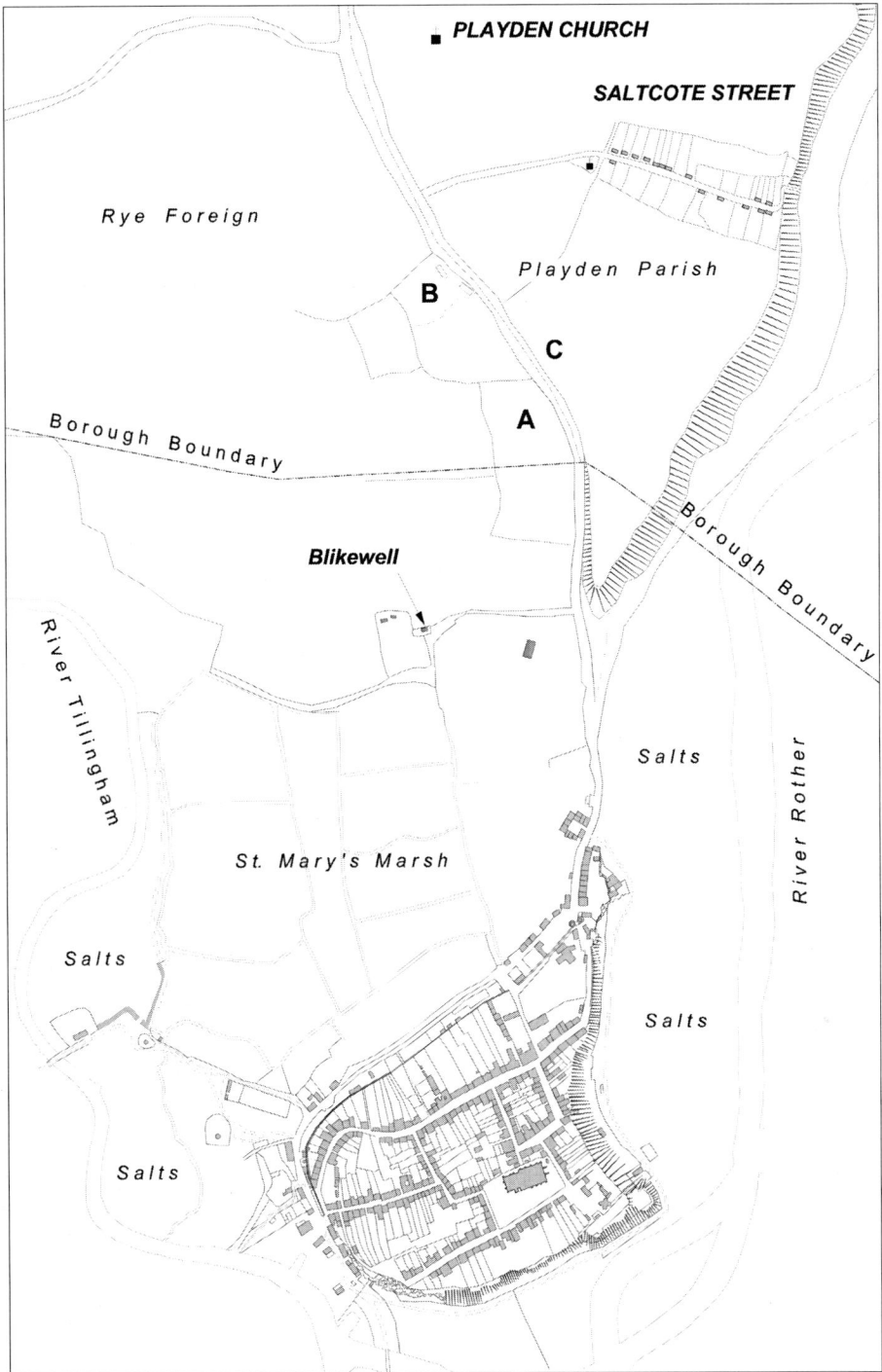

Fig. 7.1 Rye town and Rye Foreign showing possible locations of the Leper Hospital (A, B, C), and also Blikewell and Saltcote Street.

CHAPTER 7

The Leper Hospital of St Bartholomew

Introduction: The Location of the Hospital

The leper hospital of Rye, dedicated to St Bartholomew the Apostle, was founded in the late 12th century and lay in Rye Foreign, an administrative unit, and what became the parish of Playden.[1] No remnants of its buildings, a chapel and a house, now survive. Its close connections with the leading townsmen of Rye were well known and it was, for example, described as 'the hospital of lepers of St Bartholomew, by la Rye' in 1344. However, over time it became known instead as 'the hospital of Plaiden by Rye', or similar, because of its location on the route leading north out of Rye towards Playden.[2] This chapter examines the evidence for the location of the hospital lands and buildings, and then goes on to explore the lives of the inmates.[3]

Deeds of 1339 and 1340 confirm that the hospital lands lay to the west of the Rye-Playden route, which is known nowadays as Rye Hill. The garden of the hospital abutted on lands which were in 'the borgh (tithing) of Goldspur of the Norman virgate', perhaps a reference to the half virgate with which the hospital was endowed at an early period by Fécamp Abbey (*Chapter 1*).[4] The borgh of Goldspur lay immediately to the north of Rye town. The garden, and the fields which were tilled until at least 1380, and the barns where the wheat and other corn were stored, must have lain close to the buildings for security.[5] Holloway and Vidler each identified locations for the hospital, labelled A, B and C on Figure 7.1; Holloway suggested two, A and C, and Vidler one, B.[6] In 1989 an archaeological assessment provided no positive evidence for site B, *The King's Head Inn*, which by 1990 was called the *Top of the Hill Pub*. The assessment concluded that this re-opened the question of the hospital's location.[7] The location proposed by Holloway at A certainly included hospital land (Spittal Field) and was near the southern boundary of the hospital lands.[8] The northern boundary of the liberty of Rye included the land of the hospital of St Bartholomew. Together with deeds re-examined for this project, the boundaries confirm that the land of the hospital lay to the north of the highway which ran from near the northern exit of Rye (later the Landgate area) to the spring at Blikewell and then westwards on towards Leasam along the north side of North Marsh, later called St Mary's Marsh (*Chapters 1*, *9*).[9] Finds from tile and pottery kilns were made by Vidler at location A.[10] In addition to these, a kiln-waster assemblage of the late 13th and early 14th centuries was found some 500 metres north of site B, and further up Rye Hill, approximately marked by the street name Kiln Drive. Other finds included a 'lead token' called 'Abbot's money' and a number of musket balls, and many post-medieval and modern items.[11] A watching brief was kept in 2007 at the site of this kiln-waster assemblage where a new doctor's surgery was built. There was lots of disturbance of the ground and no information in relation to a possible hospital site here was found either.[12]

After the Dissolution the hospital became known as the free chapel of Playden. Holloway stated in 1863 that an old stone foundation alongside the path could be seen in one of two fields called Parvis and Paradise. He suggested that the stone foundation represented part of this free chapel, which was his second suggestion for the location of the hospital buildings, at C, on the eastern side of the road.[13] By *c.*1670 the former hospital property was called the manor of Playden St Bartholomew in a survey which dealt only with the demesne of the manor which then formed part of the extensive estates of the Tufton family. The survey describes a demesne farm of 32½ acres in extent, with a house and barn upon it. The farm lay in four detached portions and all but one acre was located in Rye Foreign. Of this farm the house, barn and four parcels of meadow (ten acres and two rods) were called St Bartholomew's. They abutted east on the London road, south on lands of Sir John Fagg and Colonel Austen, and north and west on lands of Mr Norton and Mr Halsey.[14] In addition one small plot lying in Playden parish was described in the survey as 'a little piece whereon formerly the manor house stood'. This little piece lay immediately to the east of the London road and abutted the lands of Mr Norton on the south, east and north.[15] Mr Norton's lands included the holdings of Parvis and Paradise where Holloway noted the old stone foundation.[16] By 1735 the former manor house site had been subsumed into Norton property.[17] A draft map of this date of the demesne of Playden St Bartholomew shows the farmhouse and all the lands described above, except the site of the manor house. The farmhouse is identifiable on the map as occupying the site of the present-day *Top of the Hill Pub* on the west side of the road (site B). The adjacent lands of the demesne of St Bartholomew were also on the west side in the location where a fair was held until 1858, possibly its original location. The manor house site, however, was according to the 1670 survey on the east side of the road (site C), now the Mill Road housing estate. It is thus possible that the site of the hospital building and that of St Bartholomew's manor house in the 17th century were one and the same, the stone foundation which Holloway observed locating them on the east side of the road, with the hospital garden, fair ground and lands on the western side. However, although reasonable detail is known about the location of the fields which made up the demesne during the post-medieval period, neither the written sources nor the map evidence reveals the exact extent, location or boundaries of the hospital lands during the medieval period. Although the general location of the hospital lands are known to have been on the western side of the route north out of the town, the exact site of its buildings remains unknown.

The location of St Bartholomew's hospital on the route out of Rye parallels that of the New Romney leper hospital, which was founded in the late 12th century, and lay on the edge of the town on the only land route leading inland at this time, to Ashford. The leper hospitals at Rye and at New Romney thus stood on routes which led through the Weald and east Kent respectively, and finally on towards London.[18] The locations allowed the hospital inmates to be kept out of town but in a place where they could be noticed and patronised by almsgivers travelling into town. After the resumption of Rye into royal hands, Henry III confirmed the rents, possessions and all the other goods of the hospital of St Bartholomew the Apostle of Rye to the barons of the town on 14 December 1249. The rents, lands and woods were not to be alienated without advice and agreement. At that time the numbers at the hospital were set at 12 brothers and/or sisters, with some lepers, and there was of course a chaplain.[19] The hospital's own muniments did not survive the wardenship of Roger de Burton in the late 14th century. However, the material in royal records, deeds and bishops' registers reveals the hospital's relationship with the town government, its endowments, a little of the lives of its inmates, and much about its fortunes, particularly as they were affected by war with France and the 1377 raid on Rye. The hospital fulfilled its function of caring for lepers and others until the late 14th century, after which it became a sinecure for clerks who were royal officials. In this it is again paralleled by the leper hospital of New Romney which, after its re-invention as a merchant family chantry in the early 14th century, became a base for members of the *familia* of the Archbishop of Canterbury in the 15th century.[20]

The Inmates of the Hospital

The Rye hospital was recorded in 1249 as taking in lepers and described as a leper hospital four times in the 1340s.[21] Nevertheless, the 1249 reference makes clear that others besides lepers were accommodated, and these others were perhaps the great majority. The other inmates were described as the poor in 1380, 1420 and 1442. Both women and men were accommodated, as was common in medieval hospitals which had originated as leper houses. Since the hospital had a garden, able-bodied inmates may have taken part in cultivating it as they did at other hospitals, such as St John's, Sandwich, or Maynard's Spital, Canterbury. The Rye inmates may even have worked in the fields belonging to the hospital which before 1380, at least, were tilled. The inmates may also have offered a daily and yearly round of commemoration. In 1380 the Rye hospital was noted to have owned indulgences worth 40s. yearly in offerings. These indulgences may have been purely to show to potential almsgivers to the Hospital, or they may suggest that almsgivers also expected to benefit from the prayer of the inmates, a frequent practice.[22]

The surviving precedent book and custumal of Rye were compiled between the late 15th and the mid-16th centuries; however, they record earlier provisions concerning the medieval hospital, perhaps dating from records of custom made in the Cinque Ports in *c.*1356.[23] The provisions in these books reflect practice at that time, and indeed go back to the origins of the hospital in the late 12th century. The most important aspect was the extensive involvement of the town government in running the hospital. These provisions relate to the appointment of its chaplain, its property and its inmates, in particular to the rules on admission. The rules did not restrict the numbers of inmates, but the mayor and commonalty had to agree to all admissions. In addition the mayor, with the agreement of the jurats, could nominate any 'good man or woman' from among the commons of the town for free admission and maintenance on the basis that 'they had competently borne charges in their time for the welfare of the town, if they be impoverished and impotent, decayed of their goods and chattels, and little goods have to live with'. The rules and statutes of the hospital were read to any potential inmate of the hospital before admission, apparently in the presence of the brothers and sisters who were already resident, and the new inmate then had to accept those rules.[24]

Control of the Hospital and the Appointment of its Chaplains (Wardens)

The hospital was in the charge of a priest, who was both its chaplain and its warden. There was a tripartite arrangement in which the townsmen nominated the chaplain and presented his name to Fécamp Abbey for its agreement, and the chaplain was then presented to the bishop of Chichester for institution. This arrangement between Fécamp and the townsmen dated from the earliest origins of the town when the Abbey nominated the priest in charge of the hospital with the advice of the *prudhommes* (*Chapter 1*). However, subsequently the mayor, jurats and commonalty had greater control, choosing their own man as chaplain and submitting his name to Fécamp. The mayor could also audit the accounts of the chaplain as warden four times a year if he chose.[25] The change in the balance of control in the appointment process probably derived from the resumption of the town of Rye from Fécamp by Henry III in 1247, although Fécamp's bailiff remained in control of Rye Foreign where the hospital lay (*Chapter 1*). Until the final resumption of the property of all alien priories in England in 1415, Fécamp Abbey continued to have rights over the hospital. In wartime, however, i.e. from 1337, the king took the temporalities of Fécamp Abbey in England into his own hands, the main income from the Rye hospital being the revenue from its endowments and the tolls of the fair. The king also took into his own hands the right to appoint the chaplain or warden. He explained that the appointment was in his gift 'by reason of the temporalities of the abbot of Fécamp, an alien, being in his hands ... on account of the war with France.[26]

The chaplains of the early 14th century, before the outbreak of war, were local men. Robert de Southmallyng, a place near Lewes, was appointed chaplain in 1319 and died in 1329.[27] In the following year *dominus* Richard de Garlethorpe, chaplain, was warden of the hospital. He acted as first witness to a record concerning the important marshland called *Levedimerss* in Iden parish, the next witnesses being the barons of Rye (*Chapter 5*). Garlethorpe's premier position among the witnesses firmly associates him with the governing elite of the town. This was the only occasion between the 13th and 16th centuries when the chaplain of the hospital was a witness to a charter in conjunction with members of the town government. The naming of Garlethorpe as first witness, even before the barons of Rye, emphasises the significance of his new appointment and his role in the town.

In 1343 Hugh Pipard was appointed as the chaplain or warden of the Rye hospital 'by the king's gift' and was described as a king's clerk. Pipard was granted custody of the hospital of lepers at Rye and then presented to the bishop of Chichester for institution. However, a few months later the mayor and commonalty of Rye asserted their right to nominate the warden, and the king 'for certain causes' revoked Pipard's appointment. Pipard was replaced by Ranulph de Wyke, chaplain, the town's nominee.[28] Although Edward III had taken the temporalities of the hospital from Fécamp because of the war with France, he nevertheless had to take into account the customary rights of the town government to nominate the warden, since at this time he was relying heavily on Rye's ship service, shipbuilding facilities and the important anchorage between Rye and New Winchelsea. Ranulph de Wyke may have died in the Black Death, for in 1348 a new appointment was made, one John; John was followed by a chaplain called William atte Nesshe.[29] William's surname indicates that he was a local man from Rye, and indeed part of the family of whom one, Thomas ate Nesse, was mayor at this period.[30]

The next known warden was Robert de Burton, clerk, who was appointed in the spring of 1379, the grant noting that the temporalities were still in the king's hands. This was the first occasion on which a grant of the wardenship was noted as being 'for life'.[31] In 1379 Rye had recently suffered a severe French raid and a serious loss of population due to the plague epidemics of 1348 onwards.[32] The townsfolk had responded to these disasters by a show of support for the town's new Austin Friary which had recently been founded by leading families, and which was moved in 1378 to a new site within the defences which were being rapidly strengthened.[33] From this period onwards it seems that the hospital, an old institution lying outside the town and its defences, ceased to be the focus of civic pride, control and commemoration, which were transferred to the new Friary. Robert de Burton, the new warden of 1379, had no known connections with Rye.[34] He arrived at the hospital and found it occupied and its lands properly enclosed and being cultivated. Within a few months he had sold off the grain in the fields and barns for £10 and kept the money for himself. No money was directed to the maintenance of the poor at the hospital who found themselves obliged to walk into town and beg in the streets. This came to the attention of the town authorities in the January following Burton's appointment and the king then ordered an investigation by two local lords, William Horne and William de Battesford.[35] They reported that not only had Burton sold the grain, but he had left the hospital's fields uncultivated and its woods unenclosed. He had sold a large number of trees from its woodland and had carried off documents, particularly bulls of indulgences which had produced an income of £2 a year for the hospital inmates. Burton had even taken the brass vessels which the inmates used for cooking, claiming that they owed rent. The commissioners concluded that 'the waste done by the said Robert will be the final destruction of the hospital unless a remedy is speedily applied'.[36]

There is no record of a remedy being speedily applied nor of the removal of Burton as warden. It was not until 24 April 1391 that another man, John Waldeby, clerk, received a grant of the wardenship, again a royal grant for life.[37] One John Waldeby was an Austin Friar, preacher and writer, and Prior Provincial of the order, perhaps originally from Waldeby near Hull.[38] If this Waldeby was the man who received the grant of the Rye hospital wardenship, then it was probably a financial contribution for his maintenance in late life. It does not necessarily indicate that he came to live at Rye, although as Prior Provincial he would certainly have known of the new Austin Friary foundation there. The royal Patent Rolls record that John Waldeby, warden of the Rye hospital, was replaced by Robert Longe, chaplain, in a grant made on 2 October 1391 because John Waldeby had died.[39] Robert's surname suggests that he was related to the other members of the Longe family of Rye (*Chapter 3*). This family supplied members of the town government from the early 13th century.[40] Robert Longe was warden of the hospital for a few months only. He died and was replaced by Ralph Repyndon, king's clerk, on 3 October 1392.[41]

Ralph Repyndon was not a local man but parson of the church of Walesby in the diocese of Lincoln. Repyndon was not instituted and inducted personally to the wardenship but instead appointed John de Ivelich, clerk, as his attorney to take possession. Repyndon remained as warden, that is, collected the hospital revenues, for about eighteen months and then resigned. He was replaced by Thomas de la Chambre, chaplain, who was warden for two years and then replaced by John Bowetby in a grant of 18 June 1395.[42] In September 1395 Ralph Repyndon, described at that time as clerk and official within the king's household, instructed his attorney, John Dent, to ask John Bowetby, then warden, to repay him £7 13s. 4d. from the hospital revenues 'which he had recovered in the King's Court at la Rye'.[43] Bowetby was followed as warden by John Sharp, chaplain, in 1396 and subsequently by Thomas Brigge, clerk, in 1397.[44] This may have been Thomas Brigge who was named as a burgess of Lydd when he was executor of a will in 1415, and as the lessee of Scotney manor on Romney Marsh in 1423.[45] Brigge was one of two patrons of the leper Hospital of Saints Stephen and Thomas, New Romney, at the appointment of *dominus* Andrew Aylwyn, priest of Lydd, to the mastership there in 1436.[46]

Until 1393 most chaplains of the Rye hospital remained in place until death and some were probably appointed late in life. From 1393 until 1407 the wardenship seems to have been effectively granted only for a year or two at a time, with new grants sometimes stating that the previous warden had resigned.[47] All the grants dating between 1393 and 1420 mention that the man appointed had been nominated by the mayor and barons, or on occasion the bailiffs, of Rye. However this appears to have been a mere formality rather than reassertion of control over the wardenship by the town government, since it is clear that the appointees were chaplains or parsons of churches elsewhere, or were royal servants of various sorts. For example,

John Deye, warden in 1400, was chaplain of the chantry at the altar of St Margaret in the chapel of St Katherine in the cathedral church of St Paul, London.[48] Joseph Scovill, warden in 1403, was parson of the parish church of Leyham in the diocese of Norwich.[49] John Elmeton, warden from 1406, was described as king's clerk.[50] Elmeton apparently remained warden until Nicolas Colnet, king's clerk, sergeant, and physician was appointed in 1413.[51] Colnet attended Henry V during the Agincourt campaign and possibly also Charles, Duke of Orléans, after his capture (1415), since the Duke gave Colnet a ewer which he subsequently bequeathed. Colnet made his will in advance of preparations for leaving for France again in 1417 and cannot, as a royal physician, have been a resident warden of the Rye hospital. However, he bequeathed 20s. to the 'hospital of the poor' of Rye in his will which was proved in 1420. This may indicate that some paupers were maintained there at this time or it may have been a gesture on Colnet's part to acknowledge the support which the hospital revenues gave him for several years.[52]

Thomas Chace, chancellor of Oxford University, was appointed warden in 1420 following a royal letter to the mayor and barons nominating him.[53] At this time Chace was one of a group of masters and doctors of theology gathered by Bishop Philip Repingdon (d. 1424) in his diocese of Lincoln to combat Wycliffism.[54] Chace was also appointed to the wardenship of the Hospital of St John Baptist, Huntingdon, in the diocese of Lincoln. At that time the assets of the Rye hospital were said to be worth no more than nine marks (£6) a year, although this may have been a round figure since it was also applied to the assets of the Huntingdon hospital. In 1426 Chace was granted a papal dispensation for 10 years to hold these two wardenships together with the prebend of Kylardry in Cashel (Tipperary).[55] In 1435 or 1436 William Parker was appointed and kept the hospital in a dilapidated state (below).

The careers and actions of the men appointed in this period indicate that after Robert de Burton's depredations of the hospital's assets in 1379, the hospital did not provide accommodation for inmates or alms for the poor, certainly not after 1420, the year of Colnet's death, and this is confirmed by the state of its buildings which was made clear in a visitation of 1442. This was held in the chapel of the hospital on Sunday 20 January 1442 by William Rowe, clerk, commissary of the bishop of Chichester. Rowe found that the warden of the hospital, William Parker, had been absent for six or seven years without licence. Parker had leased the revenues of the hospital to lay people; the chapel and the house (*mansio*) of the warden and paupers were in complete ruin, and no paupers maintained there.[56] Parker was promptly deprived of the living and replaced as warden by John Faukes, a clerk of the Chancery.[57]

The Transfer of the Hospital to Syon Abbey in the 15th Century

The hospital and revenues had been in the king's hands since 1337 as the property of an alien house. The final resumption of alien priories into royal hands in 1415 thus made little effective difference to the hospital, although in common with that of many others, its property was ultimately reallocated to a religious house in England in return for prayers for the royal family. The hospital, described as 'sometime belonging to the abbey of Fécamp', was granted to the abbey of Syon, Middlesex, which itself was founded in 1415. Syon Abbey was also granted other former Fécamp property in east Sussex: the advowsons of the churches of St Clement and All Saints, Hastings, the church of Brede and the church of St Leonard in Yham (New Winchelsea). Syon's title to the lands of former alien properties was later called into question but in 1443 Syon sought and received confirmation of its title to its Sussex and Gloucestershire properties, i.e. those formerly belonging to Fécamp.[58] The custody of the hospital continued to be assigned to chaplains and royal servants after the grant to Syon. The first appointment was to William Tracy, chaplain, on 24 December 1461, an appointment perhaps made by Syon itself.[59] Tracy remained until his death and in 1478 Master John More, clerk of the king's closet, was appointed to the custody in his place.[60] John More was followed by the clerk, Master Thomas Brent, the queen's almoner, who surrendered the custody on 1 February 1503. This was followed on 23 July 1503 by the grant of the advowson of what was called the free chapel of Playden by Rye to John Islip, Abbot of St Peter's, Westminster, and to the prior and convent there, in the place of Syon Abbey.[61] On 13 July 1504 the temporalities were also granted to Westminster Abbey probably to support the Lady Chapel which was Henry VII's memorial.[62] The hospital was not formally appropriated to the Abbey until some years later, possibly in 1521.[63]

It is impossible to envisage that there was any revival of an active spiritual or communal role for the hospital in the 15th century with the transfer to Syon Abbey and the continued appointments of royal servants to the wardenship or custody. Indeed it is probable that such a role ended with the mastership of Robert de Burton in 1379 and this is confirmed by the absence of any bequests to it by local people or by more distant gentry. In this the Rye hospital differed from that of St John, New Romney, the town's second hospital; that remained in active use until the 1470s, and received support and donations from the townsfolk, particularly the jurats, and was a focus for their burials and collective memorialisation. In the 16th century St John's was transformed by the townsfolk into an almshouse, Southlands, which continued in operation in the same premises until the 19th century. This kind of continuity between medieval hospital and almshouse also occurred at the Cinque Ports of Sandwich and Hythe, as well as at Canterbury, Rochester, Faversham and possibly Lewisham and Deptford. At New Winchelsea two of three hospitals survived in some form until the mid-1560s.[64] The fate of the former leper hospital at Rye was different for three reasons. It lay outside the town where it could be largely unnoticed by the townsfolk on a day-to-day basis. It was in a location which would have appeared particularly vulnerable after the 1377 raid and subsequent fortification of the town. The Austin Friary, particularly once it had moved to its new site inside the town, provided a new and attractive focus for almsgiving and commemoration. The Friary, rather than the hospital, became the institution which the town governors and elite families patronised and supported. Furthermore, with the loss of an active hospital, the poor of Rye were deprived of a place which had supported them. From the late 14th to the late 15th centuries, there is no evidence about the care of the poor of Rye. In a period of much reduced population but greater individual wealth, the poor may have been supported by individual charity or increased employment opportunities and higher daily wage rates.[65] However, at the end of the 15th century and in the early 16th century, a period of sharp population increase, there were beggars in the town and the jurats of Rye set them to work on the town walls and cleaning the castle, probably the Ypres tower, paying them to do so.[66] After the Reformation the corporation continued to provide some relief for the deserving poor and accommodation in the new almshouse which was set up in 1551 (*Chapter 6*).

The Dispersal of the Assets of the Hospital

The dispersal and use of the assets of the hospital in the 16th and 17th centuries was tied up with the nature of Rye's society and economy, and particularly the fortunes and careers of those who had an interest in those assets. On 12 February 1530 Abbot John Islip of Westminster drew up an indenture about the site and other lands of the hospital, which were leased to Nicholas Tufton (I). These lands were said to be in Rye, Playden, Saltcote, Peasmarsh, Beckley, Brede, Udimore, Iden, Ewhurst and Northiam. Playden included the site of the hospital, and Iden, immediately to the north, may have been mentioned in case any of the hospital lands, such as its fields, in fact lay in that parish. Brede was included because Fécamp, and subsequently Syon Abbey, then Westminster Abbey, held the advowson of the church, and also the manor of Brede, part of which may have been thought to lie in the adjacent parish of Udimore. Ewhurst and Northiam are both likely to have been mentioned since the hospital's woodlands lay in Ewhurst but near the parish boundary with Northiam

(*Chapter 3*). In making the indenture Abbot Islip and his lawyers were covering all eventualities as to the location of the lands, a common practice. The site of 'the late hospital of St Bartholomew of Pleydon beside Rye' and its lands were conveyed to Andrew, Lord Windsor, at the Dissolution in 1542.[67] His son and grandson held the former hospital property until at least 1558. In 1560 it was held by William Scott, and Henry Peck and John Tufton were also linked to its ownership. One John Tufton held it in 1601.[68] On 8 July 1611 the Earl of Northampton wrote to an unknown recipient that 'out of the regard I have for the poor estate of the town of Rye' he wished him 'to send me particulars of the estate of the Hospital' so that he could decide whether to delay a grant of the former hospital to Tufton.[69] Some twenty-six acres of the hospital lands between Rye and Playden seem to have been in use by Rye inhabitants for grazing land, and the Earl may have been considering their interests rather than wishing to see the lands treated as a private estate. However, the grant to Sir John Tufton was subsequently made, and members of the Tufton family held the estate until Nicholas Tufton (II), the Earl of Thanet, conveyed the property, then called a manor, to Sir Clifford Clifton in 1664.[70] In 1669 the twenty-six acres of grazing lands were in the hands of Mr John Halsey of Lincoln's Inn and leased out to Mr Thomas Tutty; they had previously been leased to the widow Carey. The question of their management and the benefits which Rye inhabitants might have from them was raised in a letter of September 1669 from Richard Kilburne, the lawyer and antiquarian, to his 'much respected friend' Samuel Jeake the elder.[71] Kilburne was steward of Brede and Bodiam manors, and his residence was in Hawkhurst on the London to Rye road.[72] Kilburne was concerned that the former hospital lands should be managed so that Rye inhabitants could benefit from their use for grazing: the tenant Mr Tutty was not to plough any part of them nor to put up permanent hedges which would have excluded common grazing. Kilburne had close connections with Rye though his stewardship of local manors and particularly through his two marriages, which were to women who were descended by birth or marriage from mayoral and commercial families of Rye of the late 16th century, firstly Elizabeth Davy and secondly Sarah Burchit, a widow.[73] In the 17th century, some gentry and noble families like the Tuftons built up estates around Rye from property such as that of the hospital, but others like the Earl of Northampton and Kilburne were worried about the sad state of Rye and the effects of its decay on the residents. This was expressed in their concern that the residents should be able to make some use of the hospital lands in which the townsfolk had had an interest since the 12th century.

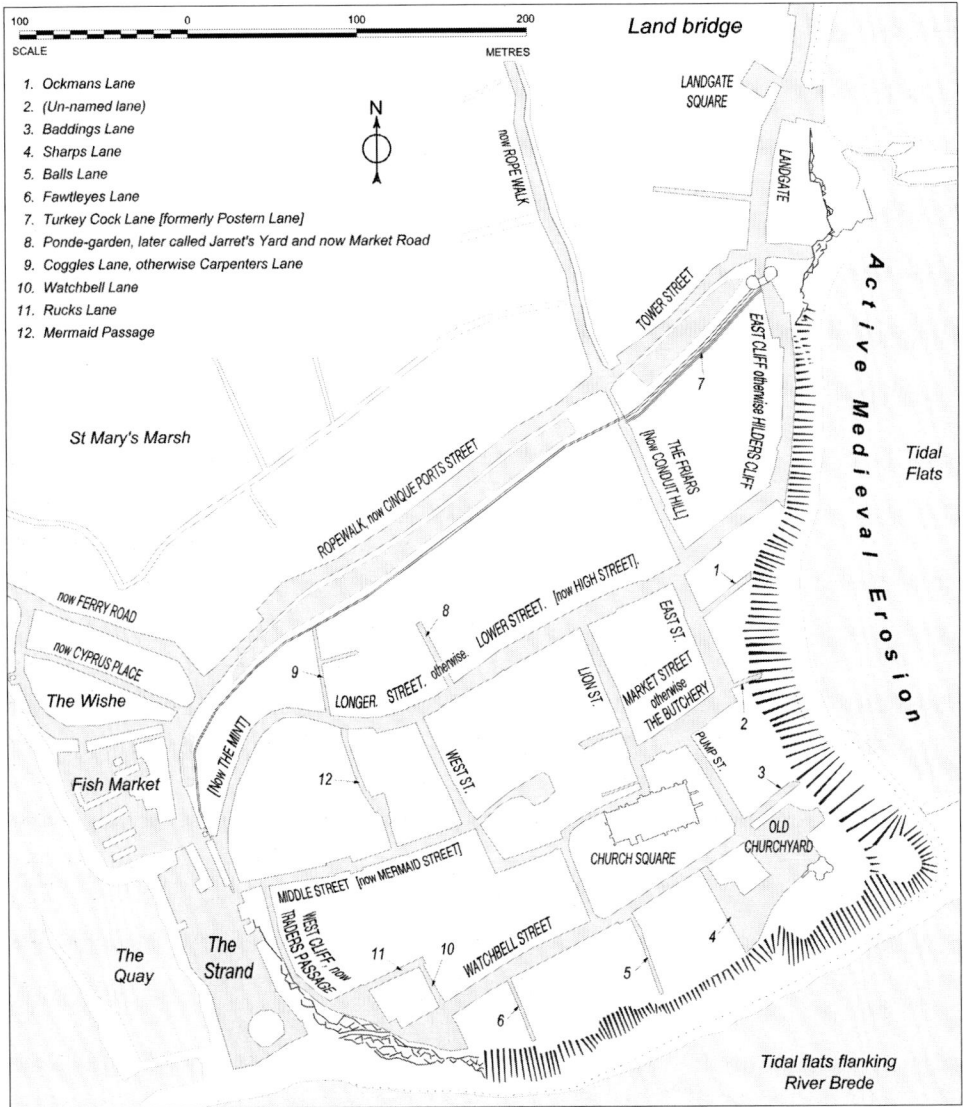

Fig. 8.1 Names of Rye streets and lanes based on Samuel Jeake's map which was drawn in 1667 and copied by William Wybourn in 1728, RYE/132/15.

CHAPTER 8

The Environment, Assets and Defences of Rye, c.1086 to c.1660

Introduction

The defences and street pattern are immediate visual components of an historic town such as Rye and the factors influencing their development are essential to any urban study. At Rye these include the site's natural geography and its access by land and water, access which came to be restricted and defended by gates and towers. The limited size of the site of Rye on its rock promontory and its location on an estuary were also major influences (Plate IV). The land below the five-metre contour has been prone to periodic flooding and change during the historic period.[1]

Fécamp Abbey founded the new borough of Rye to take advantage of a growing population in its hinterlands, its protected estuarine site, and the local natural resources such as salt, wood, fish and iron (*Chapters 1, 3*). Rye was a relatively small town in the medieval period but its port facilities gave it local significance for the inhabitants and regional significance for the monarchy in wartime. Fishing was based on the creeks and strands which gave immediate access to the town for vessels. The protected natural harbour which Rye shared with Winchelsea sheltered a versatile fleet of boats and ships which could be used for fishing, trade, war and the transport of royalty and troops. The local inhabitants also used their vessels for piracy and privateering, activities which proved almost impossible to eradicate (*Chapters 2, 4*). This versatility of Rye's vessels and the adaptability of its economy were vital to its success. The principal exports from its immediate Wealden area were bulky and of low value, consisting mostly of wood, timber and iron, but they were crucial in wartime. The naturally defensive, dry, raised location of the site, with its protected access to the sea, made Rye a good location for colonisation and development, and gave it advantages over towns such as Old Winchelsea and New Romney which lay on vulnerable shingle banks close to the open sea. Those towns developed early from coastal fishing and trading settlements. Rye in contrast was established after the Conquest to take advantage of increasing population, production and demand in its hinterlands. Transport links by land and water to these hinterlands were vital and helped to shape the character of the town.

Routes In and Out of Rye

The medieval road out of Rye ran across the land bridge towards the adjacent upland at Playden on which the leper hospital stood (Figure 8.1) (*Chapter 1*). It led from the north-eastern corner of Rye and connected with the crossing of the River Rother at Newenden and then with the important route to London (later the A21) via places with medieval markets where fish could be sold: Hawkhurst, Combwell, Lamberhurst, Tonbridge, Sevenoaks, Chipstead, Chelsfield, Farnborough, Orpington, St Mary Cray, Bromley and Lewisham, which is known as a market in 1086.[2] The recorded market days suggest that Rye fish distributors travelled to the markets of Hawkhurst and Combwell on Tuesdays, then went on to Farnborough, Bromley and Bexley, returning the next day via the markets of Orpington, St Mary Cray and the surrounding villages.[3] This route out of Rye also had links to the medieval markets in the Weald at Cranbrook, Bodiam, Salehurst and Robertsbridge, where Rye fishing families had connections. Rye fishermen included the Lambin family who also held property at Robertsbridge and were fishmongers at London in the 14th century.[4] The markets at these local places were held on Mondays at Robertsbridge, on Wednesdays at Salehurst, and on Saturdays at Bodiam and Cranbrook, suggesting that Rye fishermen supplied these places when not occupied with markets on the main route towards London on Tuesdays, or at Rye on Fridays. Markets at Rye were held on Wednesdays and on Fridays, the main fish-eating day, until 1404, when the Friday market was moved to Saturday at the request of the townsfolk.[5] At this low point for the Rye fishing industry, its fishermen may have been selling only locally on Saturdays and not finding it worthwhile to go as far as Bodiam and Cranbrook, if indeed their markets were still functioning then.

The place-name Chipstead means market place and is recorded in 1191. It was an important point on the medieval fish route to London, which crossed nearby places called Mackerel Plains and Salters Heath. Mackerel was one of the main catches at Rye (*Chapters 3, 4*). In 1348 John of Chipstead was described as a fishmonger and in 1374 a London fishmonger acquired property in Knockholt, also on this route. In 1414 John de Baye, purchaser of fish for the royal household, used the market at Chipstead. The journey from Rye as far as London could be undertaken quickly.

On 18 March 1360, following the signing of the Treaty of Brétigny, Edward III landed at Rye in the evening and travelled overnight on horseback to London, a journey of sixty miles, taking fifteen hours at most, with frequent changes of horse. By the end of his reign Edward III had staging-posts established on this route at Flimwell near Hawkhurst and at Chipstead to provide for changes of horse. The route between London and Rye also provided shorter overland journeys for those travelling to Paris than going via Dover. The importance of the Rye route for royal travel and the transport of fish to London and local markets cannot be overstated.[6]

The land bridge provided what was normally a dry route into Rye, although fears that its southern end near the Landgate might be flooded were expressed in 1573 when a stone wall costing £140 was built by the town to protect its southern end.[7] The area to the east of the land bridge is depicted on the Prowez map of *c.*1570 as a large area of sands where barrels of water or other goods were laden onto small boats to be taken out to larger vessels anchored in the channels (Plate V).[8] The land bridge itself is depicted by Prowez as protected from salt water on the east by a series of breakwaters, and similarly on Van Dyck's view of the town from the north in 1633[9] and on Jeake's map of 1667 (Figure 8.1).[10] The area to the west of the land bridge was described as 'salt marsh now submerged' in the mid-16th century (1547, and again in 1584) and at this time the land bridge was referred to as a causeway, no doubt because of the surrounding water.[11] The flooding of St Mary's Marsh which lay on the west side of the land bridge or causeway contributed to the submersion of land here (*Chapter 9*).

By water the medieval routes into the town were via the estuary and the two strands, one on the east side and the other on the west. The east strand below the east cliff was lost to the sea in the early 14th century, and the west strand then became the town's main landing place and quayside for fishing and trading vessels. From at least the early 14th century access into Rye from the land bridge and the west strand was protected and controlled by gates, the Landgate and Strandgate (below).

Rye also had a minor route to the low-lying land known as St Mary's Marsh which surrounded the town on the north. This area had to be crossed by the inhabitants to reach two of the three natural springs ('wells') that formed the main water supply in the medieval period (*Chapter 9*). St Mary's Marsh was called North Marsh in the mid-13th century, St Mary's Croft in 15th century and St Mary's Marsh in the 16th and 17th centuries. It was reached from the town centre via its own lane or street, now called Conduit Hill, at the lower end of which a postern gate gave access over the town dyke or ditch. Jeake's map shows a straight track, now Rope Walk, extending from the postern gate and crossing St Mary's Marsh north towards

Blikewell, which was alternatively known as Brickwell or Dodes Well, and from the later 16th century as Queen Elizabeth's Well. From here a narrow road now called Deadman's Lane links to the main route into and out of Rye via the land bridge, and may have done so in the historic period. Those collecting water at Blikewell could also have turned west and taken a route along the north side of St Mary's Marsh towards the spring under the cliff at Leasam, one of the earliest known settlements around Rye, recorded from 1200 (*Chapter 1*).[12]

The Ferry Routes from Saltcote and the Strand or Wishe Suburb

There was also access to Rye via two ferry routes. One ferry crossed the Rother estuary towards the east. This may have developed as a fixed route to East Guldeford after 1478 when the church there was built following large-scale marshland reclamation on the eastern side of the Rother estuary over the course of the 15th century (*Chapter 2*). In the 16th century the ferry to East Guldeford departed from Saltcote Street in Playden parish, a point one kilometre to the north east of the town (Figure 7.1). Saltcote changed in nature and grew in significance after the mid- to late 13th- century storms diverted the main course of the Rother past it and on towards Rye (*Chapter 1*).[13] In the late 14th century (1385) Saltcote Street was recorded as a fishing settlement when a levy was made on fishermen in Playden.[14] There was a piece of land and woods called the Grene Okes near Saltcot in Playden which was adjacent to the 'sea shore', i.e. the Rother estuary.[15] The name Grene Okes suggests that timber was grown there, and it is likely to have been shipped from a hythe at Saltcote just as it was from Scots Float which lay approximately one kilometre further up the estuary.[16] Sir John Scott greatly enlarged the hythe at Scots Float to serve as a loading place for firewood for Calais in the 1480s. In the 1390s members of the Rye town elite, the Taillours, held property at Saltcote next to the Grene Okes, property which had been formerly held by the Ambroys family (Ambroysestonne). Richard at Wode, citizen and fishmonger of London, acquired the land and woods at Grene Okes in 1422; the term green oaks suggests the trees were immature or unseasoned and perhaps had been planted when demand for timber was high in the later 14th century (*Chapter 3*).[17] Richard at Wode also held 10 acres in the 'new marsh' at Rye, St Mary's Marsh (*Chapter 9*).[18] As the landholding by the Rye elite and a Londoner suggest, Saltcote may have grown in importance as a fishing settlement and as a small port in the late Middle Ages, flourishing partly on the growing and export of timber and firewood. Rye inhabitants walked out of the town across the land bridge and down to the shore at Playden to catch the Saltcote ferry, or travelled to Playden by boat to do so. The Saltcote ferry, with its two boats, was a valuable asset to the Guldeforde (Guildford) family which reclaimed Guldeford Level and established the church at East Guldeford in 1505. In 1601 it was confirmed that Sir Henry Guldeforde of Hempsted, Kent, knight, was to hold the ferry, together with the advowson of the rectory of East Guldeford and the beer house at Saltcote. Sir Henry also held a windmill in Rye and Playden, and lands called Dennyses in Peasmarsh, paying a total rent of 100 marks.[19] The existence of a beer house at the departure point of the Saltcote ferry is paralleled by a beer brewhouse at Smallhythe further up the Rother where a ferry also crossed the river.[20] The settlement at Saltcote Street, which had its own chapel, is shown in Figure 7.1 as it existed in the late 16th century. By 1771 it was all but gone.

There was a second ferry route which was on the western side of Rye, and known as the Town Ferry or West Ferry in the 16th century. This ferry would have crossed to the important ridgeway leading towards Battle via Udimore and Brede and to an under-cliff track which gave access to the ferry to New Winchelsea.[21] It also ferried passengers to Cadborough Hill (Cliffs) near Leasam (Figure 1.2).[22] In the 14th century there was an established link between Rye families and the sale of fish at the fish shelter (*fyssheltre*) in Udimore, a link which would have used this ferry.[23] Before the 16th century this westwards ferry link probably departed from the western strand and was accessed via the Strandgate. However, from the 16th century a road from the Town or West Ferry entered Rye through a suburb on the north-west side called The Wishe (Figure 8.3). There was no direct land route into Rye through the Wishe suburb except a possible pedestrian gate known only from a 1771 map. The suburb existed by the late 13th century when at least four notable inhabitants of Rye were named from it: Richard de la Wisse, William ate Wische, Stephen Wise and Joan le Wise. Stephen Wise's tenement as recorded in the rental of Edward I's reign was subsequently held by Pharon Ion, mayor of Rye in 1304.[24] William ate Wische was a member of the town government between 1311 and 1316 and his lands were spacious, indicating that they lay outside the walls.[25] By 1316 Joan le Wise was the widow of Henry Aumbroys (Ambreis), and of sufficient status to possess a personal seal to confirm her property transactions. The Aumbroys family, like that of Pharon Ion, was important in the town government and parish church in the first half of the 14th century but disappeared from the town at the time of the Black Death (*Chapters 5, 7*).[26] Property was thus held by the town elite in the Wishe suburb until the mid-14th century, but not apparently after that time when the suburb seems to have shrunk or declined alongside the loss of population from plague and the French attacks of *c*.1340 and 1377.[27] However, the Wishe suburb appears to have subsequently expanded and the ferry road to have developed during the period of Rye's later boom between *c*.1490 and 1580 (*Chapter 5*). The Wishe had nevertheless been part of Rye as the medieval walls, gates and layout of the town were established.

The Development of Settlement at Rye

Limited archaeological investigation has been undertaken at Rye, but the development of settlement there can be considered from documentary sources and the street pattern, access points, strands and defences. The earliest evidence is the record of 64 townsfolk (*burgensi*) in Domesday Book, the development of the church and the market functions (*Chapter 1*). These townsfolk would have needed a location in which to dwell and trade and it is possible that their tenements were clustered adjacent to the church and market place. There were four shamells (stalls) in the market place during Edward I's reign.[28] Deeds of the early 14th century mention properties in or next to the market place, including a principal tenement. The market place, described as 'of the lord king', lay to the north of the church by 1374 and this was probably its earlier location. In 1374 Reginald Bocher (butcher) had a stall (*selda*) near the east side of the market place, which was later held by Stephen de Wye, described as a butcher of Rye, but whose surname suggests his origins in Wye in east Kent.[29] The market place in Market Street and the Butchery was strongly associated with the sale of meat and leather, important Rye trades which are frequently represented among the occupations (*Chapter 4*).[30] The medieval market area may also have included an area to the north west of the church which later became part of Red Lion Yard. In this area land appears to have been reserved too for courts (the Courton) and, perhaps, for an official local headquarters of the seigneurial lord (*Chapter 5*). The temporary stalls of the 13th-century market place were replaced by more permanent structures and enclosures between the 14th and the early 16th centuries.[31] The town's second market place, for fish, was at the Strand (below) which grew greatly in significance from the late 15th century as it supplied the town's expanding population.

The Medieval Street Pattern

The street layout of Rye was influenced by the location of the early access routes and the fixing of the entrance points as the walls and gates were developed in the 13th and 14th centuries (below). The parish church was also a fixed point within the street layout from the mid- to late 12th century. On maps and at first sight, the street layout of Rye appears rectilinear with some streets intersecting roughly at right angles to one another. However the layout does not form a rigid grid and the layout is dominated by three principal east-west aligned streets with short, randomly placed, lesser streets (Figure 8.1). The three main streets were, however, by no means straight and were disjointed in nature, as their names reflect. They were known by the 16th century as Longer or Lower Street (now High Street and the Mint), Middle Street (now Mermaid Street and Market Square or the Butchery) and Watchbell Street, part of which is formed by Church Square. The arrangement of the three principal streets is similar to that of medieval New Romney which in the 11th and 12th centuries had a simple layout including a beach trackway, which later became the 'old' high street, and a small network of roads around St Lawrence's church. In the early 13th century, however, the streets of New Romney were re-laid out with a new high street running roughly parallel to the old one, a third parallel street, and a widened market place and short cross streets at variable distances apart. The principal streets and cross streets give an impression of a rectilinear plan at New Romney, and it was assumed by Beresford that this derived from the immediate post-Conquest period. This proves not to have been the case, and similarly no assumptions can be made that the roughly rectilinear layout of Rye derives from one period of planning and laying out of its streets at the time of its foundation.[32] The same is true of Ludlow, Shropshire, a classic 'planted' town, as plan analysis of the rectilinear street layout has demonstrated.[33] Rye should not therefore be included as an example of a grid system in discussions of 'planned' urban sites.

The names of some of the medieval streets of Rye are known but the sources do not allow them to be located: *Le Pygge Lane, Schytbourglane, Lane leading to M[i]lnerstrete, Merstret* and *Potepiriestrete*.[34] Some of these may equate to the short cross streets or lanes which appear in deeds but are not usually specifically named; instead such lanes are identified by reference to the streets which they linked. For example, 'the lane to the market' which is known in 1305 and 1500 may equate with 'the comon street leading from the longer street to the market' of 1657, presumably modern Lion Street.[35] Despite their lack of names, the deeds which mention lanes give a vivid picture of the nature of Rye at certain periods. For example, in 1476 a woman of New Winchelsea and her husband made a grant of property to four men of Rye and two others from Romney Marsh, John Lye of Brookland and Henry Bate of Lydd. Bate was from an important family of butcher-graziers of Lydd in the late 15th century.[36] The property was a messuage (a house perhaps with garden or courtyard) in Rye 'with shops in the Market Place and a small stable annexed'; while the messuage, shops and stable were all part of the same transaction they were not necessarily located together on the ground. The messuage itself was described as surrounded by the lands of various people and by a highway on the north. On the west side of the shops and stable in the market place lay another shop; on the east side lay a lane from the cemetery to the market place, and on the north the market place. Although it is not possible to locate the messuage, shops and stable precisely on the ground, their nature as an economic unit is clear. When women feature in deeds in this locality it is usually because they have inherited property, and houses were often sublet, both of which may apply here.[37] Henry Bate of Lydd, and perhaps John Lye of Brookland too, may have required the shops in the market place of Rye as an outlet for the animals they raised on Romney Marsh, and the small stable for their horses on market day.

The Strands at Rye: East Strand, West Strand and La Nesse

The first mention of a strand at Rye occurs in 1272 when the name of Michael de la Stronde was recorded among the fines of the Rye town court.[38] The strand also appears in the rental of Edward I's reign (1272-1307) as a tenement held by John de Ihame which had formerly been held by Bate atte Stronde.[39] In the first half of the 14th century, documents refer to two strands, *Estronde* and *Westronde*, on the low-lying areas on either side of the promontory on which the main part of Rye town stood.

Estronde appears in deeds in the early 14th century and was the location of a salt house and mill (*Hegeteghe*) both of which also appear in the Edward I rental.[40] The rents of three tenements at *Estronde* are given in the bailiff's account of Rye for 1343: Hugo de Rumenale (Romney) paid a quit rent of 2d. for the tenement formerly of Henry near *Estronde*; Joanna daughter of John Ryd paid 2d. for her tenement near *Estronde*; the heirs of Pharon Johan paid 6d. for their tenement named *Storme* near *Estronde*; and Thomas Muryel [Muriel] paid 6d. for his tenement near *Estronde* which had formerly been Stephen Packet's.[41] Thomas Muriel was a pirate. Two barges belonging to Muriel and others of Rye were used in an attack on merchants travelling between Dover and Calais, and their goods taken as far away as Weymouth in the barges.[42] Barges were shallow-draught vessels and it is likely that Muriel and the other Rye mariners beached their barges at *Estronde*.

Eighteen tenements were described as 'submerged' in the Rye bailiffs' account of 1342 including *Hegetege*, which was a mill lying at *Estronde* (below), and *Estronde* itself.[43] Documents concerned with the establishment of the Austin Friary on its first site in this area make clear that the submersion was caused by tidal action (*Chapter 6*). The 18 tenements were still listed as submerged in 1344 and also in a schedule of decayed rents dated simply to Edward III's reign (1327-77). These sources do not give the date when these tenements, *Estronde* and the mill became submerged, nor do they suggest that they were ever recovered.[44] *Estronde* was sited below what appears to have been a cliff-top promontory, *La Nesse*. *La Nesse* perhaps also referred to an area of rocks below the cliff which may be identified with a degraded outcrop of rocks known in the 17th century as Gungarden Rocks. This projected eastwards from the south-eastern corner of town. *La Nesse* was an important area in medieval Rye and its inhabitants formed part of the town elite. There are references to nine people named atte Nesse or de la Nesse in Rye between 1258 and 1341. For example, Thomas de la Nesse was among seven 'barons of the Port of Winchelese and la Rye' who were deputed to attack the king's enemies in the Channel in 1267 (*Chapter 4*).[45] Thomas de la Nesse was described as a clerk in 1311. His daughter Sarra transacted property with the town clerk of Rye of this period, Peter de Heghtone, using her own seal on the deed which confirmed the transaction. Thomas atte Nesse, brother of Sarra, was mayor in 1341.[46] Nicolas Paulyn, mayor in 1338, had a house at *La Nesse* which was taken down and rebuilt in 1341, presumably on the cliff, due to the submersion of the lower ground.[47] *La Nesse* gave its name to a ward of the town until at least 1415, with the other named wards given as Watermelle, Ward outside the Gate and Market Ward.[48] In the 16th century the wards were increased in number and known by different names since the topography and administrative structure of Rye had been affected firstly by inundation, erosion and slippage where *Estronde* and *La Nesse* lay, secondly by the mortality caused by plague and raids and the consequent economic downturn until the later 15th century, and finally by a temporary boom and period of population growth.

La Westronde (west strand), named in opposition to *Estronde*, is known in 1353, with a reference to messuages at *la Westronde* in Rye which had formerly belonged to John Eppelman. These messuages (dwellings or other buildings) were conveyed from John Peytevyn to James Boniour of Rye and Sarah his wife for a payment of 10s. a year, a high rent. There was a covenant which required James and Sarah to keep the buildings 'roofftight' and watertight, i.e. fully protected from rain and wind, a necessary requirement for buildings on a strand.[49] From this date onwards documents no longer differentiate between the east strand and the west strand, suggesting that only the latter survived, and supporting the evidence of submersion of the tenements at east strand in the 1340s. Thus as the east strand below the east cliff was lost to the sea in the mid-14th century, the west strand became the town's main landing place and quayside for fishing and trading vessels, the one later known simply as 'the Strand'. The evidence from the late medieval period about the Strand is limited but shows the economic activities known from earlier still occurring, i.e. fishing and the import of salt (*Chapter 3*), and the town government paying out small sums for routine maintenance of the quay there. In 1448 the town government sent for Janyn, a carpenter of Ewhurst, to come and inspect the quay on the strand and paid for twigs, probably brushwood, to 'make' or repair it.[50] Between 1474 and 1476 the town paid Edward Carpenter 20d. for materials and labour in repairing the quay and also in making the stocks.[51] In 1466 an important grant of a vacant piece of land at the Strand (Lestronde) was made by the mayor, Babilon Grauntford, jurats and commonalty to Robert Crowche of Rye in return for a rent for 2s. a year. The parcel was 34 feet by 20 feet and a 'shop' was subsequently erected on it.[52] This was probably a forerunner of the many grants of vacant parcels on the Strand side of Rye just outside the wall there which were made in increasing numbers from the 1480s.[53] Grauntford also paid 12d. rent to the town government for his own workshop on the Strand, and 6s. 8d. for dues on a vessel laden with salt which docked there. Robert Hekke, a ripier (a carrier of fresh fish by pack-horses), paid the same amount 'for his heap upon the Stronde', that is the due paid by fishermen to the town for landing fish on the quayside.[54]

The town government had a new quayside created at the Strand in 1480 and new shops built there in the mid-1480s, as Rye entered a period of growth and investment.[55] A shop was a workshop or 'a room or building used as a place of business by a victualer, craftsman, etc'.[56] Some of those on the Strand were used for the fish trade, with, for example, shops at the 'Fishmarket Place' being described as near the Strand in 1498.[57] The rents of assize of thirteen or more of such shops were noted in a rental of 1575, representing these early shops at the Strand.[58] The rents varied from 16d. to 20d. to, exceptionally, 12s. One was held by the heirs of John Potten, who included his son Thomas, a wealthy fisherman who lived in Landgate ward.[59] Another of these shops was held by Thomas Radford, cordwainer (*Chapter 5*).

In the mid-1540s two new rows of shops were built at the strand, some with lofts and garrets above them. The first row had five shops, 10 lofts and two garrets, one specified as being over the loft. The ratio of shops to lofts suggests that each shop had two lofts. The shops, lofts and garrets were mostly let separately, although one man rented both a loft and the garret over it. Their rents were not fixed rents of assize like those of the earlier shops but were economic rents: shops were let at 16s. a year each and lofts and garrets at 8s. each. All those holding lofts and garrets whose occupations are known were fishermen, fishing masters or mariners.[60] Of those holding shops, one was a wholesale fishmonger ('feter') and another a jurat who acted as royal purveyor of fish and was an 'ost', who both sold fish wholesale and acted as an agent for the London Company of Fishmongers.[61] The second row of shops comprised six shops, and nine lofts of which one had a garret, and a 'great house and garret'. The rents of the nine lofts and one shop were 8s., and of the other five shops 16s. The tenant of the great house and garret paid 11s. and the tenant of the one loft with a garret 12s. Two shops were held by Robert Brown and Richard Daneill, both wholesale fishmongers, with Richard Daneill also being a principal agent for cloth exporters and London importers. Another shop was held by Robert Daneill, a tailor and wool draper, and the other shops by William Ratcliff, a jurat, tailor and vintner, Peter Kelinge, a yeoman, merchant and shipowner, and John Belveridge, a fishing master and ship owner.[62] The lofts and garrets and great house were occupied, like those of the first row, by fishing masters and mariners.

Other property recorded at the Strand in 1575 gives a further clear indication of its nature at that time. A property described as stables at the Strand was held by members of the Wodd family, either John Wodd, a mariner, or Matthew, a fisherman, or Robert, a merchant of Strandgate ward.[63] Two men jointly held a tenement on the new quay at the Strand and also a 'ground' there, paying large rents, respectively 30s. and 16s. There was a storehouse whose tenant paid a rent of 1d., and a piece of land enclosed to one of the shops with the same rent. These were rents of assize perhaps indicating that this storehouse was of the early period like the 13 or more shops whose tenants also paid rents of assize. The town itself had a storehouse erected in 1552 which brought in a much more substantial rent until the early 1590s. All traders had to pay to store their goods at the town's storehouse or pay for the right to store them in their own garrets. Another new 'Great Storehouse' was erected in 1555 and a crane in 1556. The custom house also stood on the Strand.[64] In 1575 Nicholas Harrold paid a rent of 3s. 4d. on a void piece of ground next to the custom house. Harrold was a yeoman, merchant and an agent for London cloth importers, and this piece of ground was perhaps used for storage.[65] Similarly in 1587 Robert Castleden, mercer, held a piece of 'empty ground' at the Strand next to Thomas Byrchett's shop on the quay.[66] Thus until the late 16th century the quayside at the Strand was an active centre of mainly maritime activity, largely fishing, together with commerce which depended on water transport, notably cloth importing and exporting. However Rye was reaching the end of this period of economic boom and many men in Rye diversified into various craft, victualling and mercantile activities at this time in an attempt to make a living.[67] Mr Robert Carpenter is a notable example. He was once a wealthy jurat and mayor who held the stables at the Strand following the Wodd family and was occupied in brewing, an occupation entailing heavy capital expenditure. By the end of the 16th century Carpenter was failing to pay his yearly rent to the town and could not afford, or did not bother, to have a noisome dunghill cleared away from the door of his stable. He actively sought the repayment of his dues from a London grocer to whom wares had been sent but he eventually died in poverty.[68]

A rental of 1670 seems to reflect the severe downturn in the economy of Rye and the silting of the harbour which occurred between c.1590 and 1610 (*Chapter 5*), perhaps exacerbated by the occurrence of epidemic disease in the early 1590s. This rental records rents by ward under the heading of king's rents of assize paid to the king's bailiff, but it is not clear whether it is directly comparable with the rental of 1575. Nevertheless it can be noted that only two rents were recorded under Strandgate ward. One was 14d. for a tenement (house) near the Strandgate; the other rent was 7d. for property in the area between the western end of Longer Street and the town wall described as 'a piece of ground where late stood a tenement'.[69]

The Mills of Rye

Medieval Rye possessed both water mills and windmills which were important assets to the monarch and the individuals who held them. In the early 13th century Ellis de Rye had a lease of mills near Rye, probably water mills (*Chapter 4*). The suggestion of a least one water mill at Rye is strengthened by an event in 1234 in which Ralph the son of Nigel the miller was drowned 'in the water of Rye'.[70] On 20 January 1256 Walter de Winchelese, clerk of Old Winchelsea and Rye, was commissioned to farm (lease) the assets and profits of these towns, including their mills, for six years. He was to render 220 marks (£146 13s. 4d.) a year and maintain the mills at his own cost, but it was agreed that he would not be answerable for any misadventure to the mills.[71] On 5 November 1273 a royal order was made to the bailiff of Winchelsea and Rye 'to cause the mills of La Rye and the sea walls (*wallis*) of the same to be repaired and amended where necessary'.[72] The linking of the mills and the sea walls in this royal order suggests that these were tide mills.

Besides the mills which Ellis leased from Fécamp Abbey and which Walter de Winchelese leased from the king after Rye and Old Winchelsea were resumed into royal hands, there were other mills belonging to individuals within Rye. These can be identified from several sources. One was a windmill on the cliff at *La Nesse*. The deed of 1358 in which this windmill appears gives the *portum maris* as lying to its south.[73] The term *portum maris* appears in the records of many medieval ports and seems on occasion to refer to the bounds of port activity, but in this Rye deed should probably be interpreted simply as a reference to the port or sheltered anchorage shared between Rye and New Winchelsea, which lay on the south-eastern side of Rye.[74] In 1330 this mill on the cliff was described in a conveyance as 'lately built' by Richard Portesmouth of Rye upon the cliff near *La Nesse* in Rye.[75] In that year

Richard's widow, Juliana, conveyed her part of the mill and its associated lands and ways to Margery, the widow of Thomas Hallere of Rye. Margery was to pay two loads of good wheat each year to Juliana or her representative. The possibility that the mill might be moved from the site on the cliff during Juliana's lifetime was envisaged, and if this was done Juliana was to pay her share of the cost. The division of the profits of, and responsibility for, the mill between the two women suggests they were relatives, probably sisters.

There are two or possibly three men called Richard (de) Portesmouth known between 1272 and 1312, sometimes distinguished as junior and senior, and as Richard the mayor (*Chapter 5*). In the rental of Edward I's reign, the heirs of Richard de Portesmuthe junior were responsible for the rent of a tenement next to the *melflet*, i.e. mill fleet or mill stream. This suggests that a water mill may have been a predecessor to the recently built windmill on the cliff at *La Nesse*. Margery's husband, Thomas Hallere, had held a tenement on *La Estronde* below *La Nesse* in 1323, suggesting that *Estronde* was the location of such a watermill, with the windmill on the cliff replacing it because of the submersion of the east strand by 1342. Milling and selling wheat in a town like Rye was a crucial and profitable activity. Richard de Portesmuthe junior had a tenement in the market of Rye where much of the wheat was no doubt sold.[76] The families with interests in the east strand and the mill on *Estronde* and later on the cliff were the Portesmuthes, the Halleres and also the Rakeles. These families were among the wealthy and governing elite of Rye. Reginald de Rakele of Rye and his wife Matilda held a house which lay between two tenements (holdings) at *Estronde*, those of Thomas Hallere and one John Pocok. A highway, i.e. a public route, lay alongside the Rakeles' house at *Estronde*. In 1323, before the submersion of the east strand, the Rakeles conveyed their house to another couple.[77] Reginald de Rakele was from the family which produced the earliest known mayor of Rye. The surnames (by-names) of families holding property at *Estronde* and *La Nesse*, Hallere, Portesmouth, Rakele and Nesse, do not appear under Nesse Ward in the 1415 scot list.[78] These families were among those which disappeared from Rye during the mortality of the late 14th century and were replaced by a new town elite (*Chapter 6*).[79]

Three further mills in Rye are recorded in the rental dated between 1272 and 1307: one 'on the cliff', one of the Marchant family and one called *heheteyhe*.[80] These are considered in turn. The mill on the cliff was held by Robert Vincent, for which he paid a quit rent of 2½d. Jacob Marchant held the second mill but two other men, Robert Marchant and Robert Michel, were responsible for paying the rent. These two men were probably his heirs, perhaps his son and son-in-law, paying respectively 20d. and 6d. rent each. Robert Michel also held a principal tenement in Rye for a rent of 12d. and another tenement for 3d. These were considerably higher than most Rye rents, some of which were as low as a halfpenny.[81] Besides the mill Jacob Marchant paid 6d. rent 'for the salt house which was had previously been Henry Bone's'. This might possibly suggest that the Marchants' mill was in a low-lying location near a salt house, perhaps on *Estronde*. Members of the Bone family also held land to the east of Iden where salt was made.[82]

In the rental Geoffrey Solas or Solaz was recorded as paying a rent of 10d. for the third mill, called *heheteyhe*. He appears as a witness to numerous Rye deeds between 1305 and 1321 as part of the town government.[83] In 1321 *Heghetheghe* was described as a windmill. This mill was called *Heytehy* at *Estronde* in Rye in a deed of 1325, and *Heghetegh* in Rye in 1338. In 1321 John Kyttey and Martha his wife of Rye acquired a quarter of the profits of the windmill called *Heghetheghe*. The consideration of 40s. which they paid for this emphasises the true economic value of the Rye mills as compared with the small fixed quit rents which were due to the king's bailiff every year.[84] John and Martha Kyttey also had a salt house (*domo salina*) at *La Estronde* from 1320.[85] A deed of 1325 in which the mill is passed on to John Kyttey's heirs specifies that the mill called *Heytehy* lay at *Estronde*, indicating its general location near the Kytteys' salt house there. By 1325 John Kyttey had died and his rights in the mill passed to his sons John junior and Geoffrey. They passed their rights to their mother Martha who was still alive, John junior doing so in 1325 and Geoffrey in 1338.[86] Although the mill *Heghetegh* was still a valuable asset in 1338, by 1342 both *hegetehe* and *Estronde* were submerged by the tides. At that time one other mill and 52 tenements were additionally described as burnt by the French, so that the king received no rent from them.[87] Besides the mills recorded in the rental, one Henry Sliphe also owed 12d. rent for 'mill land' which may have been close to one of the mills. In *c*.1260 Sliphe also held a tavern which was described as being at the strand (*Chapter 4*).[88] In ports such as Rye, as at Sandwich and New Romney, taverners and innkeepers were important not only in providing accommodation but were also business contacts for traders across the Channel.[89]

The important economic assets of medieval Rye were the natural features and the structures built on them which enabled the local resources, salt, fish, water and wind power, to be exploited. Mills and salt houses were vital assets for a medieval port and town like Rye to supply the inhabitants and the local and export markets with grain, and the fishing industry with salt for preservation (*Chapter 4*). A small number of individuals and families held one or more of these assets which formed the basis of their wealth and their dominance of the town government. Those who held taverns where trading deals could be made such as Henry Sliphe, William the taverner (Tabernar) and Brice Palmer were among the richest men in town (*Chapter 4*).

After the 1350s the name of only one mill, *Hothemill* in the parish of Rye, appears in the medieval records, in 1480.[90] This mention of only one mill between the late 1340s and 1480 probably reflects the loss of population and economic activity in the town. *Hothemill* was linked to holdings at both Rye and Iden and may have been on north side of town.[91] From the early 16th century, the number of mills increased greatly. In the 1510s Robert Shepherd (I) of Rye owned land at Windmill Hill, presumably Rye Hill. The Prowez map of *c*.1570 shows two post windmills on the wall at the western end of St Mary's Marsh (*Chapter 9*) and two post mills with fantails between Land Gate and Playden Church, perhaps intended to represent those on Rye Hill. These are labelled 'The mylles at begger hill'.[92] In the late 16th century there were windmills to the north west of the Wishe suburb (the Strand mills) at the site of a new sluice (*Chapter 9*).[93] In 1583 a carpenter of Rye, John Stonham, made an agreement with Hugh Robinson of New Romney, Kent, miller, about the rebuilding of a windmill at a place called 'the mylles' in Rye, which was leased from Thomas Colbrand, jurat.[94] There continued to be several windmills located on Rye Hill to the north of the town and three windmills on the flat land around the town.[95]

The Defences of Rye: Introduction

Rye's need for defences developed from the early 13th century as it eclipsed New Romney as an important entry point to England (*Chapter 1*).[96] An awareness of the need to fortify Rye was expressed repeatedly throughout the 13th and 14th centuries and on until the late 16th century, not least because of the important anchorage, the Camber, to the south east of Rye (*Chapter 2*); it not only sheltered trading and naval vessels near Rye but was part of the access by water to the town, so that defences, whether built or artillery, remained important. Rye's significance as a port revived under the Tudor monarchs, and it provided several ships on five occasions between 1481 and 1557 mainly for transporting troops (*Chapter 5*).[97] Rye had a large mercantile fleet by tonnage, ranked 11th in the country, which needed protection as it lay at anchor. Rye harbour, which consisted of both the Camber and Rye Creek (the Strand area) was thus in full use in the 16th century. The harbour and the defences which protected it from attack received attention and support from both the monarch and the town government (below). However, the Camber was damaged by the dumping of ballast, the reclamation of marshes and the consequent failure of the ebb tides to scour the harbour in the mid-15th century. In 1548 it was claimed that the Camber had once been able to hold 300 or 400 ships but by then only 30 or 40 with difficulty.[98] It became known, perhaps contemptuously, as the Puddle. In the late 16th century only small (fishing) vessels used the Strand on the western side, with large vessels remaining anchored in the Camber and being provisioned by small boats sailing out from the east side of town, but the need to defend the harbour was largely over.

The Organisation of Defences: The 'Castle', Walls and Gates

The hilltop site on which Rye was built was to some extent naturally defended against enemy attack. It was partly surrounded by tidal water and protected on its eastern, southern and south-western sides by cliffs, although over time they became rather degraded in places (Figures 8.2, 8.3). Under conditions of war from the early 13th century onwards, additional defence in the form of walls and towers would have been desirable at the south-eastern corner where the cliff is less defined, and here the Baddings or Ypres Tower was constructed. However, the principal weak zone was the northern and north-western side of Rye where the hill slopes naturally down to marshland. Once Rye's walls were constructed, apparently over a period of time, they ran on the northern side of the town from the eastern side of the Landgate to the Strand, a length of approximately 575 metres. A surviving length of c.60 metres is currently visible from Cinque Ports Street, its nature suggesting different periods of construction. Also visible from Cinque Ports Street is the base of an 'interval tower' to the west of the Postern Gate. There was one western bastion and possibly one eastern bastion, neither of which survive. Between the Landgate and the western bastion there was an extra-mural ditch (fosse), usually filled with water.[99]

The first definite indication of the intention to raise military defences at Rye occurs in 1226 when Henry III opened negotiations with the Abbey of Fécamp in Normandy for an exchange of the town: one reason given was that the king wished to build a castle there.[100] In 1249 Henry III committed the income of a wardship and certain lands including the honour of Hastings to Peter of Savoy in order that he should 'fortify the castles of Hastings and la Rye'; more specifically he was to fortify Hastings first and Rye afterwards if there was sufficient money.[101] Baddings (later Ypres) Tower, which occupies an exposed location in the south-eastern corner of the town, is thus usually considered to be Rye's castle and to date from the 13th century (Figure 8.4).[102] However there is an absence of closely dateable architectural features and it may perhaps have been built as late as the second half of the 14th century, at which time the name of the Baddings family was attached to it. Richard Baddyng was a ship owner and mayor, MP and bailiff of Rye between 1352 and 1371, and

John Baddyng, his immediate descendant, fulfilled the same roles in various years between 1386 and 1407, as well as that of churchwarden in 1399 (*Chapter 5*).[103] A bond for the large sum of £120 was made in 1392 between John Baddyng and four stonemasons from Kent. It is likely to relate to a building contract, probably the Baddings Tower or perhaps the town walls.[104] The first stonemason, William Londoneys, came from St Margaret's parish, Canterbury, although his surname Londoneys indicates his family origins in London. Canterbury was a centre of building expertise in stone in the late 14th century at the Cathedral, Castle, city walls and the Westgate under the royal master mason Henry Yevele.[105] The three other stonemasons came from East Malling and Boxley, which were centres of expertise in the supply and cutting of sandstone, of which the Baddings Tower was largely built.[106] The role of the tower seems to have been that of a blockhouse attached to, and projecting forward from, an isolated length of town wall which protected this vulnerable part of the town. In the 16th century the Baddings Tower doubled as the town's courthouse and possibly its prison, as did the Landgate.[107] The existence of the king's prison of Rye is mentioned in 1261 when Ralf and Margaret Brichewald and William and Agnes Page were detained there in connection with the death of Thomas Rumbirg.[108] The location of this prison is not given and so this early reference does not assist in dating either the Baddings Tower or Landgate.

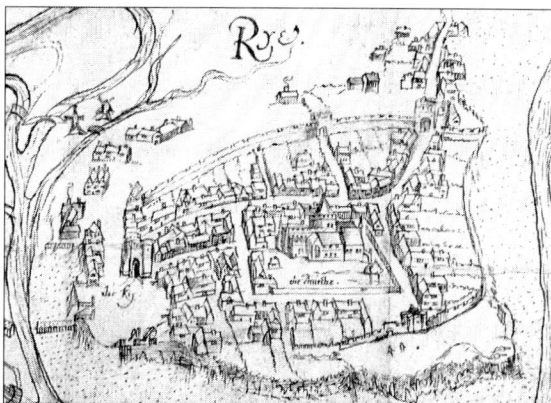

Fig. 8.2 Extract from the 'Plott of the Towne of Rye' of 1591, TNA MPF 1/3.

Having acquired the town from Fécamp, Henry III evidently wished to see it adequately protected with walls against enemy attack, for in 1246 an instruction was issued to Bertram de Croyl (Criol), trusted courtier of Henry III, that 'where necessary' he was to make repairs to the walls around the towns of Rye and Old Winchelsea. Criol was also instructed to entrust the guarding of the towns to those whom he believed effective and faithful.[109] This instruction suggests that walls already existed and it appears clear that some length of stone wall was in position by the 1270s. In 1272 one Denis (*Dyonisis*) de Stonwall is named as the tenant of land in the Rye bailiff's account as paying 4s. rent.[110] In *c*.1285 Wymund atte Walle witnessed a Rye deed.[111] The rental of the reign of Edward I (1272-1307) also refers to a *walle lapidee*, i.e. a stone wall.[112]

The town gate also featured in a personal name, that of Pharon *de porta* (*c*.1260), who a little later was called Pharon atte Gate in the town rental of Edward I's reign (1272-1307).[113] The rental refers to three properties 'outside the gate' and it appears that this was the North or Land Gate, protecting the landward link from Rye. The town also had a man at this period whose job it was to guard or keep the gate, Adam portour.[114]

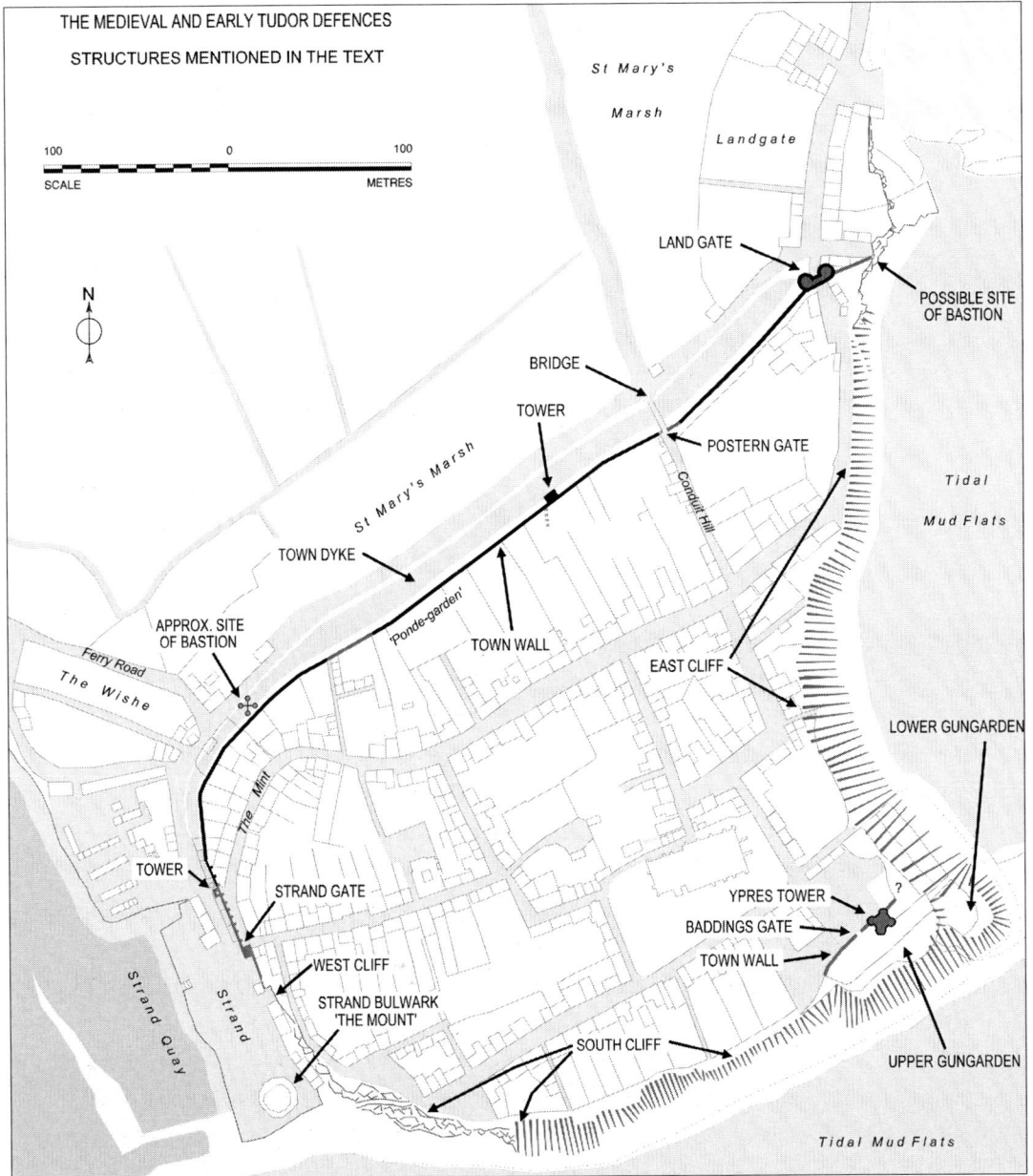

THE MEDIEVAL AND EARLY TUDOR DEFENCES

STRUCTURES MENTIONED IN THE TEXT

Fig. 8.3 The Medieval and Early Tudor Defences.

Deeds of 1323 and 1325 refer to property 'outside the gate'.[115] Another deed of 1335 refers to 'a tenement lying within the north gate of Rye', i.e. Landgate. This specific reference to a north gate may suggest the existence of the south (Strand) gate also at that time.[116] There is no documentary evidence of the early existence of Strandgate, but it is mentioned in the town accounts as the Water Gate (*porta aquatica*) in 1448 when it was extensively repaired.[117] In 1473 the Strandgate was described as lying next to a section of town wall.[118] It was partly demolished in the late 18th century and completely by 1815.[119]

The Landgate (Figure 3.3) presents an impressive north-facing elevation to visitors, but is far more austere on its townward side and has very little depth viewed sideways on. It appears as an entrance arch flanked by two round towers which project forward on the extra-mural face and rise from stepped, two-tiered plinths. The Landgate is a three-storeyed structure faced in mixed Tilgate and brown ironstone rubble. It is usually said to have been built *c*.1340 and the existence of references to the 'gate' by *c*.1260 and in the rental of 1272-1307 and specifically to the north gate in 1335 might suggest that it replaced an earlier structure; alternatively it may be that the date of *c*.1340 should be revised. It may be that the proposed 'castle' of 1226 (above) refers not to the Baddings Tower but to the Land Gate.

As is often the case with other medieval towns, it is not possible to determine for Rye precise dates or periods when stone walls or towers were built, altered or

Fig. 8.4 The Baddings or Ypres Tower (after *VCH Sussex*, 9).

improved. The sections of wall which survive between the Landgate and the site of the Strandgate indicate that wall building was not a process of completing a long stretch at one time, but was more *ad hoc*.[120] The early walls may have comprised a mixture of timber and stone sections in parts next to the fosse (ditch). After the commencement of war in 1337, there were several grants of 'murage' to the town government of Rye, allowing the inhabitants to be taxed to pay for the building or maintenance of walls. However, such grants could also refer to sea defence walls; at Old Winchelsea, for instance, in 1269, the grant was for 'the protection of the town on account of the peril continually threatening it through floods and the violence of the sea' and may refer to sea defences.[121] These defences in any case prevented the enemy's galleys getting close to Rye to attack, as the murage grant of 1348 noted, and so served both purposes.[122] A memorandum was made in the mid-14th century between the people of Rye, New Winchelsea, Hastings and the areas around on the state of their defences. Rye and Hastings had poor defences, and the people of Hastings were in great peril, apparently from archers. The defences of New Winchelsea were satisfactory and, significantly, it was noted that this town, at least, was not harbouring aliens.[123] The poor state of Rye's defences allowed it to be raided by the French in 1339. In 1369 the mayor and bailiffs resolved to impose a weekly charge on the inhabitants to enclose the town, referring to a recent raid which had taken place. The power to do so was granted by a royal 'licence to crenellate' which stated that the mayor and commonalty of Rye had shown that their town had recently been burned in the course of the war by the king's foreign enemies 'for lack of enclosure'. The mayor and commonalty had agreed among themselves a levy of 1½d. weekly on every 20s. of rent in the town, and ¼d. weekly on every 20s. of goods and money, to be applied to the enclosure of the town until it was complete. The king empowered the mayor and bailiffs to distrain on any of the townsfolk who would not pay their portion of the assessment.[124] The French returned again in 1377 with devastating results, although the town had been ordered the previous year to fortify the town, arm the inhabitants and prevent any of them from fleeing in fear of an attack.[125]

The Economics of Defence

On 15 September 1372 the mayor, bailiffs and commonalty of Rye were granted the profits (revenues) of the town as well as eight pounds of yearly rent from the manor of Iden for three years. This was to help them make 'certain walls, dykes, gates and palings in and around their town'.[126] This provoked protests from two parties who had already been assigned some of the profits of Rye and rents of Iden. There was a complaint within a week to the king from William Passelewe, 'seaman', of a cadet branch of the Pashley family which had provided the warden of Rye in 1324 in the person of Sir Edmund de Pashley (*Chapter 3*). William Passelewe had previously been granted 6d. a day for life from the revenues of Rye for his service to the king, equivalent to £9 2s. 6d. a year. Other evidence of Passelewe's finances on occasions between 1371 and 1395 when he was outlawed and imprisoned on a plea of debt suggests they were stretched in the late 14th century, perhaps as part of the economic downturn at Rye (*Chapter 6*).[127] In December 1372 there was also a complaint from Elizabeth, widow of John, Earl of Kent, and subsequently wife of Eustace Dabrichecourt, knight, who had received a grant of £4 16s. 8d. yearly from the profits of Rye and Iden at the time of her first marriage. The king ordered that Rye town continue to pay William Passelewe after the new grant to the town to help with the defences in 1372, but temporised over Elizabeth's grant which Rye town was refusing to pay.[128] In 1362, the nearest year for comparison, the rents of the free tenements of Rye had produced £10 5s., and those of the Courton and the king's ditch 5s.; landing dues, fishing customs, market tolls and court fines produced 45s. 8d., making a total of £12 15s. 8d.[129] It seems that if Rye town paid William Passelewe's 6d. a day, amounting to over £9 a year, there would have been little left for expenditure on walls, dykes, gates and palings from the profits of Rye. The rents of Iden would also have contributed £8 a year, or rather less (only £3 3s. 4d.) if Elizabeth Dabrichecourt eventually received her share of them. The profits of Rye which the town government received in the years after the Black Death were in any case down by 38 per cent, comparing 1362 with 1344, when the yearly profits had been nearly £20.[130]

Whatever Rye town did spend on defences after 1372 was largely ineffective against the severe raid of 1377, which according to the chronicler Walsingham involved as many as fifty ships and five thousand men. The town government apparently attributed the raid to traitors among the townsfolk rather than to inadequate defences.[131] Money may have been spent on works of timber such as palings, or perhaps only on part of the circuit of walls since in 1382 the barons, mayor and bailiffs undertook to build a wall of lime and stone within three years 'in the necessary places sufficient to enclose' the town, using the revenues of Rye which were re-granted.[132] There was to be a penalty of £100 if the mayor and commonalty failed to do so. The wall was not built as required by 1385 but the penalty was reduced by half because of the town's poverty which is evident from the bailiffs' accounts.[133] As a result of this poverty and after the 1377 raid the town may have relied mostly on the Baddings (Ypres) Tower, the Landgate and the Strandgate for defence. In any case no defences were effective if, as the mayor and bailiff suggested, some of the townsfolk were responsible for allowing the French to enter the town and wealthy men to be captured for ransom.[134]

Perhaps because of the town's poverty, the mayor and commonalty decided in 1430 to convey the Baddings Tower to a private individual as a dwelling, John de Iprys (Ypres). Access to the tower from the highway with horses, carts and wagons, was also granted and a reasonable amount of ground on the south of the tower as far as the cliff. This land was to be at least the same breadth as the tower. For the defence of the town in any time of future hostilities or war, the town government and a reasonable number of the commonalty were to be able to enter the tower, presumably for safety, provided they brought sufficient victuals with them.[135] The town's economic circumstances do not appear to have improved since in 1449 Tenterden was formally incorporated into the Cinque Ports confederation in order to help Rye with its ship service.[136] Tenterden included the important shipbuilding centre at Smallhythe which was eight miles upstream on the Rother from Rye. Here the great ship *Jesus* of 1,000 tons had been built for Henry V in 1416 and a balinger called the *George* of 120 tons, which was in royal service until 1423 when it was sold for £20.[137]

The Baddings Tower and an adjacent house and cellar were used between 1430 and 1452 as a private dwelling by John de Ypres, esquire, his wife Elizabeth and their servants, the tower becoming known by their surname. John's name appears as Jehan Ypres on his armorial seal, both names suggesting his origins in the Low Countries. The Ypres (Baddings) Tower was subsequently held by Thomas Stoghton, fishmonger of London, until about 1456. The access to the Ypres Tower by horses, carts and wagons which was specified in the 1430 grant suggests that the Ypres family and then Thomas Stoghton valued it for reasons of both status and practicality. Stoghton also had other tenements in Rye which he sublet, with one James Hyde of Rye collecting the rents between 1454 and 1456. In 1456 James Hyde enfeoffed a relative, John Hyde, and two local men, John Passhele of Rye and Thomas Wodeward of New Winchelsea, with the tower and other property. This suggests that the tower was already effectively being taken back into the town's control, or leased to the town, as does a reference in the chamberlains' account to the mayor and his brethren using it as a meeting place in connection with town ceremony and hospitality from 1475 to 1477. John Hyde and Joan Hyde, James Hyde's daughter, remained the owners of the Ypres Tower until 1477 when Thomas Lord Stanley, Steward of the King's Household, purchased it.[138] By 1495 the town had bought back the Ypres Tower (below).

From the mid-15th century, with the south coast towns again under threat and Calais the sole remnant of English possessions in France, the town of Rye looked to artillery, placed on its built defences, to ensure its safety. The Rye accounts make clear that the mayor and commonalty of the town anxiously kept their defences in readiness against anticipated French attacks. An alleged burning of the town by the French in 1448 appears to be unsupported by evidence, but the corporation was clearly expecting such an attack, for guns were provided at this time for the defences of the town. In 1453 the king sent a message to Rye to have a ship or two ready to keep the sea, that is to keep a look out. In the same year a pit was made beside the Landgate in which to lay a gun. In 1457 a gun was brought to Baddings, presumably to overlook the estuary from the south-eastern corner of the hilltop where the town's permanent gun garden was later established. French attacks were once more feared in 1459, at which time works were carried out at both the Landgate and Strandgate. This action was repeated in 1474 when the townsfolk paid 8d. for four watchmen to look out for the French outside the town.[139] A similar concern to watch and defend against the French was expressed at New Romney between 1385 and the 16th century, where the surviving town accounts cover a longer period than those of Rye. The references in the accounts to purchases of weaponry such as 'bows and arrows for Common House' and two guns with six chambers are echoed in the unusual finds of lead shot and a powder-measure cap on the New Romney sea front.[140]

During the closing decade of the 15th century and in the early 16th century, the need for the Ypres Tower as a site for weaponry was appreciated by the town because of the increased use of artillery on board ship. The town's growth in population and wealth allowed some investment in weapons. By the early years of the Tudor dynasty the town seems to have possessed at least three and possibly four pieces of ordnance, including a great serpentine. In 1493 two more guns were purchased and in 1513 a further two serpentines were acquired, each with three chambers and forelocks. At this time an arsenal of at least four guns was stored at Ypres Tower, which in 1495 had been bought back by the town. Further purchases and loans meant that by 1515 the town must have had 10 or 11 guns at its disposal.[141]

These new artillery defences within the town became concentrated in two locations: a gun garden on the cliff to the south of the Ypres Tower and a bulwark at the southern end of the Strand. Both were strategic locations for defence of the harbour and estuary. Some form of bulwark had probably existed on the Strand by 1491 and certainly it existed by 1513 when money was expended upon it. It was rebuilt as a 'new fortress' in 1544, in which year major improvements were also made to the Gun Garden at Ypres Tower. These included the construction of the

Lower Gun Garden and the making of a gate, called Baddings Gate, in the town wall adjacent to the tower so as to improve access. In order to store the munitions required by the ordnance as well as other weapons and armaments, an aisle in the parish church to the north of the chancel was taken over as a store.[142]

During this period the crown showed further interest in assisting both Rye and New Winchelsea by taking steps to protect the mouth of their shared harbour. With the heightened threat to the south coast Sir Edward Guldeford received a substantial contribution (£1300) between 1511 and 1514 from the crown towards making 'a bridge and tower' in Iham Marshes, on the end of a shingle spit at the entrance to the estuary. Sir Edward's father, Sir Richard, had been granted the lordship of Iham in 1486, on condition that he maintained a tower to be built in the marshes there within the next two years for the defence of the port. The payments in 1511 to 1514 suggest that this had not been done. It seems likely that even in 1514 the work remained incomplete, for in 1521 the corporation sent one of their leading barons, Mr Wymond, 'to sue for the same to be finished'. This was the forerunner to Henry VIII's new artillery fort, Camber Castle, initially known as Winchelsea Castle, which was finally completed in 1544. The Guldeford family's earlier tower was incorporated as the central tower of the new fort.[143]

Even with the substantial arsenal the town had at its disposal by the 1520s, it was nevertheless vulnerable. In 1528 it was reported that 'ships could lie at a stone cast from the town wall and the town would not be able to resist them'.[144] The chief area of concern must have been to the west of the town, adjacent to the Strand and Wishe (in Prowez's terms, Rye Creek).[145] Once past the ordnance stationed at the Ypres Tower and Strand Bulwark, enemy ships, at least small ones, could potentially sail into Rye Creek and wreak havoc. On account of the wide inter-tidal zone, the eastern side of the town probably gave less concern, but nonetheless was considered in need of some extra protection. In response to these problems, a series of stone-filled wooden groynes and jetties, in some instances with thorns as extra protection, were built in the inner harbour area and, in 1544, against the land bridge outside the Landgate. In 1558 palisade fencing was added on the seaward side of the land bridge, extending up to the Landgate, presumably to give protection against enemy fire to people using the causeway. There was a further expense for similar fencing in 1562. In the case of the groynes and jetties it is often difficult to differentiate within the accounts between harbour improvements, sea defences, and defence against enemy action, though peaks in expenditure during periods of known threat give some guidance.[146] In 1573 the mayor and jurats warned the Lord Warden of the Cinque Ports that the Landgate was in imminent danger of being washed away, which would take at least £1,000 to replace, and stated that they had spent £140 on a stone wall built to defend it from the force of the sea, i.e. tides.[147]

Despite the ever-increasing reliance upon artillery and the inevitable focus of this towards the harbour mouth to the south, Rye's north-facing wall between the 'Friars and the Bulwark' was white limed in 1501 at a cost of 2s. This small expenditure was perhaps to protect the wall or to make it more visible.[148] Water still flowed in the town ditch here which was from time to time scoured. When the town leased out a small vacant parcel of land outside the walls in 1511 it reserved the right of re-entry to repair and remake the walls if necessary. The section of the town ditch immediately to the west of the Landgate was still in water in 1511.[149] Sections of the wall which had fallen into the ditch were rebuilt in 1513, at which time the top of the Landgate was defoliated and repaired. Major works were underway on the wall in 1544, showing that even at this late date not all the town's efforts were directed towards its artillery. This work included the section of wall to the east of Landgate, extending up to the cliff edge. One area of wall was evidently strengthened to carry ordnance: this may have been at the rear of Mr Eston's property where it is known that ordnance was placed. Two pieces of ordnance were sited at the Landgate in 1557, whilst new portcullises were fitted to both the Landgate and Strandgate in 1559. This was part of what appears to have been a major programme of repairs to the town wall and ditch, which included cleaning, and perhaps deepening, the town ditch. In 1588, during the Armada scare, both the Gun Garden and Strand Fortress were repaired and at this time 'gunholes' arched with brick were made through the walls of the Landgate and work was undertaken to 'hedge in the flanker there'.[150] However generally from this time onwards concern for defence at Rye diminished. Already by 1576 'new buildings' had been erected 'along the town ditch', in the area near the Wishe. Van Dyck's drawing indicates that in the early 1630s the section of town ditch to the west of Landgate had largely been filled in. In this area the drawing indicates that the wall had by then lost its crenellations, despite their depiction in the Jeake plan of 1666, although the section of wall to the west of the postern gate still retained its crenellations.[151]

The surviving defensive structures at Rye are the Landgate and Ypres Tower, and part of the curtain wall. A bastion in Cinque Ports Street still remains although it is reduced in height and mostly hidden by later buildings. A section of wall near Market Street was demolished soon after 1766 and the length against The Mint was totally rebuilt in the 19th century as the eastern wall of a new building. Of the Tudor defences, the bulwark or fort on the Strand survived as an earthwork called The Mount in 1666, but was subsequently removed to make way for a warehouse. Limited earthworks are still visible in the Gun Garden.

Fig. 9.1 St Mary's Marsh is the large area between Rye town and the name 'John Prowez' on this map of *c*.1572 (see also Plate V). North is at the lower edge.

CHAPTER 9

St Mary's Marsh:
The Physical and Historical Evidence

Introduction

St Mary's Marsh is an important area of land whose history illustrates developments in the immediate vicinity of the town of Rye over many centuries. The name St Mary's Marsh has been given in both the past and present to the area just to the north of the hill on which Rye stands. The usage of the term is not precise but generally includes some or all of the area from the Landgate on the north-east side of the town to Rye Creek on the north west.[1] St Mary's Marsh was of great significance to the medieval town and the parish church, and also to individuals concerned with large-scale reclamation in the 16th and 17th centuries. Reclamation of the western end of St Mary's Marsh at this time was entwined with the plans of the town government to prevent the decay of Rye harbour, producing a multitude of records.[2] The physical, historical, topographical and cartographic evidence has therefore been re-examined to produce a detailed interpretation of this important marshland area between the 11th and 17th centuries.

North Marys or Northmarays: The 11th to the 14th Centuries

Between the 11th and 14th centuries St Mary's Marsh was known as *North Marys* or *Northmarays* (Plate V, Figure 9.1). It was of value to Fécamp Abbey as an asset of the parish church. North Marsh was a freshwater marsh or peatlands lying on the western side of the land bridge and the road out of Rye (Figure 8.1). North Marsh is first recorded by name in May 1247 when the liberty of Rye was resumed from Fécamp into royal hands. Henry III resumed Fécamp's property including the advowson of the church and the fourth part of North Marsh with its rent of 3s. 9d.

However, in June 1247 he agreed that Fécamp should continue to receive a payment of 13 marks a year from St Mary's church and its assets, specifically from North Marsh, a payment which it had received from the priest of the church since the late 12th century.[3] In 1333 Edward III ordered an examination of the banks in *Northmersh* by Rye following the dramatic flooding of the area in the late 13th century which had occurred widely across Romney Marsh and up the River Rother.[4]

The historic physical environment of this vicinity was investigated in August 2007. The investigation focused on the areas on either side of two causeways or embankments leading north out of Rye: the land bridge, i.e. the route towards Playden (A268), and the Grove causeway or, more properly, embankment. This embankment ran from the road now called Rope Walk along The Grove to the foot of Deadmans Lane (Figure 9.2). Boreholes were sunk using a gouge auger at the landbridge and the Grove embankment by Professor Martyn Waller and Michael Grant of the University of Kingston.[5] They found a two metre layer of silty clays representing an occurrence of marine or brackish conditions during the historical period. This was not precisely dateable but they judged that it most probably occurred after *c*.A.D. 700 and in fact probably as a result of the mid- to late 13th-century storms, with the bulk of the silty clays being deposited quite rapidly after these storms. The silty clays were found on both the east and west sides of the Grove embankment.[6] The presence of the silty clays on both sides indicates that the embankment was constructed after this period of marine or brackish conditions. The borehole evidence also indicated that from about 1000 B.C. onwards the marshlands in this area would have been dry enough to 'almost certainly have been used for grazing animals and may have been cropped for reeds and sedges'.[7] This fits well with the documentary evidence of the financial value of *North Marys* or *Northmarays* to Fécamp as the lord of Rye which is known as soon as relevant records begin. The townsfolk would have crossed this relatively dry marshland by a short direct route from the town to the closest of the medieval freshwater supplies, Blykewell or Blikewell, known in 1305 (Figure 7.1).

St Mary's Croft

The Grove embankment crossed a part of the eastern end of St Mary's Marsh which was known as St Mary's Croft in the late 14th and 15th centuries. St Mary's Croft was reclaimed by the late 14th century following the marine or brackish conditions temporarily induced by the 13th-century storms. The term croft always implies enclosed land used for agricultural purposes, that is, not open grazing marsh but more intensively used land.[8] The marsh was reclaimed into smallish plots, some known themselves as crofts, which were mainly held by individuals. There were channels

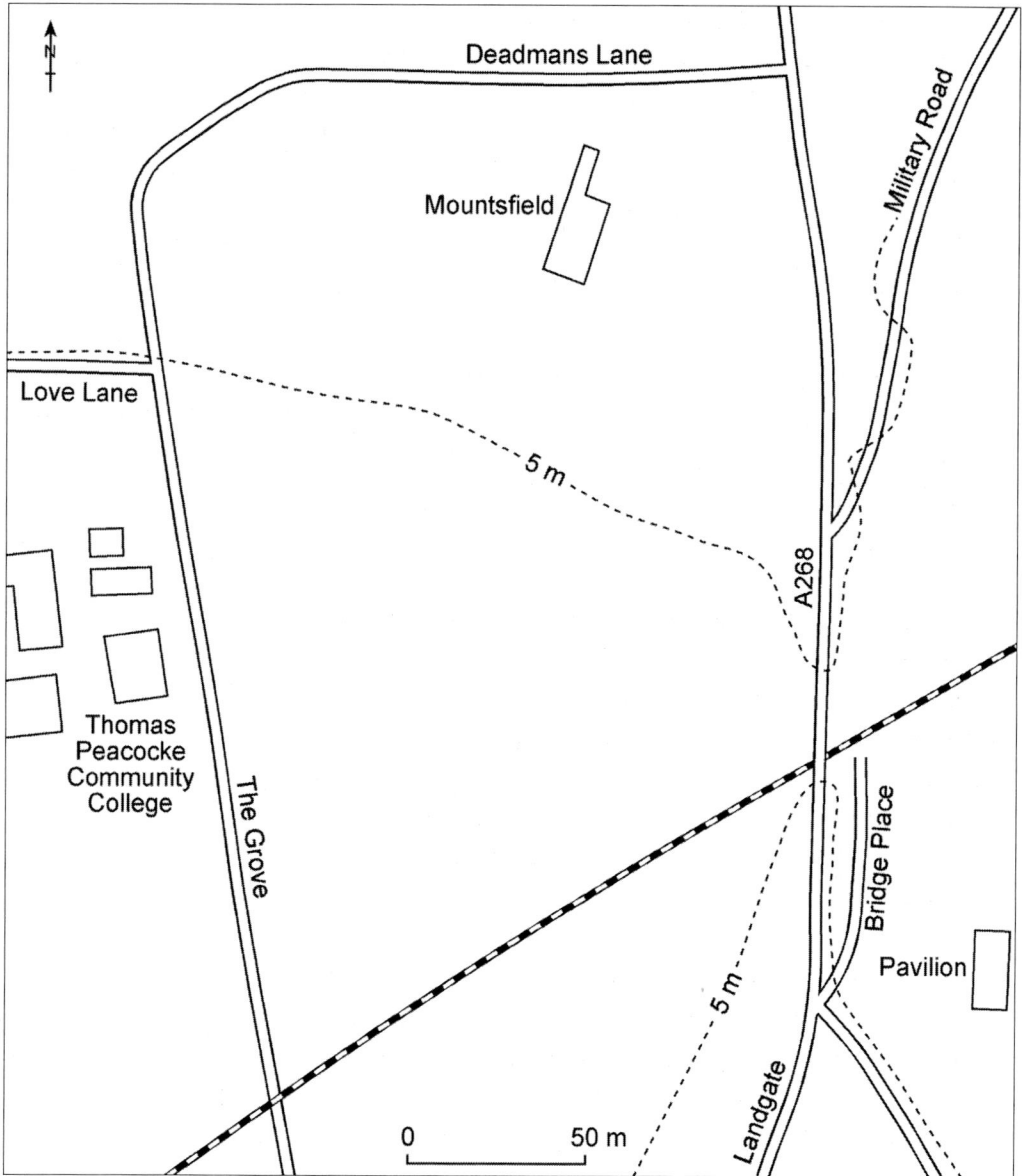

Fig. 9.2 Location map showing the area where boreholes were sunk: the Grove embankment which crosses St Mary's Marsh and the A268 route out of Rye from the Landgate (after Waller and Grant 2008).

of water or creeks between some of these crofts, whose remnants can still be seen to the east of the Grove embankment. This kind of reclamation is known from nearby in the Romney Marshes at this period.[9]

The southern boundary of St Mary's Croft was the town ditch, and the western boundary was the Grove embankment, otherwise known as the 'way leading from

Rye to the spring called Blykewelle'. On the northern side lay a street or lane, Blikelane, which ran westwards from the land bridge, past Blykewell, and on towards one of the other medieval springs above the River Tillingham and under Leasam cliff (Figure 8.1).[10] There is little information as to the nature of St Mary's Marsh beyond the western side of the Grove embankment at this period: however, there was apparently tidal flooding of St Mary's Croft in 1414 suggesting that at times tides flowed up as far as the Grove embankment from the vicinity of Rye Creek. A piece of land in this marsh called St Mary's Croft in 1407 lay immediately to the east of the 'ditch of the wall', i.e. the Grove embankment, and to the south of a 'gutter'. This was perhaps the 'old gutter', that is, channel or sluice, in the embankment through which the marsh was said to be flooded in 1414.[11] The 'ditch of the wall' known in 1407 is clearly visible on the inside of the Grove embankment on the Tithe Map.

Some of the plots in St Mary's Croft were held by members of the town elite such as John Baddyng, Joan, widow of Richard Baddyng, Robert Tayllour, Thomas Longe, the heirs of Robert Onewyn, and John Yprys, esquire, and his wife Elizabeth. John and Elizabeth conveyed their plot to Godard Pulham of New Winchelsea and his wife Agnes. One plot was held by James Godard of the Romney Marsh family which had extensive leases of marshland around Fairfield, Kent, and another by two members of rural or urban gentry families, Robert Echynghame and Robert Oxenbregge. Yet another piece was held and conveyed together with other 'new marsh' in Rye by two men, William Acdenne of Wittersham, and Richard atte Wode, a citizen and fishmonger of London.[12] William Broughton, mayor and MP of Rye, leased 18 acres to Thomas Pope, bailiff and MP, in 1444 for seven years.[13] Besides these pieces in private hands some land in, or adjacent to, St Mary's Croft was common land, presumably used for grazing. The parish church also held a small parcel in St Mary's Marsh sometimes described as two acres, sometimes as three acres; this was associated by tenure with the *Vyne Inn* and lay towards the western end of St Mary's Marsh; the church also held another parcel of marshland at the Muntes (Mountfield), lying close to St Mary's Croft outside the Landgate.[14]

People crossing St Mary's Croft left Rye via the postern gate at the lower end of what is now Conduit Hill and then crossed the embankment. The postern gate was the back door for Rye inhabitants, allowing them access to St Mary's Croft, the spring of Blykewell and another spring to the west of it along Blikelane, near Leasam.[15] The existence of the route and postern thus influenced both the line of Conduit Hill and the location of the Austin Friary on its second site. In the 16th century Rye's water supply was insufficient for its population. Over the course of the century, conduits, cisterns, taps and pipes replaced, or at least supplemented, the collection of water by hand from the springs. The way across St Mary's Marsh on the Grove embankment was utilised for laying pipes from the springs to cisterns in the town. A brick cistern, which still exists, was also built at Blykewell, accounting for its post-medieval name, Brickwell, which was also later known as Queen's Well; a cistern was also built at the postern gate.[16] The right of way from the postern gate to Brickwell continued to be preserved in late 16th-century deeds.[17]

The Large-Scale Reclamation of St Mary's Marsh in the Mid-16th Century

The mid-16th century was a period of change for St Mary's Marsh. From this time members of the local gentry such as John Tufton, esquire, and the Shepherd family, were intensely interested in the reclamation of large areas of St Mary's Marsh to the west of the Grove embankment, an interest springing from the ongoing profitability of 'inning' marshland and river valleys.[18] It received a stimulus from the involvement of Sussex gentry in land acquisitions in the county at the Dissolution.[19] The interests of these gentry and the town government of Rye were often incompatible with regard to the part of Rye harbour known as Rye Creek, i.e. the inner harbour on the west side of the town adjacent to the Strand. The main part of Rye harbour was the Puddle or Camber to the south of the town. Here large vessels could anchor and goods could be transported to and fro by smaller vessels which could sail up to Rye Creek, which was also used by fishing vessels. The successful continuation of the town's trade and fishing industry depended on keeping Rye Creek open at least for smaller vessels, and contemporaries perceived that marshland inning, as much as natural processes of silting, threatened this.

The main protagonists in the reclamation of St Mary's Marsh in the 1550s were Robert Shepherd (III) and Alexander Shepherd, who were members of a family of Rye and Peasmarsh which already had interests in inning marshland at Rye.[20] Soon after 1554 Robert Shepherd and Alexander Shepherd, together with Elizabeth Blechenden, widow, and others, erected a curving reclamation wall at the western end of St Mary's Marsh (Plate V).[21] The wall protected a barn and 15 houses inhabited by fishermen which lay in St Mary's Marsh.[22] This part of St Mary's Marsh was on the eastern side of Rye Creek in which the Prowez map shows vessels of moderate size, close to where the remains of wooden vessels, one probably carvel-built, have been found.[23] The Shepherds' reclamation wall was described in 1563 as 'the high wall towards the Channel', i.e. Rye Creek.[24] It is shown on the Prowez map as a curving black line which reaches to the end of the 16th-century strand, an area which has since undergone much change. When the wall was built it effectively defined the western end of St Mary's Marsh, which is shown in pale orange-brown on the Prowez map. At its north-eastern end the wall may have joined the medieval route known as the highway called Blikelane which ran westwards along the north side of St Mary's Marsh from the land bridge towards Leasam.[25]

On 1 November 1570 this reclamation wall was breached following some extreme winds, weather and tides and, as the Shepherds claimed, the making of a trench through the wall by Rye's inhabitants to convey water to the town.[26] This trench was undoubtedly made in connection with a contract by the town with a London plumber for a further set of pipes to bring 'new water' from Leasam to the Strand in 1570. The contract was recorded in the hundred and assembly book which noted both recurrent and extraordinary expenditure by the chamberlains on the town conduits.[27] The breach in the Shepherds' reclamation wall, allegedly caused by this work on the town water supply, was mapped by Prowez as 'The Brache in to Mr Sheppardes marshes'. Within six days of the breach occurring in November 1570, the Shepherds and other owners provided materials and sixty workmen to mend the breach, but mayor's bailiff 'and others of the meaner sort to the number of an hundred persons in evil and unlawful manner assembled' prevented this, claiming that the inflow and outflow of water was 'to the amendment of the said haven', i.e. Rye Creek. The mayor and jurats had conveyed this claim concerning the breach and the trench to the Privy Council and the Shepherds had promptly received a letter from the Lord Warden of the Cinque Ports ordering them not to repair the breach until the Queen's wish was known on this matter. The Shepherds for their part wished the Privy Council to order the mayor and jurats to allow them to mend the breach because of the financial implications for themselves; they claimed that the houses and mills there were worth £100, and were in particular danger at spring tides.[28] A letter from the Privy Council of 7 July 1571 emphasises the conflict which had occurred over this between the town inhabitants on one hand and Robert Shepherd and his associates on the other.[29] The inhabitants were keen to ensure a good water supply to Rye and to keep the Creek open for the vessels which were still able to use it, and felt that the Crown had a similar interest in this part of the harbour.[30]

In 1573 there was a dispute between Mr Shepherd and one Mr Jacson, servant of the Lord Warden of the Cinque Ports, over the rent of Shepherd's property in St Mary Marsh, and also of a brewhouse and mill, possibly one of the windmills which had been built on the reclamation wall. Jacson had failed to pay the £50 rent which was due and Shepherd demanded a hearing at the town court from the mayor and jurats of Rye to determine the case.[31] The Lord Warden supported Jacson and also stated that it had been the wish of the Queen and Privy Council that St Mary's Marsh should be enclosed and remain so.[32] Although the Shepherds pressed hard to be allowed to mend the breach, it remained unrepaired for several decades and some inhabitants of Rye exploited this access through the wall.[33] The breach is clearly shown on the Prowez map with channels flowing through it into St Mary's Marsh, and in 1582 access by very small boats was possible nearly as far as the postern gate. On a February night in that year about midnight the town watchmen caught two men smuggling in a small batch of leather worth 6s. 8d. aboard a little cockboat near to the conduit outside the postern gate. These small-time smugglers were 'one Butler [living] in the Fryars' just up Conduit Hill and another 'little fellow'. The watchmen reported that they had taken the leather, sold it to 'Old Scragge' and divided the proceeds between themselves.[34] Cockboats were used in the shallow creeks of north Kent, for example, around Faversham and Oare, for similar access.[35] Although very small boats could navigate channels in St Mary's Marsh in 1582, it is clear that this much of this area was solid land, since it was noted in 1596 that two pieces had been marked out, one of which was a piece 158 feet by 122 feet on which the town's dung and filth was to be laid.[36]

From 1589 the possible use of St Mary's Marsh as an indraught to pen water and release it to scour Rye Creek was under frequent discussion by the corporation. This was not in fact carried out although it remained an active possibility until at least 1613.[37] In this year the mayor and jurats made a detailed agreement for an indraught to be made in the 27 acres of St Mary's Marsh in the occupation of William Shephard of Mereworth in Kent, gentleman, which were said to be flooded at the spring tides which fell into the Rye Channel. These marshes were allegedly formerly good firm ground, which it was thought might be regained without prejudice to the town by laying a sluice and making an indraught to receive the water. Detailed plans were made to build a sluice in the middle of the creek running out of St Mary's Marsh into the Tillingham channel next to the windmills there and to close the creek up to the sluice.[38] However, the written agreement was peppered with marginal notes such as 'time too short', and 'failed in his covenant not being sufficient; not performed in any part'. Finally, instead, agreement was reached in 1617 to allow Shepherd to continue to inn the Tillingham level without interference and in return to convey 33½ acres of St Mary's Marsh to trustees of the town.[39] William's father, Alexander Shepherd, had been enclosing marsh in the Tillingham level since at least 1597.[40] Previously the town government had feared that inning Tillingham level would be prejudicial to Rye haven and harbour, but on mature consideration it agreed that the ownership of St Mary's Marsh would be more beneficial for the harbour and town. William Shepherd himself had been enclosing parts of Tillingham level since at least 1604, and in 1612 was 'an earnest sutor unto Corporacion of this Towne' to be allowed to inn about 125 acres of salts in Tillingham level. The town assembly referred the request to a committee to survey the salts and return their opinion and the proposal was approved with certain conditions.[41] This resulted in the failed agreement of 1613 for the related proposal for the indraught and the conveyance of St Mary's Marsh to the town in 1617.

This is a simplified account of the complexities involved in maintaining and managing St Mary's Marsh in the 16th and 17th centuries. St Mary's Marsh was only part of the corporation's concern in relation to Rye Creek. The indraught there was not the scheme first proposed in 1589 involving a 'Great Scluse' in Mr Tufton's marshes on the west side of Rye in the Tillingham valley, which sluice in 1595 had 'to be once again repaired and set going again and a new wall constructed to help pen in the water there'; nor was it part of another scheme of large-scale works undertaken from 1596 to the north west of Rye, involving a different sluice.[42] In that year, to avert the shallowing of Rye Creek, the corporation took a gamble on a plan to divert the waters of the Rother through marshland to the north of the town into the Tillingham river in the hope of deepening the water in the Creek. The scheme was unsuccessful and very expensive, nearly bankrupting the town, and led in 1610 to the dismantling of the sluice.[43] The town imposed higher taxes and sold assets in the early 17th century to try other means to save the harbour but these damaged the town's already declining economy. Unsuccessful efforts to save Rye Creek as a significant harbour continued to be made until the 1650s and beyond, but they were doomed to failure when faced with the interests of the local gentry in extensive reclamation, and the natural processes of silting and coastal change in Rye Creek and the wider harbour area.[44]

The interests of the gentry such as the Shepherds of Peasmarsh living in the immediate hinterlands of Rye were opposed to those of the townsfolk. The gentry could turn a good profit from reclaimed grazing marsh. The townsmen hoped to preserve the prosperity of Rye based on its port and fishing industry by keeping the Creek open. The gentry reclaimers stressed their rights of ownership and the inheritance of property but also the benefit to the town of their provision of housing for fishermen. They hinted that the breach in their reclamation wall was deliberately facilitated by the trench for the town's water supply and made snide remarks to the Privy Council about the low status of those who opposed them.[45] For their part the townsfolk, led by the mayor and jurats, believed that the Privy Council would find arguments for the preservation of the harbour and the fishing industry convincing, and complained that the Commissioners for the Marsh had supported Mr Shepherd.[46] Their view was retrospective; they feared that Rye harbour would go the same way as that of New Romney which had in fact been lost by the end of the 15th century.[47] In contrast the gentry from the hinterlands anticipated that profit and prosperity would come, at least to themselves, from marshland reclamation around Rye, as it had for many years, and took steps to make it happen.

Postscript on St Mary's Marsh

St Mary's Marsh was apparently fully walled again until two extraordinary tides in the winter of 1720 washed away a wall which protected it. The corporation had the wall repaired and the question arose as to who was responsible for the costs. A commentator of the 19th century interpreted the papers of a suit in chancery to mean that the corporation in the 18th century owned 18 acres of St Mary's Marsh and the defendants in the suit owned the remaining 30 acres. The marsh contained 48 acres of which the corporation had once owned all, as inned by William Shepherd and others, but had sold 16 acres to John Fowtrall, one man called French and others in 1596, and a further 14 acres to one Welsh in 1668. Subsequently the town government acquired more of St Mary's Marsh from Henry Montague. The corporation continued to be concerned and responsible for its maintenance until the 19th century.

CHAPTER 10

Conclusions

The late 14th century was the pivotal period in the history of medieval Rye, transforming it from a small but moderately prosperous town into one sunk in economic stagnation for a century, whose townsfolk were seriously concerned for their lives and souls. The mortality of the mid-14th-century plagues followed by the 1377 French raid affected Rye much more severely than other towns nearby. In addition famine may have occurred in Rye in the 1330s and inundations certainly did take place on the low-lying side of the town in the 1340s, leading to the loss of land and houses. Long-term issues were also at play in Rye's decline in the 14th century, in particular the downturn in the Yarmouth herring fishery and the rise of the south-western fishing industry centred on Exeter, which increasingly competed with that of the south-eastern ports.

Rye had started well in the 11th century with a good location and a rich and distant overlord. It was admirably placed to market the resources of its Wealden hinterland which were being opened up to commercial exploitation, particularly timber and firewood. Its major commodity, fish, was sold in the town and also at inland market villages, notably those on the route to London. The existence of Fécamp Abbey as lord gave Rye some advantages. The Abbey provided a large and beautiful church which fulfilled the needs of the town for both a place for worship and a look-out tower. There was no struggle for urban control between various lords as there was at other Cinque Ports such as New Romney and many towns elsewhere. Fécamp Abbey was happy to agree terms with the leading townsmen on which to share the revenues of Rye from fishing, rents and the tolls and customs of the market and fair, and then to leave its running to the townsmen. The bailiffs appointed to collect rents and hold the town court after the resumption of Rye into royal hands were barons of Rye or Old Winchelsea. The revenues of the two towns were assigned as dower to Henry III's widow, Queen Eleanor of Provence, between 1275 and 1291, and formed part of her estate of Aquila in Kent and Sussex. Her bailiffs were not local men but there is no sign of conflict with the townsmen. After Eleanor's death the estate reverted to Edward I and from that time Rye had its own mayor. Most importantly, Edward also proceeded with the foundation of New Winchelsea whose main function was the import of Gascon wine. New Winchelsea was a very different town from Rye, producing a much greater revenue for the king, but Rye was able to continue to develop as a fishing and market town, not least because of its good inland connections by road to the north and north west. Rye and New Winchelsea were not active competitors as towns for three reasons. Firstly, they were under the same lord; secondly, some of the leading families, including those involved in high-level lending, were associated with both towns in the 13th and early 14th centuries; thirdly, New Winchelsea's local market activity was orientated towards settlements to its west such as Icklesham and did not obviously overlap with the economic hinterland of Rye.

Rye had just one central market space next to the church and the Courton but there is little doubt that fish was also sold on the strands. The Rye market was the outlet for the trades and crafts in the town which produced the vital goods needed both to sustain everyday life and to supply shipping: grain, bread, meat, salt, cloth, leather and pottery. Rye had a range of more specialised goods such as spices, shoes, gloves and ready-prepared food, and services such as medical attention and taverns. They all point to its role as a regional, and not merely a local, market. Customers included the townspeople, merchants and fishermen in port, and the residents of local villages to the north and north west which did not have their own markets. Market activity and fishing in Rye held up right until after the Black Death but the loss of population and low demand then affected them badly, and also ancillary services such as carting, food preparation and petty retailing.

The two or three taverns in medieval Rye were undoubtedly more than mere drinking places or hostels, but provided contact points for those making deals, needing or offering credit, arranging the shipping or the onward carriage of goods by boat, cart or horse, or looking to find a carpenter or other specialist workers to build a ship or house. Fécamp and the townsmen expected a large income from the fair which was held in August near St Bartholomew's Hospital. The fair had a good site on a route out of town which would attract both the townsfolk and people from villages around. Pottery made at the kilns near the Hospital is likely to have been a major product sold at the fair, both for domestic and industrial use.

Rye pottery is found quite widely on coastal sites in Sussex and Kent, presumably in some cases being carried or used on board ship. Apart from the Rye kilns, the nearest known site for large-scale pottery production at this period was over fifteen miles away at Ashford in Kent.

If freedom from the immediate control of its lord or traditional structures helped commerce, then Rye was again well placed. The dependence of the monarch on the goodwill and co-operation of the Cinque Ports confederation resulted in the charter of the late 12th century which liberated Rye from the administrative demands of the county and hundred. Ship service was not an onerous burden given that the townspeople already had the necessary vessels which they used for fishing or trade; at least until the 1330s they were not required to provide the vessels frequently, nor for long periods, nor for demanding roles. The Ports' importance was not simply ship service but their function as entry and exit points to the kingdom, which gave the townsmen some power as they could chose whom to support. In 1066 William the Conqueror had landed at Pevensey, and after his victory over Harold near Hastings his soldiers travelled on towards New Romney, which they sacked, and then to Dover. In 1216 Louis the Dauphin arrived at Rye and his fleet was subsequently blockaded by Philip de Albini in the shared anchorage between Rye and Old Winchelsea. The existence of an anchorage which could accommodate a fleet of vessels of some size gave these towns greater significance than places like Pevensey and New Romney where vessels were merely beached; New Romney's haven, although used by merchants, does not appear ever to have had this kind of significance. The importance of Rye was reinforced by the damage caused to Pevensey and New Romney by the 13th-century storms, and also to Seaford, Hastings, Hythe and Dover, which caused them to lose their harbour facilities over the next century. The storms also diverted the course of the Rother away from New Romney and south towards Rye and Winchelsea and the anchorage there. Although Old Winchelsea was destroyed by the storms, New Winchelsea was established and its private harbour plots for merchants and the common quay were much in demand until the mid-14th century. There is strong evidence of the transport of firewood and timber down the Rother river and more circumstantial evidence of its use by travellers such as pilgrims; the carriage of goods and people would have contributed to the solid prosperity of the two towns until the disaster of the Black Death.

From 1337 the Hundred Years' War opened up further opportunities for Rye as a focus for royal shipbuilding and the export of timber, firewood and horses to France, especially Calais. Plague and war disrupted Rye's other trade in a variety of goods with the Low Countries to some extent, but it was merchant shipping which was most severely affected by the piracy to which the men of Rye and New Winchelsea turned in periods of truce or changing political alliances. It was difficult to eradicate because the pirates were embedded in urban society in the Ports. A very serious consequence of war for Rye was the French raid of 1377 in which many inhabitants were killed and much damage caused to buildings. There had also been an earlier raid in 1339 and attacks on other coastal towns, including New Winchelsea, in 1360. The raid of 1377 kept the population low, with no evidence of the recovery which was experienced by some inland towns or ports elsewhere. The danger of attacks also made Rye an undesirable place to live. The townsfolk responded in two ways to the raid: a revenge attack in 1378 and a heightened concern for their own safety, which built on their experience of severe mortality in the Black Death and subsequent epidemics. There was little enthusiasm or money for strengthening the town's gates and walls against further raids, although some efforts were made and the Baddings or Ypres Tower may date from the later 14th century. But the townsfolk looked primarily to God to save them, setting up new chantries in the church and founding a new Austin Friary, whose major function was prayer for the health and souls of the founders. These founders were part of a new town elite which had replaced the previous one largely because of the high mortality: the changed conditions also offered opportunities for ambitious families such as the Taillours and Celys. The wealth of some surviving townspeople allowed them to beautify the parish church with new windows and wooden fittings in the 15th century. At the same time support for St Bartholomew's Hospital faded, even though its origins had been partly an expression of the urban nature of Rye and the independence of the town's leaders. After the 1377 raid the mayor and commonalty ceased to assert their right to nominate the warden of the Hospital and allowed the office to become a sinecure for royal clerks. In the late 1370s poor people still lived at the Hospital, an indication that at Rye the loss of population and changed economic circumstances had not produced new opportunities and higher incomes for all. However, the deterioration of the hospital building and the withdrawal of care for the poor were not remedied by the members of the town government, perhaps because the Austin Friary was providing them with a spiritual focus which was both new and lay within the relative safety of the town walls.

The Taillour family, leading members of the new elite, remained in Rye only until the late 14th century when they moved to a nearby rural manor. The mortality from plague and raids reduced the number of wealthy and ruling families in Rye from about forty to about a dozen. Over the course of the 15th century this number fell much further, although there were still important and energetic men who found profitable activity in the town to sustain them while they helped to run it, such as Richard Baddyng, John Baddyng, John de Ypres and Babilon Grauntford. Members of three other elite families, the Estons, Oxenbridges and the Wymonds, also remained in Rye and then benefitted, along with many others, from the rapid rise in population from the 1490s which stimulated demand for grain, meat and leather goods. This growth was partly based on the final decline of other Cinque Port harbours and of New Winchelsea as a trading town of any significance, some of whose merchants may have migrated to Rye. Some recovery of demand for land and trading places was satisfied by the letting of vacant plots around the largely empty quarter where the Austin Friary stood, and by the building of some shops and a new quayside at the strand. Rye's fair which was active between the 12th and early 14th centuries may have been in abeyance in the later Middle Ages, when there are no records of it, but was evidently taking place in the 16th century. This century marked the peak of prosperity as Rye capitalised on its harbour which remained in good condition for vessels for both trade and war. It is no surprise that it was from Rye that Sir Richard Guldeford sailed on his pilgrimage in 1506. Until the early 17th century, when the port of Dover revived, Rye's harbour was the biggest and best of the confederation ports. Large vessels could not come right into Rye Creek but could still anchor safely in the Camber and be provisioned by smaller vessels from Rye. The military and naval adventures of the Tudor monarchs assisted Rye since they ensured royal support. A temporary boom in the demand for firewood for Calais and Boulogne also helped, particularly in the mid-16th century, as did the subsequent arrival of many Huguenots, some of them craftspeople, who worked hard and created demand for food, goods and housing. Two of Rye's early industries, butchery and leather processing, had a strong revival, along with the usual wide range of urban trades and crafts. Rye again provided some of London's requirement for fish, as it had done much earlier. Increased population and activity at the port required more inns and victualling houses, and more ship carpenters and specialist workers to build ships.

The population of Rye was perhaps just over a thousand in the 15th century, with some growth towards the end of the century. By the early 1520s, however, Rye's population was something over two thousand people, and then perhaps doubled again by the 1550s to just over four thousand. Rye was larger and wealthier than any other town in Sussex or Kent. Demand for permanent housing and temporary accommodation was extraordinary and is the explanation for Rye's building boom from the late 15th century. Since Rye had almost no room to expand physically, this building at first consisted of infilling between houses which were then almost all quite recently built and which lay on spacious plots. In the second half of the 16th century properties were subdivided and many people were crowded into lofts and garrets.[1] The numbers of permanent residents was also swelled by temporary visitors such as mariners, freebooters and those travelling on board ship. The arrival of Huguenots in the 1570s boosted the population much further, although only temporarily, and the overall number of residents in Rye was sharply reduced at the start of the 17th century. The loss of Calais and Boulogne, the departure of many Huguenots, the final silting of Rye harbour and the lack of local control of important commercial activity contributed to the end of Rye's boom. By 1660 Rye's population was perhaps only a quarter of its size at its height in the late 16th century but it was still much larger than the nearby town of Battle, and almost as large as the county town of Lewes. The area of the town where the fishing industry was concentrated, the Wishe, remained depressed and impoverished but some merchants and traders made a good living. The availability of the former Hospital and Austin Friary lands attracted gentry and noble families who built up private estates between the mid-16th and the mid-17th centuries, as did others through the reclamation at St Mary's Marsh and other marshes and river valleys around the town. Some of the successful urban gentry families left town in the first half of the 17th century, refocusing their attention on rural estates in parishes in east Sussex and beyond. Rye nevertheless retained some wealthy families and an active intellectual community in the mid-17th century, which was encouraged, at least until the Restoration, by the presence of people like Samuel Jeake the elder. In the 1650s and 1660s Rye was entering a new period of its history, no longer a flourishing port but a local market town served by a small riverside quay. The fortunes of Rye up until the mid-17th century, and especially its prosperity in the 16th century which is epitomised in Hartshorne House, the residence of the Palmers and the Jeakes, were crucial in forming the appearance of the town as it remains today.

Notes

Chapter 1   The Origins of the Town of Rye c.1000 to c.1250

1. Thomson 1998, 8.
2. Gardiner 1999a, 30-1. The historical and archaeological evidence about southern Sussex between *c*.450 and *c*.650 is extremely limited, White 1999, 28-9.
3. *PNS* 1, xxiv-v. The *burgensi* of Domesday Book should be translated as 'townspeople' or 'townsmen' rather than burgesses. The term *burgus*, from which the word *burgensi* is derived, can be translated as 'borough' but the translation 'town' is better, since Domesday Book, as an inquisition compiled from many different contributions, has no consistent terminology for towns, Reynolds 1987, 295-300.
4. The settlements discussed in this and later chapters have many varieties of spellings of their names, which have generally been standardised. The early forms are given in *PNS* and *PNK*. The *Haestingas* may originally have been a group partly based in Kent until their defeat by Offa in 771, after which they were attached to the south Saxon province and bishopric, Welch 2007, 194.
5. Davison 1972, 123-7; Kitchen 1984, 175-7; *DB Sussex*, 'The Rapes' in Notes section (n.p.); Jones 1999, 50; Gardiner 1999a, 30. Castle Toll fits better with the hidation and defensive circuit and is on land at Beckley probably mentioned in King's Alfred's will, which was apparently a necessary precursor to all the *de novo burh* foundations, S. Brookes, pers. comm.
6. Gardiner 1999a, 30-1; Adams 1999, 41; *DB Sussex*, 'Outliers' in Notes section (n.p.). Fairlight has been suggested for Guestling. A (late) hundred meeting place of Gostrow hundred, earlier Babinerode hundred, which lay to the west of Rye was the Hundred House in Brede, *PNS* 2, 507, 514, 526, 534. Changes in Babinerode/Gostrow and Goldspur, including in relation to Rye, between 1086 and 1661 are given in *VCH Sussex* 9, 164, and indicate the impossibility of any argument about Rye as an early hundred meeting place.
7. Brookes and Milne 2006, 5-13; Brookes 2007, 1-18; Brookes 2003, 86-7, 93. The width and significance of fleets (channels) such as *Meacesfleote*, later called the Wantsum, may be overstated by Brookes 2003, fig. 8.1, by the use of the 10m. contour, cf. Long, Waller and Plater 2007, 201.
8. Riddler 2004, 28; Welch 2007, 193.
9. Metcalf 2003, 39-41; Brookes 2003, 85; Tummuscheit 2003, 219-20.
10. Murray 1935, 231; Early Medieval Corpus and Sylloge of Coins of the British Isles http://www.fitzmuseum.cam.ac.uk/emc/emc_search.php. Two coins of A.D. 680-710 have been

found on the western and northern fringes of Romney Marsh, one at Stone-cum-Ebony and one at Warehorne. Romney Marsh and the Western River Valleys: an archaeological gazetteer, http://www.arac50.dsl.pipex.com/gazetteer.pdf.

11. Two coins are known from the end of Edgar's reign with the legend WENCLES, an abbreviated town name, possibly the earliest reference to Winchelsea. Other coins with somewhat similar legends have been attributed to a mint at Winchcombe, Glos., but equal weight can be placed on either, Metcalf 1998, 231, 236. However the legend includes the letter L, similar to the early charter form of Winchelsea, *Wincenesel, PNS* 2, 537; Ballard 1904, 9, n.1,120.

12. Le Maho 2003, 236, 244-5.

13. Matthew 1962, 25. Greenwich was granted to St Peter's as part of the large estate of Lewisham in north Kent.

14. Brookes 2003, 93; Draper and Meddens (forthcoming), chapter 2.

15. Blair 2007, 12-13. Palmer seems not to have fully appreciated the extent of navigable rivers and thus of trade at the East Kent *wics*, Palmer 2003, 52, 55, fig. 5.2 , which can be contrasted with those shown in Sussex and Kent by Budgen's map of 1724.

16. Eddison 1998, fig. 5.10, 68-9.

17. Long, Waller and Plater 2007, 202-3.

18. Long, Waller, Stupples and Schofield 2007, 83, 92-3, 99, 106; Schofield and Schofield 2007, 12, fig. 2.1. Such storms are recorded as occurring between 1236 and December 1287 and early 1288, those of the latter period being the most severe, i.e. in 1236, 1250 (1 October?), 1252 (October?), 1261 (?), 1271, 1287 (December) and 1288 (January?), Eddison 2002, 130; Scott Robertson 1880, 241; Matthew Paris, *Chronica Major*, 176, 272-3; Gardiner 1988, 112.

19. M. Waller, pers. comm.

20. Burke 2004, 11; Lawson 2004, 32.

21. Charter S911 in P. Sawyer, *Anglo-Saxon Charters: an Annotated List and Bibliography*, http://www.trin.cam.ac.uk/chartwww/eSawyer.99/eSawyer2.html.

22. Subsequent grants of land further to the west near the Sussex coast and, after the Conquest, at inland places such as Cogges, Oxfordshire are discussed in Blair, Steane *et al* 1983, 37-125.

23. Haskins 1918, 344-5.

24. Charters S949 and S982, Sawyer, *Anglo-Saxon Charters* (above). This amplification may be suspect since the monks of Fécamp may have added the record of these valuable rights later but it is just as likely that Cnut had specified the tolls of Winchelsea and land at Brede, with Harthacnut confirming this by 1042, Matthew 1962, 20; Keynes 1997, 208, n. 30, gives S982 as 'suspect' on the basis that it contains an amplification.

25. Gardiner 2000, 86, n. 80.

26. Henry I, the Abbot of Fécamp and Henry Count of Eu agreed that the King and the Count would share half the tolls of Winchelsea for stalls (*trusselle*) and for maintaining bridges (*pontage*), and the Abbey would have the other half, plus all the rest of the dues. Ships belonging to men of Hastings driven to put into Winchelsea by storms were excepted from this arrangement, presumably because the Count of Eu was the major lord of Hastings, *Cal. Docs France*, 41-2. *Cal. Docs France* includes excerpts from Fécamp's cartulary which is in La Bibliothèque Municipale, Rouen, Y51. La Bibliothèque Nationale de France holds an 18th-century copy of the cartulary but apparently no other records of direct relevance to its Sussex possessions, P.-J. Riamond, pers. comm. Other records of Fécamp's English

possessions are in Archives Departémentales Seine-Maritime, Rouen, 7H57. Photographic copies were reviewed by the author for this project. They are deposited in the Thompson Archive, Steyning Museum, Sussex, and were calendared in Whittick 2004.

27. A. Du Monstier, *Neustria Pia* (Rouen, 1663), 223; J. Mabillon, 'Annales Ordinis Sancti Benedicti' 5, 503, given by Matthew 1962, 20.

28. *PNS* 2, 430, 444, 534; Gardiner 2003, 157.

29. Matthew 1962, 21; *Cal. Docs France*, 38.

30. *DB Sussex* 5: 1. Guestling hundred lay between Rye and Hastings but as noted above the boundaries changed between the 10th and 13th centuries and no arguments can be built on those boundaries.

31. *DB Sussex* renders the punctuation between the Rameslie and the Hastings section incorrectly in the English version, using a comma to separate them. The accompanying Latin version shows the sections separated by (the equivalent of) a full stop and the Hastings town section starting with a capital letter. The heading Rameslie in the Latin section is given as Rye in English but Rameslie referred to the whole estate not just the town of Rye.

32. Morris in *DB Sussex*; *PNS* 2, vi-vii. Occasionally Hastings and even Old Winchelsea were floated as possible identities for this new borough. *VCH Sussex* 9, 49, stated that the new borough almost certainly refers to Rye, and argued against the identification of the new borough as Hastings which had earlier been made in *VCH Sussex* 1, 385, 391; Hinde and Hallam 1985, 272-3, adopted the rendering of Rameslie as Rye by *DB Sussex* and accepted the weight of evidence for Rye being the new borough. Hastings was clearly established as a town before the Conquest, having a mint by reign of Æthelred II (978-1016). The 'Old English burgesses' or *burhware* (early citizens or portsmen) of Hastings had their own hythe, Bulverhythe, *PNS* 1, xxii; *PNS* 2, 535. The four *burgensi* of Hastings belonging to Fécamp appear under their own entry in Domesday Book and some twenty *burgensi* of the major lord of Hastings, the Count of Eu, appear under Bullington, Bexhill hundred, which lay to the west of Hastings and included its castelry, *DB Sussex*, 9:11,13, and notes (n.p.). Domesday Book was compiled shortly before the time when the lands and income of the Count of Eu, the major lord of Hastings rape, were passing to his son and heir William, accounting for the eccentric entry for the part of Hastings belonging to them, Warren Hollister 1987, 226-7. A 'new town' suggested to have been built at Hastings in the 1180s cannot be that of Domesday Book in 1086, Rudling *et al.* 1993, 72-77. A report on Hastings castle by Archaeology South-East dates the castle to the immediate post-Conquest period, constructed on an existing earthwork, but this does not demonstrate a new town was founded there at that time, ESRO HBR1/1359 (1999). Old Winchelsea was a trading place with tolls before 1042 and possibly a mint, which required it under the law of Aethelstan (925-39) to be a borough, and thus cannot have been the new town of 1086, Ballard 1904, 9, n.1, 120.

33. http://www.spink.com/news/current_news/4018b.asp [consulted 3 December 2007].

34. The absence of a reference to minting under Rameslie in Domesday is attributable to the early but restricted tradition of certain bishops or abbots receiving royal rights such as having a mint, Metcalf 1987, 281; Reynolds 1987, 300-1.

35. M. Allen, pers. comm. Romney Marsh and the Western River Valleys: An archaeological gazetteer, http://www.arac50.dsl.pipex.com/gazetteer.pdf. A hammer cross silver coin of *c.*1059-62 from the York mint found at Rye cannot be taken as a clear indication of trade there in the 1060s since its condition and the circumstances and location of the find are unknown.

36. In 1127 one Robert (*Rotberto*) de Rye witnessed a charter of William Count of Ponthieu. This granted land at St Germain of Montaigu, and the tithe there, to the Abbey of St Sauver le Vicomte, diocese of Coutances (Manche), *Cal. Docs France*, 346; Matthew 1962, 12. The earliest reference to Rye (as *Ria, Rya*), given by *PNS* from the English royal records used, the Pipe Rolls, is of 1130, the next of 1165, *PNS* 2, 536. The widow of Hubert de Ria is known probably in 1131 and certainly by 1146, when the manor of Horton (Glos.) was given to Worcester Cathedral by Agnes de Bellofago, wife of Hubert de Ria, 'Prebendaries: Horton', Fasti Ecclesiae Anglicanae 1066-1300: volume 4: Salisbury (1991), pp. 77-8. URL: http://www.british-history.ac.uk/report.aspx?compid=34255&strquery=ria. Date accessed: 26 February 2008.

37. Cf. Dyer 1992, 143-4.

38. Hope Marsh had already been reclaimed and grants were made to reclaim further land in the vicinity, Salzman 1902, nos. 4, 12.

39. Between 1196 and 1199 Laurence, the parson of Brede, and James son of Alard were in dispute with Fécamp Abbey over the tithes of Winchelsea and White Fleet marsh (if Wlfedemareis equates to White Fleet marsh). The tithes were judged to have been worth 33 marks (£22) during this time and Laurence and James were to pay 10 marks compensation and 20 marks 'by taxation', *Cal. Docs France*, 49-51; Whittick 2004, R2.

40. A charter records that for 100s. Robert de Hughtham gave up to William, Abbot of Fécamp, 'his right across the end of the water in the marshes (*in moris*) of Brede to the north [of those marshes?], which water runs from the bridge of Brede to Iham', Whittick 2004, R60. This charter can be approximately dated by the name of the abbot and also by those of the witnesses, who included Paulyn de Winchelsea, as well as Sir Robert de Aubervill', Reynold, chaplain of Hastings, Henry son of Reginald de Winchelsea and Robert de Brede. The last witness and clerk, who wrote and recorded this charter in the court of Brede, was named Nicholas. Lawrence, the rector of Brede, had disputed the tithes of moors and marshes (i.e. *moris*) of Brede with Fécamp (those which did not form part of the demesne) in 1203, Whittick 2004, R17. In 1245 Lawrence's successor as rector of Brede, Master William of Fécamp, leased these tithes for life for 28s. 4d., presumably yearly, making an annual payment of 25s. from the church to Fécamp, Whittick 2004, R58. He subsequently disputed with the Abbey over these tithes, claiming they belonged to Brede church and therefore to him by common law, but was ordered to allow the Abbey to possess the tithes in peace in 1252, Whittick 2004, R37.

41. Gardiner 1988, 112.

42. Long, Waller and Plater, 2007, 201-4, figs. 6.6, 6.7.

43. The physical evidence comes from sites in the former Brede estuary, West Winchelsea and White Fleet, Long, Waller, Stupples and Schofield 2007, 93, 99.

44. Long, Waller, Stupples and Schofield 2007, 94; Gardiner 1995, 128-31.

45. Gardiner 1988, 114-15. Fines nos 5, 12, 25 in 'Sussex Fines: 1-5 John (nos. 15-93)', An abstract of Feet of Fines for the County of Sussex: vol. 1: 1190-1248 (1903), pp. 5-22. URL: http://www.british-history.ac.uk/report.aspx?compid=65764. Date accessed: 26 February 2008.

46. Further details of this family are given in Draper, 'Failing Friaries?' (in prep.)

47. Gardiner 1988, 112-13, and fig. 10.1.

48. *PNS* 2, 529.

49. Gardiner 1988, 125-6.

50. *VCH Sussex* 9, 149-50.

51. Durrant Cooper 1850, 9, cited by Gardiner 1988, 119.

52. Gardiner 1988, 116. The land of Scotney mentioned in a bailiff's account of 1394 included *herbagium* in *hokkysland* and *Ockholte* which, as an *inspeximus* of an inquisition and commission of 1365 into the Broomhill marshes makes clear, bordered Broomhill Marsh, Bodl. MS dd All Souls c183, item 51, c184, item 1 in wooden box.

53. The witnesses were Stephen Andr[ew], Henry Alard, Henry[?] Mainard, Nicholas de Kareta, Godfrey Poun, Alan Poun, Reinger Paris, John Pret, Ralph de Brede, Geoffrey son of Mabel, David de Walla, Augustine his brother, Hamon Love, Walter Jordan, RYE 138/1, 2. The Mainard family were associated with both Old Winchelsea and Rye (*Chapter 2*).

54. Shipbuilding is documented in 1259 when a writ was sent to the bailiffs of Winchelsea to ensure that the king's galleys and barges newly made there and at Rye were kept in a roofed building to prevent damage, *Cal. Lib. Rolls* 4, 446. On 22 February 1252 a writ was sent to the sheriff of Sussex to go in person with four knights to Rye and see that the king's galleys were safely kept without damage and placed in a building or as they could best be kept, *Cal. Lib. Rolls* 4, 79. The year 1223 provides the earliest documentary indication of shipbuilding for the monarch at Rye, in the forbidding of the export of timber as the king was planning to build ships and galleys, *CPR 1216-35*, 374.

55. This shipbuilding family is known from 1341 onwards at Smallhythe in the person of Stephen Donet and later other Donets, James, Draper and Martin 2005, 57.

56. In his glossary of 16th-century Rye, Mayhew 1987, 313, gives *feter* as such. Neither this word nor variants appear with this meaning in MED for the medieval period but for this locality Mayhew's definition should be accepted as Martin Fetere's occupation.

57. Whittick 2004, R9.

58. They were granted 2s. on every ship carrying 80 tuns of wine and over for one year. A year later this grant was renewed although ships from Gascony were exempted, *CPR 1232-47*, 427, 454.

59. The harbour at New Romney appears to date from this period also, Draper and Meddens (forthcoming), chapter 3.

60. *CPR 1247-58*, 90.

61. Eddison 2004, 4-5.

62. By the end of this period some pottery was imported from the Continent and the rest came from kilns at Rye and Ashford, to which New Romney had a road by 1220, Reeves 1995, 78-91; Draper and Meddens (forthcoming), chapter 2.

63. The town of Battle was established with market rights in William I's reign and perhaps with borough rights by *c*.1180, Bleach and Gardiner 1999, 43. Battle is a pointer to the development of inland towns in addition to those already well established on the coast of Sussex and Kent.

64. Vollans 1995, 120, 126.

65. The centre of ironworking is *una ferraria* at an unnamed site in the hundred of East Grinstead, to the north west of Rotherfield, *DB Sussex* 10, 102. Other centres of ironworking were in Cheshire, Devon, Hampshire, Herefordshire, Lincolnshire, Northamptonshire, Surrey, Warwickshire, Wiltshire and Yorkshire, Britnell and Campbell 1995, 36.

66. Holden *et al.* (forthcoming).

67. Crossley 1999, 62-3; Howard 1999, 55; Williams 1999, 2.

68. Clarke and Milne 2002, 13.

69. Rushton 1999, 37.

70. Bynames such as de Maghfeld became fixed in this locality in the first half of the 14th century. Gilbert traded in Spanish iron, woad and alum, Bolton 1980, 302.

71. Coates 1999, 32-3.
72. Damien Goodburn identified the nails, Wetherill 1992, 22, 48.
73. *PNS* 2, 533.
74. Battle's main interest in the Rye area, around 1100, appears to have been at Dengemarsh, with holdings at Broomhill, which was located beyond Winchelsea, but adjacent to Dengemarsh. Dengemarsh clearly had a sea beach since both fish (*craspeis*), probably whales and porpoises, could fetch up on it and vessels be wrecked there. Dengemarsh appears contiguous with its neighbour Broomhill, Searle 1980, 123.
75. In the late 13th century the Archbishop was receiving rents from at least 50 salt-pits at New Romney. There are physical remains of this saltmaking but the precise relationship to the estuary and haven cannot be mapped because of later landscape changes. Salt-making continued at New Romney at least until the mid-15th century when it was recorded repeatedly at Geffes Saltcote and the town's saltcote, with a mention of Cotehelle, one of the many artificial mounds left by the salt-making process here and at Belgar near Lydd, Draper and Meddens (forthcoming), chapter 4. At Bishop's (later King's) Lynn the settlement developed on the marshes from their use as a landing place by traders purchasing salt which was being producing in nearby vills; in the late 11th century Lynn had houses, a market, fair and church. Rye's development, with the 100 saltpans of Domesday under Rameslie, parallels this, just as Romney and Hythe parallel the growth of Yarmouth from fishing settlements, Gardiner 2000, 85-6, citing Owen 1979, 141-53.
76. Vollans 1995, 118, for the name and nature of *Saltcoteshelle*. Salt-making in the lower reaches of the strongly tidal and originally estuarine River Adur in West Sussex is known from at least the late 13th century, Ridgeway 2000, 135.
77. Sources for this figure: the Romney Marsh Research Trust archaeological gazetteer; *HAS*; *HAK*; *PNS*; *DB Sussex*; British History Online (town histories); *VCH Sussex*; Gardiner 1988; Gardiner 2000; individual church guides and leaflets; the Cnut/Harthacnut charter for Brede.
78. Brooks 1988, 94, 100-1, fig. 8.7.
79. Eddison and Draper 1997, 82.
80. For the route through Brede, Babinerode (1086) and Babirote (1130), which appears later as 'a high road called Babaoestret' in the court rolls of Brede in 1406, *VCH Sussex* 9, 164; *PNS* 2, 514; a memorandum of a grant, c.1300, of two plots with houses in Brede which abutted the great street of Brede to the east, Whittick 2004, R31.
81. Waller and Grant 2008, 22-5.
82. Cf. James, Draper and Martin 2005, 12-15.
83. Jessup 1974, 49; *DB Kent*, 2, 25, 43; 5, 178.
84. Cf. Gardiner 2000, 81.
85. Postan 1972, 212.
86. The charter is dated by the name of the abbot to 1140-89, *Cal. Docs France*, 42-3. The collection of this amount of 33s. 4d. from assized rents by the mayor and commonalty appears in the 1343 bailiffs' account, TNA SC6/1028/12. Accounts covering the period of a year such as Michaelmas 1343 to Michaelmas 1344, or mayoral years, are cited by their year of commencement, and similarly other documents such as rentals dated by regnal year.
87. The hospital was described as a hospital for lepers in 1249 and again in the 1340s (*Chapter 7*). Its small size may account for its omission from the gazetteer in Rawcliffe 2006, who noted that there were more to be identified.

88. *Cal. Docs France*, 52. It was witnessed by Vincent of Rye, 'Nigasio' (possibly Nicasius of Rye, known 1203) and Gerard of Luvesham. Luvesham, also known as Levisham, Leflesham, Lewisham and other variants, and finally as Leasam, was an early and important settlement or manor to the north west of Rye, *VCH Sussex* 9, 56; *PNS* 2, 537.

89. *DB Sussex*, appendix, contains a modern discussion of the virgate, a quarter of a hide, as a taxation unit.

90. *Cal. Docs France*, 52.

91. This is stated in the cartulary, the seals themselves not surviving.

92. Fairfield was shown on the 6-inch OS map, *PNS* 2, 537, which also gives *Fayrfeld* known in 1574. Absence of an earlier reference may suggest the fair was in abeyance in the late Middle Ages as Rye suffered economic decline and the hospital became inactive (*Chapter 7*).

93. There are many other examples such St Nicholas' fair at Royston near St Albans, and the Stourbridge fair near Cambridge, Rawcliffe 2006, 314-15.

94. '*Quieti de syres et de hundredis*', Murray 1935, 235.

95. The original is in Archives Departémentales Seine-Maritime, Rouen, *liasse* 7H57, with a photograph and drawing in ESRO AMS 4947; Whittick 2004, R68. The seal is assigned to *c*.1190 and is of white wax, supported on four doubled threads of blue silk. Ellis's seal was also attached but only the tag remains.

96. 'Administrative History' of the Rye corporation, ESRO catalogue. In the medieval period the mayor was probably chosen in the open area called Courton. It is discussed in the companion volume to this history, D. Martin, B. Martin with J. Clubb and G. Draper, *Rye Rebuilt: regeneration and decline within a Sussex port town, 1350-1660* [hereafter Martin, *Rye Rebuilt*], chapter 2.

97. *DB Kent*, D2; 2, 2; 5,178.

98. Murray 1935, 12-13, appendix I; Rodger 1997, 25, 124; Rodger 1996, 644.

99. Murray 1935, 232-4.

100. Carpenter 1990, 160, 237, 261. In 1253 the men of Sandwich, Old Winchelsea, Rye, Yarmouth and Dunwich were warned that the king would take retribution if any further mutual attacks occurred, but these may have been empty words, *CPR 1247-58*, 225, 239.

101. Murray 1935, 1, 6, 14, 18, 19, 44. *Lestage* was 'a toll paid by merchants, etc., for the privilege of trading at fairs and markets, or a toll or tax paid for the privilege of loading a ship; *rivage* was a tax on arrival at shore; *passage* was a toll for passing over a bridge or through a place', MED.

102. Rye and Old Winchelsea were each requested to supply two ships for royal service in 1235, *CPR 1232-47*, 92. A late copy of a list of the five Head Ports with their members gives Rye and Winchelsea and other places as members of Hastings which together owed 21 ships, Parker Library, Corpus Christi College Cambridge, ms. 189, f. 35. Hastings objected in 1199 to Rye's and Winchelsea's charter of 1191 as restricting the service due of old, Murray 1935, 15, 44, appendices IF, IIC.

103. Carpenter 1990, xvi-xvii, 12-13, 19-20, 31-5; Painter 1933, 208; Philip de Albini was constable of Ludlow castle (1204) and keeper of the Channel Islands between 1207 and 1219, after which the office went to his nephew of the same name.

104. Vidler 1934, 7.

105. In April 1216 four townsmen were ordered to report the shipping details of the port to the king and the bailiffs, perhaps these keepers, who were told to send all the town's vessels to the Thames. The Cinque Ports had mainly been loyal to John but wavered in the middle of

his reign and near the end, *VCH Sussex* 2, 130. John made William de Warenne, Earl of Surrey, warden of the Cinque Ports in 1216, telling them that he did not want to put an alien over them, i.e. an Anglo-Norman magnate who might have been perceived as more French than English, Carpenter 1990, 261.

106. Vidler 1934, 7.

107. *CPR 1216-25*, 102, 108, 248-9.

108. [No named author], 'Worthy man of English Blood: William of Cassingham, a Forgotten Hero', Kent Archaeological Society newsletter 75 (winter 2007/8), 11. The loyalties of the men of the Cinque Port confederation were more complex than suggested by Rodger 1997, 54.

109. Carpenter 1990, 121, 27, 36, 44. Philip d'Albini fought with the king's army at the battle of Lincoln in May 1217, and in August commanded one of the king's ships at the naval battle off Sandwich.

110. It was founded before 1227, *VCH Kent*, 2, 226-7. http://www.british-history.ac.uk/report. aspx?compid=38241. Date accessed: 13 September 2008.

111. Carpenter 1990, 343-4.

112. The confederation limb of Pevensey was also named, as were Kingston and Pagham in west Sussex, and Portsmouth, Hull, Norwich, Ipswich, Shoreham, Exeter, Lynn, Southampton, Bristol, Orford, Orwell, Seaford, Dartmouth, Dunwich, Yarmouth (Norfolk) and Yarmouth (Isle of Wight), *CPR 1216-35*, 484.

113. *CPR 1216-35*, 476.

114. Carpenter 1990, 379. In 1225 royal letters of protection were also issued to various men and merchants travelling along or across the channel: William, the parson of St Giles' church, Winchelsea, Paulin of Winchelsea, William son of Alard, and Thomas son of Godfrey, also of Winchelsea. Furthermore neither Godfrey de Lucy, Keeper of the King's Galleys and Ports, nor the barons were to try again to prevent one John Bonin of Bruges from completing his voyage. Bonin, who was travelling with a cargo of grain from Flanders to Bishop's (King's) Lynn, had put into Old Winchelsea because of a storm, *CPR 1216-35*, 504.

115. *VCH Sussex* 9, 40.

116. A similar mandate was sent to Drogo de Barentin, warden of the Channel Islands, *CPR 1232-47*, 405, 424.

117. *Calendar of the Charter Rolls* 1, 321.

118. Matthew 1962, 75-6. The manor of Brede as well as Rye Foreign still belonged to Fécamp in 1324, at which point it came into the king's hand 'owing to war with France', Vidler 1934, 9, 19.

119. Brooks 1925, 579; *VCH Sussex* 2, 130-1; *CPR 1216-35*, 465; Murray 1935, 139-41.

120. Vidler 1934, 9; *Cal. Charter Rolls 1226-57*, 321.

121. RYE 139/50 (1589), enrolled in RYE 33/16, f. 206.

122. A conveyance dated 15 April 1470 helps locate the fee of Sir William de Etchingham (d.1262) on the west side of Rye. It was made by Thomas Echyngham, knight, lord of Udimore, and his wife Margaret and conveyed to Robert A' Crowche and his wife Margaret salt marsh in Rye marsh, bounding west on Gatebrigh (Cadborough) dyke, for a yearly rent of 26s. 8d. It also conveyed fields called Great and Little Ileland in Rye and Udimore, RYE 57/7. Cadborough marsh was the general term for the marsh on the west and south-west side of Rye to the north of the river Brede; it was one of two parts of the demesne lands of the manor of Udimore, Gardiner 1995, fig. 10.1,133.

123. In 1366 the marshes of the liberty were described reaching the highway from Playden to Rye on the east, the town on the south, the banks of the sea called 'Melflet' (i.e. probably where the mill race was) on the west, and the lands called 'Kyngeswyssh' and 'Bernardeshill' on the north (*Chapter 8*), *CPR 1364-67*, 284.

124. *CCLR 1247-51*, 32. Vidler 1934, 9, argued that the boundaries of the 13th-century parish, borough, liberty and Foreign would have been identical with those of the 19th century, but given the changing landscape that is unlikely. Some late medieval deeds of St Mary's Croft noted that it was within and without the liberty because it was not certain, or relevant, even then, where the precise boundary lay (*Chapter 9*).

125. Dyer 1992, 144, 152.

Chapter 2   Mariners, Pilgrims and Pirates

1. The seals of the barons, commonalty, mayor and churchwardens of Rye are the subject of a future study by G. Draper and C. Whittick.

2. Carpenter 1990, 374-9; Sylvester 2004, 8.

3. The fleet gathered at Portsmouth in 1225, *CPR 1216-35*, 514.

4. In addition there were 12 other ships, mostly from Wales, one from London and two foreign mercenaries, Sylvester 2004, 14, fig 2.7.

5. Dunwich was one of the five wealthiest ports in England in 1200, owing a fee-farm of £80 13s. 4d., Bailey 1991, 194-7.

6. Rudling *et al.* 1993, fig. 4, 75, 77.

7. Gardiner 2000, 85-6, 88-92; Pelham 1929, 93-4; Murray 1935, 209-11, 243; Taylor 1999, 46-7; Dulley 1966, 42; Draper and Meddens (forthcoming), chapter 4; *HMC* 5, 533-53. Smallhythe became a member of Rye in 1448.

8. Clarke 2005, 13-15; H. Clarke, pers. comm. At that time there were 810 inhabited houses in the town, with the population estimated at over 3,000, Parkin 1984, 199. Milne suggested from a 14th-century 'census' that the population was 2,000, including 400 mariners, Milne *et al.* 2004, 260.

9. E.g. *CPR 1232-47*, 92; *CPR 1422-29*, 192.

10. Gardiner 2007, 102.

11. A record of piracy in 1404 suggests contemporaries regarded the port of Rye or Winchelsea as much the same thing. A mass attack by Cinque Portsmen took place on a cargo of mixed and valuable goods from Biscay being carried to Southampton or Sluys. It was led by those of Rye, including William Longe, and seven balingers were used, three from Rye. Two mariners of the merchant vessel were killed and the rest wounded. In the royal commission to enquire into this, the captured vessel and goods were described as being taken to Rye or Winchelsea; at the inquisition which followed they were described as taken 'to the port of Rye', *Cal. Inq. Misc.* 7, 144-5, item 276; *CPR 1401-05*, 431.

12. A licence allowed hides to be imported and beans exported from Rye in return, *CPR 1364-67*, 1.

13. Murray 1935, 55.

14. Pelham 1928, 182.

15. *CPR 1422-29*, 192.

16. *Calendar of State Papers Venice* 1 (1864), nos 120, 126, 209, in which the chart is shown (frontispiece) in a Victorian copy.

17. Martin *et al.* 2004, 26-7; Long, Waller and Plater 2007, fig. 6.7, 204.

18. TNA MPF 212.

19. Draper and Meddens (forthcoming), chapter 4.

20. *CPR 1324-27*, 26.

21. In 1587 there were said to be no ships, captains or mariners living in New Winchelsea and just one sailor. When 20 tons of iron were shipped from New Winchelsea to London in 1595 a vessel from Hastings was used, Martin *et al.* 2004, 22, 36-8.

22. *Rough's Register*, 189; Boys 1792, 800; *CPR 1358-61*, 482-3, 516; Mate 2006, 86; Draper and Meddens (forthcoming), chapter 5; Pelham 1930, 177. A shallop was a local name for small boats usually under 25 tuns with fore and aft sails, and oars, and sometimes launched from a strand and used in shallow waters.

23. *CPR 1370-74*, 460, 485, 492; *CCLR* 1374-77, 48.

24. *CCLR 1405-1411*, 27.

25. Martin *et al.* 2004, 19, 101, 196.

26. In 1404 the Portsmen 'in warlike array' captured a merchant vessel between the Isles of Guernsey and Wight, dividing the goods at Rye. Of the Rye men, Stephen Scherman had captured the barge and salt, iron and other goods. William Longe and Robert Taillour had done similar, as had the masters of the balingers, *Cal. Inq. Misc.* 7, item 276, 144-5.

27. Vidler 1934, 44.

28. Sources for ships of medieval Rye: TNA E101/3/1; SC6/1028/15; *CPR 1216-35*, 514, 516; *CPR 1232-47*, 98; *CPR 1301-07*, 499; *CPR 1345-49*, 216; *CPR 1350-54*, 352, *CPR 1358-61*, 586; *CPR 1232-47*, 85, 309; *CCLR 1385-89*, 330; *CPR 1321-24*, 371; RYE 136/26, 33; Sylvester 2004, 13, citing TNA E101/19/22; *Cal. Inq. Misc.* 7, item 276, 144-5; Langdon 2007, 115, n. 21; Vidler 1934, 8, 16, 19, 44. Vidler 1934, 23, appears incorrect in stating that Salerne was the owner of *La Nicholas*, and indeed that Bynedenne owned a separate vessel. A 'snake' was a warship, i.e. a vessel long in the beam, Rodger 1997, 12.

29. *CPR 1258-66*, 661.

30. Sweetinburgh 2006, 103-4; Sweetinburgh 2008a, 16-24; *CPR 1266-72*, 233.

31. *CPR 1232-47*, 98, 309; RYE 136/7. Similarly Andrew de Poddepyrie (Potepirie), who was master of a vessel which travelled to Bordeaux 'with the King's treasure' in 1242, lent his surname to a street in Rye, Vidler 1934, 8. The street name Longer perhaps derived from the important Longe family rather than its length (*Chapter 8*).

32. RYE 136/26, 27, 33. Some land belonging to this man or his family, *Torelesakre*, lay north of Rye near Lee or Legh brokes (meadows) and the land of Brocale Sampson of Lewleshamme or Leasam in 1307, RYE 136/28.

33. Langdon 2007, 129.

34. Sylvester 2004, 12.

35. A tun (ton) cask was equivalent to a cylinder 60 inches long and almost 36 inches in diameter, weighing about 2,048 pounds. Although the tun was the accounting unit for customs, etc., wine was probably transported in casks called hogsheads which were one-quarter the size of a tun, *Vaults of Ancient Winchelsea* [Winchelsea Archaeology Society, n.d., n.p], drawing on Sylvester 2004, 7-19. Pelham 1929, 116, noted that these accounts recorded that the *Lebanon* of Winchelsea exported 135 casks from Bordeaux on 17 May 1308. Martin *et al.* 2004, 122-3, record from Homan's work that 15 New Winchelsea vessels appear in the Bordeaux accounts in 1306-7. In 21 shipments they transported 2923.25 tuns, equivalent to nearly three-quarters of a million gallons of red Gascon wine, and well over 1,000 tuns per shipment, a remarkable amount. It is not known how many brought the wine to New Winchelsea or how many non-Winchelsea vessels were also involved.

36. The size, shapes and capacities of vessels are discussed in Langdon 2007, 122-5. The *Jesus* built at Smallhythe in 1416 was a 1000 tun ship, making it 46m. long with a 32m. keel and 14m. in breadth, Taylor and Aston 1999, 38.
37. This was the case in the 16th century, Mayhew 1987, 163.
38. *CPR 1358-61*, 586.
39. In 1389 pilgrims could only leave from Dover and Plymouth without special licence from the king, unless they were going to Ireland to where they could pass from wherever they liked, *Statutes of the Realm*, 12 Richard II, c.20. However an order of the Council in the same year acknowledged that in reality pilgrims, or those posing as such, were likely to depart from a great variety of ports. It was addressed to the keepers of the passage at Newcastle upon Tyne, Scarborough, Kingston upon Hull, Boston, Lynn, Great Yarmouth, Kirkelerode, Ipswich, Orwell, Harwich, Chichester, Southampton; Melcombe, Exeter, Plymouth, Dartmouth, Bristol, Dover, Sandwich, New Winchelsea and Rye, *CCLR 1385-89*, 592.
40. *CPR 1381-85*, 1; [no named authors], *The English Channel: the link in the History of Kent and Pas-de-Calais* (Maidstone, Kent County Council, 2008), 18; East Kent Archives Centre Do/CPi 4.
41. *Rough's Register*, 160; *HMC 5*, 538.
42. Martin *et al.* 2004, 21.
43. Webb 2001, 8, 167-9.
44. Draper and Meddens (forthcoming), chapter 2.
45. D. Martin, pers. comm.; Webb 1994, 62.
46. Rawcliffe 2006, 342.
47. The following draws on Lutton 2009, 9-16; Ellis 1851. Kyriel, through which Guldeford travelled, was probably modern Crieul-sur-Mer between Le Tréport to the east and Dieppe to the west.
48. E.g. *CPR 1232-47*, 64, *CPR 1232-47*, 309; *CPR 1360-64*, 29.
49. The area in which they could operate was between the race (*sappum*) of St Mathieu and the foreland of Thanet. The race was probably that of the mills near Rye or Old Winchelsea (*Chapter 1*). A protection for two years for the brethren of the hospital or hermitage of St Antony in the port of Winchelsea was also granted, *CPR 1266-72*, 59, 91. The hermitage has been identified as lying across a channel from the possible site of Old Winchelsea, Gardiner 1988, fig. 10.1, 113. Eddison 1998, 75, queried this exact location.
50. *Rough's Register*, 128, n.1, 157.
51. MED.
52. Pelham 1930, 184-5.
53. The mandate for action against them was addressed to the ports and limbs of the confederation indicating that it was on Romney Marsh that William and Robert were based, as does the record of 1212, *CPR 1232-47*, 187.
54. Saul 1986, 53. Relations between England and France were strained in 1325 to 1328 and in the customs accounts alien wool merchants were absent from East Sussex ports, something that was attributed to the 'war', Pelham 1929, 97.
55. On 24 July 1323 a commission of oyer and terminer was ordered in response to the complaint that Richard de Pulteneye, merchant of Coventry, freighted his ship with goods at Rouen to take to Southampton and then John de Shotteby, John Payn of Wynchelse and others entered his ship at anchor in Portsmouth and carried away his goods, *CPR 1321-24*, 374-5.

56. *CPR 1321-24*, 160. The merchants were perhaps from Cologne, cf. the alien Peter Herman living at New Winchelsea in 1436 who was from Cologne in Almain, *CPR 1429-36*, 586.

57. There were two men named Gervase Alard, senior and junior, Martin *et al.* 2004, 67, 69. The references here are probably both to Alard junior. On 4 February 1303 Gervase Alard was appointed admiral of the fleet of the Cinque Ports and of all ports from Dover to Cornwall, setting forth for Scotland, *CPR 1301-07*, 111. Vidler 1934, 16, citing *Sussex Notes and Queries* 1,78, recorded 39 vessels assembling at New Winchelsea in 1300 under Alard and four captains. The Rye vessels had among them had two masters and 30 crew. They served between 20 June and 26 September. The masters were paid 6d. a day and the men 3d. The Alard family were notable members of the town elite of New Winchelsea with two chantries in St Thomas's church there, Martin *et al.* 2004, 78-79.

58. *CPR 1321-24*, 371.

59. *CPR 1301-07*, 499.

60. TNA SC6/1028/12; RYE 136/45, 46.

61. *CPR 1321-24*, 151, 313, 375, 449.

62. *CPR 1321-24*, 375, 389. Hardyng is also recorded involved in a similar action under the name John Hardi of Winchelsea, *CPR 1321-24*, 310. Nicholas Hardying was also of New Winchelsea. On 10 March a ship was seized by the bailiff of Southampton in order to carry victuals to Scotland and handed over to Robert de Wynter, who sold it to Nicholas Hardyng of Winchelsea and refused to restore it to its owners, or pay for it, to the damage of the owners and delay of the Scottish expedition, *CPR 1301-07*, 187.

63. Thomas Pharon, Robert Pharon, Pharon atte Gate/*de porta*, Richard Pharon, Robert Pharon, Pharonsson, Pharon Ion, Thomas Pharon, Laurence Pharon, TNA SC12/15/73; RYE 136/1, 3, 4, 36, 15, 17, 20, 24, 25, 27, 29, 36, 37, 40, 43, 50, 55, 64. After 1325 the only record found is of another Laurence Pharon who appears once in the town records in 1415, paying a local tax on a tenement in Watermelle Ward, RYE 77/1.

64. J. Kirkham, pers. comm., drawing on A. Stenning, extracts from 'Return of Members of Parliament ordered by the House of Commons', 1878. A Dutch ship owner petitioned the king and council for justice after Longe, and others of Rye including Robert Webbe, attacked the Dutch ship with five of their own, captured the merchants in it and threatened to kill them when Longe could not get a warrant from the Lord Warden to leave Rye, TNA SC8/127/6331.

65. *CPR 1324-27*, 317; *CPR 1327-30*, 155; *CPR 1338-40*, 26; Barron and Saul 1995, 3-4.

66. E.g. *CPR 1301-07*, 273; *CPR 1350-54*, 520; *CPR 1358-61*, 482-83, 516; *CPR 1396-99*, 101.

67. *CPR 1361-66*, 150; Archaeological Gazetteer of Wrecks on and around Romney Marsh and the southerly Cinque Ports, www.rmrt.org.uk.

68. Claesius de Grave of Sluys was master of the ship. There were also ashes, for tanning, among the goods which came from Almain and were said to be worth 1800 florins in total, *CPR 1350-54*, 165.

69. On 2 May 1347 such protection had also been ordered for the galleys of the merchants of Venice, the king addressing Sandwich and Winchelsea as well as such ports as Portsmouth, Southampton, Dartmouth, Fowey and Weymouth, *CCLR 1346-48*, 220.

70. Barron and Saul 1995, 4-5.

71. The Flemish mariners were in many cases primarily carriers rather than merchants, Harding 1995, 155-62.

72. *CPR 1374-77*, 48-9, 65.

73. Mercer 2005, 56-7. Prendergast's activities at New Romney, where his relative Dame Beatrix Prendergast ran the Rome tavern, are described in Draper and Meddens (forthcoming), chapter 6; *HMC* 5, 533-5, 539.

74. The agreement, written in French, concerned the ransoms of Frenchmen from 'Harfleu as far as Hendrenesce' when they were captured during the course of *skumerie*. The aim was ensure a minimum rate of ransoms for different classes of masters or mariners, while enabling those of Romney or Lydd to extract higher payments from a gentlemen or a merchant if they could. The French could apply the same rates to any captured masters and mariners from places between Southampton and the Isle of Thanet, *HMC* 5, 538-9.

75. Murray 1935, 9.

76. Mercer 2005, 60-2; Draper and Meddens (forthcoming), chapter 2.

77. Murray 1935, 133.

78. The townsmen made their oath in person to the Abbot. This and the witnesses suggest that they travelled to Fécamp rather than the Abbot to Rye, *Cal. Docs France*, 42-3.

79. Dulley 1969, 47-8. The men of Rye exercised a degree of caution over swearing to enforce the Abbey's share of the catch; they would ensure that no one living in the town would be allowed to fish without paying the Abbey's shares but some who landed and sold fish at Rye were not townsmen and there might be no way to make them pay if they refused. The Rye bailiff's account of 1343 recognised the status of fishermen making payment in relation to the lord's share as different from that of residents and non-residents making other customary payments. It is headed (in translation) 'the profits and perquisites of the court of the town of Rye from 18th day of June, year 17 (1343) until Michaelmas next following and from the said Michaelmas until Michaelmas, year 18 (September 1344), for one year both residents of the said town and of fishermen and strangers, plus the fines of millers from the enacting of the assize of bread', TNA SC6/1028/12, m.1.

80. This Rye agreement is the earliest evidence for fishing in this area. Much discussion of fishing and in particular the share system depends on reading back from later evidence and practice from other Sussex towns, particularly Brighton, Dulley 1969, 37-8, 42-3. The shares recorded in the accounts represent a literal fraction of the value of the catch, perhaps a quarter or half share at Winchelsea, so that calculations of the fishing industry's worth must be multiplied several times depending on the number of shares per vessel. Using comparative evidence from Brighton from the 16th century, Sylvester proposed values for the Winchelsea industry, noting that others doubted that such calculations had validity. He accepted Dulley's comparisons between Old Winchelsea and Rye, i.e. that the fish shares collected at the former were worth six times those of Rye in 1267 and five times in 1272, Sylvester 2004, 16, n. 87; Sylvester 1999, 232-6.

81. Called 'certain customs called cristschar' arising from fishing boats' in the account of 1362 following a dispute when William Taillour was bailiff of Rye, TNA SC6/1028/15. The parson of Rye brought a petition complaining, like his predecessor, that since 1247 the tithe of fish known as Christ's Share which belonged to the church had been collected by the bailiffs to the king's use. A commission under Robert Herle, the Lord Warden of the Cinque Ports, took evidence from the parson and from William Taillour, William de Brampton, and four good men of Rye, including Benedict Cely, mayor, *Cal. Inq. Misc.* 3, 182, item 490; TNA E101/28/7. Christ's Share escaped alienation at that time and also alienation to Stanley Abbey with the advowson of the church in 1363, *CPR 1361-66*, 327, 329. In the chamberlains' accounts of the mid-15th century onwards, it was taken by the vicar and churchwardens as St Mary's Share, Dulley 1969, 41-2. There seems no evidence

for the suggestion that Stanley Abbey received Christ's share and the town the king's share, Vidler 1934, 25. In 1401 a similar agreement to that of Rye was made between the king and Hugh Setour, parson of New Winchelsea, stating that in time of peace the custom known as Christ's Share there was worth 20s., 40s. or 100s. or 10 marks yearly, but in wartime little or nothing, *CPR 1399-1401*, 460.

82. Gardiner 2000, 87; Parker Library, Corpus Christi College, Cambridge, ms. 189. These categories of ship applied not only to Rye vessels but more generally to those fishing on this coast.

83. Sweetinburgh 2008a, 18; Murray 1935, 236-9. In 1303 the fishermen of New Winchelsea, Rye and Hastings still took a vigorous part in the herring fishing off Yarmouth, protesting loudly about their great losses when they were prevented from selling at the Yarmouth herring fair, Sylvester 2004, 16.

84. Rye bailiffs' accounts of 1272 to 1363 containing useful material on fishing are discussed below. Accounts are referred to throughout by their year of commencement. The following ones include Rye but contain no useful detailed information: the ministers' and receivers' accounts for farms in the Honor of Aquila in Sussex, Kent and Essex for some years of the reigns of Edward I and Edward II, TNA SC6/1089/21, membranes 1-8 (1283-90); a summary in fragmentary condition, listing sums due from king's officers for places in the whole country including Rye, in 1337-9, SC6/1090/10; a minister's account for the receipts of alien priories in wartime including Rye, SC6/1127/4. SC6/1028/9 is a fragment of an account covering Rye in which not even the bailiff's name is legible. SC6/1028/14 is a post-Black Death four-year summary of 1355-9 referring to a particular account which does not survive and to Thomas de Wynchelse's name.

85. TNA SC6/1031/19 (1266) contains at the end the farm of the town of Rye at £40. It is a long account of Old Winchelsea, recording taxes on ships and giving masters and cross-Channel ports, e.g. Le Tréport, Crotay, Dieppe, and also Yarmouth, under custom received, revealing a very busy port. There is a very long list of shares and also perquisites of court. The Winchelsea ferry is accounted for although the sum is illegible. 1028/8 covers Rye (6 May 1272 to 6 May 1273); 1028/11 covers Rye from Michaelmas 1342 to 18 June 1343; 1028/12 covers 18 June 1343 to Michaelmas 1343 then to Michaelmas 1344; 1028/13 covers Rye in 1344-5, includes fishing shares in January and August. 1032/7 is the particular account of John Longe for Winchelsea, Iham and Rye in 1351. 1032/8 (1352) is similar and shows more goods being loaded and unloaded at Winchelsea than at Rye, including featherbeds, and at Rye more fishermen and mariners than at Winchelsea. Iham is different, its part of the account being more like that of a traditional rural manor.

86. Dulley 1969, 39-41.

87. Fifty-six at Rye in 1343 was in fact an exceptional number because the account covers over 15 months, TNA SC6/1028/12.

88. TNA SC6/1028/11-14. The four-year summary of 1355-9 gives the amount received by the bailiff from the custom of fishing boats as follows: 1355-6, 46s.; 1356-7, 52s.; 1357-8, 44s. This compares with a regular annual income of £10 2s. 4d. from rents of assize and from 'farm of stalls' of 40d. The income from pleas and perquisites of court varied between 18s. in 1354-5, in which year the fishing custom is illegible, to 46s. 4d. in 1357-8, SC6/1028/14. The total sum collected as Christ's Share in 1362 (£3 17s. 4d.) was a little larger than that received by the bailiff from 'the custom of fishing boats' in the 1350s which ranged from £2 6s. to £2 12s.

89. Bailey 1991, 198, 205.

90. Sylvester 2004, 16.
91. TNA SC6/1028/12, 15.
92. Kowaleski 2000, 429-54.
93. The town fair received a charter in 1290 for the original date of 8 September, *Calendar of Charter Rolls, 1257-1300*, 342; *Calendar of Charter Rolls, 1300-26*, 61. This was linked with the parishioners' oblations, who in 1476 were said to have been formerly obliged to pay on the feast of the Assumption (8 September) but who were often abroad, fishing for herring in distant parts or frequenting 'fairs in neighbouring places', presumably the one near the hospital, since there are no other possible candidates. The bishop of Chichester made a mandate addressed to the vicar of Rye, William Wykwyk, that they should make their oblations on the Nativity of Mary, 15 September, *HMC* 5, 496.
94. The Scarborough fair was held between 15 August and 29 September, Sylvester 2004, 16; Sweetinburgh 2008a,18.
95. Dulley 1969, 38-9. Fish assemblages at Dover in the late 12th and 13th centuries were dominated by herring, cod and mackerel, suggesting that fishing was predominantly in the Channel and southern North Sea rather than around the south-west coast, Parfitt *et al.*, 365-69.
96. Participation in fishing in the spring and summer is evidenced in Rye accounts of 1272 and 1343. The 1272 account records 'town' fishing shares paid at St John Baptist (24 June), at St Peter *ad vincula* (1 August) and at mid-Lent; unspecified fishing shares paid at Easter and also Yarmouth shares, TNA SC6/1028/8. The 1343-4 account records share paid in September 1342 (20 men), October 1342 (16 men), April 1343 (20 men), July 1343 (31 men), and September 1343 (21 men). They were not all different men each time, SC6/1028/12. In 1362 the account has a record of share payments only at three terms: the feast of St Andrew, i.e. 30 November, Christmas and Easter, SC6/1028/15.
97. Herbows were in general used during the summer months, primarily to catch conger, although in this perhaps exceptional year were being used at Rye in the Lent season. The herbows or harbews of the account might refer to the hooks themselves rather than vessels. Flew nets were drift nets used for herring in the local, coastal waters. They might also be used in the North Sea, although there the deeper norward nets were often used. Fishing vessels and economics in Lydd, New Romney and Hythe are discussed in Sweetinburgh 2008a, 16-23.
98. *Cal. Inq. Misc.* 3, 182, item 490; TNA E101/28/7. The names of some of the fishermen in 1362 are those of Rye families, e.g. Finch and Sam(p)son. Robert Vynch (Finch) witnessed a feoffment of 1306, in which John Torel, the merchant or carrier, conveyed *Crockeresfeld* in Playden to Richard de Portesmouthe, junior, RYE 136/26. The Sampson family is discussed in *Chapter 4*.
99. Sweetinburgh 2008a, 21. Another possibility is that for the purposes of shares, the Rye town government recognised four categories as in the 12th-century agreement.
100. *Rough's Register*, x. Herring from eight boats operating out of New Romney were assessed for a local tax in 1340, which raised £4 13s. 4d. for the town compared with over £5 from the butchers, Boys 1792, 799.
101. Draper and Meddens (forthcoming), chapter 3.
102. *Rough's Register*, 28-30.
103. Dulley 1969, 41. The evidence lies in the chamberlains' accounts which do not themselves survive until this time. The peak was passed in 1570-90 with the silting of Rye Creek, Mayhew 1987, 262-6; see also *Chapter 9*.

Chapter 3   Rye and its Hinterlands in the Middle Ages: War and Trade

1. Barron 1995, 3.
2. Romney Marsh contains very little in the way of woodland except for an ancient holly forest at Lydd, Beck 2004, 19-21.
3. In 1327 a grant was made to Queen Isabella for life of the king's town of Rye which was valued at £15 a year, and of the manor and marsh of Iham (at New Winchelsea) valued at £34. Other places elsewhere were granted which were valued at £37, *CPR 1327-30*, 123.
4. In 1387 the parks and woods of the queen consort, Anne of Bohemia, were described as being in the Rape of Hastings and were presumably held by her as dower, just as Philippa had held them, *CPR 1385-89*, 306; Juliet Vale, 'Philippa (1310x15?–1369)', *Oxford Dictionary of National Biography*, Oxford University Press, Sept 2004; online edn, Jan 2008 [http://www.oxforddnb.com/view/article/22110, accessed 31 July 2008].
5. Sir William II held manors in Etchingham, Salehurst, Mountfield and Udimore. In 1366 he also held manors at Beddingham and Peakdean in Sussex, and in Kent at Brenzett (Romney Marsh), Hempsted (now represented by Hempstead Forest, Cranbrook, in the Weald) and Lullingstone in west Kent. Seventy-five years earlier his great-uncle, also a Sir William (I), had also held manors in Stopham, Yapton and Linch in Sussex and Bryanston and Bradford Bryan in Dorset, and a town house in New Winchelsea, Saul 1986, 3, 178.
6. Batlesforde also leased arable, marshland and 'broci', possibly thickets, to Aschbournham, *CPR 1389-92*, 76.
7. *CPR 1350-54*, 287. These lands lay in the most of the hundreds forming the Rape of Hastings, Shoyswell, Hawksborough, Ninfield, Netherfield, Foxearle, Battle, Bexhill, Henhurst, Guestling, Staple and Goldspur hundreds, although not in Gostrow hundred which covered Brede and Udimore, *PNS* 2, 450-534.
8. Gardiner 1999b, 38-9; Williams 1999, 6-7.
9. ESRO HBR/1; Hughes and Martin 1999, 61.
10. Langdon 2007, 115, n.21.
11. *CPR 1350-54*, 18.
12. Matthew 1962, 166-7.
13. Gardiner 1995, 131.
14. Burke 2008, 7-9. Winchelsea's cellars were primarily for wine storage but a possible secondary retail use has also been suggested for the cellars, Martin *et al.* 2004, 105, 123. In 1360 two men were ordered to rescue as much wine as possible from the wreck of *La Katerine* of Simon Salerne of New Winchelsea and have it stored in cellars. Richard Blake and John de Wylyngham were to search carefully 'along the coast of Kent and Essex for 138 tuns, 1 pipe of the king's wine, signed with the sign of the merchants from whom it was bought', and put them in cellars. These the king had lately exported in a ship called *la Katerine* of Winchelsea, but it had been broken near the coast by stormy seas and much of the wine washed ashore in those counties, *CPR 1358-61*, 377. *La Katerine* of Simon Salerne of Winchelsea, was described as a crayer in 1387. Salerne had caused it to be loaded with salt and other wares to the value of 500 marks at the 'Baye' in Poitou many years previously 'in the time of truce'. The goods were captured off the coast of Brittany by subjects of Charles de Bloys, and acquired by the captain of Auroy castle. In 1387 Salerne was still seeking redress, *CCLR 1385-1389*, 330.
15. These cellars and those of other coastal and southern towns are reviewed and illustrated in Martin, *Rye Rebuilt*, chapter 6.
16. Pelham 1928, 170.

17. Pelham 1928, 170; *Cal. Inq. Misc.* 4, 67, no. 109.

18. At TQ8124, Explorer OS map; *Cal. Inq. Misc. 4*, 67, no. 109; *PNS* 2, 522, gives under Ewhurst parish: 'Spital Wood, cf. Speteslond 1406 Ct, Spittlewyshe, terr.voc. Spyttles 1574 Ct'. 'Ct' refers to unspecified court rolls as the source for these names. Brokelond itself does not appear under Ewhurst.

19. In 1225 an order was made that timber and other necessaries be sent to Dartmouth to repair the king's ships. They were to be transported in the ship of Rayner, son of David (or Daniel) of Romney, and he was not to be impeded in any way by the bailiffs or barons of the Cinque Ports. Before the storms of the 13th century, New Romney was a more significant port than Rye and the River Rother which passed through the Weald had its major exit to the sea there, *CPR 1216-35*, 504. On the early development of Boston, Gardiner 2000, 85.

20. The bridge for which timber was supplied renewed an earlier one and was so substantial that it did not apparently need repair until 1500, Thompson 1856, 250, 317.

21. *CPR 1358-61*, 96, 119.

22. Draper forthcoming.

23. *CPR 1385-89*, 306.

24. Rye and New Winchelsea remained in the king's hands because of war until 1415, and also afterwards when the property of all alien priories in England was permanently absorbed by the monarch, some of which was later redistributed largely to the then queen consort and subsequently to English monasteries.

25. On 1 March 1360 the French who had recently entered England at Winchelsea were described as 'a host of armed men and vessels, [who] took the town, slew the men therein, and rode about the country [locality] committing homicides, burnings and other mischief'. The king ordered that four named French lords were to be held in custody in the castles or towns where they lived in places as far away as Pontefract, Bristol and Gloucester. They were to swear an oath to ensure their loyalty, *CPR 1360-64*, 14-15, 29.

26. *CPR 1358-61*, 350.

27. *CPR 1216-35*, 374. Smallhythe was very important for royal shipbuilding from at least 1401, Bellamy and Milne 2003, 354.

28. E.g., *CPR 1232-47*, 293; *CPR 1247-58*, 363.

29. Or perhaps only 25,000 foot soldiers, the calculation of the figures being uncertain; the ships left from Winchelsea and Portsmouth, Martin *et al.* 2004,13, n. 55.

30. *CPR 1340-43*, 272.

31. Langdon 2007, 113.

32. *CPR 1345-48*, 215.

33. *CCLR 1346-49*, 95; listings of officers on boards at Winchelsea Court Hall.

34. *CCLR 1346-49*, 149-51, 164, 169.

35. The other lords would have included Edmund de Passeleye [Pashley] who had woodland in Peasmarsh and many other places around, *CPR 1327-30*, 556. Some of the Pashley family were mariners with Rye connections. Edmund was appointed warden of the town and port of Rye at the same time as Etchingham (I) was appointed to New Winchelsea, *CPR 1324-1327*, 26.

36. *CCLR 1377-81*, 276. This may have been part of ongoing friction between the town government of New Winchelsea and an earlier Sir William Etchingham (I), great-uncle of Etchingham II, who was appointed warden of the town by Edward III in 1324 in the run-up to war, *CPR 1324-1327*, 26. The Cinque Ports disliked what they saw as any infringement of their rights of self-government. By 1311 Etchingham (I)'s wealth was sufficient for him

to be summoned to Parliament as a lord, sitting with the earls and barons; he had earlier been elected to the Commons as a knight of the shire for Sussex. Etchingham (II) was disliked and attacked locally as a collector of customs and later of the poll tax of 1381 in Sussex, Saul 1986, 3, 6, 81-2.

37. Portsmouth suffered a French raid in 1369 as war resumed. Both Winchelsea and Gravesend would be burnt by the French in 1380, Thomson 1983, 137. Rye had previously been raided in 1339 (*Chapter 8*).

38. Mercer 2005, 51, 56, 57; Vidler 1934, 21, 30-32, 39.

39. This wood was described as between Bodyham pond and the lands of Thomas Colpepere, knight, in Wigeshull, with the right of entry for five years (after 1376), the soil then belonging to Edward Dalyngridde, knight; this right explains the felling in 1381, *CPR 1377-81*, 4.

40. Draper forthcoming.

41. Like many others of the new English population, Adam and his heirs were to render a yearly or reasonable farm, and the rents and services from the inn which were due to the church and the hospital of St Nicholas at Calais, *CPR 1345-48*, 546-68.

42. Some timber was also re-loaded at Knelle dam, west of the Isle of Oxney, Gardiner 2007, 101. 'Shout' derived from the Dutch *schuit* or *schuyt*, the cross-Channel trade between the Low Countries with Rye and Winchelsea suggesting how the term and type was introduced, Langdon 2007, 115, n.21.

43. Its possible transport by 'carriages' is mentioned although difficult to envisage in the Weald in winter, *CPR 1350-54*, 192. Firewood was not usually carried more than 12 to 18 miles overland in the early 14th century, and less after the Black Death as costs rose, Galloway, Keene and Murphy 1996, 468. Small quays at *Damme* in the lower Brede valley and at Bodiam, Newenden, Maytham and Reading Street on the Rother were used to load firewood or timber onto boats, Gardiner 1995, 131. Scots Float to the north of Rye was enlarged and used from 1480 to load firewood for Calais, Gardiner 2007, 101.

44. It was apparently rare, from 'incidental references', for the hinterlands of Rye and New Winchelsea to supply London with firewood in the 14th century, at least regularly, 'although both ports had close connections with the capital through trade in more valuable goods', Galloway, Keene and Murphy 1996, 467.

45. For this paragraph see Pelham 1928, 170-82. These customs accounts presents some difficulties by their inconsistent format, particularly in relation to the head customs ports such as Chichester, New Winchelsea or New Romney under which customs from lesser ports like Rye were recorded; there are a number of years for which they were not made or do not survive with, for example, no records of customs on exports of wood between 1329 and 1371. When the new custom of 1303 was first introduced on imports and exports it only applied to alien merchants or traders and not to native ones.

46. Pelham 1929, 104.

47. 44 ship voyages were made from New Romney with billets. Schiedam received the highest numbers of cargoes from Rye with a total of 14 ship voyages, Pelham 1930, 204.

48. *Ancorage* and *Bulcag'* were anchorage and unloading dues. The payment on the purchase/ export of talwood was simply referred to as 'custom', TNA SC6/1028/15.

49. Talwood was 'cut wood for burning, firewood; also, firewood logs in the form of whole rounds'. It can be colloquial for billets, cheaper, smaller, firewood, MED.

50. Pelham 1928, 182.

51. Galloway, Keene and Murphy, 1996, 467, citing CCA DCc/RE 258. *La Godewille* of Neuport in Flanders crossed the Channel to fetch brushwood and other victuals but was detained

at Smallhythe by the bailiffs there in 1377 because of the prohibition on ships' passage. It was permitted to leave on condition it went only to London, *CCLR 1377-81*, 38; Pelham 1930, 177-80. When the townsmen of Rye went to Tenterden they travelled via the River Rother and Smallhythe, Gardiner 2007, 103, citing the chamberlains' accounts, RYE 60/3, f. 68.

52. Pelham 1930, 187, 203-4; Pelham 1928, 174-5; John Salerne II was appointed collector of a subsidy of poundage with Laurence Corboill in 1371-2, TNA E122/147/15. Poundage was one of the two main types of customs, a proportional tax on all imported and exported goods. The other was tonnage, a tax on each tun or cask of imported wine.

53. *CCLR 1385-89*, 330; Pelham 1930, 183-5.

54. Pelham 1929, 92-103.

55. Pelham 1930, 171-204.

56. Pelham 1930, 199-200; *Rough's Register*, 156. This William Elmet is not otherwise known, but one of this name was a citizen and dyer (*tinctor*) of London in 1461, CCA DCc *Charta Antiqua* O116.

57. TNA SC6/1028/15. A trader from *douerdarr'* was also recorded in this document and given as such by Vidler.

58. Pers paid anchorage and paid *pro cust'ciser' et pisc'sals'*, TNA SC6/1028/15. On 12 August 1374 Gabriel Fogalus, a merchant of Piacenza, appointed Lewis Andreu of Florence his attorney to sue for and receive his goods which had recently been captured at Rye when they were being carried in a Genoese tarrit, *CCLR 1374-77*, 48.

59. Similar licences were issued to barons of the other Cinque Ports, specifying Nicholas Archer of Dover, Nicholas Adelard of New Winchelsea and Walter le Taverner of Sandwich, *CPR 1301-07*, 499. Harding 1995, 163, mentions the possible role of taverners and innkeepers not only in providing accommodation but also business contacts for traders across the Channel.

60. Hockley 1962, 703-4; Langdon 2007, 127.

61. E.g., on 4 February 1303 Gervase Alard of New Winchelsea was appointed as admiral of the fleet of the Cinque Ports and of all ports from Dover to Cornwall, setting forth for Scotland, *CPR 1301-07*, 111. On 12 August 1302 a pardon by reason of service in the Scottish war was given to various men held in Norwich gaol for larceny, including Thomas de Hull of Winchelsea, *CPR 1301-07*, 54.

62. Pelham 1929, 117.

63. *CPR 1345-48*, 59, 216, 311, 313, 319. Clapitus became sheriff of London in 1347, Barron 2005, 330. *VCH Kent*, 2, 181, states that he was a vintner. He founded the house of nuns of the order of Preachers at Dartford, *CPR 1345-48*, 77. He was granted wood for the construction of the house by the king, which could easily be transported there by water, Lee 2001, 16-17, 51. The *La Katerine* of Rye, master Walter Salerne, might perhaps have been the same as that of New Winchelsea owned later by Simon Salerne, although this female saint's name was commonly used for vessels in this locality, Sweetinburgh 2008a, 22-3.

64. Accounts for the late 14th century show the large quantities grown on Romney Marsh, Pelham 1930, 190; Gross and Butcher 1995, 109; Gardiner 1995, 133.

65. Clapitus also had to bring back letters of testimonial to confirm its delivery, *CCLR 1374-77*, 48.

66. *CPR 1350-54*, 352, 384; *CCLR 1374-77*, 48. The record does not state where Bynedenne was a merchant. Lyons was a vintner, sheriff of London, impeached in the Good Parliament and murdered in the Peasants' Revolt, Barron 2004, 138, n.119, 143, 277, 303, 333.

67. *CCLR 1389-92*, 287. The tenement was among the 39 described as *forinsec* in the chamberlains' account of 1405, RYE 60/1, f. 2r, probably Rye Foreign. Paul Portesmouth, mayor and churchwarden of Rye, sublet one there too.
68. Harding 1995, 157-9.

Chapter 4   The People of Rye: Economic and Occupational Activity c.1260 to c.1660

1. A. Leach, 'Schools', in *VCH Sussex* 2, 425.
2. Goddard 2004, xi. For example, all the references to Rye and the settlements in its hinterlands in the Close and Patent Rolls and in the various rentals and accounts of the king's bailiffs were collected and entered as well as those from the town records.
3. G. Draper, 'Did the Cinque Ports Matter: the Place of the Ports in the Maritime Economy of South East England *c.*1000-*c.*1600?', paper at International Maritime History Conference 2008.
4. TNA SC12/15/73. The names of some who appear in the rental are known from other sources to have been dead by the early 14th century, suggesting that it dates from early rather than late in the reign.
5. These rents were also recorded in the bailiffs' accounts of the 14th century, e.g. TNA SC6/1028/13.
6. RYE 136/33. Considerations varied from 40d. upwards but were often £1 or £2; Holloway 1847, 323-6, gave the 1670 rental.
7. Biller 2000, 10-11.
8. In 1343 it was *terra plesanns iuxta curton* (Courton), a general description typical of medieval material which is sufficient to place it in this location, TNA SC6/1028/15.
9. By 1343 the rents of some holdings described as burgages, and perhaps the burgages themselves, had been subdivided between up to four people with rights in them. A quarter of one held by Valentine in the rental was held by Walter de Rakele, and a quarter of another by a member of the Paulyn family, TNA SC6/1028/12.
10. Reginald de Rakele, whose forebear Henry was the first known mayor of Rye (RYE 136/7), and Matilda his wife conveyed a property at Estronde to Thomas Hallere in 1323 for a consideration of £4 sterling, with 4d. reserved rent to the town, RYE 136/58. One tenant in the rental had the byname *burgeys*.
11. At New Romney the Tithe Map shows what might be interpreted as 'burgess plots', i.e. long, narrow tenements with boundaries onto which others abut, and which front onto the market area and town centre streets. In fact these plots date not from the 11th century, but from the re-laying out of the market and town in the early 13th century, Draper and Meddens (forthcoming), chapter 2.
12. This definition and those of occupations, following, are taken from MED. There is much variation in spellings of Sliphe in Rye and Winchelsea records, which like other names have been standardised in this study.
13. TNA SC6/1028/8, 14.
14. Bleach and Gardiner 1999, 43. These places may have had small unrecorded markets.
15. Account of 18 June 1343 to Michaelmas 1344; the bailiff accounted for 'the profits, fines and perquisites of the court of the town of Rye both from residents and from strangers [*extraneis*] and fishermen of the same', TNA SC6/1028/12, 13.
16. *PNS* 2, 456, 477, 527-8; Bleach and Gardiner 1999, 43.
17. TNA SC6/1028/12, 13.
18. TNA SC6 /1028/8; SC12/15/73.

19. Plegge is also found as a surname elsewhere than Rye, MED.
20. Other pleas were called 'of covenants' and 'of trespass' but no more detail is given. Fines for breaking the assize of bread were 21d., of which six were imposed on men and one on a woman, TNA SC6/1028/12. Fines were imposed in 1272 for such things as not turning up to court or not having a plea, for contempt, for retained debts (*pro debito retento*), or for breaking distraint (*pro infracta districtione*), as well as such things as drawing blood (*pro sanguine fuso*), SC6/1028/8.
21. Petronilla Lamb' perhaps Lamb*in*, TNA SC6/1028/13.
22. Butcher 2001, 17-20.
23. *CCLR 1272-79*, 180.
24. Stacey 1995, 82-93; Hunt and Murray 1999, 36.
25. Small communities of Jews possibly continued to live elsewhere in England, particularly in towns or cities with trading links to Europe, Nenk 2003, 206.
26. On 11 July 1250 Henry III sent two representatives to all the Cinque Ports and Ancient Towns, and also to Pevensey and Bulverhythe, to enquire about the goods of Jews which were believed to be concealed or hidden in those towns. The bailiffs of the confederation ports were ordered to co-operate with the king's representatives, *CPR 1247-58*, 71.
27. Draper and Meddens (forthcoming), chapter 3.
28. Homan 1949, 29; RYE 133/1, RYE 136/2; CCA DCc CA R69, A171.
29. Geoffrey Russell, a man described as bailiff, possibly of Legat and Langsters, acted as intermediary in this transaction, Sawyer 1887, 90.
30. *CCLR 1272-79*, 50.
31. Vidler 1934, 13-14; CCLR 1272-79, 180, 182, 396.
32. *Calendar of Plea Rolls of the Exchequer of Jews* 1, 137; 4, 58, 138; 5, 72, 96, 126; 6, 288, 305.
33. *Plea Rolls of the Exchequer of Jews* 6, 288, 305. The surname was also given as Slipe, Sype, Slyphe, Shype, Shipe, Shepe and Shype in the Rye records (below).
34. Robert and Martha Sampson, and Sampson Sliphe, also all had tenements at Rye, TNA SC12/15/73.
35. A deed of *c*.1260 in which Henry Sliphe conveyed a messuage in Rye to Brice in return for one from Brice has two endorsements. The first was 'Henr' Slippe de taberna [ad] Stronde' [13th cent.], Henry being the grantor. The second was 'Bricio Cantare Sancte Marie' [14th cent.] Members of the Sliphe (Slipe, Sype, Slyphe, Shype, Shipe, Shepe, Shype) family, Laurence, Henry and Sampson, appear in both deeds of this period and the Edward I rental, where one William Tabernar, i.e. taverner, held Laurence's tenement. Neither the grant nor the endorsements clearly indicate that the properties conveyed were the tavern or related to the chantry, but they may have been. Brice's father was called Nicholas, RYE 136/2.
36. For the following see CCA DCc CA G138A, 1-5. The agreement between Alice and Henry of Bocland was witnessed by the Prior of Canterbury Cathedral, Henry of Eastry, and various other priory officers. The original charter by which Alice had acquired *la hoke* was in the form of a chirograph from Benjamin de la Hoke and his wife and had been enrolled in the King's bench in November 1265 before one of the royal justices, Gilbert de Preston, and others.
37. *CCLR 1272-79*, 518.
38. *CCLR 1272-79*, 229, 234; *CCLR 1279-88*, 52, 194, 394; TNA E326/2384.
39. The clerics of Rye are discussed in *Chapter 7*.

40. RYE 136/14, 15, 53.
41. TNA SC12/15/73; RYE 136/43.
42. Hanley and Chalklin 1964, 71-172. Goddard 2004, 218-19, suggested that in Coventry bynames had become inherited surnames by the second decade of the 14th century and could not be used after that as evidence of occupation. Kowaleski 1995, 120, n. 3, criticised the use of occupational bynames until the end of the 14th century as evidence, noting that 37 per cent of occupational groups in Exeter had no correspondence with bynames in 1377, meaning of course that 73 per cent did, even after the changes of the Black Death period. This chapter on Rye uses occupational bynames as evidence only until the Black Death.
43. William the tanner, for example, was son of Gilbert the tanner, RYE 136/8.
44. *Cal. Inq. Misc.* 1, 184; TNA SC12/15/73. William called cod and Henry le Cod witnessed a Rye deed in which a tanner conveyed a half-acre on the road near the early market of Yalding, Kent, perhaps for marketing purposes. The tanner had purchased it from Peter Harang. The presence of the deed among the Rye records suggests that Rye people were involved, perhaps one or more of the female parties who had married and moved from the town, RYE 136/8. *Chapter 8* discusses Rye fishermen as market traders on the routes towards London.
45. *Bruiningo piscator* is named in the bailiff's account of 1272-3, TNA SC6/1028/8.
46. *Rough's Register*, x.
47. RYE 136/3, 34 34.
48. 'A certain field of land called Crockeresfeld in the vill of Pleydenne', RYE 136/57, 64. William and Walter Poteman (who witnessed a Rye deed but may not have lived there), Poteman Lambyn, Martin Potery RYE 136/8; TNA SC12/15/73; Andrew and William Potepirie, who shared a name with *Potepirie Lane* in Rye, may also have been potters, RYE 136/4, 20 (*Chapter 8*); Vidler 1934, 8, 12. Robert Croker (potter) is known slightly later in 1344 to 1345, TNA SC6/1028/13.
49. *VCH Sussex* 9, 56.
50. Draper and Meddens (forthcoming), chapter 2. Pottery finds at New Winchelsea including Rye wares and the so-called 'Winchelsea' black wares are discussed in Martin *et al.* 2004, 177-84. Rye jugs of the 13th century were not apparently traded or carried to London, Vince 1985, 78.
51. John called le Blodletere, witness and grantor, RYE 136/37, 38, 42; John Fitzjohn, barber, and Walter Blodletere, TNA SC12/15/73.
52. Michael Carpentar, Kyngemyn Carpenter, Roger le carpenter, TNA SC12/15/73; Nicholas Carpenter, witness, RYE 136/63.
53. RYE 136/54, i.e., a 'shipwright's able clincher', as later described, Mayhew 1987, 154.
54. Luke la salater, RYE 136/40 (1314).
55. TNA SC12/15/73. The other occupations which follow are also from this rental unless stated; MED.
56. Smiths produced a variety of metal goods including perhaps horseshoes, since blacksmithing was a well-known trade later at Rye. Medieval blacksmiths who produced and fitted horseshoes (ferours) are rarely found in records in the south east although they are known at Tonbridge and horseshoes were apparently produced at medieval Tenterden, Furley 1882, 37.
57. TNA SC6/1028/12, 13. Paganus le veriere, was the maker of glass, possibly stained glass. The term is known from 1245 in the online Anglo-Norman Dictionary. There were also three 'markeres', Geoffrey, Robert and William, who perhaps stamped trade marks.

58. RYE 136/59.

59. Henry was related to one Laurence Sliphe, also known in 1258, RYE 136/55, 2, 69; TNA SC6/1028/13. The many alehouses and victualling houses of poor repute in 16th-century Rye were suspected of harbouring prostitutes as was the *Jerusalem* tavern at New Romney in the early 15th century, Mayhew 1987, 206-26; Draper and Meddens (forthcoming), chapter 3.

60. A Laurence the taverner is known as a member of the town government in 1354 and 1371 and may have been part of the Sliphe family, RYE 136/1, 2, 4, 97, 116.

61. The tenement was close to a highway and those of notable people, including the king's warden and mayor, suggesting that it lay near the Courton (*Chapters 5, 8*), RYE 136/67, 79.

62. RYE 77/1.

63. RYE 47/2/32; RYE 33/20, f. 370v. John Allin moved to London and practised medicine there; it is likely that he previously used his skills in Rye too.

64. Ellis was son of Engelbert of Rye. The lease stated that neither Ellis nor his ancestors had any previous right in the mills, and that the lease was for the duration of his life, or until he took the religious habit, a standard clause in Fécamp's charters at this time, Whittick 2004, R68 (n.d., date assigned *c.*1190). In 1195/6 Master Ellis of Rye (*Helia de Ria*), presumably the lessee of the mills, witnessed a notification concerning the tithes of the church of Cogges in Oxfordshire, which belonged to Fécamp, *Cal. Docs France*, 49. A mill of 1220 near Old Winchelsea was suggested to have been a tide mill because of its proximity to the sea and the likely low flow of the river near it, Gardiner 2002, 102. Similar is likely to have applied to Ellis's mills near Rye.

65. Nicasius is given as of Rye in a document of 1203; this document records the witnesses gathered together at St Mary's church, Oxford, before the abbot of Eynsham, the prior of Oseney and the sub-prior of St Frideswide of Oxford. These three men had been appointed to hear witnesses in the dispute over the tithes of the marshes of Brede between Lawrence, the parson of Brede and Fécamp. Other witnesses came from Oxford, London (two men) and Cogges in Oxfordshire, Whittick 2004, R17.

66. James, Draper and Martin 2005, 25. In 1201 Gerard de Witeflet and Gerard de Leflesham made an agreement about the transfer of 10 acres of land in Rye, for which the former paid the latter seven marcs, Fine no. 49 in 'Sussex Fines: 1-5 John (nos. 15-93)', An abstract of Feet of Fines for the County of Sussex: vol. 1: 1190-1248 (1903), pp. 5-22. URL: http://www.british-history.ac.uk/report.aspx?compid=65764. Date accessed: 26 February 2008.

67. *CPR 1232-1247*, 64. Feoffment from Stephen called Skynnere of Rye to Thomas called Pyron, miller, of all that messuage in the town of Rye which he had by demise (lease) from Agnes called Sonke, RYE 136/43. Thomas Molend*arius* (miller or of the mill) is recorded in 1343/4, TNA SC6/ 1028/12.

68. Nathaniel *pistor*, Coldynger *pistor*, TNA SC12/15/73; Walter Belde, RYE 136/7. An earlier John the baker appeared as a witness, ie member of the town government, to a feoffment of *c.*1285, RYE 136/15.

69. RYE 136/62. The tenement was acquired by Robert called Archer of Wynchelese and Margery his wife from Richard, son and heir of Roger Belde of Rye. It was then conveyed to Robert called Holstok', baker, of New Winchelsea and Joan his wife. The consideration for the feoffment was 60s. sterling, with a yearly rent to the town of Rye of 6s. 9d. silver. A member of the Gaylard family, William, below, was a witness.

70. John Bakere's land lay to the south of a half-acre which was in Rye 'in the borgh of Goldspur of the Norman virgate which Margery Red onetime held of the manor of Brede'. The half-

acre was on the west of the highway, presumably the road from the Landgate to Playden, i.e. Rye Hill, RYE 136/75, 76. Goldspur hundred lay north of Rye (*Chapter 1*).

71. TNA SC12/15/73; SC6/1028/12. This assumes that their names are compounds of mele/ mule (meal/grain) and ward, i.e. keeper.

72. Thomas and William Taillour acknowledged the receipt of 48s. 4d. being the rent of the manor of Iden at Michaelmas from William Upton on 7 April 1379, RYE 138/5.

73. RYE 136/100.

74. RYE 136/99. Richard Gayllard was a relative, probably son, of William Gaylard, who as a member of the town government of Rye witnessed 11 deeds between 1318 and 1332, RYE 136/50-54, 57, 60, 62-4, 69. Richard himself similarly witnessed one in 1354, RYE 136/97. After this the Gaylards disappear from the records.

75. From Robert Dyne, RYE 60/1.

76. This was a quitclaim for which Parnel received the sum of 30s. 6d., RYE 136/1.

77. It was held from Samsone de Levelishame (Leasam) and from Julia, late the wife of Ralph ate Welle, locating it on the north side of Rye (*Chapter 9*). Julia's principal tenement was at Colspur, the usual term for land within the liberty but not the urban area of Rye, on the north side. The quitclaim was made for a consideration of two marks (26s. 8d.), a substantial sum, RYE 136/22.

78. Unusually for this locality Emetota was not named as her father's daughter on the seal, but rather Le Webbe, Draper 2005, 28-40.

79. RYE 136/48, 49, 65.

80. The name *Le Teynton* at Rye, by analogy with the *Courton* for the place where the courts were held, seems to be the tenter-ground, RYE 136/107; Martin, *Rye Rebuilt*, chapter 2. Laurence le Teynturer was named among the barons of the Cinque Ports in 1266 (town not given), *CPR 1268-66*, 575. This occupational name was derived from *tenteren*, 'to stretch (cloth) on a tenter', MED.

81. RYE 136/102, 104.

82. RYE 136/107. Others called *tixtor* or Webbe appear in the bailiffs' accounts but weaving may not have been their only activity; they were not necessarily related to those described above. Robert *tixtor* paid 6d. for breaking a distraint in 1272, TNA SC6/1028/8. In 1343 Walter Webbe paid a market toll of 2d. on a bundle of goods, indicating he was not a Rye man; Joanna Webbe was fined 21d. for breaking the assize of bread, and Juliana Webbe 6d. in a plea of debt, TNA SC6/1028/12.

83. RYE 77/1; RYE 136/180, 186. In 1442 Robert Onewyne (II) alias Taylour, was described as son and heir of Robert Onewyne alias [blank] late of Rye, RYE/136/194, although was also sometimes called Robert Taylor. Both Onewyns were mayors of Rye, Roskell *et al.* 1993, 3. It is not clear whether they were related to William Taillour.

84. RYE 136/39.

85. John de Pritelwell, citizen and spicer of London, acquired valuable lands in Icklesham and Guestling in 1348. His acquisition was witnessed by other citizens of London (Thomas de Maryns, Thomas de Walden and Roger de Frowyk), and by Henry and Vincent Finch, members of a leading New Winchelsea family. The route from New Winchelsea towards London via Battle leads along the ridge through Icklesham and Guestling and Pritelwell's acquisition was presumably connected with trading in spices, *CCLR 1346-48*, 604.

86. RYE 136/138, 139.

87. RYE 136/108.

88. RYE 136/108, 119; CCA DCc CA R60; Vidler 1934, 159.

89. Or 1456: this is recorded in the chamberlains' account book (RYE 60/2) in which the accounts ran from the yearly choosing of the mayor on St Bartholomew's day, 24 August; *HMC* 5, 492. These accounts cover most years between 1448 to 1464.

90. MED, citing *Early English Meals and Manners*, ed. F. Furnivall, Early English Text Society 32 (1868, reprinted 1973), 57.

91. The mayor and the jurats, acting in the court where the Rye market was regulated, reallocated the plot to William Pashelewe, seaman, of a junior branch of the Pashley family which had provided the king's warden of the town and port of Rye in 1324, RYE 136/144.

92. Stephen skinner, or called Skynnere, TNA SC12/15/73; Philip Skynnere, RYE 136/80; Thomas the tanner, or Thomas Tannere, RYE 136/53, 63, 64 (1321, 1325); William and Gilbert, tanners, RYE 136/8; Laurence the dyer, RYE 136/8, 14, 17; William Hetherst, dyer, RYE 136/37.

93. TNA SC12/15/73; RYE 136/7, 34, 66.

94. MED.

95. John de Kent, John de Roger, cordwainers, and Walter Ganter, glover, RYE 136/71, 72.

96. RYE 136/43.

97. *CPR 1350-54*, 165.

98. TNA SC12/15/73.

99. RYE 136/71.

100. Draper 2008, 230.

101. RYE 136/83.

102. Richard Wyke, tanner, is the last known in 1363, RYE 136/107.

103. *Levedimerss* was also spelt *Lewedymers*, *Levediesmersch*, etc., *PNS* II, 527. By 1298 Kechenour was part of the extensive holdings of Edmund Passhley (d.1327), Martin and Martin, Iden and Playden Tenement Analysis. Kechynore was called a manor in 1498, ESRO AMS/635.

104. RYE 136/19. William was described in this deed as of Peasmarsh; at this period the boundaries of these various places may not have been fully settled. This marsh *Levedimerss* is presumably to be equated with the marshland of 240 acres known to have been part of the manor of Legh or La Mote in 1634, Martin 1993.

105. RYE 136/68, 72, 81.

106. John de Kechenore (II) and William de Wyghtresham (Wittersham, Isle of Oxney, Kent) were servants of Geoffrey de Say, a soldier and admiral. Thomas de Passele, knight, William de Pagham and others were accused of carrying away Say's goods at Beckley, Peasmarsh and Iden on 25 March 1352. They also besieged and assaulted William de Wyghtresham and John de Kechenore II as they were coming out of the house there, and a commission of enquiry was set up into this, *CPR 1350-54*, 281; Peter Fleming, 'Say, Geoffrey de, second Lord de Say (1304/5–1359)', *Oxford Dictionary of National Biography*, Oxford University Press, 2004 [http://www.oxforddnb.com/view/article/24763, accessed 4 Jan 2009]. William de Pagham, who was alleged to be the leading assailant, was a steward of Battle Abbey until this year, Saul 1986, 45. It is likely that John de Kechenore II and William de Wyghtresham acted as similar officers for Say. In 1361 Richard Kechenore, brother of William Kechenore, witnessed a grant to an Iden man of land to the north of Rye, with William Pagham being the second witness to this deed. In 1363 Richard Kechenore witnessed the conveyance of land at Peasmarsh, RYE 136/104, 110.

107. TNA SC12/15/73.

108. The rent was to be paid at the Heghtones' principal tenement in the town, RYE 126/124.

109. RYE 136/45, 49. Beneyt the butcher was a witness as a member of the town government rather than as a neighbour of the property, and witnessed many more transactions between 1304 and 1316, RYE 136/24, 34, 42, 44.

110. RYE 136/49. Harvey and McGuiness 1996, 89. A full study of the nearly 300 seals on medieval and early modern documents conveying property in and around Rye is beyond the scope of this book but is intended as the subject of a future study.

111. TNA SC6/1028/13.

112. Peter Bocher (II) was a descendant, probably grandson, of Robert senior who was alive in the 1340s, RYE 136/138. The consistent spelling of the surname and the holding of a shop in the market place suggest they were members of one family, RYE 136/118, 120, 121, 127, 144, 155; RYE 137/6. No butcher (Bocher) is recorded in the legible part of the earliest chamberlains' account of 1405-6; however, this part covers the 'forinsec' tenements which were not in the town centre, RYE 60/1.

113. RYE 136/122, 123.

114. The Holstoks were not described as of Rye nor do they reappear in the Rye records, RYE 136/131. An earlier Robert called Holstok was in 1334 described as a baker, who acquired a tenement in Rye via a baker of New Winchelsea from the Belde family of Rye, one of whom at least was a baker, RYE 136/62. A Robert Holstok who was alive in 1415 was associated with Northiam, as were John Holstok, father and son, in the first half of the 15th century, ESRO FRE/6920, 6925, 6928, 7011.

115. RYE 136/151, 152.

116. Tychebourne was also a witness to deeds, and recipient of property recorded in them, RYE 136/143, 144, 147, 149, 151, 152, 154, 158, 166, 167 (1393-1411).

117. RYE 77/1.

118. William Benet, perhaps a descendant of Richard Beneyt, butcher, also appears in the scot assessment of 1415, although under Nesse Ward not Market Ward, RYE 77/1.

119. RYE 136/201.

120. RYE 136/186.

121. Mayhew 1987, 32, 120, 117, 293; Draper 2007b, 11-15.

122. The number of surviving deeds is similar before and after the Black Death, for example in the class RYE 136 there are 86 from the 90 years between 1258 and 1347, and 105 for the next 90 years. However, occupations largely cease to be mentioned in them, nor do they appear in the 1415 scot list, and only very rarely in the few surviving chamberlains' accounts. None are recorded in the legible part of the account of 1405; however, this part covers the 'forinsec' tenements which were not in any case in the town centre, RYE 60/1. The account covering 1474-6 mentions only the ripiers of the fishing industry, and the choice by the mayor, jurats and commons of John Notyngham, alias Sextene, for the office of collector of the box of the ripiers on the Strand, *HMC* V, 493-4 (the original account has been missing since c.1854, RYE 51/9). The king's bailiffs' accounts cease to survive after 1363. There is no surviving rental like that of Edward I's reign. Following the changes to the town elite after the Black Death, very few of the 'new' men had occupational surnames, although they could not necessarily be used as direct evidence of occupation at that period.

123. *CPR 1429-36*, 561, 565, 569, 576, 582-3, 586. In 1436 large numbers of aliens living and working in southern England took an oath of fealty to Henry VI following the decision of Philip the Good, Duke of Burgundy, to give his support to Charles VII of France and the subsequent fall of Paris to the French, M. Carlin, pers. comm.; Thomson 1983, 192.

124. *CPR 1346-1441*, 576-77; TNA E179/235/55.

125. East Kent Archives Centre, LY 2/1/1/1, f.51v; *HMC* 5, 492.

126. Dover had four householders and 12 lodgers, Mate 2006, 114-16.

127. Durrant Cooper 1867, 149-52.

128. Mayhew 1987, 81.

129. For this and the following see Mayhew 1987, 107-10, 154-5.

130. Lutton 2008, 12; James, Draper and Martin 2005, 10.

131. For example, on 13 September 1578 [?] Richard Holdbrooke of Rye, mariner, leased a ship 'to freight' to Thomas Bromrick and Richard Killingback of London, merchants, RYE 140/9. On 19 March 1589, the sale of a ship was agreed from John Taylor, gentleman, and Thomas Forde, merchant tailor, both of London, to John Ollyver of Rye, mariner, RYE 140/37.

132. RYE 140/19.

133. Occupational activity in early modern Rye was explored by Mate 2006, 81-2 (until 1550); Mayhew 1987, 124, 147-69 (until 1603); Hipkin 1995a, 1995b, 1998-9 (until *c*.1640). It is re-examined in Martin, *Rye Rebuilt*, chapter 6, particularly in relation to location.

134. These premises are discussed in detail in Martin, *Rye Rebuilt*, chapter 7.

135. RYE 140/32.

136. Mayhew 1987, 37, 157, 181-2, 184-6, 282, 288.

137. *HMC* 5, 490, 492.

138. There were more butchers, beerbrewers and bakers than cordwainers but these were not artisans but rather part of the important early modern victualling trade of Rye, Mayhew 1987, 109.

139. There were two Thomas Radfords known in 1575. Radford senior was a merchant and Common Councillor who lived in Middle Street ward. Radford junior was the cordwainer who had the shop on the Strand, Mayhew 1987, 229, 277, 288.

140. Radford's holdings are reconstructed from RYE 60/9, f. 60v; RYE 130/33, 34, 38. The rents for the plot of land behind the shop and the strip where the stall stood appear to have totalled 20d. a year.

141. Harris was active in the town magistracy from *c*.1570 to 1583, Mayhew 1987, 126, 131, 178, 275, 280.

142. Mayhew 1987, 267.

143. RYE 60/9, f. 60r; Mayhew 1987, 65, 120, 275, 277, 314.

144. RYE 130/38; Mayhew 1987, 83-4, 89, 175, 277, 282, 295.

145. There may have been several more who did not convey property or otherwise take action which caused them to appear in the Rye records.

146. RYE 33/20, f. 447v; Mayhew 1987, 83.

147. The witnesses to the apprenticeship were Samuel Landsdale and John Landsdale, RYE 29/146; RYE 33/20, f. 392r. Tallow was used not only for lighting but also for caulking vessels. In *c*.1575 the Younges were a wealthy family with two messuages in Rye (in Middle Street and outside the Strandgate), one on Beggars Hill (*Chapter 8*) and one in Playden. John, son and heir of John Younge, deceased, made a quitclaim to Richard Younge his brother of all his interests in them, RYE 139/4.

148. RYE 33/20, f. 476r.

149. RYE 33/20, ff. 443v, 514r.

150. RYE 33/20, ff. 363v, 470r, 473r.

151. Mayhew 1987, 109; RYE 138/20.

152. The occupations of the witnesses, abutters, and members of town government or officials were not usually given although they were often described as jurat, esquire or gentleman.

No ordinary (house) carpenters are given, perhaps a quirk of the records or because Rye was between its period of vigorous housing growth, which lasted until the late 16th century, and its revival in the mid-17th century, Martin, *Rye Rebuilt*, chapter 1.

153. RYE 33/20, ff. 357, 362-3, 365, 370, 380, 391-2, 396-7, 401, 412, 418, 421, 423, 431, 437, 442-4, 467, 470, 473-4, 476-7, 504, 514; RYE 137/53. In 1615 the salter, John Cooper, was also described as a feter, a wholesale fishmonger, when John Wyndle, citizen and fishmonger of London, made a sale to him of a third part of three messuages and gardens in Bawdwyns Street and Longerstreet, RYE 139/88. Tradesmen in allied crafts sometimes shared premises, as for example in a quitclaim from Christopher Gee, joiner, to Peter Cooper, cooper. This related to two small rooms over the gatehouse of Cooper, in the street from Longerstreet to Middlestreet, RYE 139/95 (8 May 1619).

154. Mayhew 1987, 252-3; e.g. a haberdasher of 1621, John Spye; RYE 137/44; a yeoman of 1600, RYE 137/42; deed of partnership in trade of ropemakers between John Nicholson and John Kempe of Rye, 20 March 1607, RYE 140/48.

155. Hipkin 1998-9, 135.

156. RYE 82, 83. This is examined in more detail in Martin, *Rye Rebuilt*, chapter 5.

157. ESRO RYE 82/82, RYE 83/5. The number of flues counted in the hearth tax indicated the size of the house and therefore wealth, but may have been a judgement made by the assessors as to what should be paid in a particular year, rather than an actual count of flues: it varied from year to year.

158. For this and the following see Draper 2007b, 10-11.

159. RYE 33/20, f. 442.

160. RYE 136/33.

161. RYE 136/65

162. RYE 136/26, 27, 34, 57, 64.

163. In the rental some women had bynames (surnames) of their own but these did not relate to occupations. Despite their rights, female heirs could be effectively sold in marriage. The wardship and marriage of Elizabeth, the cousin and heir of Joan, sister of Stephen Paulyn, were sold by John Halle of Ore, esquire, to Henry Dobyll of Wittersham, Kent, in 1420 because Joan held lands in Pett and Fairlight from Halle by military service, RYE 136/178.

164. As for other towns there is no material to produce satisfactory population estimates for Coventry before the Black Death. After great mortality there in the plague, the population was estimated at between 7,200 and 9,600 in 1377, making it the fourth largest town, Goddard 2004, 6-7, 157, 159, 160, 189, 213, 218-27, 253-4, 267-8, 294.

165. Exeter is four miles from the Exe estuary via a river and 10 miles from the open sea, a position not unlike that of Rye, but more distant from the sea, Kowaleski 1995, 4, 222.

166. Kowaleski 2000, 429-54.

167. Population estimates for medieval Rye are almost impossible, not least because of the exemption of members of the Cinque Ports confederation from national taxations; no poll tax material exists for 1377. However, after a mortality of at least 40 per cent in the second half of the 14th century (below) there seems to have been little growth over most of the 15th century. 129 people were assessed in 1415 for a half scot (tax) and 139 for an almost contemporaneous full scot, aimed at raising a fixed amount for the requirements of the town. In 1491, a period when growth had already begun, 176 people were assessed and there were two more households in addition. These three assessments are however not directly comparable, RYE 77/1, 2; Martin, *Rye Rebuilt*, chapter 5. In the 16th century

Rye's population doubled or perhaps almost tripled to reach and exceed 4,000 by the mid-century, Mayhew 1987, 6; Martin, *Rye Rebuilt*, chapter 1.

168. Kowaleski 1995, 118, chapter 4.

169. From the time of the Black Death it was recognised that pestilence arrived with people coming to a port 'in boats' and mixing with the local population, although corrupt air and urban filthiness were blamed for continued infections, Henderson 1992, 141, 146; Mayhew 1987, 47.

170. Along with vintners (apparently partly a term of status), millers and ripiers, butchers replaced fishermen, particularly kiddle-men, and perhaps a goldsmith, as the town elite of New Romney in the 14th and 15th centuries, *HMC* 5, 539; Boys 1792, 799; Draper and Meddens (forthcoming), chapter 6.

171. Britnell and Campbell 1995, 52, 190-3.

172. *HMC* 5, 489, 491.

Chapter 5   Mayors, Barons and Bailiffs: The Government and Prosperity of Rye

1. *VCH Sussex* 9, 51, read the custumal as if it could be used to interpret the town government of the medieval period.

2. In general terms the *prudhommes* of a town were worthy men, or in legal terms, law-worthy men, householders or freeholders, The Anglo-Norman Dictionary, http://www.anglo-norman. net.

3. Henry de Rakele was dead by 1300, RYE 136/7, 17. RYE 136/17. Robert Paulin was appointed bailiff in 1289, *VCH Sussex* 9, 50. The ESRO catalogue notes that the form of the charter is unaffected by the statute *Quia Emptores* of 1290, suggesting it pre-dated it. Before this time the first witnesses were men who appear frequently in the records such as John Thorell (forebear of John Torel, merchant), James Marchaunt and Brice of Rye, founder of the chantry (*Chapter 6*), RYE 136/1, 4,15.

4. RYE 136/ 25, 26, 30, 31, 33, 34, 36-8, 40-52, 54, 57-61, 62-4, 67, etc. The first witness was still being specified as mayor in 1636, RYE 137/48.

5. Magdalen College Oxford Muniments, Romney deed 40; Murray 1935, 5; Draper and Meddens (forthcoming), chapter 2.

6. Deeds involving land outside Rye but recorded by the town because of the importance of the transaction or because the parties were from Rye, were often witnessed by a small number of Rye men and some other people local to the transaction.

7. In 1397 the mayor, deputy (*locum tenens*), bailiff, clerk and three men called jurats were all named as witnesses to the grant of a tenement to the vicar of Rye. The jurats were probably so called because the roles of the others were all specified, or possibly because they had been a party to an earlier transaction of the property involved, RYE 136/147. In 1466 a feoffment was made from the mayor, Babilon Grauntford, and the jurats and whole commonalty to Robert Crowche, RYE 136/198. Much earlier a royal mandate referred to William Byaufits (Beufiz or Beaufitz), Stephen Alard and Richard Wimund and other men in the Cinque Ports as jurats as early as 1235 rather than by the usual term baron, *CCLR 1234-37*, 163. In 1235 a request was addressed to the barons of Winchelsea and Rye to let Stephen Alard and William Beufiz, jurats, have two good ships from each town, well fitted out, to go on the king's service from the port of Winchelsea with the first favourable wind, *CPR 1232-47*, 92. Beufiz exercised exceptional responsibilities on behalf of the king but may not have been a resident of the Cinque Ports and thus not himself a 'baron'. After the initial stages of the Saintonge war, in 1246, Beufiz was one

of the king's agents and bailiff of Rye, and as bailiff was appointed to receive two of the king's galleys at Rye, one of which had been kept in the port of Romney and the other at Sandwich, *CCLR 1242-47*, 176, 494-95.

8. RYE 57/1, which is quoted by Vidler 1934, 21, who discusses its contents. There is also an undated book of precedents relating to the Cinque Ports and select items from the Rye custumal (known otherwise only from later versions) in what appears to be a late 15th-century hand, RYE 157/4, f. 37-70 (original foliation). Other copies of the custumal begin *c*.1560 and were continued for many years, RYE 157/2, 3.

9. Mayhew 1987, 94-5.

10. Kowaleski 1995, 95, n. 72; *HMC* 5, 493.

11. Mayhew 1987, 92.

12. *CPR 1232-47*, 305.

13. *Calendar of Chancery Warrants Preserved in the Public Record Office, 1244-1326* (HMSO, London, 1927), 294.

14. RYE 138/1. This early deed refers to land at Hocholt which is to be identified with Ocholt near Broomhill and includes Stephen Andreu known later at Rye and Henry(?) Mainard from a Rye family.

15. They were Reginald (1258), Dyn, James (mayor) and Richard, who were brothers, Robert (mayor) and his son Paul (mayor). There may have been more than one James and Robert. One William Marchaunt is known in 1396 and 1411 but then the family disappears from the records.

16. RYE/136/4, 20.

17. E.g. RYE 136/7.

18. Archives Départementales de Seine-Maritime, Rouen, 7 H 57, includes this charter in which for 100s. Robert de Hughtham gave up to William, abbot of Fécamp, 'his right across the end of the water in the marshes of Brede', a manor and parish to the west of Rye. It can be approximately dated by the name of the abbot and also by those of the witnesses, who included Paulyn de Winchelsea (bailiff of Rye and Winchelsea 1250-2), as well as Sir Robert de Aubervill', Reynold, chaplain of Hastings, Henry son of Reginald de Winchelsea and Robert de Brede. The last witness and clerk, who wrote and recorded this charter in the court of Brede, was named Nicholas.

19. *PNS 2*, 527; RYE 136, 17, 20, 22, 24-6, 29-33, 37-40, 43, 48, 50-4, 57-60, 62, 64-5, 67, 82, 86. Peter the clerk was last witness to all the surviving deeds from Rye in this period, although the last was written by another Peter the clerk, perhaps his son.

20. Mayhew 1987, 96-9; Vidler 1934, 156-68, listed the officers and officials, as well as MPs, vicars, rectors, justices and wardens of the leper hospital.

21. RYE 33/7, f. 39r.

22. *HMC* 5, 494. Some Rye town accounts survive from 1448, with a lone survival of one from the mayoralty of John Macop in 1405 to 1406. These are generally known as the chamberlains' or town accounts, RYE 60.

23. This brief account is taken from RYE 60/3, f. 122; Vidler 1934, 40-1; Mayhew 1987, 100; ESRO catalogue, Introduction to accounts.

24. RYE 136/32.

25. RYE 136/68.

26. TNA SC6/1028/8, 9. Mathew was bailiff of Winchelsea in 1267, *CPR 1266-72*, 86.

27. ESRO AMS 6569/6, MS Rolls Sussex 10 being the microfilm, a roll of estreats held at Rye linked to bailiffs' account.

28. Winchelsea Court Hall listings of officers on display boards.
29. TNA SC6/1089/21, m.1-8. Luce de la Gare was steward to the dowager Queen Eleanor in 1284-8.
30. TNA SC6/1032/6.
31. TNA SC6/1032/7.
32. TNA SC6/1028/14 (1355-9). This refers to another more detailed account in Thomas de Wynchelse's name which no longer survives.
33. TNA E101/28/7; SC6/1028/15.
34. About 180 people around the coast were commissioned including also Henry Goldene (presumably Goldyeve), Thomas Taillour and William Holynbrok all of Rye, and Robert Baddyng, Vincent Fynch and John Peytefu (presumably Petevyn) of Winchelsea, *CPR 1364-67*, 77.
35. In 1266 they were briefly recorded at £40 at the end of a long and detailed account of Old Winchelsea, TNA SC6/1031/19. This amount does not accord with any of the later grants or amounts actually collected.
36. *CPR 1247-58*, 363.
37. TNA SC6/1028/12.
38. She was also granted the manor and marsh of Iham at New Winchelsea valued at £34. Other places elsewhere were granted which were valued at £37, *CPR 1327-30*, 123.
39. E.g., *CPR 1266-72*, 86; *CPR 1324-27*, 26.
40. Vidler 1934, 28, 156-67. Details of Vidler's later notes on the MPs and bailiffs including Tettesworth were provided by J. Kirkham. Edmund Tettesworth appears in the following as one of the King's Serjeant-at-Arms with one Thomas Hore, in 1383-4, 'Folios clxx – clxxx: Nov 1383', Calendar of letter-books of the city of London: H: 1375-1399 (1907), 224-49. URL: http://www.british-history.ac.uk/report.asp?compid=33472. Date accessed: 28 August 2007.
41. Vidler 1934, 157-8, 163-7.
42. *HMC* 5, 491. Members of his family do not appear in the Rye records examined for this study before this date.
43. In 1459 or 1460 (38 Henry VI) the men of the Earl of Warwick entered Rye 'with a strong band' and took down the quarter of a man's body and had it buried in the churchyard, *HMC* 5, 492.
44. *HMC* 5, 492. Vidler 1934, 157, 159; Babilon was also bailiff in 1476, RYE/137/21. The Grauntfords may have been in office in other years for which evidence does not survive.
45. *HMC* 5, 493.
46. *HMC* 5, 493-6 (the original account for 1474-6 has been missing since *c.*1854, RYE 51/9). Small payments of 4d. were also frequently received from non-Rye men for removing the harbour boom to allow vessels to enter, and other ones as fines for breaches of the peace and assaults. Slightly larger payments up to 6s. 8d. were paid on the import or export of salt in vessels. John Sylton, valet of the crown, was appointed king's bailiff at Rye on the death of John Grauntford, RYE 60/2.
47. This system was abolished in 1526 or 1527 by the agreement of meeting of the commonalty held in the churchyard. In future the boxes were to be opened in the town hall, not the mayor's house, and he was to receive no more than £4 for his fee for his year of mayoralty, paid quarterly. The account of 1474 said that a dinner was given on the day the mayor was chosen, *HMC* 5, 492, 494.

48. Compare the figures given in *Chapter 8* with those given by Vidler 1934, 41; Dyer 1993, 103, 217.
49. Martin, *Rye Rebuilt*, chapter 5.
50. *VCH Sussex* 9, 50.
51. E.g. RYE 136/1, 6, 20, 23, 30, 31, 52-6, 62, 69, 70, 72, 74, 78, 79, 83, 89, 101, 102, 112, 144, 147, 149, 156, 158, 173, 174, 180, 190. Not all deeds were dated except by year.
52. *CPR 1348-50*, 98; Martin, *Rye Rebuilt*, chapter 2.
53. At New Romney there was an early guildhall, perhaps where the 'halimot' met. This guildhall was sold off by 1234 and the town governors and officials may then have met in St Nicholas' church as they did for a short period later. In the late 14th century the jurats of New Romney rented a chamber in which to meet but between 1404 and 1407 held their sessions in the church of St Nicholas. The vicar disapproved of this and made a payment to the jurats to find themselves another meeting chamber; at first they rented one and then they purchased another. The jurats of New Romney met in their newly purchased common house between the mid-15th and the early 16th centuries, although after 1483 they did not entertain important visitors to the town there but rather at the houses of the town elite. In the first half of the 16th century a new meeting place, the Guildhall, was established, possibly on the site of the current Town Hall, East Kent Archives Office, NR/JB2; Salisbury 1887, 20; Draper and Meddens (forthcoming), chapter 6.
54. *HMC* 5, 492; Martin, *Rye Rebuilt*, chapter 2.
55. Protectionist guilds developed in the 1560s and 1570s in response to the arrival of many Huguenot craftsmen, Mayhew 1987, 165-9.
56. Membership was open only to men, automatically excluding about half the population, Kowaleski 1995, 95-6.
57. RYE 60/2, f.1v.
58. Kowaleski 1995, 107.
59. Kowaleski 1995, 94.
60. Hipkin 1995a, 319-29; cf. Gibson and Harvey, 211, 203-21; Mayhew 1987, 94-5.
61. Cf. Kowaleski 1995, 118-19, for the increasingly restricted franchise in 15th and 16th century Exeter; Mayhew 1987, chs 2 and 6; Draper and Meddens (forthcoming), chapter 7.
62. Kowaleski 1995, 109-11.
63. Mercer 2005, 51, 56, 57; Draper and Meddens (forthcoming), chapter 2. Another Thomas Longe, probably the one also known as senior, or the elder, was last witness to some Rye deeds, and described as clerk, in the early 14th century, RYE 136/154, 156 (1402, 1405); he was a grantor called the elder in 1439, RYE 137/12, at which time Thomas Longe junior was also active.
64. This is based on a reconstruction using RYE 130/5-9; RYE 136/71, 113,126; RYE 137/6; RYE 134/2.
65. Archaeological investigation shows that New Romney's decline began with the great storms of the late 13th century. There was contraction of the numbers of wards and people between 1415 and 1450, and commercial activity, particularly marketing, changed. Higher disposable incomes, particularly among wage labourers, contributed to change in the town's economy, with, for example, accommodation and refreshment being supplied in a number of taverns run by wealthy men rather than poorer women in their homes. One of New Romney's two hospitals became a chantry for a merchant family. Two of the three parish churches were lost in the 16th century. That some people remained reasonably wealthy in the late medieval and early modern periods is suggested by the domestic buildings, many of which

are late medieval properties refronted in the late 17th or 18th centuries, as at Rye, Draper and Meddens (forthcoming), chapters 2-7.

66. Property transactions within Rye were normally witnessed by the mayor and jurats whereas outside Rye the witnesses sometimes included a limited number of jurats and some neighbours, e.g. one 'given at Gatebergh' (Cadborough), RYE 136/35.

67. RYE 136, RYE 137. The graph ends at 1476, after which there was a change in practice and the deeds, often feoffments, were no longer witnessed by the whole town government.

68. Dyer 1993, 140, 267.

69. The following is based on an analysis of the witness names in RYE 136, 137. Those disappearing include not only those twenty families with known occupations given above but also members of families named Alard, Andreu, Blykewelle, Corboyle, Kechenore, Kyttey, Ambroys, Sliphe, Wische, Beneyt, atte Wode, Paccok, Paulyn, Pharon, Portesmouthe, Storm, Thomas, Vincent and Yevegod and others. Six members of the de Portsmouth family are known in Rye between *c.*1272 and 1405: Richard senior and Richard junior, Richard the mayor, John, Juliana, the widow of one of the Richards, and Paul, who was churchwarden in 1354, and mayor in 1351, 1354 and 1358, RYE 136/7, 14, 20, 24-30, 32-4, 66-7, 71, 86, 89, 94, 96, 97, 99, 100; TNA SC12/15/73. After that only Reginald is known, in 1378, as a witness to a quitclaim; he was referred to as a former owner in 1424, RYE/136/127, 182. There is also a reference, possibly retrospective, to Paul letting a tenement in the account of 1405, RYE 60/1, f.2.

70. John Salerne (I) is known in the 1310s as a witness but three members of the Salerne family were witnesses or mayor between 1351 and 1411, John (II), Walter and Simon. Henry Goldyeve (I) is known once as a witness in 1314 but Henry Goldyeve (II) was repeatedly a witness and mayor between 1353 and 1367. Similar is true for the Wimund (Wymond) family whose members appear repeatedly in the town government from 1354. John Salerne (II) was appointed collector of a subsidy of poundage with Laurence Corboill in 1371/2, TNA E 122/147/15

71. RYE 136/127; Vidler 1934, 158.

72. Thomson 1983, 7-8.

73. Some advocants were from Somerset, Devon and Dorset, and later some were of French and Dutch origin, *VCH Sussex* 9, 52; John Dowying, merchant of Taunton, paid 6s. 8d, and then 20d. yearly to be a 'Combaron' of Rye, and was required to keep the letters recording this, which were sealed by both the common and the mayor's seal, *HMC* 5, 492. Robert Belingham, esquire, not otherwise known as a Rye man, paid 3s. 4d. in 1474; Master John Grauntfort's payment of 6s. 8d. was returned to him 'to be goode frende unto the towne', *HMC* 5, 495.

74. Mayhew 1987, 92.

75. Mayhew 1987, 6, 20-3, 47, 92; Gunn *et al.* 2007, 47-8; Hipkin 1998-9, 108; Dyer 2000, 761-5. Rural depopulation and poverty on Romney Marsh and the decline of the port of New Romney in the early 16th century may have contributed to the numbers moving into Rye in search of work or support, Gardiner 1998, 140-1; Draper 1998, 113-15.

76. Martin, *Rye Rebuilt*, chapter 1.

77. Vidler 1934, 53, 63; Greenfeild was the king's searcher for the port of Chichester, Martin, *Rye Rebuilt*; chapter 7; Winchelsea Court Hall listings of officers on display boards.

78. Martin *et al.* 2004, 21-3; Mayhew 1987, 235-6; Martin, *Rye Rebuilt*, chapter 6.

79. Mayhew, 1987, 238.

80. Adapted from Mayhew 1987, 252-3.

81. Martin, *Rye Rebuilt*, chapter 5. It is said that 'efforts to preserve Hastings harbour began in 1562', Murray 1935, 209; Kepler 1979, 53; Palmer 2008, 266.
82. Gunn *et al.* 2007, 13, 16, 24, 60-1; TNA E179/190/200.
83. Mayhew 1987, 236.
84. RYE 47/6/48.
85. RYE 47/24/12; RYE 47/26/5; RYE 47/20/2; RYE 47/2/30,31; ESRO WIN/53, ff. 102v-103; Mayhew 1987, 86-7.
86. RYE 1/1/, f. 4
87. Mayhew 1987, 252-3.
88. Mayhew 1987, 258. There was only a small number (7) of transfers of Sandwich property to Londoners in the 15th-century Sandwich account or general memorandum books made by the town clerks. These included two feoffments to Thomas and William Stoghton (Stoughton), fishmongers of London, East Kent Archives Centre Sa/Ac 1, f. 235, 251v. The two feoffments were of a tenement with a cellar in Gascoigne Lane, Sandwich, and the Crowne in the Strand, the main commercial street of Sandwich. Other transfers to London people were mainly of property associated with the Sandwich fishmarket, quays or strand, Mate 2008. This Thomas Stoghton was a freeman of Rye and MP in 1446-7 and 1448-9, and occupier of the Baddings (Ypres) Tower there. A John Stoghton was MP for Hastings in 1446, Vidler 1934, 38; RYE 124/3.
89. Hipkin 1995b, 138-47.
90. A licence granted in 1628 for a collection in the counties and boroughs of the South East noted that Rye was 'so greatly decayed from its past wealth' that it was unable to repair the harbour walls and erect new quays and jetties. These works would require at least £3,000, RYE 99/14.
91. Hipkin, 1998-9, 131-6.
92. Mayhew 1987, ch. 7.
93. RYE 33/20, ff. 314-514. Draper 2007, 4-20.
94. 'Sussex wills', 67.
95. Martin, *Rye Rebuilt*, chapter 5.
96. RYE 1/4/228 (the 1576 sesse); RYE 139/45; TNA PROB 11/43, 11/94; Mayhew 1987, 37, 179, 279, 284. The name Tokey or Tokye is confined to this locality at this period and it can be taken these people were related.
97. RYE 60/9, ff. 59-61; RYE 137/36; RYE 138/12. His will, proved 9 October 1583, was, however, 'entirely neutral doctrinally', Mayhew 1987, 133; TNA PROB 11/66.
98. RYE 60/9 ff. 59 to 61; RYE 137/36. The tomb contains the bodies of John Fagge II and III and commemorates them, notes the existence of John Fagge I, and was erected by Sir John Fagge IV; Vidler 1934, 75, 76, 80, 166. J.T. Peacey, 'Fagge, Sir John, first baronet (1627–1701)', *Oxford Dictionary of National Biography*, Oxford University Press, 2004 http://www.oxforddnb.com/view/article/9060, accessed 15 Jan 2009].
99. For Brice and Elena Palmer see *Chapter 6*. Martin Palmere was a witness to a Rye deed which conveyed a house in the town in *c*.1260, RYE 136/4.
100. Mayhew 1987, 288; RYE 35/31.
101. Mayhew records him as having a shop and being a beer tipler, Mayhew 1987, 278, 288. His connections were local to Kent and Sussex but it is not certain that he was related to the later Palmer family of Rye.
102. RYE 140/54, 8 October 1609.
103. RYE 28/17 (1607).

104. RYE 28/22 (1610).

105. Martin, *Rye Rebuilt*, chapter 12.

106. Little is known about Henry Palmer's origins but he clearly had links to both Sussex and Kent. He had an estate at Bekesbourne, east Kent, and can probably be identified with the Henry Palmer, esquire, a commissioner for concealed lands in Kent in 1581, David Loades, 'Palmer, Sir Henry (c.1550–1611)', *Oxford Dictionary of National Biography*, Oxford University Press, Sept 2004; online edn, Jan 2008 [http://www.oxforddnb.com/view/article/21186, accessed 28 June 2008].

107. Mayhew 1987, 221.

108. RYE 29/55, 58, 59, 61, 66, 68, 71, 101.

109. RYE 65/116; RYE 35/66.

110. RYE 122/33, 39, 42-53.

111. TNA PROB/11/153. The will was proved in the same year by his widow and executrix Elizabeth Palmer. He was described as jurat in his will.

112. The heirs of Mark and Joseph Palmer had property on the north side of the Butchery in 1654, RYE 33/20, f. 401r; Vidler 1934, 73.

113. RYE 47/140-41; RYE 33/20, ff. 477r, 504r, 514r; RYE 46/12; RYE 112, 10; RYE 113/1a, 2-4. The information on the poll and hearth taxes in RYE 82/82 and 83/5 was supplied by David and Barbara Martin.

114. A reconveyance of the school property in 1690 gives him as Thomas Palmer of Wye, in Kent, RYE 113/5. A John Palmer, presumably IV, was known as a freeman of Rye in 1696, holding a lease of corporation suggesting that he, as the younger brother, remained in Rye, RYE 127/29.

115. This property was bounded on the east by the lands and tenements formerly of John Bassocke and then of Michael Jacob; on the north by the lands formerly of Mark Thomas, gentleman, deceased, and then of Edward Gee; on the west and south by the lands of Edward Gee, formerly of Edward Benbrigge gentlemen, deceased; and on the south and west (*sic*) by the lands of the heirs of Mark Carpenter and Thomas Hunter, RYE 137/54. The identification with Hartshorne House is also supported by the names of those with abutting tenements in other deeds and in the 1670 list of King's rents of Assize, RYE 137/48, 49; RYE 33/20, f.504; Holloway 1847, 323-26. In 1652 the heirs of Mark and Joseph Palmer may have been occupying this property or another to the south of Longer Street, RYE 33/20, f. 363v. Its location is confirmed by a conveyance of 1673 when Thomas Palmer's property was described as lying in this location, ESRO SAS-B/42.

116. RYE 137/54.

117. ESRO FRE/5273.

118. ESRO FRE/5255; Martin, *Rye Rebuilt*, chapter 12.

119. Hunter *et al.* 1999, xxix-xxx.

Chapter 6   Religious Rye: the Parish Church and the Friaries

1. Martin, *Rye Rebuilt*, chapters 1, 4.

2. *VCH Sussex* 9, 57-9, 161. Steyning, Fécamp's other church in Sussex, is similar to St Mary's.

3. The earliest surviving parts of the early fabric including the semi-circular aumbries on the east wall of the chancel under the window and the sedilia in the north and south transept may be of the early 12th century; the earliest structural parts, the semi-circular arches into the nave and into the main tower, are of about the middle of that century. The abbot of

Fécamp, Guillaume de Ros, visited Rye in 1103 and may have initiated the building of the current church. This cannot be conclusively demonstrated but fits well with the timing of the foundation of the new town. The current stone church would have been preceded by an earlier one, perhaps of wood, and one of the five mentioned under Rameslie in Domesday Book. For this and the following see *VCH Sussex* 9, 57-8, which discusses the church architecture in detail, and J. Kirkham, *Rye Parish Church* (Pitkin Guide, no date, n. p.). Current research has not revealed any more definitive date. There seems to be no evidence that Rye was a minster church, Rushton 1999a, 37; Rushton 1999b, 133-52.

4. Taylor, Childs and Watkiss 2003, 133.

5. The name Clare Chapel was attached to the north chancel aisle in the 19th century, J. Kirkham, pers. comm. The plan of the church in *VCH Sussex* 9 has a chapel called St Nicholas on the north side and one called St Clere on the south, but the basis for this is not given. Three 16th-century testators requested burial in St Nicholas' chancel and one in the north chancel. The editor of these wills assumed this was the 'St Clare or North Chapel', presumably because since the Victorian period the north chancel had been known as St Clare's chapel, 'Sussex Wills', 64, 67. The north chancel may in fact have been identical with St Nicholas' chancel; no reference to St Clare is found in these wills, or elsewhere.

6. *VCH Sussex* 9, 60. At Sevenoaks, Kent, for example, there is a 'parvise' room over the porch which contains a fireplace and a window, indicating clearly that is was used for accommodation and possibly for teaching by the chantry chaplain, preceding the formal foundation of the grammar school in *c*.1432, Draper 2007a, 87-8. At Rye the upper storey of the south porch was destroyed by its later use as the Lamb Vault although it was later restored.

7. RYE 136/2, 5, 6, 7; Draper 2008, 222.

8. Subsequently the north porch formed the tower (belfry) entrance and contained its 17th-century stairway.

9. Local groups such as those of New Romney performed in St Mary's church in the 1470s and 1480s, usually between Christmas and early April, perhaps giving a version of New Romney's passion play which in the latter town was associated with a procession, Draper and Meddens (forthcoming), chapter 7. The numbers of these religious, biblical or hagiographical plays fell off from the 1530s in Rye. All performances, even of music at the mayor's door, were increasingly unpopular with Rye's puritanical town government over the later 16th and early 17th centuries, Louis 2000, xxxvii-xlvi, 52-3, 146.

10. Birchett, a baker and brewer, became the first Protestant mayor of Rye, in 1539, with William Mede. Birchett was temporarily removed as mayor in 1540 and Inold was temporarily restored as vicar in 1541. However, the complete victory of the Protestant faction was established long before the counter-reformation under Mary, Mayhew 1987, 55-67, 114. Mayhew's chapter 3 discusses religion in Tudor Rye in detail.

11. Bequests to repairs of the church were very sparse in the late 15th and early 16th centuries, 'Sussex Wills', 76.

12. Vidler 1934, 74. Pecock also bequeathed 20s. for the preaching of his funeral sermon in his will dated 10 September 1638, RYE 112/2 (18th-century copy). Rye wills between 1497 and 1560 have bequests for the education of children (several boys and one girl), rather than for a school building. They name 16 clerks, curates and chaplains, besides the vicars and the parish clerks. There were generally two clerks or curates at a time, Draper 2008, 222, 224-6, 237.

13. RYE 133/1, a deed reciting the provisions of the will and testament; RYE 136/2.

14. RYE 133/2, 3.
15. The royal galleys were *in domo nostra de la Rye*, perhaps a dockyard or storehouse, *CCLR 1242-47*, 43; *Cal. Lib. Rolls* 1, 68, 134.
16. RYE 136/95.
17. At the Lynot chantry at Ivychurch on Romney Marsh the founder similarly arranged for a family member to be the chantry priest, Draper 2007a, 78.
18. Bone's seal was appended to the deed of 1281 in which this was recorded, and because it was unknown to most people, he procured the seal of the Dean of Hastings to be appended also. Bone's seal showed a mailed arm holding a hawk, and the legend read SI: JOHANNIS: BON: . The counterpart deed had the witness clause worded differently, 'I have caused these letters to be made patent to the said Sir [*dominus*] Robert', RYE 133, 2-3.
19. The consideration was 33 marks sterling, RYE 136/ 2, 4, 14. Robert the chaplain also witnessed another Rye deed in *c*.1283, RYE 136/5.
20. Bone was from Wickham in the parish of Icklesham, next to New Winchelsea, and held 29 acres in that town, from which he granted four to the Friars Minor (Grey Friars) for their new site in *c*.1285, Martin *et al.* 2004, 5.
21. Bone was following the instructions of the executors of Brice and Elena who included James Marchaunt, mayor, Master Richard de Pagelham, chancellor of Chichester, and John Samson, called of Yham, and John de Carette, RYE 133/1-3.
22. TNA SC12/15/73; RYE 133/4, 5. A grant to Brice of a messuage in Rye might represent part of the endowment of the chantry but this suggestion rests on the endorsement. The precise location of the messuage is not clear, RYE 136/2, 42.
23. The Alard chantry or chantries of Winchelsea reflects the prosperity and the significance of the family from at least the 1220s, RYE 138/1, 2. In 1235 Stephen Alard and William Beufiz, king's officers, were commissioned to receive two ships of both Old Winchelsea and Rye from the barons. The other Cinque Ports and the men of Dunwich and Southampton were also ordered to provide ships to Stephen Aylard and William Beufiz, which were to be assembled at Old Winchelsea, *CPR 1232-47*, 293. One Stephen Alard, perhaps a later one, was the founder of one of the two Alard chantries at Winchelsea. The monuments of the Stephen Alard chantry at New Winchelsea seem to have been of early 14th-century date. The wording of a foundation document is equivocal about the date of its building and it has been believed that it was originally at Old Winchelsea, Martin *et al.* 2004, 79. After the foundation of New Winchelsea, however, the Alard family was linked to that town rather than to Rye, although members of the family also refounded the hospital of Saints Stephen and Thomas at New Romney as a chantry in the 1330s, which was then taken over in the 1360s by the minor landholding family of Fraunceys, Draper and Meddens (forthcoming), chapter 2.
24. TNA SC12/15/73.
25. Alard inherited the advowson and valuable lands at Rye, Peasmarsh, Brede and Udimore from John Ambroys. John, son of Nicholas Ambroys, was a notable member of the Rye town government and elite between 1314 and 1343 but had died without an heir of his own family by 1354, the family apparently dying out in the plague. There were several earlier members of the family known in Rye in the first half of the 14th century: one John, probably a different individual from John, son of Nicholas, Henry, Stephen, Richard, Ralph (I?) and Isabella. One Ralph Ambrays (II?) was last witness to a deed in 1358, but after that the family does not appear in the records of Rye and its surrounding parishes examined for this study, RYE 136/16, 20, 21, 33, 37-8, 40, 42-55, 57-60, 62-4, 66-9, 73, 75-6, 83, 95, 101; TNA SC12/15/73.

26. This occurred at the chantry of the Fraunceys' family at New Romney, Draper 2004, 143-4. The identity of the holder of the other moiety is unknown.

27. RYE 136/60, 94, 116. The messuage in *Potepirie Street* may have been held by an earlier John Petevyn.

28. Neither this transaction nor that of John Ambroys in 1354 specify that the lands in Rye, Brede, Peasmarsh and Udimore conveyed with the advowson were endowments of the chantry, but this is possible, RYE 136/171, 172; Holloway 1847, 88. The Monyn family was associated with the town government of Dover, with Thomas Monyn, mayor of Dover, possibly being the son of John Monyn and Agnes, Hasted 1972, 9, 394-400.

29. RYE 133/4; Vidler 1934, 158. That the town governors had a role is also indicated in 1397 when Stephen Paulyn, of the family which had provided bailiffs of Rye, had nominated the chaplain 'for this time', *VCH Sussex* 9, 61, n. 9. Stephen held land at the Grene Okes at Saltcote next to the Ambroys' family home, Ambroystonne (Chapter 8).

30. RYE 133/5.

31. Pope was the bailiff or king's sergeant of Rye, appointed in 1420 and re-appointed 1420 and 1428, and mayor and MP in 1426, Vidler 1934, 157, 165. He held a principal tenement in Rye, which had formerly belonged to John Salerne of the merchant family, RYE 137/11, 17; RYE 136/191, 192, 194-5; RYE 130/1.

32. *Reg. Chich.*, 1, 260.

33. *Sussex Chantry Records*, xxi.

34. 'Sussex wills', 68; Vidler 1934, 159.

35. 'Sussex wills', 67-8, 70; MED; Vidler 1934, 159; RYE 136/199.

36. Oxenbridge was assessed at the highest amount in the local tax of 1491, 66s. 8d. on a valuation of £400, and Crowche at the second highest, with four others assessed at the same amount, RYE 77/3. Crowche came from a family of wealthy stock-raisers and butchers, Draper 2007b, 12-13; *HMC* V, 496.

37. This was the term used by the commissioners at the suppression under the Act of 1 Edward VI (1547). For this and what follows, see *Sussex Chantry Records*, xxvi-xxviii, xxx, xxxiii, 13, 31, 55, 165-6, 195.

38. The earliest so annotated was dated 1441, RYE 135/2, 3, 4, 8, 10, 11, 14, 16, 17, 22; RYE 122/9.

39. In general the testament bequeaths personal property and the will real property but the distinction is not always precise and those copied in the Rye records in any case have an unusual arrangement of clauses as between the two. 'Will' is used here to cover both.

40. RYE 77/1.

41. TNA PROB 11/2B. The bequest to St Richard is among those to Rye church.

42. 'Sussex Wills' identified the wills of 140 Rye testators proved in the Prerogative Court of Canterbury (PCC) and in local ecclesiastical courts up to 1560, giving extensive extracts concerned with saints' cults, the structure of the parish church and repairs to it, vicars and chaplains, places of interment, provisions for commemoration, charitable giving, the Austin Friary, etc. Four testators from Ticehurst, Iden, Sandwich and Pett who gave to such causes at Rye were also identified, some or all of whom had probably lived there at some time. Research for this book identified no further wills in these courts, although five more were found of which copies or extracts were kept in the Rye town records, dating between 1475 and 1505, RYE 60/4, ff. 73, 136-7, 164; Rye 60/5, f. 59r; RYE 57/5, 57/7, f. 2. This research re-examined various aspects of the 20 wills proved in the PCC up to 1499 from Rye and surrounding places: New Winchelsea, Brede, Ore, Iden, Hastings,

Ewhurst, Iden, Battle and Salehurst. It also explored the possibility that wills from Kent parishes, especially on Romney Marsh, might contain bequests to the church, friary or hospital at Rye, but there proved to be very few such bequests.

43. Martin, *Rye Rebuilt*, chapter 5.

44. There were 1,304 wills for Sussex proved in the PCC in 1500-99 of which 90 were of Rye people: this compares with 67 wills for Chichester, 44 for Lewes, 32 for Hastings, 18 each for New Winchelsea and Battle, and five for Shoreham. In the Kent Cinque Ports there were five each for New Romney, Dover and Hythe, 10 for Lydd, and 25 for Sandwich. There were 69 for Maidstone, 56 for Canterbury, 30 for Rochester, 25 for Faversham and 15 for Tonbridge. Notably there were 79 for Greenwich. Looking farther afield, Southampton had 69 and Bristol 568; Plymouth had 32, Portsmouth 16.

45. Mayhew 1987, 16; Hipkin 1998-9, 109; Martin, *Rye Rebuilt*, 7-9. The making and proving of wills in various courts did not of course depend entirely on economic and demographic circumstances, and the numbers are impressionistic rather than definitively quantitative. At the end of the 16th century probably only ten Kent towns had more than 2,000 inhabitants, and in England as a whole only 70 out of at least 600 did so, Betts 2004, 70.

46. Rye had the highest proportion of Protestant and reformist wills in Sussex towns in the reigns of Henry VIII and Edward VI, as expressed in their preambles and the number of bequests for masses, Mayhew 1987, 61-2.

47. The bequests at Rye for traditional commemoration were expressed in a great variety of words and phrases suggesting that they represented the real wishes of the testator, and not, say, those of the clerk or even the vicar in shaping the will.

48. 'Sussex Wills', 73-4; Mayhew 1987, 114.

49. Cheston specified the wife of George Colton, and the wife of Thomas Not and 'other of them', 'Sussex Wills', 74.

50. Mayhew 1987, 69. In addition to the many who simply made bequests to the poor, nine of the 18 testators who wanted traditional commemorations between 1540 and 1550 also left money for the poor.

51. The poor chest was also known as 'goddes chest' in 1548 and 1558; its location within the church is not known, 'Sussex Wills', 72, 74-5.

52. 'Sussex wills', 64-6, 70. Lutton 2006, 69-80; Draper 2007a, 80-1.

53. The Lady Chapel and St Nicholas' chancel continued to be named as places for burial but this should perhaps be regarded as referring to the structure rather than saints' cults, 'Sussex Wills', 67-8.

54. The 16th-century jurats included John Chesman alias Baker, Richard Ingelett, Alexander Wulphyn, George Mercer, Robert Maycoke, John Marche, Richard Rucke, Richard Nicholl and William Johnson, identified from Mayhew 1987. Others who asked to be buried in the church were Edward Cheston, Andrew Kirk, John Pyers, John Lumberd, Robert Bacheler and John Tokye.

55. This was vacant land, 75 feet by 24 feet, outside the Watergate at the strand for a rent of 2s. per annum, RYE 130/3, 4.

56. Crowche's will was made in 1497 although he did not die until 1500, Draper 2007b, 12.

57. The careers of these men are discussed in detail by Mayhew 1987, ch. 3.

58. Mayhew 1987, 77-8, 202.

59. Mayhew 1987, 31-2; 'Sussex Wills', 74, 78-9.

60. *VCH Sussex* 9, 60.

61. 'Sussex Wills', 67-72.

62. The will was proved in 1498. Vidler 1934, 155-6, gave Wykwyk as *artium magister*, the first vicar listed with a degree among a note of the other vicars and rectors of Rye. An addition to the list is John Coteler who was named as vicar of Rye in 1408; William Longe, mayor of Rye, witnessed the deed in which this is recorded, CCA DCc CA R62A.

63. He did not specify that it was to be chained in the nave or chancel; this might have given an indication as its availability to the parishioners, Kisby 2008, 312-14.

64. Freeth 1974; Draper 2008, 227-8.

65. Several on the chamberlains' accounts in RYE 47. Samuel Jeake used one sheet on a notebook, J. Kirkham and C. Whittick, pers comms.

66. Mayhew 1987, 113, 176.

67. After this, only Richard Inglett, jurat, a religious traditionalist, left vestments, in 1544, 'Sussex Wills', 66; Mayhew 1987, 65.

68. Kirkham 2006, 11, 21-3, 24, 26. Cf. Zell and Chalklin 2004, 75.

69. TNA PROB 11/57.

70. VCH Sussex 9, 61; Mayhew 1987, 79.

71. Vidler 1934, 76.

72. Of the 168 subscribers to the Engagement only 77 made marks rather than signatures, RYE 17; Vidler 1934, 78.

73. Hunter and Gregory 1988, xx.

74. There was a Quaker burial ground outside the walls at the Wishe in 1694, Vidler 1934, 88. The Baptists do not seem to have had a meeting house until the mid-18th century, Holloway 1847, 541-2.

75. Vidler 1934, 82-3. Samuel Jeake enrolled the deeds in the town court record book, RYE 33/20 (*Chapter 5*). His writing was neat and his spelling was consistent and conventional. In contrast the parties' own signatures generally used less standardised spellings and capitalisation than Jeake and reflected local pronunciation: for example, Richard Wilmserst as written by Jeake, Richard Wimsust in the signature. The letters to Frith are in the Frewen archive at ESRO; these remain an area for future study.

76. These are discussed in Draper, in prep.

77. Andrews 2006, 210, 213.

78. *CPR 1258-66*, 253.

79. Andrews 2006, 209, 213.

80. TNA SC/12/15/73.

81. ESRO HBR/1/0792, 2.

82. Vidler 1934, 18; Holloway 1847, 323-6, gives the rental. *VCH Sussex*, 9, 43, equates the Sack Friars' house and 40 Church Square, citing Vidler.

83. 'Whereas in England there are many cities and considerable towns in which the Augustinian hermits have no place, and many faithful desire to found places for them, they pray for licence to accept the same, and to build oratories with bell towers, and necessary offices in which they shall enjoy their privileges, immunities, and indulgences', *Cal. Pap. Reg. Petitions 1342-1419* 1, 492.

84. 'To the prior provincial and the Augustinian friars in England. Licence to acquire places in four of the cities and solemn towns of the realm of England, and to build in each a church and dwellings for twelve friars, with consent of the diocesan, saving the rights of the parish church and of all others', *Cal. Pap. Reg. Papal Letters 1362-1404* 4, 90.

85. Roth 1961, 200; Andrews 2006, 103. The patronage is discussed in Draper, in prep.

86. The defences are discussed in Martin, *Rye Rebuilt*, chapter 3.

87. *CPR 1361-64*, 440. An Inquisition *Ad Quod Damnun* of 1363/4 by the Warden of the Cinque Ports, Robert de Herle, described the proposed grant as a certain place containing two acres for an oratory and other buildings of the friars eremites house [to be] of new building. The friars were to celebrate for all faithful dead. It confirms that it was the tides or flooding (*refluxione*) of the sea which rendered the land worthless to the king, TNA C143/350/15. Roth 1961 did not give this document.

88. TNA SC/6/1028/11, m.3.

89. RYE 134/1.

90. The New Winchelsea Blackfriars had three sites in succession there, the second on the edge of marshland outside the town. In 1342 they complained about the danger of flooding there and in 1357 moved to their third site on the edge of the New Winchelsea hilltop by the Pipewell Gate, Martin *et al.* 2004, 88.

91. *CPR 1361-64*, 440.

92. His name is given as John Little in Barron 2005, 331.

93. TNA E101/28/7. In addition, William Taillour was also known as Bailiff of Rye in the previous year (1361), when a petition was brought by the parson of Our Lady of Rye against the bailiffs regarding 'Cristesshare' of the fish brought into the port; the petition also mentions Benedict Sely, *Cal. Inq. Misc. 1348-77* 3, 182, no. 490.

94. In 1354 William Taillour was a witness to a quitclaim, i.e. a member of the town government, RYE 136/95. The family consisted of William senior (the Friary founder) and his wife Agnes and their son, William junior; Thomas Taillour (the son of William senior or junior) and his wife Joan; Richard Taillour and Juliana, his wife and executor, RYE 136/89, 92, 94-7, 100, 105, 106, 107, 108, 117, 118, 120-7, 131, 135, 138, 142; RYE 137/4-6; RYE 138/5; *CCLR 1385-86*, 286; *CPR 1364-67*, 327.

95. RYE 137/5; RYE 138/5. These men were perhaps feoffees (trustees) for the Mote and its chapel.

96. E.g. *CCLR 1279-88*, 462.

97. In 1366 Sir Robert de Pashley II was lord of the manor of Mote and made a settlement concerning it, thus explaining the Taillours as new holders in 1367 and the disposal of the wood. Although the Taillours rented the manor, they had to purchase the wood of the manor which remained in the ownership of the lord. The 1366 settlement referred to the need for the Pashley feoffees, who included Robert Covert or Conert, chaplain, and the parson of Iden, to find sufficient chaplains to maintain the Pashley chantry, a free chapel with six chaplains. It was sustained by the profits of lands in Beckley, Peasmarsh, Northiam and elsewhere, and by the alienation of the advowson of Fairlight church. From *c.*1460 the Scott family owned and occupied the manor, rebuilding it and the chapel, Martin 1993, 6, 8, 10, citing BL Add. Ch. 41853-41856, and *VCH Sussex* 9, 154-7, and *Archeol. Cantiana.* 74 (1960), 1-47.

98. RYE 136/142 (1392); RYE 138/5. Vidler 1934, 158, gives William Taillour as mayor in 1394.

99. Hanham 1985, 2, 5, 6.

100. There are only two other Benedicts. This deed survives only in an 18th-century translation, RYE 137/3. The original is dated by its last witness, Henry de la Nesse, to the early part of the 14th century. Benedict Cely had a toehold in Rye in 1343 in the form of a tenement formerly of Thomas Steyn which he held for a quit rent of 2d., TNA SC6/1028/12. However,

Celys do not appear in the Edward I rental, nor in earlier deeds, nor earlier lists of rents or fines in the bailiffs' accounts.

101. *HMC* 5, 502.

102. Inspeximus of 1399, *CPR 1399-1401*, 90. Sir Benedict was executed for treason against Henry IV in 1400, Roskell *et al.* 336.

103. RYE 134/1. Similar is recorded in *Cal. Inq. Misc.*, 3, 182, no. 490.

104. The activities of Thomas Taillour and John Otringham, town clerk, demonstrate the turnover or turmoil in the landmarket in Rye in the late 14th century and how such men reworked landholding there by purchase and reconveyance, RYE 136/106, 108, 117-18, 120, 122-4, 126; RYE 137/4. This is exactly paralleled by the activities of one Thomas Godfrey at Midley near New Romney and of course elsewhere in England in the later 14th century, Draper 1998, 114-15.

105. This appears to have been a private transaction in the sense of being a grant to two individuals, RYE 136/113 (1366); RYE 136/126 (1376). Thomas Taillour and John Ivory were wardens of the works and lights of the church of the Blessed Mary of Rye, RYE 136/113. Ivory witnessed the grant of the obit by the Friary to William and Agnes Taillour in 1368, RYE 134/1.

106. E.g. RYE 136/108, 112, 114, 126.

107. The parties were Walter Ganter (Glover) and Christina his wife, and John de Kent, cordwainer. The property lay between properties the parties already held, RYE 136/71. Christina was said to have lately acquired the property transacted from John de Portesmouth, and this was probably as his heir. Much later, in 1582/3, this area still seems to have been one of leather-working: two men, one from the Friary, brought a little cock boat up a minor creek to the postern gate with a small batch of leather worth 6s. 8d. and smuggled it in, RYE 1/5, 13.

108. The Austin Friary at Canterbury was founded before the Black Death in 1318. Canterbury was crowded with people and religious establishments and the Friary therefore had to negotiate and compete for space in a way which did not apply to the Rye foundation after the Black Death, Sweetinburgh 2008b, 197-212.

109. Given at Rye, Thursday in the feast of the Translation of St Thomas the Martyr, 2 Richard II, RYE 134/2. The date of 7 July 1379 in the work of Poland and Roth (citing Poland) appears to be an error, Poland 1928, 126; Roth 1961, 215, D537.

110. In 1340 the parson of Rye church, Henry de Kendale, requested remission from a tax of a tenth 'as the church and the houses and other buildings of his parishioners in that town, the fruits and issues, whereof a part of his living consisted, have been so burnt by certain enemies of France and the other possessions of that rectory dissipated, that they are not sufficient to maintain the priest there and other charges upon the church without outside aid', *CCLR 1339-41*, 650; Johnes 1839, 58-9. In a revenge raid of 1378 after that of 1377, Rye men replicated these acts, Taylor, Childs and Watkiss 2003, 219. On 8 May 1376 it had been ordered that Rye be fortified and the townsmen furnished with arms and arrayed in case the king's enemies attacked by land or water, *CCLR 1374-44*, 349.

111. Martin *et al.* 2004, 45.

112. Dickinson 2002, 64.

113. *VCH Sussex* 9, 42.

114. Holloway 1847, 592, recorded that 'running from the north east angle of the chapel in a northerly direction and in a straight line from the eastern gable, is still traceable the foundation of a building, to the extent of 30 feet in length from south to north and 12 feet

in width from east to west. At the point of junction with the main building, some plaster is still discernable, none of which is to be seen on the other part: our opinion that this was the dormitory and refectory of the Friars'; A. Van Dyck , 'View of Rye from the North East', The Pierpont Morgan Library, New York; Martin, *Rye Rebuilt*, chapter 4.

115. Holloway 1847, 289; *VCH Sussex* 9, 41. Neither contains primary source references to the postern gate.

116. RYE 134/2.

117. This lane was in 1557 noted as being a footway seven feet wide between the town walls and the premises of one John Ford, and leading from the Landgate to the Postern gate of the town, RYE 131/1.

118. RYE 130/5-9; RYE 136/71, 113,126; RYE 137/6; RYE 134/2.

119. TNA PROB/11/8, 11/11 (wills of Robert Oxenbridge, made 1483, and Adam Oxenbridge, 1496); 'Sussex Wills', 56, 57, 81, 82, 372; Durrant Cooper 1856, 215-16, 218.

120. Colpeper's will was written in French. L.L. Duncan's transcription is available on the Kent Archaeological Society's website Medieval Wills at Lambeth, http://www.kentarchaeology. org.uk/Research/Libr/Wills/Lbth/Bk22/page%20139.htm. There is a full abstract of this will together with an account of the family by F. Attree and J. Booker in *Sussex Archaeological Collections* 47, 48. Thomas Sakevyle of Bayham Abbey also bequeathed 6s. 8d. to the Friary in 1432, 'Sussex Wills', 81. The wills of Colpeper, Sakevyle, and the rector of Snargate, above, are the only wills from or linked to Kent which have been identified with bequests to the Rye Friary. Colpeper's will was typical of the minor landholding elite of the Weald at this period in the number of its bequests to a range of friaries, priories and churches, Holden *et al.* forthcoming; Webster 1984, 217-30.

121. *Reg. Chich.*, 4, 387-9.

122. It was also stated on 14 June 1439 that the Friary 'may accept four from the province on condition that four novices are received within four years', Roth 1961, 324, D791.

123. 'Many human bones have been discovered at different times in the garden which adjoins it, indicating that a burying ground must have been attached to it', Horsfield 1835, 1, 497. Holloway 1847, 593, noted that 'when the wall was built, separating the [Friary] grounds from the highway, in 1762, five or six skeletons were found which had been interred in an upright position'. Others refer to skeletons being disinterred inside the surviving building, notably when the floor was lowered. Poland 1928, 132, followed Clark 1861, 28-9, in describing many skeletons, apparently wrapped in woollen cloth, being dug up in 1826 within the chapel 'in consequence of the floor being lowered several feet'. Construction of an air-raid shelter in 1939-40 in the area north of the surviving building led to the discovery of several skeletons. On 22-3 April 1953 two trenches were excavated in the car park adjacent to the Friary either side of the filled-in air-raid shelter. Three skeletons were found, damaged by insertion of later brick drain, all with head to west. Medieval tile and pottery were found in the lower layers. The skeletons were reburied (location unstated) and the finds sent to Rye Museum, Burstow 1954/7, 204-5. In 1989 a commercial excavation into and/or below the Victorian floor of the chapel took place. Human bone, animal bone and pottery was salvaged first by J. Kirkham and A. Dickinson and then by Hastings Area Archaeological Group, Clements 1991. The human bone was re-interred, following analysis, at unmarked location in churchyard, J. Kirkham, pers. comm.

124. Byspyn's bequest was conditional on his dying without heirs, 'Sussex Wills', 76; *VCH Sussex*, 2, 96-7.

125. E.g., RYE 136/122, 123.

126. *HMC* 5, 548. In 1505 a felon took sanctuary in the Friary, Vidler 1934, 49.

127. The Franciscan Friary at New Romney had disappeared by 1331, perhaps as the result of the severe storm damage to the town in the late 13th century, and no other friary was established later, Little 1939, 151-52.

128. 'Sussex Wills', 57, 80. The Winchelsea Court Hall listings record John Kyrkeby as mayor of Winchelsea in 1513. An earlier Kyrkeby, Ralph, had been taxed to the half scot in Rye in 1415-16 and was a party to a Rye agreement to effect a mortgage of 1416, RYE 77/1; RYE 136/174.

129. RYE 60/5, f. 140. Another bequest for repair of the Friary house was made in 1533, the substantial sum of £10 by Henry Walter of Iden, 'Sussex Wills', 82.

130. The Marshes or Marches were a wealthy and well-known Rye family whose members included a freemen and an MP in the 1550s to 1570s. Two members of this family, Robert Marche, butcher and freeman, and Simon Marche, yeoman, were assessed in 1576 in Middlestreet Ward at 13s. 4d. and 16s. 8d. respectively, both high sums, Mayhew 1987, 60-5, 75, 280.

131. *LPFD H8* 6, 1329; Butler 1865, 131; Poland 1928, 131-2; Roth 1961, 444-5, D1088.

132. *LPFD H8* 13 (2), 1058; Poland 1928, 132; Roth 1961, 486, D1143. Vidler 1934, 54, mistakenly applied to Rye Friary alone the sum of £1122 2s. 6d. that Godwyne paid for various church properties across southern England.

133. *LPFD H8* 29 (2), 340 (51).

134. TNA PROB 11/11. Adam bequeathed his chalice, gold chain, his diamond, sapphire, ruby and emerald gold rings, a gilt cup and six silver chased cups, Mayhew 1987, 33, 103, 112, 273-4.

135. Notably in the person of William Oxenbridge, who was possibly the man of this name admitted to Gray's Inn in 1527, Mayhew 1987, 65, 117. Andrew Oxenbridge, Ll. D., the son of the Thomas Oxenbridge who died *c.*1540, adhered to the Catholic faith and denied the Queen's supremacy; he was committed to Wisbech Castle in 1583 and released after signing an acknowledgement of the supremacy, Durrant Cooper 1856, 223. Nevertheless not all the Oxenbridges were recusants. Elizabeth Oxenbridge, niece of Adam, who married Sir Robert Tyrwhitt and to whom the education and governance of Princess Elizabeth was briefly committed in 1549 after the Thomas Seymour incident, was described as 'not sane (learned) in divinity and half a scripture woman', Durrant Cooper 1856, 224. As Lady Elizabeth Tyrwhitt she wrote pious Protestant poetry, and *Morning and Evening Prayer, with divers Psalmes, Himes, and Mediations* (1574). John Field dedicated his translation of the *Treatise of Christian Righteousness* (1577) to her as his 'vertuous and dear sister'.

136. McCann 1999, 28. Of the five Oxenbridge wills proved in the Prerogative Court of Canterbury between 1431 and 1497, five testators described themselves of Brede, and Adam only as of Rye. The wills were those of Robert Oxenbryigge of Brede, Sussex, proved 21 March 1431, TNA PROB 11/3; Robert Oxenbrigge or Oxenbrigg of Brede, 11 December 1488, PROB 11/8; John Oxenbrigge of Brede, 1 February 1494, PROB 11/10; Adam Oxenbrigge of Rye, 4 November 1496, PROB 11/11; Thomas Oxenbriggs of Brede, Sussex, 08 February 1497, PROB 11/11.

137. Mayhew 1987, 66, 71.

138. RYE 135/9; RYE 1/4/228; Mayhew 1987, 277-84.

139. Kirkham 2006, 8.

140. Harding 2002, 549-69.

141. RYE 139/21.

142. Norton took a lease of St Mary's Marsh from the corporation in 1617. The family seems to have originated at East Farleigh near Maidstone. By 1646 Anthony owned the site of the former Austin Friars inside the Landgate, and he and his descendants continued to acquire property in that area, ESRO PAR 465/1/1/2; RYE 128/1; RYE 47/151; Vidler 1934, 78-79, 91.

143. Also a 'deeze', ESRO DAP/Box 108/8/31-41.

144. *VCH Sussex* 9, 61. It was at one time used as a theatre for itinerant players and as a malt house. A floor was inserted in the building with the upper floor used as a wool store and the lower floor for cheese, butter and lard, Holloway 1847, 539, 592. Messrs. T. Legg and Son were the wool merchants, ESRO AMS/6196. Later it was used as a barracks for soldiers, Holloway 1863, 28; Simmons 2003; Vidler 1934, 142; Kirkham 2002.

145. Röhrkasten 1998, 81, 86.

Chapter 7   The Leper Hospital of St Bartholomew

1. The early history of the Hospital was briefly mentioned under the borough of Rye but mainly described under the term and parish of Playden, *VCH Sussex* 2, 104-5; *VCH Sussex* 9, 49, 160-1. Contemporary sources most often described it as 'the hospital of St Bartholomew of la Rye' or similar, e.g. *CPR 1405-08*, 332 (1407), *CPR 1441-46*, 37 (1442).

2. *CPR 1343-45*, 208. In 1380 it was described as 'the hospital of Plaiden by Rye, co. Sussex, by Robert de Burton, master thereof', *CPR 1377-81*, 464. On 24 December 1461 a grant for life to William Tracy, chaplain, of the custody of the hospital of St Bartholomew, Playden by Rye, co. Sussex' was made, *CPR 1461-67*, 861.

3. In addition to locations A, B, and C (below), a possible identification of the site of the hospital buildings as being close to the present Rovindene House was made by Wetherill from Philip Symondson's 1594 map of the Decayed Harborough of Rye. This places it west of Playden church and west of Rye Hill and near to the lane to Leasam. Wetherill 2001, 19-20. Symondson's religious buildings, e.g., Broomhill church, were apparently individually and 'accurately drawn', Gardiner 1988, 119, 125-6. However, the scale of the Symondson map is far too small and the detail depicted too indistinct to be helpful in locating the hospital building. Wetherill also gave an illustration of the hospital seal (B.M. CLXII.23).

4. RYE 136/78.

5. *Cal. Inq. Misc.* 4, 67, no. 109.

6. Vidler 1943, 73-99; Holloway 1863, 74; Holloway 1866, 13-17. The map also shows a chapel at Saltcote Street. In a Playden Porter manorial survey of 1567 the plot was described as a cottage and garden (1 rod) called Vyles 'whereon is now standing an old decayed chapel'. The chapel had already gone out of use by 1541 when the same plot was simply described as a cottage at the upper part of Saltcote Street, ESRO AMS 4883-4897. Playden Porter was a Robertsbridge Abbey manor which it acquired early from Tréport in Normandy, but Saltcote Street itself, i.e. the settlement to the east of the crossroads next to the chapel, was part of Iden Manor, and the origins of this chapel remain obscure, D. Martin, pers. comm.

7. There was a 'paucity of finds' at this site, Gardiner 1990, 251-2.

8. Wetherill 2001, 3.

9. E.g. RYE 136/75, 78; *Cal. Docs. France*, 52.

10. Gardiner 1990, 251; Vidler 1932, 83-101; Vidler 1933, 44-64; Vidler 1936, 106-18.

11. Found in May 1994 near the ambulance station and electricity sub-station on Rye Hill at TQ.91902155, Wetherill 2001, 1-18.

12. The watching brief was carried out by C. Johnson; J. Kirkham, pers. comm.
13. Holloway 1863, 74.
14. A little distance away, immediately to the north of Leasam Lane, were three other pieces (abutments given) called the Hare Braten Lands, amounting in all to 13 acres of meadow, arable and pasture, and some distance north of that, in the angle between the Peasmarsh road and the Iden road, were two pieces called Hoad-Millpond Land (8 acres of pasture).
15. ESRO DAP 1/3.
16. ESRO SAS/HC, Iden Manorial Records.
17. ESRO ACC 4382, Map of the estates of Ralph Norton, dated 1735.
18. Draper and Meddens (forthcoming), chapter 7.
19. WSRO Ep I/1/3, f. 67 (1249, copied in the late 15th century).
20. Draper and Meddens (forthcoming), chapter 2.
21. WSRO Ep I/1/3, f. 67; *CPR 1343-45*, 118, 120, 189, 208.
22. *Cal. Inq. Misc.* 4, 67, no. 109. The inmates of St Bartholomew's, Sandwich and St Nicholas', Canterbury may have worked on the home farms belonging to these two hospitals, Sweetinburgh 2003, 17-19, 28. For the poor of 1420 and 1442, see below.
23. The version of the Rye custumal as given by Holloway 1847, 137-58, derives from one of several records of Rye customs, decrees and precedents of the mid-16th century, RYE 57/1-4, RYE 33/7; *VCH Sussex* 9, 35.
24. The custumal (item 59 as given by Holloway) acknowledged the reality that in wartime the monarch, not Fécamp, controlled the nomination process, an acknowledgement that would be applicable by 1356. This stated that 'the mayor of Rye and jurats, forthwith the commonalty, shall have the nomination of the chaplain, which is called the Custos of the Hospital of Saint Bartholomew, besides Rye, which said chaplain in time of peace, shall be sent unto the Abbot of Fyscamp (*sic*), and, in time of war, unto the Lord Chancellor of England; and, by one of them, he shall be presented unto the Bishop of Chichester, and by him he shall have institution', Holloway 1847, 156-7.
25. *VCH Sussex* 2, 104, citing the Rye custumal as recorded by Holloway. At New Winchelsea the Hospitals of St John and St Bartholomew were similarly under the control of the mayor and commonalty, Martin *et al.* 2004, 90, 92; Draper and Meddens (forthcoming), chapter 2
26. *CPR 1343-45*, 189.
27. Vidler 1934, extended by Vidler and Kirkham, and Rye Town Hall listings, citing Chichester Cathedral Liber E, fol 228v. Roger de Southmallyng was perhaps from Lewes Priory, where the chief Cluniac house in England was sited, since Fécamp Abbey itself, while remaining independent, followed the traditions of Cluny, Burton 1994, 36.
28. *CPR 1343-45*, 118, 120, 189, 208. *VCH Sussex* 2, 105, gives a list of masters of the hospital which is extended here.
29. Vidler 1934, extended by Vidler and Kirkham, and Town Hall listings, Brede Court Rolls A 10. Cf. Hist MSS Com Rep v. 513.
30. Thomas atte Nesse was mayor in 1340, RYE 136/77. La Nesse was a low-lying area on the east side of Rye below the cliff; it was under threat from the tides by the 1340s when a house there next to one belonging to Nicholas Paulyn was dismantled and rebuilt elsewhere in Rye, RYE 136/80. One of the medieval wards·of the town was named Nesse, RYE 77/1.
31. A 'Writ de intendendo' for Roger de Burton was directed to the brothers and sisters possibly requiring them to attend on and obey the warden, *CPR 1377-81*, 336.

32. Analysis of the numbers of witnesses to Rye deeds between the early 13th and the late 15th centuries shows a distinctive drop after the Black Death, suggesting the loss of perhaps a third to a half of the population in the late 14th century
33. Draper (in prep.)
34. He may have been the man of this name who held the office of Receiver of the Chamber at the Tower of London.
35. *CPR 1377-81*, 464. William Horne was from the family of this name which owned a stone house near Appledore just north of Romney Marsh in the 14th century, one of whose forebears, Mathew, had received a royal grant to build a quay at New Romney in 1276, Draper and Meddens (forthcoming) chapter 2. William de Battesford (Batlesford, Batesford) received other royal commissions in the locality between 1364 and 1389, e.g. into repairs of the walls and ditches of Romney Marsh, *CPR 1361-66*, 544.
36. *Cal. Inq. Misc.* 4, 67, no. 109.
37. *CPR 1388-92*, 399.
38. His exact date of death is unknown, although it was certainly after 1372 and a statement in a 15th-century book of his homilies puts it in 1393 at York, J. Catto, 'Waldeby, John (d. after 1372)', *Oxford Dictionary of National Biography*, Oxford University Press, 2004 [http://www.oxforddnb.com/view/article/53112, accessed 26 May 2008].
39. *CPR 1388-92*, 483.
40. William Longe (I) was a witness to a deed which can be dated to the early 13th century concerning valuable land at *Stoburma*, perhaps near Icklesham, whose first witness was a man from the manor of Levelysham, by Rye (*chapter 1*), and whose last witness was William the clerk of Winchelsea, RYE 137/1. In 1260 Richard Longe was one of 12 witnesses to a feoffment concerning a certain house in Rye near the donor's house on the north and reached from the highway leading to the mill on the west to the land of John Le Bode on the east. This feoffment was from Roger Le Vynch with the assent of Alice his wife to Alexander Le Sweyn with Parnel, the donor's daughter, in free marriage, RYE 136/4. Richard Longe was recorded in the Edward I rental as having formerly held a tenement owing 7d. rent at Michaelmas in Rye and another one 'outside the gate' of Rye owing 10d. rent at St Andrew's term, TNA SC12/15/73. John Longhe of Winchelsea witnessed a feoffment in 1351 concerning tenements and rents in Winchelsea, Rye and Iham which was also witnessed by the mayors of both Winchelsea and Rye, RYE 136/89. John Longhe was father of William Longe (II), *CPR 1358-61*, 28. One Philip Longe also appears as a witness to town deeds, RYE 136/154, 163 (1402, 1410).
41. *CPR 1391-96*, 182.
42. *CPR 1391-96*, 275, 581.
43. *HMC* 5, 512.
44. *CPR 1396-99*, 46, 188;. Draper 2007a, 78.
45. *Reg. Chich.*, 3 404-6; Bodl MS dd All Souls c182, item 23. Thomas Brigge was also known as Thomas de Breggis, atte Bregges, etc. His career is discussed in Draper 2004, section 2.2.7.
46. The other patron was Thomas Moonie, an official of the Archbishop of Canterbury, *Reg. Chich.*, 1, 36.
47. E.g. *CPR 1391-96*, 275.
48. Deye exchanged benefices with one John Hoton, chaplain, who had been master in 1399, Deye was followed as master by Robert Kyng, chaplain, in 1401, and then swiftly by John Bedford, *CPR 1399-1401*, 31, 390, 432.

49. *CPR 1401-05*, 218, 200. Scovill was followed in 1405 by John Preston who resigned after a few months, *CPR 1405-08*, 32. Preston was nominated by the mayor and barons but is not otherwise known.

50. *CPR 1405-08*, 141.

51. *CPR 1413-16*, 19.

52. '*Item hospitali de Riam pauperibus*', *Reg. Chich.*, 2, 215-16; Colnet also bequeathed 100s. to the Hospital of St Mary of Bethlehem outside Bishopsgate, London, Linda Ehrsam Voigts, 'Colnet, Nicholas (d. 1420)', *Oxford Dictionary of National Biography*, Oxford University Press, 2004 [http://www.oxforddnb.com/view/article/52670, accessed 26 May 2008].

53. *Reg. Chich.*, 1, 197; *CPR 1416-22*, 311.

54. Stephen E. Lahey, 'Upton, Edward (d. 1419?)', *Oxford Dictionary of National Biography*, Oxford University Press, 2004 [http://www.oxforddnb.com/view/article/52686, accessed 5 Feb 2009].

55. *CPR 1417-1431*, 7, 417.

56. WSRO Ep/I /1/2, f. 80v.

57. *VCH Sussex* 2, p. 105; *CPR 1441-46*, 37.

58. Syon was granted much other property of former alien houses but it was not always immediately received, since in some cases the leases had to lapse. In the 1400s Syon feared that its endowments might be transferred to Henry VI's new foundations at Eton and Cambridge as some of its other endowments were, but this was avoided. Barron and Davies 2007, 280-3; *CPR 1441-46*, 234; *CPR 1461-67*, 144-5.

59. *CPR 1461-67*, 86.

60. *CPR 1476-85*, 105.

61. *CPR 1494-1509*, 303.

62. *CPR 1494-1509*, 374-5; Barron and Davies 2007, 69.

63. Harvey 1977, 403.

64. Draper, 2007a, 86; Martin *et al.* 2004, 90-3.

65. Wages for the relatively unskilled work of digging and ditching on Romney Marsh rose from 2d. or 3d. a day before the Black Death to 5d. or 6d. afterwards, mirroring a typical rise nationwide.

66. This is recorded in 1491 and 1508-9, Gunn *et al.* 2007, 84, citing RYE 60/3, ff. 16v, 76r. Later, in 1545, the town government used French prisoners as labourers on the town's fortifications project, Gunn *et al.* 2007, 79, citing Mayhew 1984, 113.

67. Windsor also received many other former Syon properties, *LPFD H8* 17, 167.

68. *VCH Sussex* 9, 160-1.

69. RYE 47/79/13a, 13b.

70. *VCH Sussex* 9, 161.

71. Smart 1864, 303.

72. John Whyman, 'Kilburne, Richard (1605-1678)', *Oxford Dictionary of National Biography*, Oxford University Press, 2004 [http://www.oxforddnb.com/view/article/15523, accessed 28 May 2008]; Smart 1864, 303.

73. Mr Thomas Burchit was the first Protestant mayor of Rye. He had three sons who were educated and trained at Cambridge and the Inns of Court between the years 1547 and 1564. He was a baker, brewer and merchant with two substantial and valuable houses in Mermaid (Middle) Street, Mayhew 1987, 114, 117-18, 174. Burchit and his heirs also held a tenement and two shops in Rye in the 1570s, and Sarah Burchit, formerly Short, was presumably married to one of his descendants, RYE 130/21; RYE 60/9, ff. 59-61.

Chapter 8   The Environment, Assets and Defences of Rye, c.1086 to c.1660

1. The town's infrastructure is further discussed in Martin, *Rye Rebuilt*, chapter 2.

2. This route was one of the two main routes through the Weald and part of it was the earliest to be turnpiked in Kent, Melling 1959, vii, 27; McLain 1997, map 2; Watson 1999, 28-9; Knowlden 2008, 123. In *c*.1285 Henry called le yonge of Rye enfeoffed Richard called ate Welle of Winchelsea and Joan his wife, daughter of Walter de Bromleghe, with 'a messuage with buildings built onto it' in Rye. The transaction suggests the human connections made along the route from Rye to Bromley, RYE 136/185. In the early 16th century the routes mentioned in wills included those to Newenden bridge, to Flackley (Peasmarsh) and to Udimore, 'Sussex Wills', 79-80.

3. McLain 1997, 99-103. The market days for Lewisham and Tonbridge are not known but these were early and significant markets, probably held more than once a week, Holden *et al*. (forthcoming). The market day for Chelsfield and nearby West Wickham was granted for Mondays and perhaps fish was not sold here, buyers going instead to the other nearby Tuesday markets. Traditionally fishing boats do not go out on Sundays.

4. Elyas Lambyn appears with the mariners of Rye and Winchelsea in a list of 1230. Poteman Lambyn had a tenement at Rye in the late 13th century which was subsequently held by Richard Marchant, i.e. merchant. Robert, Walter and William Lambin were among men described as burgesses and fishmongers of London in 1270. The latter, William Lambyn, witnessed a Rye feoffment of the late 13th century, and such witnesses were members of the town government and elite of Rye. One Alan Lambin of Robertsbridge is known in 1290 and it is likely that he was involved, like the other Lambins, in the London fish trade. John Lambin was also a fishmonger of London in 1340, TNA SC12/15/73; *CPR 1225-32*, 345; *CPR 1266-72*, 377, 455; *CPR 1338-40*, 390; RYE 136/3. Lambin was an uncommon name with the individuals concentrated in the period and places mentioned here, although others were citizens and mariners in ports of London and Yarmouth. A large database of individuals derived from both national and Sussex records and a further search of the Patent Rolls reveal few Lambins (Lambyns), http://www.uiowa.edu/~acadtech/patentrolls/ accessed 17 September 2008. Peter Lambyn owned a ship called *Godeyer* which he freighted at London with 200 quarters of wheat for Flanders in 1344. Edmund Lambyn, citizen of London, was keeper of the wool-beam in the port of Great Yarmouth in the 1350s. A later William Lambyn, known in the early 15th century, was master (but not owner) of *La Gracedieux* of Dartmouth, suggesting that perhaps the Lambins had moved away to the West Country with the rise of the fishing industry there, *CPR 1343-45*, 417; *CPR 1350-54*, 73; *CPR 1401-05*, 134.

5. McLain 1997, 101; Bleach and Gardiner 1997, 43.

6. Watson 1999, 26-9; Durrant Cooper 1850, 82.

7. RYE 47/6/47.

8. TNA MPF 212.

9. This is shown in Martin, *Rye Rebuilt*, fig. 2.3.

10. RYE 132/15. This was drawn by Samuel Jeake in 1667 and copied by William Wybourn in 1728, Brent 1980, doc. 5

11. *Sussex Chantry Records*, 31, 166.

12. *PNS 2*, 537.

13. In 1480 the town income from fishermen was recorded separately from those of Rye and Saltcote in a way which had not been done in the mid-14th century, Vidler 1934, 41.

14. *VCH Sussex 9*, 151.

15. The Grene Okes lay on the south side of Ambroysestonne in Playden, which also had the estuary on its east side. A channel (gutt) ran through the land to the north of Ambroysestonne draining into the estuary, RYE 136/142.

16. Joan Taillour and her daughter Juliana quitclaimed their rights in Ambroystonne, perhaps acquired by marriage and inheritance, in 1392, RYE 136/142; Gardiner 2007, 102.

17. In 1422 the manor of Marley, Peasmarsh, which included lands and rents at Saltcote, was divided between Richard ate Wode, fishmonger of London, and Henry and Elizabeth Dobyll of Wittersham in Kent, the former taking 'land and wood by The Grene Oke(s) near Salcot which Thomas Sutton lately held to farm', ESRO AMS 6800/6/1. Well-seasoned English oak was used for making barrels in the late Middle Ages, and the Lord Mayor of London made an ordinance in 1488 against 'green and sappy' timber being used instead, Kilby 2004, 22.

18. RYE 122/8.

19. RYE 138/15.

20. James, Draper and Martin 2005, 12, 19, 27-8, 42.

21. Martin, *Rye Rebuilt*, fig. 1.2. A ferry at Old Winchelsea is also known from the bailiffs' account of 1266-7, TNA SC6 1031/19.

22. Mayhew 1987, 14, 289, n. 3.

23. The fish shelter at Udimore lay next to the street of the barrel-makers, Couperestrete. Richard and Alice Hefdrop of Rye enfeoffed John Edmund and his sons of Udimore with 1½ acres next to the fish shelter and Couperestrete, which were surrounded on two sides by land the Edmunds already owned, RYE 136/132.

24. TNA SC6/1028/8. Richard atte Wysse paid a 10d. rent for a tenement in the Edward I rental, in which Stephen Wise also appears with a tenement which was one of several subsequently held by Pharon Ion, mayor of Rye, TNA SC12/15/73.

25. William was named indifferently de la Wische and atte Wische. In one deed William's lands abutted one side of a parcel of land of 1½ acres, RYE 136/31, 34, 40-1, 43, 44-6.

26. Joan quitclaimed all her right and claim by way of dower in the tenements, lands and rents of her husband to another member of the town government, John Kittey, senior (perhaps her son-in-law), for half a mark of silver, a small amount. Joan's name was spelt Wyse by the clerk of the deed and given as Le Wise on her seal, RYE 136/44.

27. A note attached to the bailiff's account of 1342/3 records that 52 tenements and a mill had, apparently recently, been burnt by the French, TNA SC 6/1028/11, m.3.

28. TNA SC12/15/73.

29. RYE 136/122, 123. Stephen Wy', perhaps the same man or his descendant, also held marshland in St Mary's Croft in 1402, RYE 122/1, 3, 10.

30. E.g., in 1446 an empty plot was conveyed which abutted east on a cottage of Robert Onwyn and the churchwardens, south on the walls of the cemetery, west on a path from the market place to the cemetery, and north on a lane between the premises and the town butchery, RYE 130/2.

31. This is discussed in detail in Martin, *Rye Rebuilt*, chapter 2.

32. Draper and Meddens (forthcoming), chapter 2.

33. Butler 1976, 32.

34. *Le Pygge Lane*, RYE 136/49, 53; RYE 124/3; *Schytbourglane*, RYE 136/112; *Lane leading to M[i]lnerstrete*, RYE 136/86; *Merstret* (1307), RYE 136/29; *Potepiriestrete*, RYE 136/60. The names of the three principal streets are not known in the medieval period but may have been similar to those used later.

35. RYE 130/11; RYE 33/20.
36. RYE 137/21, f. 2v; Draper 1998, 16.
37. The document was a feoffment which was acknowledged in Rye court by the wife, suggesting that the property was hers by inheritance, RYE 137/21, f. 2v; Draper 2005, 34-40; Draper 2007, 4-20.
38. His payment of 6d. for default of the law (*deficiet de lege*) and 10s. 'for land' are recorded among the pleas and perquisites of the court, TNA SC6/1028/8.
39. TNA SC12/15/73.
40. RYE 136/51 (1320). The spelling *Estronde* varied slightly in the records but has been standardised here.
41. The tenement *Storme* may be read as *Storine*, TNA SC6, 1028/12, but tenement *Storme* appears frequently in the Edward I rental.
42. *CPR 1321-24*, 371.
43. TNA SC 6/1028/11, m.3.
44. TNA SC 6/1028/13; SC 12/15/78.
45. *CPR 1266-72*, 59.
46. One Thomas de la Nesse is known as early as 1258 and it is clear that over the period there were two men called Thomas named from La Nesse. Henry de la Nesse was also described as clerk and last witness to a deed, RYE 136/1, 2, 4, 14, 17, 20, 30, 31, 66, 79, 82; RYE 137/3; TNA SC12/15/73.
47. Stephen Russel and Thomas Peronel also had houses on the low ground at *La Nesse*, RYE 136/74, 80.
48. The medieval wards were given in an assessment for a half scot (rate). Some people were assessed without a named ward being given, RYE 77/1. The later wards are discussed in Martin, *Rye Rebuilt*, chapter 2.
49. RYE 136, 94, cf. RYE 136/34.
50. *HMC* 5, 491.
51. The entry does not make clear whether these stocks were those set up on the Strand between the Cage and the town's house before 1587, RYE 130/136.
52. The feoffment was witnessed by local gentry such as Sir Thomas Echyngham, knight, and Robert Oxenbridge esquire, and the mayor of New Winchelsea, Thomas Thunder, since the town could not witness its own grants, RYE 136/198; Vidler 1934, 39.
53. The later grants are recorded in RYE 130.
54. Grauntford also paid 20d. for his workshop (*opella*) in the market, and 12d. for half a year's contribution towards the inning of the Gutt. He is first mentioned in the town accounts under 1448, *HMC* 5 491, 493-4.
55. Mayhew 1987, 26.
56. MED.
57. RYE 130/10.
58. The rental of 1575 records 12 rents of assize for shops at the strand, taken to represent these early shops whose rents were distinguished from the rows built in the 1540s. The rental noted past holders of the early shops suggesting they had been in existence for some time, in contrast to the new rows. A precise count of the early shops is impossible since in six entries the scribe gave shops (plural) but one rent. A tenement at the strand was also recorded, rent 16s. The rental is recorded in RYE 60/9, ff. 59-61, from which the following analysis is made.
59. Mayhew 1987, 160, 177, 277.

60. William Hailliard and John Rowes, both fishing masters, Thomas Cutthorne, Stevin Dyne and John Parkes, all fishermen, and Edward Engram, mariner. John Gogle who held a loft and a garret over it had a relative, Simon Gogle, who was a fishing master. The occupations from sources other than the 1575 rental are given in Mayhew 1987, 277, 279, 281, 283, 287.

61. Robert Walker and Mr Milles, who held two shops, Mayhew 1987, 126, 130-1, 275, 281, 313-14. There were several men surnamed Milles in Tudor Rye but the term Mr usually referred to a jurat, identifying the one in the rental as Matthew Millis.

62. Their occupations are given in Mayhew 1987, 36, 43-4, 104, 107, 113, 126, 131, 133-6, 152, 175, 178, 163-4, 156, 220, 258, 268, 276, 279-82, 287, 300.

63. Mayhew 1987, 160, 279.

64. Mayhew 1987, 26-9; Martin, *Rye Rebuilt*, chapter 7, gives the garrets in private houses.

65. Mayhew 1987, 258, 279.

66. RYE 130/40.

67. Martin, *Rye Rebuilt*, chapter 5.

68. Mayhew 1987, 43, 54, 94, 86-98, 102, 116, 120, 122, 129-33, 136-8, 234, 257, 264-5, 275, 279, 300. Carpenter also had a stable elsewhere in town behind the tenement which was in the tenure of one Mrs Tarpes (?), RYE 60/9, f. 59v.

69. There were outbreaks of plague at Rye in 1596 and 1625, and of smallpox in 1634, 1635, 1654 and 1655, Holloway 1847, 318. The rental of 1670 (or 1671) is given in Holloway 1847, 323-6. Mayhew confirmed from an analysis of baptisms, marriages and deaths certain periods which were relatively free of the high mortality associated with epidemic disease: the years around 1550, the early 1570s, the mid-1580s, and also the early 17th century. Peaks in the number of annual burials occurred in the early 1560s, the late 1570s and the early 1590s, Mayhew, 1987, 22-4.

70. Another young man, William Redburn, was suspected of causing his death but was pardoned because it might have been an accident, *CPR 1232-47*, 64.

71. *CPR 1247-58*, 477.

72. *CCLR 1272-79*, 36. The term *wallis* was usually used in coastal and marshland parts of Kent and east Sussex to mean defensive walls against tidal water, often in conjunction with *et fossatis* (and ditches), e.g. in 1339 a commission *de walliis et fossatis* was made to Thomas de Brokhull, James de Echyngham, Geoffrey de Warsham and Robert de Sharndenne for the area between Romney, a place called Longerake, the church of Lydd and the sea in the town of Lydd, *CPR 1338-40*, 362.

73. RYE 136/99.

74. http://www.archive.org/stream/gildmerchantcont02grosuoft/gildmerchantcont02grosuoft_djvu. txt accessed 4.11.2008.

75. The conveyance was a conditional feoffment, RYE 136, 67.

76. He paid 10d. rent, TNA SC12/15/73.

77. RYE 136/58.

78. RYE 77/1. Although Paul de Portesmuth and his fellows claimed in a dispute on 18 March 1349 to be simply 'poor mariners' of Rye, he was joint owner of the ship *La Nicolas* of Rye, one of the town's larger vessels, with Richard Baddyng, the mayor (*Chapter 4*), *CCLR 1349-54*, 65.

79. Neither these families, nor those with mills (below), appear in the scot list of 1415, RYE 77/1.

80. The one on the cliff cannot be identified as the windmill at the Nesse because this was built later, TNA SC12/15/73.

81. The 'considerations' which people paid to each other to convey property in Rye were considerably more than the reserved rents to the town which the deeds also recorded, which were small fixed yearly rents, e.g. a consideration of 22s. 6d compared to a reserved rent of 6d., RYE 136/50.

82. Other members of the Bone family, Adam and Simon, were tenants at *Morbrigge* in the early 14th century. This bridge may possibly have lay to the east of Boonshill in Iden where, as at Houghton Green and Saltcote Street, tracks ran eastwards from the upland towards the low-lying marsh, Gardiner 2002, 117, n.10. At Saltcote, certainly, salt was made. The daughter of Brice Palmer, founder of the chantry in Rye church, married John Bone. John's grandson was Henry Bone, Vidler 1934, 24.

83. *Molande de heheteyhe*, TNA SC12/15/73; RYE 136/17, 24, 26, 29, 31, 34, 36-8, 40-4, 48-9, 52, 54.

84. On 14 January 1321 Richard le Whyte of Rye, son of Richard, made a feoffment to them to this effect, RYE 136, 52.

85. John called le Whyte of Rye made a quitclaim to John Kyttey of the same and Martha his wife of an annual rent of 6d. arising from the Kytteys' salt house [*domo salina*] at *La Eststronde* in Rye, RYE136/51. In a deed catalogued as *c*.14th century, Nicholas de Rastronde (catalogued as ?La Stronde) appears as a witness. This deed is lost and exists only in an 18th-century transcription so the spelling of the original cannot be checked, RYE 137/3.

86. John Kyttey had died and rights in the mill passed to his sons John junior and Geoffrey. They passed their rights to their mother Martha who was still alive, John in 1325 and Geoffrey in 1338, RYE 136, 63, 74.

87. TNA SC6/1028/11, m.3.

88. TNA SC12/15/73; RYE 136/2.

89. Draper and Meddens (forthcoming), chapter 2; Harding 1995, 163. Walter le Taverner of Sandwich was among the barons of the other Cinque Ports to whom licences to export grain were issued in 1307, *CPR 1301-07*, 499.

90. On 13 May 1480 the manor or tenement of Dornydale, alias Dornedale, in Playden and Iden was recorded as descending to a list of 15 names on death of widow Agnes Clestre, together with a mill called 'Hothemille' in the parish of Rye, *CCLR 1468-85*, 193. The windmill on the cliff at *La Nesse* is last recorded in 1358 (above).

91. RYE 136/65 (1325).

92. These are labelled 'The mylles at begger hill'. The writing is partly obscured by the compass rose.

93. Mayhew 1987, 12, 267.

94. RYE 140/14. Stonham was later consulted by the town about amending the harbour. He was assessed in Market Ward in 1576, where he paid at a sum in the middle of the range, Mayhew 1987, 153, 266-67, 278.

95. Those on the flat land were Rye smock mill, one north of Ferry Road and one to the east of the new Winchelsea Road, Dickinson 2002, 54-5.

96. Most of the towns of the Cinque Ports confederation had defences, apart from New Romney. The beaching area and harbour of New Romney was severely damaged by the storms of the later 13th century so that it was not a prime candidate for raids in the warfare of the 14th century. The damage to the prosperity of New Romney meant that it was unlikely to seek to build walls or gates as an expression of status or fashion in the 13th century, or to control the entrance of merchants, since merchants had traded there since at least the

mid-11th century. It was in addition protected on the inland side by its marsh hinterland, Draper and Meddens (forthcoming), chapter 2.

97. Gunn *et al.* 2007, 60.

98. RYE 99/1; see also Hipkin 1995, 138-47.

99. The defences are examined more fully in Martin, *Rye Rebuilt*, Chapter 3.

100. *Calendar of Papal Letters* 1, 111.

101. 'Notification that, whereas the king has committed to Peter de Saboudia issues of the lands late of Theobald le Butiller and Richard de Burgo and the honour of Hastings, with the marriage of the heir of Theobald, to fortify the castles of Hastings and la Rye, he shall not be bound to render account for these. Grant to him of the wardship of the lands and heir of Richard de Burgo, to fortify the castle of Hastings out of the wardship, and then the castle of la Rye, if anything remains over', *CPR 1247-58*, 50.

102. E.g. *VCH Sussex* 9, 50.

103. RYE 136/137, 153. According to the listings on boards at the Winchelsea Court Hall, another Badding, Robert, was mayor of Winchelsea in 1363 and 1376.

104. RYE 136/139. The bond was 'received at Wittersham'. The stone masons confirmed the document with their seals, one of which bore an armorial image.

105. Lyle 1994, 22, 76-7, 81.

106. Mostly with courses of iron-stained sandstone, roughly finished, Martin, *Rye Rebuilt*, chapter 3. The Kentish sandstone called ragstone which was used for building in Kent and London was quarried from the Hythe beds. Robinson and Jarzembowski 1998, describe Kentish ragstone from around Maidstone as a hard gritty sandstone of the early Cretaceous age (120 million years ago). In the quarries which used to surround the town, the ragstone was extracted from distinct layers, or beds, of varying thickness, separated by soft shale or mudstone. Some beds contain fossil shells, mostly oysters, showing that the ragstone formed in a shallow, sandy sea. Some of the ragstone beds cut easily into near cubic rocks; others provide flat slabs.

107. RYE 1/4/24r.

108. *CCLR 1259-61*, 378.

109. *CCLR 1242-47*, 461. Criol was warden of the Ports and constable of Dover at this period, when the office of warden was being developed and gradually becoming permanently linked to that of constable, Murray 1935, 81-3. Another of the trusted courtiers was Robert Passelewe, H.W. Ridgeway, 'Henry III (1207-1272)', *Oxford Dictionary of National Biography*, Oxford University Press, Sept 2004; online edn, Jan 2007 [http://www.oxforddnb.com/view/article/12950, accessed 13 Nov 2008].

110. He was also recorded as paying 4s. for default of the law (*deficiet de lege*) among the Rye court fines (pleas and perquisites) of 1272-3, TNA SC 6/1028/8, covering 6 May 1272 to 6 May 1273.

111. RYE 136/13.

112. TNA SC12/15/73.

113. RYE 136/3. This feoffment can be dated approximately to this year by its witnesses, and it fits with the description atte Gate in the rental.

114. 18d. rent from Roger Baudechon for the tenement *Ryngelot* outside the gate; 10d. from the same Roger Baudechon for the tenement of Richard Longes outside the gate; 6d. rent from John Bochard or possibly Jacob Marchant outside the gate, TNA SC12/15/73. Portour also meant one who guards the gate of a bridge, MED.

115. The first deed of 1323 conveyed an annual rent of 7½d. arising from the principal tenement of the heirs of John Lambsyn situated outside the gate of Rye for a consideration of half a mark silver. The recipients were Goda, the daughter of John Torel (*Chapter 4*), and her husband. The words are *extra portam*, not gates (*portas*) as originally catalogued, RYE 136/57, 64.
116. RYE 136/73.
117. *HMC* 5, 490, referring to RYE 60/2.
118. A piece of vacant land, 75 feet by 24 feet lay outside the Watergate (*portam aquaticam*) at the Strand, abutting east on town land, south opposite the town walls and on the common quay, west on the Strand, north on town lands called the common Strand, RYE 130/3-4.
119. Martin, *Rye Rebuilt*, citing Holloway 1847, 77, 288-9.
120. *VCH Sussex* 9, 40.
121. *CPR 1266-72*, 357.
122. *VCH Sussex* 9, 40.
123. The memorandum is in French and survives in rather poor condition. It is undated but catalogued as of 1327x1377, TNA C47/2/48.
124. *CPR 1367-70*, 224.
125. *CCLR 1374-77*, 50. Lewes, which was left undefended, was also attacked by the French, Saul 1986, 35.
126. *CPR 1370-74*, 492. The grant of the town profits may have meant they were excused the amount they usually paid to farm (lease) these profits, which amounted to approximately £20 before 1377 and £18 afterwards, Vidler 1934, 28.
127. The grant was made by letters patent, *HMC* 5, 502; RYE 58/6.
128. *CCLR 1369-74*, 406, 408; Vidler 1934, 24.
129. TNA SC6/1028/15.
130. In 1344, the last year before the mortality of the Black Death for which an account survives, the town had received a similar amount in rents as in 1361 (because these were fixed assize rents), but much more (£9 14s. 6d.) from other income such as the landing dues and fishing customs and also the profits of the town court such as fines, and various rents for market stalls, making a total of £19 17s. 4¼d., TNA SC6/1028/13. Rental income worth 38s. 4¼d. had already been lost with the burning of a mill and 52 tenements by the French in the raid of 1339, rents which were not recovered, TNA SC6/1028/11, m.3.
131. Vidler 1934, 27. No primary source has been found for his statement that Simon Lonsford, the mayor, and Richard Baddyng, the bailiff, escaped with their lives and promptly hanged and quartered as traitors those most responsible for the loss of the town, and then set the people to work to rebuild their houses and repair the breaches in the walls. Walsingham stated that 'at dawn on the festival of the apostles Peter and Paul [29 June], the French attacked the town of Rye with fifty ships, large and small, with as many as five thousand men. They captured the town with little effort, though the townspeople, confident in their strength, had stated and made firm promise that nobody would carry off their moveable possessions from the town; so that at all events because of their love of material possessions they put up a spirited resistance in the conflict. However they acted like the sons of Ephraim, "bending and shooting with the bow, but turning back in the day of battle".' The result of their folly was that the town of Rye was captured with all their possessions, Taylor, Childs and Watkiss 2003, 133.
132. *In locis necessariis sufficienter claudere*, *HMC* 5, 497. In the 16th century this document was

endorsed as a 'Charter for building the walles of Rye' but was clearly a royal requirement in response to the grant of the town income, *VCH Sussex* 9, 40.

133. On 14 January 1385 the French were said to be scheming to seize and fortify Rye themselves, in order to use it as a base for attacking the surrounding countryside as well, as they had done in 1377, *CPR 1381-85*, 519; Taylor, Childs and Watkiss 2003, 133. Hastings was also raided in 1377, Pelham 1930, 175.

134. *HMC* 5, 501.

135. RYE 124/1.

136. Vidler 1934, 36.

137. James, Draper and Martin 2005, 25.

138. RYE 124/6, 7, 8, 12; RYE 136/187, 191; *HMC* 5, 495, reading 'Payed after the Mayer and his bretherne come owte of the Towere [of Ypres] from the affyryng [affeering or assessing] of the quest, unto Master Graunforthes, to a dyner there, with them beyne present Master Robert Oxenbregge, Sqyuer, for their expences in mete and wyne 2s. 8d.'.

139. Events recorded in the accounts are cited by their year of commencement; *HMC* 5, 490-4; *VCH Sussex* 9, 40, n.25.

140. Draper and Meddens (forthcoming), chapter 10.

141. RYE 124/13, 14, 17; Mayhew 1984, 114.

142. Mayhew 1984, 115.

143. Mayhew 1984, 114, n.39; *VCH Sussex* 9, 185; Biddle, Hiller and Scott 2002.

144. Mayhew 1984, 111, n.25.

145. The creek of Rye was a term in use in 1546, when a Dutchman was described as landing there discreetly with intelligence of the French fleet, *LPFD H8*, 400, no. 803.

146. Mayhew 1984, 111, n.25.

147. 18 September 1573, RYE 47/6/47.

148. Vidler 1934, 47.

149. RYE 130/15.

150. Mayhew 1984, 111-15; Mayhew 1987, 35.

151. Mayhew 1987, 283; RYE 127/12-13; RYE 130/38-44.

Chapter 9   St Mary's Marsh: The Physical and Historical Evidence

1. In 1541 Gateborough marsh was described as lying within the marsh called 'Seynt Mary Marshe', *LPFD H8* 16, 505. In the 13th to 15th centuries Cadborough Marsh, or Gateborough marsh, lay between Winchelsea and Rye to the north of the River Brede. However, the landscape there was so transformed by flooding, reclamation and the shrinkage of fleets that by the early 16th century there was much dispute over place-names and boundaries of marshes in this area, Gardiner 1995, 128-9.

2. Hipkin 1995b, 138-47.

3. North Marsh may have been an asset of the church from as early as 1197 when there was a dispute between William de Marinis, the vicar of Rye, and Fécamp Abbey which claimed that he owed a yearly payment of 13 marks (£8 13s. 4d.) from the church and its assets, which by 1247 included North Marsh, *Cal. Docs France*, 49-50; Vidler 1934, 9; *CPR 1232-47*, 503. At the time of the final resumption of the alien priories in England in 1416, Fécamp was still trying to claim this income from the priest of Rye. A memoir of instructions for the Abbey's agent visiting England included '*Item de demander au cure de la Rye xiii marcs dargent, quil doit a leglise de Fescamp chacun an*', Matthew 1962, 167.

4. On 22 January 1333 there was a 'commission de *walliis et fossatiis* to Thomas de Faversham,

Richard de Grofherste and Robert de Bataille in the marshes of Northmersh by La Rye and of Spadelond between the town of Wynchelse and Daunsewalle and in other marshes and places adjoining', *CPR 1330-34*, 391, cf. Lovegrove 1964, 120. The banks of Northmersh may be represented by a surviving embankment at the back of Tillingham Avenue, Rye, protecting Northmersh from the tidal Tillingham river with a creek allowing access to the (West) Strand, T. Burke, pers. comm. A similar commission for other marshes, some near Rye, was appointed in 1331, but it is not clear whether this was concerned with the initial reclamation or their subsequent defence from the sea. They were named as *Laddesmarsh, Bodyhammesmersh*, Whiteflete marsh and Cadborough Marsh. A deed of 1332 mentions that a 'new marsh', *Pipenesell* marsh near Rye, had been re-inclosed, Gardiner 1995, 131; RYE 136/70

5. Waller and Grant 2008, 22-6. Rye was not literally an island although it had access to tidal water on the western side in from *c*.700-800. Tidal water flowed through marshland on the eastern and southern sides of the hill on which the town stood by the 13th century. After the storms of the mid- to later part of the 13th century the marshland on the eastern side would have been buried or the sediment eroded away, M. Waller, pers. comm.

6. The silty clays lay above a thick peat layer which is interpreted as a fen carr environment from about 4000 B.C. to 1000 B.C. Subsequently the marshlands here, as in the Brede valley/levels and Tillingham valley, may have been used for grazing and perhaps cropped for reed and sedges. This may be represented by a thin organic layer of buried soil between the peat and the silty clays, which in fact was found only on the west and not the east side of the Grove causeway, where it may have been washed away. The peat may have been exploited later for fuel as suggested by the record of 'a saltmarsh called Colpit near the Wish in St. Mary's Marsh' in 1589, RYE 139/50, enrolled in RYE 33/16, f. 206. 'Col' was sometimes a general term for fuel, MED. This 'saltmarsh called colpit' may be equivalent to Colemersh, one of the bounds of Rye at the resumption (*Chapter 1*).

7. Waller and Grant 2008, 24.

8. MED.

9. RYE 136/168, 184; RYE 122/3, 4; Eddison and Draper 1997, 82-4.

10. RYE 136/107, 137, 184, 191; RYE 136/22, 184; RYE 122/1, 4, 6, 9; RYE 124/3; RYE 135/16, 24. This highway is also referred to in 1413 as abutting north on two acres in St Mary Croft, RYE 122/4. This important route is known too from a deed of 1452 of land and a garden near to the land of John Doune and of the Hospital of St Bartholomew, abutting south on a lane from the highway to Blekewell, north on the land of the heirs of Stephen Langporte, RYE 124/3. What were possibly the same two acres abutting north on the east-west highway called Blikelane were described in 1596 as two acres of salt marshes (lately fresh marsh, in 1586) abutting north on a way from Leasam manor to Rye, RYE 135/16, 24.

11. RYE 122/3; Lovegrove 1964, 120.

12. The new marsh was called Corboyllesmersch and may have been inned considerably earlier by the Corboil family, RYE 136/168, 175, 184; RYE 122/3, 4, 8.

13. RYE 122/1, 6, 10, 11; RYE 136/137.

14. RYE 136/107; RYE 135/8, 16, 17, 22, 26 (1563, 1586, 1588, 1594, 1600); RYE 139/23 (1585).

15. A third spring lay under the cliffs to the north east of Rye on the way from the foot of Playden Hill to Saltcote, along what is now Military Road, Dickinson 2002, 64. Neither Holloway nor the Victoria County History contain primary sources for their references to the postern gate, Holloway 1847, 289; *VCH Sussex* 9, 41.

16. Dickinson 2002, 64.

17. WSRO WISTON 22 (1575); RYE 135/24 (1596).

18. E.g. the church's two- or three-acre parcel abutted south on the lands of Alexander Shepherd, gentleman, and east on the lands of John Tufton, esquire, RYE 135/24.

19. E.g., 'The Manor of Peasmarsh Prebend was granted after the Dissolution to Sir Anthony Browne of Battle Abbey and his wife Elizabeth. Their son Sir Anthony Viscount Montague sold the manor in 1557 to Robert Sheppard of Peasmarsh and his son Alexander. Alexander Sheppard inherited the manor in 1575 and his son, William, died seised of the manor in 1634', ESRO catalogue under Administrative History; ESRO AMS 6200/6.

20. Robert Shepherd (I) of Rye had interests in the Rye marshland at Goldhope or Newland's Garden, land at Windmill Hill, the Budgewell and the Town Salts in 1510 to 1513, including some marshland which he inned. There were also Robert Shepherd (II), gentleman of Peasmarsh, father of Robert (III) and Alexander, and William (son of Alexander), of Mereworth in Kent, RYE 122/87; RYE 123/3, 10-14.

21. TNA PSP 12/254 75. Two deeds transferred as evidence of title when Alexander's Shepherd's son, William, conveyed this part of St Mary's Marsh to the Rye corporation confirm that the land for this inning had been acquired by 1559. These two deeds refer to the acquisition of part of St Mary's Marsh by Robert Shepherd in 1559. There are also a subsequent common recovery (1570) and a marriage settlement (1603) concerned with those lands. The latter was between Alexander Shepherd and his son William Shepherd and other parties and witnessed by Robert Shepherd, Alexander's brother, RYE 122/22-24, 27.

22. There were also two windmills on the wall, TNA PRO SP 12/254 75.

23. Tyler 2004, 10-11. The Prowez map labels the creek as 'The Crek of Rye goinge up towards Udimore'.

24. RYE 135/8.

25. It was said in 1596 that the wall, then described as decayed, had at one time led from the Strand to Deadmans Lane, which led off from Blikelane, RYE 135/24.

26. The petition of the Shepherds and others to the Privy Council (TNA PRO SP 12/254 75) and the records of the mayoralty of John Donnyng date this breach to 1570, not 1571 as Bendall suggested, nor 1595 as the Calendar of State Papers gave it, Bendall 1995, 44; Hipkin 1995b, 140. The petition was written in November (no year given). In a draft letter to the Privy Council of August of the year of John Donnying's mayoralty, from late August 1571 to late August 1572, the mayor and jurats noted the flooding of the Marsh at All Saints the previous twelvemonth, i.e. November 1570. They objected to its being inned 'absolutely', but wanted left 'such ditches and sluice thereto', i.e. where the breach had occurred, 'whereby our creek may receive some nourishment by letting out the indraught at quarter ebb'. This they claimed would benefit 'her majesty's poor town and common weal'. They deleted from the draft 'fishing' and 'fishing masters' as also standing to benefit but planned to have the letter signed or marked by the town's fishermen and seafaring men, RYE 47/3 (15).

27. Mayhew 1987, 29; RYE 1/4/66, 69v. Huge expenditure by the chamberlains on new arrangements with various workmen and plumbers to maintain and update the conduits may have prompted a new resolution by the assembly to form a short-lived experimental council of 'prudent commons' in 1563, one of whose functions was to oversee the chamberlains' decisions and expenditure, Introduction to the hundreds and assemblies and sessions of Rye, ESRO catalogue.

28. TNA PRO SP 12/254 75

29. Dasent 1894, 34.

30. RYE 47/3 (15).
31. RYE 47/6/14. The rent was £30 from the brewhouse and mill and £20 for the marsh.
32. RYE 47/6/12. Letter from Lord Cobham at London to the Mayor and Jurats of Rye, 1573, November 29. The dispute then disappears from the correspondence, etc., of the mayor of this period, John Donnyng, which is fully calendared.
33. The wall was clearly not repaired in 1586 when the church's two- or three-acre parcel was subject to flooding, being described at that time as salt marsh which had lately been fresh marsh, RYE 135/16. In 1596 the wall was described as 'decayed', RYE 135/24.
34. RYE 1/5, 13, February 1582/3. A cockboat was a small boat used in and around the harbour including for lading goods onto larger vessels and also for small-scale fishing, Mayhew 1987, 313.
35. Draper (forthcoming.)
36. RYE 135/24.
37. Mayhew 1987, 266-7, 311, n.59; 'Articles to be mynystred to certaine men to be sworne to enquire of upon the cause of the Decaye of Rye haven' [2 April 1595]; four articles concerning the proposal to channel Appledore water around the north and west of the town through St Mary's Marshes, RYE 98/8, cf. RYE 97/1 .
38. RYE 122/87.
39. RYE 122/33 (a deed dated 2 September 1617); RYE 122/89, no date [c.1617]
40. A note of 'the reasons & occasion of the session of Sewers at Rye x mo. Octobr' laste' stated that the purpose of the commission of sewers which was procured at the sole cost of Rye and that a session for 10 October had been hastily called owing to work on innings of Alexander Shepherd, who refused to defer action. The session rehearsed the ordinances of the last session (2 September 1597) against innings and the reasons for doing so. The paper ends by drawing a comparison between the decay of New Romney and Rye, praying that their lordships would construe their actions favourably. The sheet was found pinned to RYE 98/11, RYE 98/12 [1604].
41. RYE 122/88 [c.1613]. cf. a decree of 13 December 1604, engrossed 31 December, stating 'that William Shepherd shall cease to make innings in the Salt Marshes adjoining Tillingham water and shall remove all dams and stops in the creeks leading to the marshes which are prejudiciall and hurtefull to the said Channell', RYE 97/2, 3.
42. Mayhew 1987, 266-9.
43. Hipkin 1995b, 138-9; Mayhew 1987, 311, n.59.
44. Hipkin 1995b, 140-7.
45. TNA PRO SP 12/254 75.
46. RYE 47/3 (15).
47. RYE 98/12 [1604].

Chapter 10   Conclusions
1. Martin, *Rye Rebuilt*, chs 6, 7.

Bibliography

Adams, C. 1999, 'Medieval administration', in Leslie and Short, 1999

Andrews, F. 2006, *The other friars: the Carmelite, Augustinian, Sack and Pied Friars in the Middle Ages* [Woodbridge]

Bailey, M. 1991, '*Per impetum maris*: natural disaster and economic decline in eastern England, 1275-1350', in Campbell, B. (ed.), *Before the Black Death: studies in the 'crisis' of the early fourteenth century* [Manchester]

Ballard, A. 1904, *Domesday Boroughs* [Oxford]

Barron, C. 1995, 'Introduction: England and the Low countries 1327 to 1477', in Barron and Saul, 1995

Barron, C. 2005, *London in the later Middle Ages: government and people 1200-1500* [Oxford]

Barron, C. and Davies, M. (eds) 2007, *The religious houses of London and Middlesex* [London]

Barron, C. and Saul, N. (eds) 1995, *England and the Low Countries in the late Middle Ages* [Stroud]

Barron, C. and Stratford, J. (eds) 2002, *The Church and Learning in later medieval society: essay in honour of R.B. Dobson*, Proceedings of the Harlaxton Medieval Symposium 1999 [Donnington]

Beck, D. 2004, 'Can't see the wood for the trees?', *Romney Marsh Irregular* [Newsletter of the Romney Marsh Research Trust] 22

Bellamy, P. and Milne, G. 2003, 'An archaeological evaluation of the shipbuilding facilities at Small Hythe', *Archaeol. Cantiana*, 123

Bendall, S. 1995, 'Enquire "When the same platte was made and by whom and to what intent": sixteenth-century maps of Romney Marsh', *Imago Mundi*, 47

Betts, P. 2004, 'The Rural Landscape' in Lawson and Killingray, 2004

Biddle, M., Hiller, J. and Scott, I. 2001, *Henry VIII's coastal artillery fort at Camber Castle, Rye, East Sussex: an archaeological, structural and historical investigation* [Oxford]

Biller, P. 2000, *The Measure of Multitude: Population in Medieval Thought* [Oxford]

Blair, J. (ed.) 2007, *Waterways and canal-building in Medieval England* [Oxford]

Blair, J., Steane, J., Gardiner, J. and Wilson, B. 1983, 'Investigations at Cogges, Oxon., 1978-81: the priory and parish church', *Oxoniensia*, 47

Bleach, J. and Gardiner, M. 1999, 'Medieval markets and ports', in Leslie and Short, 1999

Bolton, J. 1980, *The Medieval English Economy 1150-1500* [London]

Boys, W. 1792, *Collections for an history of Sandwich in Kent with notices of the other Cinque Ports, …* [Canterbury]

Brent, C. 1980, *The maritime economy of eastern Sussex 1550-1700* [unpub. typescript, Local Hist. Res. Unit, East Sussex Record Office]

Britnell, R. and Campbell, B. (eds) 1995, *A commercialising economy: England 1086 to c.1300* [Manchester]

Brooks, F. 1925, 'William de Wrotham and the office of Keeper of the King's Ports and Galleys', *English Hist. Rev.*, 40

Brooks, N. 1988, 'Romney Marsh in the early Middle Ages', in Eddison and Green, 1988

Brookes, S. 2003, 'The early Anglo-Saxon framework for middle Anglo-Saxon economics: the case for east Kent', in Pestell and Ulmschneider, 2003

Brookes, S. 2007, 'Boat-rivets in graves in pre-Viking Kent: reassessing Anglo-Saxon boat-burial traditions', *Medieval Archaeol.*, 51

Brookes, S. and Milne, G. 2006, 'Towns and trade on an unkind coast: rewriting the history and maritime archaeology of the Cinque Ports', *Romney Marsh Irregular*, 28

Burke, T. 2004, 'The tithe map and the search for a small port at Appledore', *Romney Marsh Irregular*, 23

Burke, T. 2008, 'Winchelsea cellar visit', *Romney Marsh Irregular*, 23

Burstow, G. 1954/57, 'Excavations at the Friary of St Austin, Rye', *Sussex Notes Queries*, 14

Burton, J. 1994, *Monastic and Religious Orders in Britain, 1000-1300* [Cambridge]

Butcher, A. 2001, 'At the death of Emma Gobilonde', *Romney Marsh Irregular*, 17

Butler, G. (ed.) 1865, 'Notes on Rye and its inhabitants', *Sussex Archaeol. Collect.*, 17

Butler, L. 1976, 'The evolution of towns: planted towns after 1066', in Barley, M. (ed.) *The Plans and Topography of Medieval towns in England and Wales*, Counc. Brit. Archaeol. Res. Rep. 14

Carpenter, D. 1990, *The minority of Henry III* [London]

Clark, H. 1861, *Clark's guide and history of Rye* [Rye]

Clarke, H. 2005, 'Sandwich before the Cinque Port: initial finds of the Sandwich project', *Kent Archaeol. Soc. Newsletter*

Clarke, H. and Milne, G. 2002, 'A Medieval Shipyard at Smallhythe', *Romney Marsh Irregular*, 19

Clements, J. (ed.) 1991, *Rescue research at the old monastery, Rye* [unpub. rep. Hastings Area Archaeol. Res. Group]

Coates, R. 1999, 'Place-names before 1066', in Leslie and Short, 1999

Crossley, D. 1999, 'Iron and glass industries', in Leslie and Short, 1999

Dasent, J. (ed.) 1894, *Acts of the Privy Council 1571-1575*, 8 [London]

Davison, B. 1972, 'The Burghal Hidage fort of *Eorpeburnan*: a suggested identification', *Medieval Archaeol.*, 16

Dickinson, A. 2002, *Britain in old photographs: Rye and Winchelsea* [Stroud]

Draper, G. 1998, 'The farmers of Canterbury Cathedral Priory and All Souls College Oxford on Romney Marsh c.1443-1545', in Eddison, Gardiner and Long, 1998

Draper, G. 2004, 'Literacy and its transmission in the Romney Marsh area c.1150-1550' [unpub. Ph.D thesis, University of Kent]

Draper, G. 2005, 'Small fields and wet land: inheritance practices and the transmission of real property in the Romney Marshes c.1150-1390', *Landscapes*, 6

Draper, G. 2007a, 'There hath not bene any gramar scole kepte, preacher maytened or pore people releved, other then ... by the same chauntreye: educational provision and piety in Kent c.1400 to 1640', in Lutton, R. and Salter, E. (eds) *Pieties in transition: religious practices and experiences, c.1400-1640* [Farnham]

Draper, G. 2007b, 'Owners and occupiers of houses and other buildings in Rye and its hinterlands, *c*.1650 to 1665', *Romney Marsh Irregular*, 29

Draper, G. 2008, 'The education of children in Kent and Sussex: interpreting the medieval and Tudor ways', *Nottingham Medieval Stud.*, 52

Draper, G. (in prep.), 'Failing friaries? The mendicants in the Cinque Ports', Proceedings of the Harlaxton Medieval Symposium, July 2007

Draper, G. (forthcoming), 'Timber and iron: natural resources for the late medieval shipbuilding industry in Kent', in Sweetinburgh, S. (ed.) *Late Medieval Kent*, Kent History Project

Draper, G. and Meddens, F. with Armitage, P., Egan, G., Goodburn, D. and Jarrett, C. (forthcoming) *The sea and the marsh: the medieval Cinque Port of New Romney*, Pre-Construct Archaeol. Monogr., 10

Dulley, A. 1966, 'The level and port of Pevensey in the Middle Ages', *Sussex Archaeol. Collect.*, 104

Dulley, A. 1969, 'The early history of the Rye fishing industry', *Sussex Archaeol. Collect.*, 107

Durrant Cooper, W. 1850, *The History of Winchelsea, one of the Ancient Towns added to the Cinque Ports* [London and Hastings]

Durrant Cooper, W. 1856, 'Notices of Winchelsea in and after the fifteenth century', *Sussex Archaeol. Collect.*, 8

Durrant Cooper, W. 1867, 'Aliens in Rye, temp. Henry VIII', *Sussex Archaeol. Collect.*, 19

Dyer, A. 2000, 'Appendix: Ranking lists of English medieval towns', in Palliser, D. (ed.), *Cambridge Urban History of Britain* 1, 600-1540 [Cambridge]

Dyer, C. 1992, 'The hidden trade of the Middle Ages: evidence from the west midlands of England', *J. Hist. Geogr.*, 18 (2)

Dyer, C. 1993, *Standards of living in the Middle Ages: social change in England c.1200-1520* [Cambridge]

Eddison, J. (ed.) 1995, *Romney Marsh: the debatable ground*, Oxford Univ. Comm. Archaeol. Monogr., 41

Eddison, J. 1998, 'Catastrophic changes: a multidisciplinary study of the evolution of the barrier beaches of Rye Bay', in Eddison, Gardiner and Long, 1998

Eddison, J. 2002, 'The purpose, construction and operation of a 13th-century watercourse: the Rhee, Romney Marsh, Kent', in Long, Hipkin and Clarke, 2002

Eddison, J. 2004, 'The origins of Winchelsea' in Martin and Martin, 2004

Eddison, J. and Draper, G. 1997, 'A landscape of medieval reclamation: Walland Marsh, Kent', *Landscape Hist.*, 19

Eddison, J. and Green, C. (eds) 1988, *Romney Marsh: evolution, occupation, reclamation*, Oxford Univ. Comm. Archaeol. Monogr., 24

Eddison, J., Gardiner, M. and Long, A. (eds) 1998, *Romney Marsh: environmental change and human occupation in a coastal lowland*. Oxford Univ. Comm. Archaeol. Monogr., 46

Ellis, H. (ed.) 1851, *The pylgrymage of Sir Richard Guylforde to the Holy Land, A.D. 1506*, The Camden Society, old ser., 51 [London]

Formoy, B. 1926, 'A maritime indenture of 1212', *English Hist. Rev.*, 41

Freeth, S. 1974, *Catalogue of medieval fragments* [unpag. typescript, Kent Archives Office]

Furley, R. 1882, 'The early history of Tenterden', *Archaeol. Cantiana*, 14

Galloway, J., Keene, D. and Murphy, M. 1996, 'Fuelling the city: production and distribution of firewood and fuel in London's region, 1290-1400', *Econ. Hist. Rev.*, 49 (3)

Gardiner, M. 1988, 'Medieval settlement and society in the Broomhill area and excavations at Broomhill church', in Eddison and Green, 1988

Gardiner, M. 1990, 'The site of St. Bartholomew's Hospital, Rye', *Sussex Archaeol. Collect.*, 128

Gardiner, M. 1995, 'Medieval farming and flooding in the Brede Valley', in Eddison, 1995

Gardiner, M. 1998, 'Settlement change on Denge and Walland Marshes, 1400-1550', in Eddison, Gardiner and Long, 1998

Gardiner, M. 1999a, 'Late Saxon Sussex *c.*650-1066', in Leslie and Short, 1999

Gardiner, M. 1999b, 'The Medieval rural economy and landscape', in Leslie and Short, 1999

Gardiner, M. 2000, 'Shipping and trade between England and the Continent during the eleventh century', in Harper-Bill, C. (ed.), *Proceedings of the Battle Conference, 1999*, Anglo-Norman Stud., 22 [Woodbridge]

Gardiner, M. 2002, 'The late medieval "antediluvian" landscape of Walland Marsh', in Long, Hipkin and Clarke, 2002

Gardiner, M. 2003, 'Economy and landscape change in post-Roman and early medieval Sussex, 450-1175', in Rudling, D. (ed.), *The archaeology of Sussex to AD 2000* [King's Lynn]

Gardiner, M. 2007, 'Hythes, small ports, and other landing places in medieval England', in Blair, 2007

Gibson J. and Harvey, I. 2000, 'A sociological study of the New Romney Passion Play', *Research Opportunities in Renaissance Drama*, 39

Goddard, R. 2004, *Lordship and medieval urbanisation: Coventry, 1043-1355* [Woodbridge]

Gross, A. and Butcher, A. 1995, 'Agricultural policy on the manors of the Romney Marshes and the marshland fringe', in Eddison, 1995

Gunn, S., Grummit, D. and Cools, H. 2007, *War, state and society in England and the Netherlands 1477-1559* [Oxford]

Hanham, A. 1985, *The Celys and their world: an English merchant family of the fifteenth century* [Cambridge]

Hanley, H. and Chalklin, C. 1964, 'The Kent Lay Subsidy Roll of 1334/5', in Du Boulay, F. (ed.), *Documents illustrative of Medieval Kentish Society*, Kent Records, 18 [Ashford]

Harding, V. 1995, 'Cross-channel trade and cultural contacts: London and the Low Countries in the later fourteenth century', in Barron and Saul, 1995

Harding, V. 2002, 'Space, property, and propriety in urban England', *J. Interdisciplinary Hist.*, 32 (4)

Harvey, B. 1977, *Westminster Abbey and its estates in the Middle Ages* [Oxford]

Harvey, P. and McGuiness, A. 1996, *A guide to British medieval seals* [London]

Haskins, C. 1918, 'A charter of Canute for Fécamp', *English Hist. Rev.*, 33

Hasted, E. 1972 (repr.), *The History and Topographical Survey of the County of Kent* [Wakefield]

Henderson, J. 1992, 'The Black Death in Florence: medical and communal responses', in Bassett, S. (ed.), *Death in Towns: urban responses to the dying and the dead, 100-1600* [Leicester]

Hinde, T. and Hallam, E. 1985, *The Domesday Book* [London]

Hipkin, S. 1995a, 'Closing ranks: oligarchy and government at Rye, 1570-1640', *Urban Hist.*, 22

Hipkin, S. 1995b, 'The impact of marshland drainage on Rye Harbour, 1550-1650', in Eddison, 1995

Hipkin, S. 1998-9, 'The maritime economy of Rye, 1560-1640', *Southern Hist.*, 20/21

Hockley, S. 1962, 'The transport of Isle of Wight corn to feed Edward I's army in Scotland', *English Hist. Rev.*, 77

Holden, S., Draper, G., Jarrett, C. and Goodburn, D. (forthcoming), *The development of Tonbridge seen through the gate of its castle: recent excavations at the former Tonbridge stock and cattle market*

Holloway, W. 1847, *The history and antiquities of the Ancient Town and port of Rye, in the County of Sussex* [London]

Holloway, W. 1863, *Antiquarian rambles through Rye* (1st ser.) [Rye]

Holloway, W. 1866, *Antiquarian rambles through Rye* (2nd ser.) [Rye]

Holt, J. (ed.) 1987, *Domesday Studies: papers read at the Novocentenary conference of the Royal Historical Society and the Institute of British Geographers Winchester, 1986* [Woodbridge]

Homan, W. 1949, 'The founding of New Winchelsea', *Sussex Archaeol. Collect.*, 88

Horsfield, T. 1835, *The history, antiquities and topography of the County of Sussex* (2 vols) [Lewes]

Howard, M. 1999, 'Tudor and Stuart great houses', in Leslie and Short, 1999

Hughes, A. and Martin, D. 1999, 'Timber-framed buildings', in Leslie and Short, 1999

Hunnisett, R. 1985, 'Sussex coroners' inquests 1485-1558', *Sussex Rec. Soc.*, 74

Hunt, E. and Murray, J. 1999, *A History of Business in Medieval Europe 1200-1550* [Cambridge]

Hunter, M. and Gregory, A. (eds) 1988, *An Astrological Diary of the Seventeenth Century: Samuel Jeake of Rye 1652-1699* [Oxford]

Hunter, M., Mandelbrote, G., Ovenden, R. and Smith, N. 1999, *A radical's books: the library catalogue of Samuel Jeake of Rye, 1623-90* [Woodbridge]

James, R., Draper, G. and Martin, D. 2005, *Archaeological and landscape survey: Smallhythe Place, Kent* [Archaeol. South-East, Unpub. Rep. Proj. No. 1967]

Jessup, F. 1974, *The History of Kent* [Chichester]

Johnes, T. (trans.) 1839, Sir John Froissart, *Chronicles of England, France, Spain and the adjoining countries ...* [London]

Jones, E. 2001, 'Illicit business: accounting for smuggling in mid-sixteenth-century Bristol', *Econ. Hist. Rev.*, 54 (1)

Jones, R. 1999, 'Castles and other defensive sites', in Leslie and Short, 1999

Kepler, J. 1979, 'Entrepôt policy versus projects for perquisites in the administration of Dover Harbour: the dispute over charges for passing the boom, 1635-53', *Archaeol. Cantiana*, 95

Keynes, S. 1997, 'Giso, Bishop of Wells (1061-88)', in: Harper-Bill, C. (ed.), *Proceedings of the Battle Conference, 1996*, Anglo-Norman Stud., 19 [Woodbridge]

Kilby, K. 2004, *Coopers and Coopering* [Princes Risborough]

Kirkham, J. 2002, *Rye's War* [Rye]

Kirkham, J. 2006, *The Huguenots in Rye and Winchelsea* [Rye]

Kisby, F. 2002, 'Books in London Parish Churches before 1603: some preliminary observations', in Barron and Stratford, 2002

Kitchen, F. 1984, 'Towards an identification of *Eorpeburnan*', *Medieval Archaeol.*, 28

Knowlden, P. 2008, 'A Kent market town and the Great Rebellion: Bromley 1642-1660', *Local Hist.*, 38 (2)

Kowaleski, M. 1995, *Local markets and regional trade in medieval Exeter* [Cambridge]

Kowaleski, M. 2000, 'The expansion of the south-western fisheries in late medieval England', *Econ. Hist. Rev.*, 53 (3)

Langdon, J. 2007, 'The efficiency of inland water transport', in Blair, 2007

Lawson, T. 2004, 'The Viking incursions' in Lawson and Killingray, 2004

Lawson, T. and Killingray, D. 2004, *An Historical Atlas of Kent* [Chichester]

Lee, P. 2001, *Nunneries, learning and spirituality in late medieval English Society: the Dominican priory of Dartford* [York]

Leslie, K. and Short, B. 1999, *An Historical Atlas of Sussex* [Chichester]

Little, A. 1939, 'The Franciscan Friary at Romney', *Archaeol. Cantiana*, 50

Long, A., Hipkin S. and Clarke H. (eds) 2002, *Romney Marsh: coastal and landscape change through the ages*, Oxford Univ. School Archaeol. Monogr., 56

Long, A., Waller, M. and Plater, A. (eds) 2007, *Dungeness and the Romney Marsh: barrier dynamics and marshland evolution* [Oxford]

Long, A., Waller, M. and Plater, A. 2007, 'The late Holocene development of the Romney Marsh/ Dungeness foreland depositional complex', in Long, Waller and Plater, 2007

Long, A., Waller, M., Stupples, P. and Schofield, J. 2007, 'The Rye area: the timing of inundations and post-breach coastal evolution', in Long, Waller and Plater, 2007

Louis C. (ed.) 2000, *Records of Early English Drama: Sussex* [Toronto]

Lovegrove, H. 1964, 'Remains of two old vessels found at Rye', *Mariners Mirror* [J. Soc. Nautical Res.] 50 (2)

Lower, M. 1848, 'Observations of the Seals of the Cinque-Ports', *Sussex Archaeol. Collect.* 1

Luard, H. (ed.) 1872/83, Matthew Paris, *Chronica majora*, Rolls Series, 57 (5)

Lutton, R. 2006, *Lollardy and orthodox religion in pre-Reformation England: reconstructing piety* [Woodbridge]

Lutton, R. 2009, 'Leaving from Rye: Sir Richard Guldeford and his Holy Land pilgrimage of 1506', *Romney Marsh Irregular*, 33

Lyle, M. 1994, *English Heritage book of Canterbury* [London]

McCann, T. 1999, 'Religious observance in the 17th century', in Leslie and Short, 1999

McLain, B. 1997, 'Factors in market establishment in medieval England: the evidence from Kent 1086-1350', *Archaeol. Cantiana*, 117

Le Maho, J. 2003, 'The fate of the ports of the lower Seine valley and the end of the ninth century', in Pestell and Ulmschneider, 2003

Martin, D. and Martin, B. 1993, *Sussex topographical surveys, tenement analyses, Iden and Playden parishes* [unpub. rep., ESRO]

Martin, D. and Martin, B. with Eddison, J., Rudling, D. and Sylvester, D. 2004, *New Winchelsea, Sussex: a medieval port town*, UCL Field Archaeol. Unit Monogr. 2 [King's Lynn]

Martin, D. and Martin, B. with Clubb, J. and Draper, G. (forthcoming 2009) *Rye Rebuilt: regeneration and decline within a Sussex port town, 1350-1660*

Mate, M. 2006, *Trade and economic developments, 1450-1550: the experience of Kent, Surrey and Sussex* [Woodbridge]

Mate, M. 2008, 'London and Sandwich in the Later Middle Ages', Seminar in Medieval and Tudor History, Institute of Historical Research, 19 June 2008

Matthew, D. 1962, *Norman monasteries and their English possessions* [London]

Mayhew, G. 1984, 'Rye and the defence of the Narrow Seas: a sixteenth century town at war', *Sussex Archaeol. Collect.*, 127

Mayhew, G. 1987, *Tudor Rye* [Falmer]

Melling, E. 1959, *Kentish Sources 1: some roads and bridges* [Maidstone]

Mercer, M. 2005, 'The administration of the Cinque Ports in the early Lancastrian period', in Dockray, K. and Fleming, P. (eds), *People, places and perspectives: essays on later Medieval and early Tudor England in honour of Ralph A. Griffiths* [Stroud]

Metcalf, M. 1987, 'Taxation of moneyers', in Holt, 1987

Metcalf, M. 1998, *An atlas of Anglo-Norman coins, c.973-1086* [London and Oxford]

Metcalf, M. 2003, 'Variations in the composition of the currency at different places in England', in Pestell and Ulmschneider, 2003

Milne, G. 2004, 'The fourteenth-century merchant ship from Sandwich: a study in medieval maritime archaeology', *Archaeol. Cantiana*, 124

Murray, K. 1935, *The Constitutional History of the Cinque Ports* [Manchester]

Nenk, B. 2003, 'Public Worship, Private Devotion: The Crypto-Jews of Reformation England', in Gaimster D. and Gilchrist, R., *The Archaeology of Reformation 1480-1580*, Society for Post-Medieval Archaeology Monograph 1 [Leeds]

Owen, D. 1979, 'Bishop's Lynn: the first century of a new town', in Allen Brown, R. (ed.), *Proceedings of the Battle Conference, 1979*. Anglo-Norman Stud., 2 [Woodbridge]

Painter, S. 1933, *William Marshal: Knight-Errant, Baron and Regent of England* [Baltimore]

Palmer, B. 2003, 'The hinterlands of three southern English emporia: some common themes', in Pestell and Ulmschneider, 2003

Palmer, S. 2008, 'Kent and the sea', *Archaeol. Cantiana*, 128

Parfitt, K., Corke, B. and Cotter, J. with Allison, E. and Sweetinburgh, S. 2006, *Townwall Street, Dover: excavations 1996* [Canterbury]

Parkin, E. 1984, 'The ancient Cinque Port of Sandwich', *Archaeol. Cantiana*, 100

Pelham, R. 1928, 'Timber exports from the Weald during the fourteenth century', *Sussex Archaeol. Collect.*, 69

Pelham, R. 1929, 'The foreign trade of Sussex, 1300-1500', *Sussex Archaeol. Collect.*, 70

Pelham, R. 1930, 'Some further aspects of Sussex trade during the fourteenth century', *Sussex Archaeol. Collect.*, 71

Pestell, T. and Ulmschneider, K. (eds) 2003, *Markets in early medieval Europe: trading and productive sites, 650-850* [Macclesfield]

Poland, E. 1928, *The Friars in Sussex 1228-1928* [Hove]

Postan, M. 1972, *The medieval economy and society: an economic history of Britain in the Middle Ages* [London]

Rawcliffe, C. 2006, *Leprosy in medieval England* [Woodbridge]

Reeves, A. 1995, 'Romney Marsh: the field-walking evidence', in Eddison, 1995

Reynolds, S. 1987, 'Towns in Domesday Book', in Holt, 1987

Riddler, I. 2004, 'Anglo-Saxon Kent: early development *c*.450-*c*.800', in Lawson and Killingray, 2004

Ridgeway, V. 2000, 'A medieval saltern mound at Millfields Caravan Park, Bramber, West Sussex', *Sussex Archaeol. Collect.*, 138

Robinson, E. and Jarzembowski, E. 1998, *The building stones of Maidstone: town centre geological walk* [Maidstone]

Rodger, N. 1996, 'The naval service of the Cinque Ports', *English Hist. Rev.*, 111

Rodger, N. 1997, *The safeguard of the sea: a naval history of Britain, 1, 660-1649* [London]

Röhrkasten, J. 1998, 'The origin and early development of the London mendicant houses', in Slater, T. and Rosser, G. (eds), *The church in the medieval town* [Aldershot]

Roskell, J., Clark, L. and Rawcliffe, C. (eds) 1993, *The House of Commons, 1386-1421* (4 vols) [Stroud]

Ross, T. 1865, 'Old seals of the Cinque Ports and notices of the Barons: Temp. Edw. III', *Sussex Archaeol. Collect.*, 17

Roth, F. 1961, *The English Austin Friars 1249-1538* [New York]

Rudling, D. and Barber, L. with Martin, D. 1993, 'Excavations at the Phoenix Brewery Site, Hastings, 1988', *Sussex Archaeol. Collect.*, 131

Rushton, N. 1999a, 'The parochialisation of Sussex 1000-1086-1291', in Leslie and Short, 1999

Rushton, N. 1999b, 'Parochialization and patterns of patronage in 11th -century Sussex', *Sussex Archaeol. Collect.*, 137

Salisbury, E. 1887, 'Mr Edward Salisbury's report of the records of New Romney', *Archaeol. Cantiana*, 17

Salzman, L. (ed.) 1902, *An abstract of the Feet of Fines relating to the County of Sussex from 2 Richard I to 33 Henry III*, Sussex Record Soc., 2 [Lewes]

Saul, N. 1986, *Scenes from provincial life: knightly families in Sussex 1280-1400* [Oxford]

Sawyer, F. 1887, '1279 Sussex Assize Roll', *Sussex Archaeol. Collect.*, 35

Schofield, M. and Schofield, J. 2007, 'The Rye area: pre-inundation landscape and vegetation history', in Long, Waller and Plater, 2007

Scott Robertson, W. 1880, 'Destroyed churches of New Romney', *Archaeol. Cantiana*, 13

Searle, E. (ed.) 1980, *The Chronicle of Battle Abbey* [Oxford]

Simmons, M. 2003, *Hallelujah Hastings* [unpub. typescript, Salvation Army, Hastings]

Smart, T. (1864), 'Notes and Queries: The Frewen manuscripts', *Sussex Archaeol. Collect.*, 16

Stacey, R. 1995, 'Jewish lending and the medieval English economy', in Britnell and Campbell, 1995

Sweetinburgh, S. 200, 'Joining the sisters: female inmates of late medieval hospitals', *Archaeol. Cantiana*, 123

Sweetinburgh, S. 2006, 'Strategies of inheritance among Kentish fishing communities in the later Middle Ages', *History of the Family*, 11

Sweetinburgh, S. 2008a, 'Fishing and fishermen in medieval Romney Marsh', *Romney Marsh Irregular*, 32

Sweetinburgh, S. 2008b, 'The Austin Friars in late medieval Canterbury: negotiating spaces', in Burton, J. and Stöber, K. (eds), *Monasteries and society in the British Isles in the later Middle Ages*, Studies in the History of Medieval Religion, 35 [Woodbridge]

Sylvester, D. 1999, *Maritime communities in pre-plague England: Winchelsea and the Cinque Ports* [unpub. PhD thesis, Fordham University, New York, USA]

Sylvester, D. 2004, 'The development of Winchelsea and its maritime economy', in Martin and Martin, 2004

Taylor, J., Childs, W. and Watkiss, L. (eds) 2003, *The St Albans Chronicle: the Chronica maiora of Thomas Walsingham* [Oxford]

Taylor, M. 1999, 'Religious foundations', in Leslie and Short, 1999

Taylor, T. and Aston, M. 1999, *Time Team 99: the site reports* [London]

Thomson, J. 1983, *The transformation of medieval England, 1370-1529* [London]

Thomson, J. (ed.) 1998, *Towns and townspeople in the fifteenth century* [Gloucester]

Thompson, P. 1856, *The history and antiquities of Boston, …* [Boston]

Tummuscheit, A. 2003, 'Groß Strömkendorf: a market site of the eighth century on the Baltic sea coast', in Pestell and Ulmschneider, 2003

Tyler, A. 2004, 'Ships of the Marsh', *Romney Marsh Irregular*, 24

Vidler, L. 1932, 'Floor tiles and kilns near the site of St Bartholomew's Hospital, Rye', *Sussex Archaeol. Collect.*, 73

Vidler, L. 1933, 'Medieval pottery and kilns found at Rye', *Sussex Archaeol. Collect.*, 74

Vidler, L. 1934, *A new history of Rye* [Hove]

Vidler, L. 1936, Medieval pottery, tiles and kilns found at Rye: final report', *Sussex Archaeol. Collect.*, 77

Vidler, L. 1943, 'St. Bartholomew's Hospital at Rye', *Sussex Archaeol. Collect.*, 83

Vince, A. 1985, 'The Saxon and medieval pottery of London', *Medieval Archaeol.*, 29

Vollans, E. 1988, 'New Romney and the "River of Newenden", in Eddison and Green, 1988

Vollans, E. 1995, 'Medieval salt-making and the inning of the tidal marshes at Belgar, Lydd', in Eddison, 1995

Waller, M. and Grant, M. 2008 'The isle of Rye?', *Romney Marsh Irregular*, 31

Warren Hollister, C. 1987, 'The greater Domesday tenants-in-chief', in Holt, 1987

Watson, I. (ed.) 1999, *The history of the parish of Chevening* [Sevenoaks]

Webb, D. 2001, *Pilgrims and pilgrimage in the medieval west* [London]

Webb, D. 1994, 'The Church of San Frediano, Lucca', *History Today*, 44

Webster, B. 1984, 'The community of Kent in the reign of Richard II', *Archaeol. Cantiana*, 100

Welch, M. 2007, 'Anglo-Saxon Kent', in Williams, J. (ed.), *The Archaeology of Kent* [Woodbridge]

Wetherill, E. 1992, *Antiquarian rambles through Saltcote*: *Playden* ... [Hastings]

Wetherill, E. 2001, *A medieval kiln-waste tip on Rye Hill* [Hastings]

White, S. 1999, 'Early Saxon Sussex *c*.410-*c*.650', in Leslie and Short, 1999

Whittick, C. 2004, *Calendar of documents relating to the English possession of the abbey of Holy Trinity, Fécamp, at the Archives Departémentales de la Seine-Maritime, Rouen, liasse 7H57* [unpub. typescript, ESRO]

Williams, R. 1999, 'Natural regions', in: Leslie and Short, 1999

Zell, M. and Chalklin, C. 2004, 'Old and New Industries 1500-1700', in Lawson and Killingray, 2004

Index